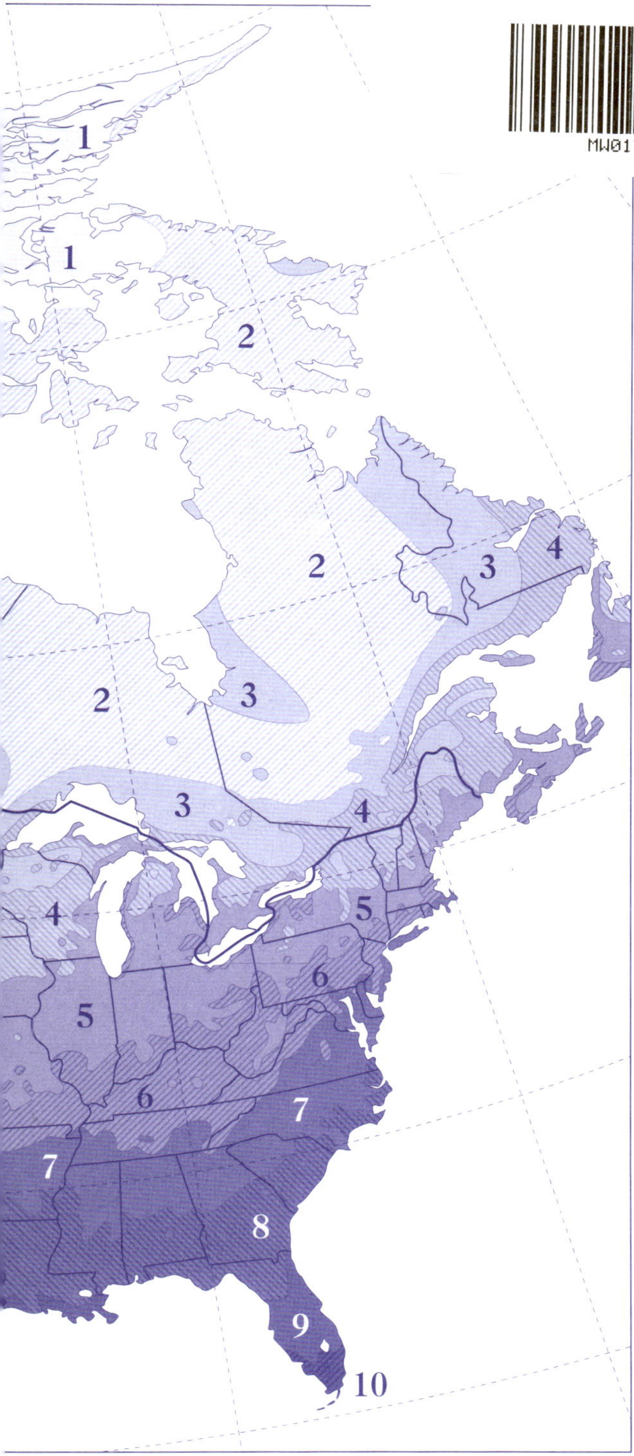

numbers accompanying the plants in this book indicate their lower limits of winter cold hardiness. Extreme summer heat and humidity also play a part in a plant's adaptability; many plants hardy in colder zones grow poorly in warmer, wetter ones.

1	BELOW –50°F BELOW –46°C
2	–50° TO –40°F –46° TO –40°C
3	–40° TO –30°F –40° TO –34°C
4	–30° TO –20°F –34° TO –29°C
5	–20° TO –10°F –29° TO –23°C
6	–10° TO 0°F –23° TO –18°C
7	0° TO 10°F –18° TO –12°C
8	10° TO 20°F –12° TO –7°C
9	20° TO 30°F –7° TO –1°C
10	30° TO 40°F –1° TO 4°C
11	ABOVE 40°F ABOVE 4°C

CAVENDISH

PLANT & GUIDES

PERENNIALS

CAVENDISH

PLANT & GUIDES

PERENNIALS

CAVENDISH BOOKS
VANCOUVER

A DK PUBLISHING BOOK

Produced for Dorling Kindersley by PAGE One
Cairn House, Elgiva Lane, Chesham, Buckinghamshire, UK

EDITOR Helen Parker
DESIGNER Bob Gordon
MANAGING EDITOR Francis Ritter
MANAGING ART EDITOR Derek Coombes
PRODUCTION Adrian Gathercole
PICTURE RESEARCH Sharon Southren

First Canadian Edition 1996
2 4 6 8 10 9 7 5 3
Published in Canada by Cavendish Books Inc.,
Unit 5, 801 West 1st Street, North Vancouver, B.C. V7P 1A4

Reprinted 1997

Canadian Cataloguing in Publication Data
Main entry under title:
Perennials
(Cavendish plant guides)

Includes index
ISBN 0-929050-47-9

1. Perennials. 2. Perennials–Pictorial works. I. Series.
SB434.P47 1996 635.9'327 C95-911078-X

Color reproduction by Colourscan, Singapore
Printed and bound in Singapore by Star Standard Industries

CONTENTS

Contributors

Linden Hawthorne
Writer

Michael Upward
Perennials in the Garden, Catalog of Perennials, Guide to Perennial Care, Daylilies, Asters, Penstemons, Peonies, Phlox

Larry Barlow *Chrysanthemums*
Eric Catterall *Begonias*
Diana Grenfell *Hostas*
David Hitchcock
Carnations and Pinks
Hazel Key *Pelargoniums*
Sidney Linnegar *Irises*
David McClintock *Grasses*
Diana Miller *African Violets*
Philip Swindells
Primroses, Ferns
John Thirkell *Delphiniums*

How to use this Book

THIS BOOK PROVIDES the ideal quick reference guide to selecting and identifying perennials for the garden.

The **Perennials in the Garden** section is a helpful introduction to perennials and gives advice on choosing a suitable plant for a particular site or purpose, such as for a border, container, or simply as a specimen.

To choose or identify a perennial, turn to the **Catalog of Perennials**, where photographs are accompanied by concise plant descriptions and useful tips on cultivation and propagation. The entries are grouped by size, season of interest, as well as by color (see the color wheel below) to make selection easier.

For additional information on perennial cultivation, routine care, and propagation, turn to the **Guide to Perennial Care**, where general advice on all aspects of caring for your perennials can be found.

At the end of the book, a useful two-page glossary explains key terms, and a comprehensive index of every perennial, its synonyms, and common names, together with a brief genus description, allows quick and easy access to the book by plant name.

The color wheel

All the perennials in the book are grouped according to the color of their main feature of interest. They are always arranged in the same order, indicated by the color wheel below, from white

The Symbols

The symbols below are used throughout the **Catalog of Perennials** to indicate a plant's preferred growing conditions and hardiness. However, both the climate and soil conditions of your particular site should also be taken into account, as they may affect a plant's growth.

- Prefers full sun
- Prefers partial shade
- Tolerates full shade
- Prefers well-drained soil
- Prefers moist soil
- Prefers wet soil
- pH Needs acid soil

Hardiness
The range of winter temperatures that each plant is able to withstand is shown by the USDA plant hardiness zone numbers that are given in each entry. The temperature ranges for each zone are shown on the endpaper map in this book.

through reds and blues, to yellows and oranges. Variegated plants are categorized by the color of their variegation, for example, white or yellow.

Perennial size categories

The perennials featured in the Catalog are divided according to the average height they attain. However, heights may vary from the ones given, according to site, climate, and age.

The categories are as follows:
LARGE
Over 4ft (1.2m)
MEDIUM
2–4ft (60cm–1.2m)
SMALL
Up to 2ft (60cm)

How to use the Catalog of Perennials

Headings

Each chapter is subdivided into sections, according to the average size of the plants and their main season of interest.

The plant's *family name* appears here.

The plant's *common name(s)* appear here.

The plant's *botanical name* appears here.

Plant Portraits

The color photographs show each plant's main features and color (see the color wheel on previous page).

Entries

A brief plant description giving details of growing habit, flowers, fruits, and leaves, followed by information on native habitat tips on cultivation, and propagation and a list of other botanical names.

Feature Pages

Plant groups or genera of special interest to the gardener are presented on separate feature pages. A brief introduction giving general information on appearance, use, cultivation and propagation is followed by concise plant entries.

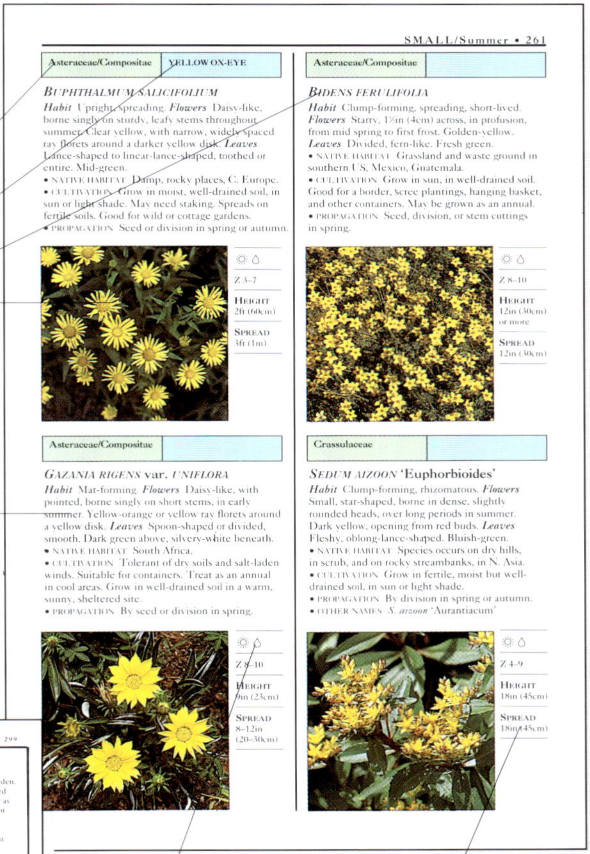

SMALL/Summer • 261

Asteraceae/Compositae | YELLOW OX-EYE

BUPHTHALMUM SALICIFOLIUM
Habit Upright, spreading. ***Flowers*** Daisy-like, borne singly on sturdy, leafy stems throughout summer. Clear yellow, with narrow, widely spaced ray florets around a darker yellow disk. ***Leaves*** Lance-shaped to linear-lance-shaped, toothed or entire. Mid-green.
• NATIVE HABITAT Damp, rocky places, C. Europe.
• CULTIVATION Grow in moist, well-drained soil, in sun or light shade. May need staking. Spreads on fertile soils. Good for wild or cottage gardens.
• PROPAGATION Seed or division in spring or autumn.

Z 3–7
HEIGHT 2ft (60cm)
SPREAD 3ft (1m)

Asteraceae/Compositae

BIDENS FERULIFOLIA
Habit Clump-forming, spreading, short-lived. ***Flowers*** Starry, 1½in (4cm) across, in profusion, from mid spring to first frost. Golden-yellow. ***Leaves*** Divided, fern-like. Fresh green.
• NATIVE HABITAT Grassland and waste ground in southern US, Mexico, Guatemala.
• CULTIVATION Grow in sun, in well-drained soil. Good for a border, scree plantings, hanging basket, and other containers. May be grown as an annual.
• PROPAGATION Seed, division, or stem cuttings in spring.

Z 8–10
HEIGHT 12in (30cm) or more
SPREAD 12in (30cm)

Asteraceae/Compositae

GAZANIA RIGENS var. *UNIFLORA*
Habit Mat-forming. ***Flowers*** Daisy-like, with pointed, borne singly on short stems, in early summer. Yellow-orange or yellow ray florets around a yellow disk. ***Leaves*** Spoon-shaped or divided, smooth. Dark green above, silvery-white beneath.
• NATIVE HABITAT South Africa.
• CULTIVATION Tolerant of dry soils and salt-laden winds. Suitable for containers. Treat as an annual in cool areas. Grow in well-drained soil in a warm, sunny, sheltered site.
• PROPAGATION By seed or division in spring.

Z 8–10
HEIGHT 9in (23cm)
SPREAD 8–12in (20–30cm)

Crassulaceae

SEDUM AIZOON 'Euphorbioides'
Habit Clump-forming, rhizomatous. ***Flowers*** Small, star-shaped, borne in dense, slightly rounded heads, over long periods in summer. Dark yellow, opening from red buds. ***Leaves*** Fleshy, oblong-lance-shaped. Bluish-green.
• NATIVE HABITAT Species occurs on dry hills, in scrub, and on rocky streambanks, in N. Asia.
• CULTIVATION Grow in fertile, moist but well-drained soil, in sun or light shade.
• PROPAGATION By division in spring or autumn.
• OTHER NAMES *S. aizoon* 'Aurantiacum'

Z 4–9
HEIGHT 18in (45cm)
SPREAD 18in (45cm)

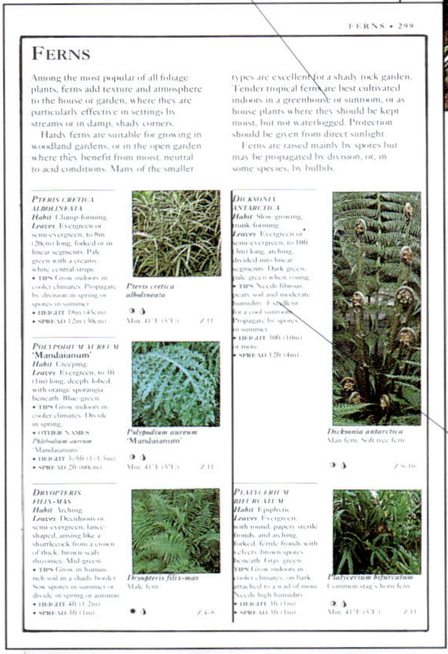

FERNS • 299

FERNS

Among the most popular of all foliage plants, ferns add texture and atmosphere to the house or garden, where they are particularly effective in settings by streams or in damp, shady corners.

Hardy ferns are suitable for growing in woodland gardens, or in the open garden where they benefit from moist, neutral to acid conditions. Many of the smaller types are excellent for a shady rock garden. Tender tropical ferns are best cultivated indoors in a greenhouse or sunroom, or as house plants where they should be kept moist, but not waterlogged. Protection should be given from direct sunlight.

Ferns are raised mainly by spores but may be propagated by division, or, in some species, by bulbils.

PTERIS CRETICA ALBOLINEATA
Habit Clump-forming. ***Leaves*** Evergreen or semi-evergreen, to 8in (20cm) long, forked or in linear segments. Pale green with a creamy-white central stripe.
• TIPS Grow indoors in cooler climates. Propagate by division in spring or spores in summer.
• HEIGHT 18in (45cm)
• SPREAD 12in (30cm)

Pteris cretica albolineata
Min. 41°F (5°C) Z 11

POLYPODIUM AUREUM 'Mandaianum'
Habit Creeping. ***Leaves*** Evergreen, to 3ft (1m) long, deeply lobed, with orange sporangia beneath. Blue-green.
• TIPS Grow indoors in cooler climates. Divide in spring.
• OTHER NAMES *Phlebodium aureum* 'Mandaianum'
• HEIGHT 3–5ft (1–1.5m)
• SPREAD 2ft (60cm)

Polypodium aureum 'Mandaianum'
Min. 41°F (5°C) Z 11

DRYOPTERIS FILIX-MAS
Habit Arching. ***Leaves*** Deciduous or semi-evergreen, lance-shaped, arising like a shuttlecock from a crown of thick, brown-scaly rhizomes. Mid-green.
• TIPS Grow in humus-rich soil in a shady border. Sow spores in summer or divide in spring or autumn.
• HEIGHT 4ft (1.2m)
• SPREAD 3ft (1m)

Dryopteris filix-mas
Male fern
Z 4–8

DICKSONIA ANTARCTICA
Habit Slow-growing, trunk-forming. ***Leaves*** Evergreen or semi-evergreen, to 10ft (3m) long, arching, divided into linear segments. Dark green, pale green when young.
• TIPS Needs fibrous, peaty soil and moderate humidity. Excellent for a cool sunroom. Propagate by spores in summer.
• HEIGHT 30ft (10m) or more.
• SPREAD 12ft (4m)

Dicksonia antarctica
Man fern, Soft tree fern
Z 8–10

PLATYCERIUM BIFURCATUM
Habit Epiphytic. ***Leaves*** Evergreen, with round, papery sterile fronds, and arching, forked, fertile fronds with velvety brown spores beneath. Gray-green.
• TIPS Grow indoors in cooler climates, on bark attached to a wad of moss. Needs high humidity.
• HEIGHT 3ft (1m)
• SPREAD 3ft (1m)

Platycerium bifurcatum
Common stag's horn fern
Min. 41°F (5°C) Z 11

Symbols

The symbols indicate the sun, soil and temperature requirements (see The Symbols on previous page). Ideal temperatures are given for plants that cannot survive below 32°F (0°C).

Sizes

The average height and spread of the plants are given, although these may vary according to site, growing conditions, climate, and age.

Feature Plant Descriptions

As with the main Catalog entries, a brief plant description is followed by useful tips on cultivation and propagation where these are not already given in the general introduction.

PERENNIALS IN THE GARDEN

PERENNIALS, PERHAPS MORE than any other group of plants, offer an infinitely rich palette of color, form, fragrance, and texture. There are perennials suitable for almost every area in the garden, however large or small, and whatever the mood or style.

Perennials are defined as non-woody plants that live for two or more years. Some, such as *Helleborus niger*, are evergreen, and so provide valuable winter interest. Most, however, are herbaceous, and die back in autumn. While this has the disadvantage of leaving bare beds in winter, many gardeners enjoy this seasonality, if only because the burgeoning new growth heralds the onset of spring.

With thoughtful selection, perennials can be used to create borders with a prolonged season of interest. They can be used in a mixed border with shrubs to give long-term structure, or with spring bulbs and long-flowering annuals to fill in during the quieter periods that precede and follow the glorious, if short-lived, midsummer flush of bloom.

Formal border
This traditional formal border is laid out in broad, straight beds flanking a path of smooth, fresh green turf. There is a gentle graduation of height, both from front to back and along the long axis of the border.

Choosing perennials

All successful planting designs depend on thoroughly analyzing the site before carefully selecting plants to suit the conditions that exist in the garden. It is always preferable to select perennials that suit the soil type, climate, and exposure than to struggle to keep plants alive in unsuitable conditions.

With their broad spectrum of color and scent, perennials are obviously valued for their flowers. A number also have very attractive foliage, ranging from the emerald-green, neatly pleated leaves of *Veratrum* to the delicate tracery of *Dicentra*. The beauty of foliage nearly always outlasts that of the flowers, and the variety of textures and colors of leaves provides great potential for extending the season of interest – especially important in a smaller garden.

Summer border
Here hot-colored flowers are offset by the cooler grays of the foreground foliage, and low, rounded plants provide a horizontal foil to the strongly upright spikes of red-hot pokers (Kniphofia).

Perennials range in height from the architectural grandeur of the cardoon (*Cynara cardunculus*), to the lowest of groundcover plants, permitting infinite variations of form, perspective, and composition. Their versatility can be applied to a range of planting themes and situations.

Herbaceous border

The herbaceous border may be designed in a variety of styles to set or enhance the overall character and tone of the garden. Since late Victorian times, herbaceous borders have proved to be an enduringly popular means of displaying perennials. In traditional borders, the usually rectangular beds were flanked by smooth green lawns, often with a backdrop of warm brick or precision-cut hedging. The profusion of summer and autumn-flowering perennials was banked according to height and arranged in bold and distinct drifts to provide tones and contrast of color, form, and texture. These well-proven principles apply equally to more modern designs, even where space is limited and borders must be created on a more modest scale.

The ordered elegance of a traditional border suits a formal garden, or, for a more contemporary style, an island bed set in a sea of grass, gravel, or paving. A cottage garden relies on the deceptively random placement of fluid and informal drifts, set to spill over and disguise the hard lines and edges of paving.

Mixed border
Here the season of interest is extended beyond the midsummer peak of the perennials by tulips in spring, and into autumn with the golden leaves of Euphorbia.

The mixed border

As its name suggests, the mixed border may contain a combination of small trees, shrubs, bulbs, annuals, and biennials to complement the often short-lived beauty of perennial plants. This mixed planting is invaluable in small gardens, where empty beds in winter may appear tediously dominant. Mixed borders provide the greatest opportunity for creating year-round interest and imaginative plant associations, but need very careful planning if they are to ensure an attractive seasonal progression, especially in the duller months between autumn and spring.

While the volume of space given over to each type of plant will vary according to taste, the allocation of one-third to one-half of the space to the planting of shrubs offers the best potential for a varied design that provides year-round interest. Use a mixture of evergreen and deciduous shrubs to impart structure and substance to the design, and consider carefully their habit, form, flowering, and fruiting period. Bear in mind that their summer foliage will provide a foil and backdrop to the summer-flowering perennials. Shrubs with attractive, glossy foliage are usually preferable, but even those with dull summer leaves have a place. They can be used as a support for scrambling herbaceous plants such as *Clematis recta*.

In the early months of the year, the emerging foliage of the perennials can be enhanced and enlivened by a successional display of spring and early summer bulbs. A sequence that includes snowdrops, narcissus, *Muscari*, fritillaries, and tulips, from the single earlies such as *Tulipa* 'Diana' to the single late-flowering tulips such as *T.* 'Queen of Night', will provide interest from late winter through to early summer. Later in the season, use summer-flowering bulbs such as *Allium sphaerocephalum* or *Galtonia candicans* to grow through and complement perennials in full bloom. Later still, sun-loving bulbs such as *Nerine bowdenii* and *Amaryllis belladonna* prolong the display well into autumn.

Annuals and biennials also make useful contributions to the mixed border. They may be used as "fillers" until other plants reach their mature dimensions, and are indispensable when used to mask gaps left by perennials such as *Papaver orientale*, that die back after flowering. Select annuals carefully; the vivid colors of many modern seed races can appear garish when set against perennials of soft and subtle color.

Designing beds and borders

When making a planting plan, the basic principles are essentially the same, whether planning a herbaceous border, island bed, or mixed border. Considerations of height, mass, shape, and sequential interest, in combination with texture and color are all variable

factors that may be exploited to achieve particular design effects. It is also vital to research an individual plant's natural preferences in cultivation, and to choose plants that are suitable for the soil type, exposure, and climate that exist in the garden. Imagination and personal taste will inevitably influence your designs, but there are a few basic guidelines to follow.

General principles

It is important at the outset to decide on the preferred style of planting, since this provides a clear suggestion as to the size, shape, and form of the beds to be planted. The choice of style will be dictated in part by personal taste and imagination, but it may also be guided by observation of the architectural style of the house and any existing hard landscaping in the garden, such as walls, steps, and paving. A formally elegant and well-ordered style usually succeeds best when planted into a straight-edged and symmetrical border. A more relaxed and informal planting, with irregular drifts of plants, is more likely to succeed in borders with irregular, curved outlines.

Informal planting
The hard edges and lines of the steps are masked and softened here by an informal profusion of foliage and flowers set to spill gracefully over them. The bold sculptural forms of hostas and Carex elata *'Aurea' are used to add focus and a strong structural element to the design.*

The size of the border will vary, but as a guide, the larger the garden the bigger the border should be to maintain a sense of proportion and scale with the house and its surroundings. A width of 5ft (1.5m) is the minimum necessary to permit balanced grouping of plants and graduations of height and form; a width of 9ft (2.7m) lends much more versatility, where space permits.

When planning a planting design, consider the space required for individual plants at maturity and take into account their rate of growth, so that the smallest are not overwhelmed. Large clumps or drifts can be planted in extensive borders, but take care to plant smaller clumps in tiny gardens. Do not be afraid to make fine adjustments to the plan when setting it out.

Contrasting foliage
The success of this sophisticated planting relies on strong contrasts of texture and form provided by the jagged foliage of Rheum palmatum *(rear), the heart-shaped leaves of* Ligularia dentata, *and the arching, strap-shaped leaves of an ornamental grass.*

Height, form, texture, and color

Borders are generally planted with the tallest plants at the back and the lowest at the front. The aim is to create undulating graduations of mass and height, from front to back and along the long axis of the border. In an island bed, taller plants are set along the central axis, with lower ones at the margins, to give tiered effects in which no one plant hides another. This rule, though, is not immutable, and the occasional use of taller plants with an airy habit at the border front can add great individuality to a design.

For greatest impact, small and medium plants are best massed in groups of one type, with taller, more substantial species used singly to form dynamic focus and counterpoint. Set out smaller plants in random blocks 3, 5 or 7 (depending on size) to form natural and irregular drifts of contrasting color, form, and texture.

Perennials range widely in habit from low, spreading forms that provide strong horizontal lines, through rounded mound-forming types to those with a narrowly upright silhouette that are used to give vertical emphasis. Juxtapose contrasting forms to create a composition in which strong horizontal and vertical elements

Planting in drifts
Planting random and odd-numbered groups of plants creates bold and irregular drifts of varying size, shape, and color. Subtle graduations of height and texture along the long axis of the border creates a sense of perspective.

are balanced by a mass of softer, rounded shapes, and use plants with a strong, spiky outline, like the red-hot pokers, to provide emphatic contrasts and dynamic diagonals.

Foliage constitutes the greatest mass in a border, and so has strong impact and great potential for contrast and harmony. Textural variety depends on both leaf shape and surface texture. Harmonize finely cut or delicate leaves with those of substantial size and simple outline such as *Rheum palmatum,* and use matte or silky surface textures in contrast with glossy and light-reflecting leaves. Color associations in a border may be daring and experimental or subtle and restrained. Color affects the mood of a planting design, perhaps more than any other factor. Monochromatic themes may appear simple to plan, but without carefully placed contrasts of small areas of strong and intense hues they can become monotonous. Soft pastels set against cool blue or intense violet creates restful and sophisticated effects, whereas hot shades of orange, yellow, and rich red lend warmth and exuberance. When combining hot and cool shades, use foliage to separate blocks of strong or clashing colors. Plants with silver or gray leaves are useful in this respect, since their cool neutrals associate well with almost every color of the spectrum.

Harmonizing textures
A tiered arrangement of plants with airy and feathery flowers, such as Astilbe, Lythrum, *and* Filipendula, *with the golden spires of* Ligularia stenocephala *in the background, forms a satisfying contrast of texture and form.*

Planters' Guide to Perennials

For exposed sites
Anemone hupehensis
Centaurea hypoleuca cvs
Centranthus ruber
Kniphofia caulescens
Limonium latifolium
Phlomis russeliana
Phormium tenax
Sedum spectabile
Stachys byzantina

Air pollution-tolerant
Aquilegia vulgaris
Bergenia cordifolia
Euphorbia amygdaloides
Geranium endressii
Helleborus niger, H. orientalis
Hemerocallis most
Heuchera most
Hosta most
Lamium maculatum
Leucanthemum x *superbum*
Polemonium most
Polygonatum some
Pulmonaria species
Rudbeckia most
Sedum spectabile
Sisyrinchium striatum
Smilacina racemosa
Symphytum most
Thalictrum most
Tiarella most
Veronica gentianoides

For moist shade
Astilbe most
Astrantia major
Bergenia all
Brunnera macrophylla
Cimifuga simplex
Convallaria majalis
Gentiana asclepiadea
Hemerocallis
Hosta
Kirengeshoma palmata
Ligularia przewalskii
Peltiphyllum peltatum
Platycodon grandiflorus
Polygonum bistorta
Rodgersia species
Thalictrum species
Trilllium species
Veratrum species

For dry shade
Acanthus mollis
Aconitum carmichaelii
Anemone hupehensis,
A. x *hybrida*
Dicentra
Epimedium
Euphorbia amygdaloides
Geranium some
Helleborus orientalis
Tellima grandiflora

Winter interest
Decorative flowers
Bergenia 'Ballawley',
B. cordifolia
Euphorbia amygdaloides var. *robbiae*
Helleborus argutifolius,
H. niger
Pulmonaria some
Decorative leaves
Bergenia 'Ballawley',
B. cordifolia
Euphorbia amygdaloides var. *robbiae*
Helleborus argutifolius
Heuchera micrantha 'Palace Purple'
Lamium maculatum
Ophiopogon planiscapus 'Nigrescens'
Phormium cvs.
Stachys byzantina

Fragrant flowers
Centranthus ruber
Convallaria majalis
Cosmos atrosanguineus
Dianthus many
Erysimum many
Filipendula ulmaria

Hesperis matronalis
Nicotiana many
Paeonia lactiflora
Phlox paniculata
Primula many

Architectural plants
Acanthus most
Angelica archangelica
Cortaderia selloana
Crambe cordifolia
Cynara cardunculus
Foeniculum vulgare
Gunnera manicata
Helleborus argutifolius
Hosta sieboldiana var. elegans
Phormium tenax
Rheum palmatum
Rodgersia species

Fast-growing perennials
Artemisia lactiflora
Campanula lactiflora
Centaurea macrocephala
Cephalaria gigantea
Crambe cordifolia
Cynara cardunculus
Ferula communis
Filipendula rubra
Galega x *hartlandii*
Gunnera manicata
Helianthus most
Kniphofia caulescens
Ligularia stenocephala
Phormium tenax
Rheum palmatum
Romneya coulteri
Salvia concertiflora

CATALOG OF PERENNIALS

Onagraceae	WHITE ROSEBAY

EPILOBIUM ANGUSTIFOLIUM ALBUM

Habit Vigorous, upright, rhizomatous, spreading. ***Flowers*** Small, 4-petaled, in long, open, erect spires, in late summer. White. ***Leaves*** Narrowly lance-shaped, wavy-edged. Dark green.
• NATIVE HABITAT Woodland edge, roadsides, waste ground, Europe, Asia, North America.
• CULTIVATION Grow in moist, well-drained soil, in sun or shade. Good for a wild garden.
• PROPAGATION By softwood cuttings of sideshoots in spring.
• OTHER NAMES *Chamaenerion angustifolium album.*

Z 3–7

HEIGHT
4–5ft
(1.2–1.5m)

SPREAD
20in
(50cm) or
more

Solanaceae	FLOWERING TOBACCO

NICOTIANA SYLVESTRIS

Habit Vigorous, upright, branching. ***Flowers*** Night-scented, tubular, produced in large, open clusters, in summer. White. ***Leaves*** Large, broadly elliptic, wrinkled. Blue-green.
• NATIVE HABITAT Argentina.
• CULTIVATION Tolerant of shade. Grow in any fertile, well-drained soil. The plant will perform best if planted in sheltered areas where the heavy fragrance can be appreciated. May also be grown as an annual.
• PROPAGATION By seed in spring.

Z 9–10

HEIGHT
5ft (1.5m)
or more

SPREAD
30in (75cm)

Papaveraceae	CALIFORNIA POPPY

ROMNEYA COULTERI

Habit Vigorous, woody-based, rhizomatous. ***Flowers*** Large, fragrant, with white, crêpe-textured petals around a boss of golden stamens, in late summer. ***Leaves*** Deeply divided. Blue-gray.
• NATIVE HABITAT Dry canyons in mountain foothills of California and Mexico.
• CULTIVATION Grow in a warm, sunny, sheltered site, in deep, well-drained soil. In cold areas, provide a dry mulch in winter. Resents transplanting.
• PROPAGATION By basal cuttings in early spring, by seed in autumn, or by root cuttings in winter.

Z 8–10

HEIGHT
5–6ft
(1.5–2m)

SPREAD
6ft (2m)

Brassicaceae/Cruciferae	HEARTLEAF CRAMBE

CRAMBE CORDIFOLIA

Habit Vigorous, multi-branched, with a woody rootstock. ***Flowers*** Small, fragrant, 4-petaled, in large, open, airy sprays, in summer. White. ***Leaves*** Large, lobed, heart-shaped, crinkled. Dark green.
• NATIVE HABITAT Open areas in rocky soils, Caucasus mountains.
• CULTIVATION Tolerates semi-shade but flowers best in full sun. Grow in any well-drained soil. A beautiful specimen for a large border.
• PROPAGATION By division in spring, or by seed in autumn or spring.

Z 6–9

HEIGHT
6ft (2m)

SPREAD
4ft (1.2m)
or more

Apiaceae/Umbelliferae

ERYNGIUM EBURNEUM

Habit Clump-forming. ***Flowers*** Small, rounded, thistle-like, on branched stems, in late summer. Green with white stamens. ***Leaves*** Evergreen, arching, sword-shaped, spined at the margin. Gray-green.
- NATIVE HABITAT Damp grasslands, South America.
- CULTIVATION Grow in fertile, moist but well-drained soil, in a warm, sunny site. Flowers dry well for winter arrangements; cut before fully open.
- PROPAGATION By seed in autumn, division in spring, or root cuttings in winter.

Z 9–10

HEIGHT 5–6ft (1.5–2m)

SPREAD 2ft (60cm)

Asteraceae/Compositae

ECHINOPS SPHAEROCEPHALUS

Habit Clump-forming. ***Flowers*** Tiny, in tight, globular heads borne on long, gray-white stems in late summer. Gray-white. ***Leaves*** Deeply divided, spiny. Gray-green above, white-downy beneath.
- NATIVE HABITAT Scrub, grasslands, from S. and C. Europe to Russia.
- CULTIVATION Grow in an open position in well-drained, not too fertile soil. Tolerates poor, dry soils.
- PROPAGATION By division or seed in autumn, or by root cuttings in winter.
- OTHER NAMES *E. paniculatus.*

Z 3–9

HEIGHT 6ft (2m)

SPREAD 3ft (1m)

Asphodelaceae/ Liliaceae

EREMURUS HIMALAICUS

Habit Upright, with fleshy rhizomes. ***Flowers*** Small, shallowly cup-shaped, in long, dense spires, in early summer. White. ***Leaves*** Strap-shaped, smooth, in basal clumps. Mid-green.
- NATIVE HABITAT Dry, rocky areas, Afghanistan, N.W. Himalayas.
- CULTIVATION Grow in a warm, sheltered site in well-drained, sandy soil. Rarely needs staking. Over winter protect crowns with a mulch of dry straw.
- PROPAGATION By division in spring or early autumn, or by seed in autumn.

Z 5–8

HEIGHT 6–8ft (2–2.5m)

SPREAD 3ft (1m)

Rosaceae	GOATSBEARD

ARUNCUS DIOICUS

Habit Clump-forming, rhizomatous. ***Flowers*** Tiny, carried in airy, branching, pyramidal plumes above the foliage, in midsummer. Creamy-white. ***Leaves*** Large, long-stalked, divided into lance-shaped, toothed leaflets. Dark green.

• NATIVE HABITAT Damp, shady woods, and streambanks, often in mountainous areas, from W. and C. Europe, Caucasus, S. Russia, and E. North America.

• CULTIVATION Thrives in moist soils and tolerates semi-shade. Grow in any moderately fertile, moisture-retentive but well-drained soil. Suitable for the back of an herbaceous border, and in a wild or woodland garden. Makes a magnificent specimen for waterside plantings.

• PROPAGATION By seed in autumn, or division in spring or autumn.

• OTHER NAMES *A. plumosus, A. sylvester, Spiraea aruncus.*

Z 3–7

HEIGHT
5ft (1.5m)

SPREAD
3ft (1m)

Ranunculaceae	GROUND CLEMATIS

CLEMATIS RECTA

Habit Upright, clump-forming. ***Flowers*** Sweetly scented, star-shaped, upright, borne in many-flowered terminal clusters in mid summer. Milky-white. ***Leaves*** Divided into pointed, oval-lance-shaped segments. Dark blue-green or gray-green.
• NATIVE HABITAT Scrub, on sunny hillsides, in S. and C. Europe, to Russia, and the Caucasus.
• CULTIVATION Grow in fertile, well-drained soil in sun. Cut down old flower stems in late winter.
• PROPAGATION By seed in autumn, or division in spring.

Z 3–7

HEIGHT
4–5ft
(1.2–1.5m)

SPREAD
3ft (1m)

Rosaceae	GREAT AMERICAN BURNET

SANGUISORBA CANADENSIS

Habit Clump-forming, rhizomatous. ***Flowers*** Tiny, in dense, slightly arching, bottle-brush spikes borne above the foliage in late summer. White. ***Leaves*** Divided, with 7–17 lance-shaped, toothed, leaflets, heart-shaped at the base. Mid-green.
• NATIVE HABITAT Marshes, N.E. North America.
• CULTIVATION Tolerates semi-shade. Grow in fertile, moist, well-drained soil. Good for woodland gardens and streambank or waterside plantings.
• PROPAGATION By division in spring, or by seed in autumn.

Z 3–8

HEIGHT
4–5ft
(1.2–1.5m)

SPREAD
2–3ft
(0.6–1m)

Papaveraceae	PLUME POPPY

MACLEAYA CORDATA

Habit Clump-forming, rhizomatous. ***Flowers*** Tiny, without petals, borne in dense, feathery, plume-like sprays in summer. Creamy-white. ***Leaves*** Large, rounded-heart-shaped, toothed and lobed, mostly basal. Gray to olive-green above, white beneath.
• NATIVE HABITAT Grassland in China and Japan.
• CULTIVATION Grow in moist but well-drained soil. Excellent at the back of an herbaceous border.
• PROPAGATION By division in early spring, or root cuttings in winter.

Z 4–9

HEIGHT
5–6ft
(1.5–2m)

SPREAD
4ft (1.2m)

Asteraceae/Compositae	WHITE MUGWORT, GHOSTPLANT

ARTEMISIA LACTIFLORA

Habit Vigorous, upright, clump-forming. ***Flowers*** Tiny, in large, open sprays, in summer. Creamy-yellow, opening from creamy-white buds. ***Leaves*** Divided into jagged-toothed segments. Dark green.
• NATIVE HABITAT Scrub, open areas in forests, W. China.
• CULTIVATION Tolerates partial shade. Grow in moisture-retentive, but well-drained soil. Needs unobtrusive staking. It makes a useful foliage plant as a backdrop for stronger colors.
• PROPAGATION By division in spring or autumn.

Z 5–8

HEIGHT
5–6ft
(1.5–2m)

SPREAD
2–3ft
(0.6–1m)

Zingiberaceae	SHELL FLOWER, SHELL GINGER

ALPINIA ZERUMBET

Habit Clump-forming with fleshy, ginger-scented rhizomes. ***Flowers*** Tubular in drooping clusters, mainly in summer. White, with yellow lips, marked pink at the throat. ***Leaves*** Evergreen, lance-shaped with fringed margins, borne on reed-like stems.
• NATIVE HABITAT Tropical forest margins, E. Asia.
• CULTIVATION Grow as a house or greenhouse plant in cooler climates. Water freely and fertilize every two weeks in growth. Needs high humidity.
• PROPAGATION Division in spring or early summer.
• OTHER NAMES *A. nutans*, *A. speciosa*.

Min. 64°F (18°C)

HEIGHT 10ft (3m)

SPREAD 3ft (1m)

Papaveraceae	PLUME POPPY

MACLEAYA MICROCARPA 'Coral Plume'

Habit Clump-forming, rhizomatous. ***Flowers*** Tiny, borne in airy, branched plumes in summer. Rich pink-buff. ***Leaves*** Large, rounded, lobed, heart-shaped at base. Gray-green above, downy beneath.
• NATIVE HABITAT Garden origin.
• CULTIVATION Tolerates partial shade. Grow in any well-drained soil. May be invasive but can be confined by slicing through and removing the roots at the margins of the clump.
• PROPAGATION By division in early spring, or root cuttings in winter.

Z 4–9

HEIGHT 6–8ft (2–2.5m)

SPREAD 3–4ft (1–1.2m)

Asphodelaceae/ Liliaceae	

EREMURUS ROBUSTUS

Habit Upright, with fleshy rhizomes. ***Flowers*** Small, shallowly cup-shaped, in long, dense spires on thick stems, in summer. Pink. ***Leaves*** Strap-shaped, smooth, in basal clumps, dying back in summer. Mid-green.
• NATIVE HABITAT Dry, rocky areas, C. Asia.
• CULTIVATION Grow in a warm, sheltered site in very well-drained, sandy soil. Needs staking. Mulch crowns in winter with straw.
• PROPAGATION By division in spring or early autumn, or by seed in autumn.

Z 5–8

HEIGHT 7ft (2.2m)

SPREAD 3ft (1m)

Malvaceae	

LAVATERA CACHEMIRIANA

Habit Short-lived, wiry-stemmed, woody-based. ***Flowers*** Cup-shaped, with widely spaced, silky petals, notched at the tip, in summer. Clear pink. ***Leaves*** Semi-evergreen, 3–5 lobed, rounded, heart-shaped at the base. Green, downy beneath.

- NATIVE HABITAT Meadows, W. Himalayas.
- CULTIVATION Tolerates partial shade. Grow in any fertile, well-drained soil.
- PROPAGATION By softwood cuttings in early spring or summer.
- OTHER NAMES *L. cachemirica.*

Z 6–8

HEIGHT 5–6ft (1.5–2m)

SPREAD 3ft (1m)

Ranunculaceae	

THALICTRUM DELAVAYI 'Hewitt's Double'

Habit Dense, clump-forming. ***Flowers*** Tiny, double, nodding, borne in open, fluffy, terminal sprays in mid- to late summer. Lilac-pink. ***Leaves*** Smooth, finely divided, resembling those of maidenhair fern. Mid-green.

- NATIVE HABITAT Garden origin.
- CULTIVATION Grow in cool, humus-rich, moist but well-drained, fertile soil, in sun or light, dappled shade. An elegant border perennial.
- PROPAGATION By division in spring.

Z 5–9

HEIGHT 5–6ft (1.5–2m)

SPREAD 2ft (60cm)

Malvaceae	TREE LAVATERA

LAVATERA 'Kew Rose'

Habit Robust, woody-based, sub-shrubby. ***Flowers*** Cup-shaped, with silky petals notched at the tip, borne on purple-tinted stems, in summer. Clear deep pink, with darker veining. ***Leaves*** Evergreen or semi-evergreen, 3–5 lobed, rounded, heart-shaped at base. Green, downy beneath.

- NATIVE HABITAT Garden origin.
- CULTIVATION Tolerates partial shade, but best in full sun. Grow in any fertile, well-drained soil.
- PROPAGATION By softwood cuttings in early spring or summer.

Z 7–10

HEIGHT 5–6ft (1.5–2m) or more

SPREAD 3ft (1m)

Apiaceae/Umbelliferae	

PIMPINELLA MAJOR 'Rosea'

Habit Robust, clump-forming. ***Flowers*** Tiny, borne in small umbels on thick, upright stems, in mid summer. Pink. ***Leaves*** Large, simply divided into toothed, almost heart-shaped segments. Dark green.

• NATIVE HABITAT Species occurs in scrub and grassland in Europe as far east as the Caucasus.

• CULTIVATION Grow in moist, fertile soil in sun or partial shade. Suitable for borders, wild gardens and wildflower borders.

• PROPAGATION By seed or division in early spring.

Z 5–9

HEIGHT to 4ft (1.2m)

SPREAD 2ft (60cm)

Rosaceae	MEADOWSWEET

FILIPENDULA PALMATA 'Rubra'

Habit Vigorous, upright. ***Flowers*** Tiny, in feathery plumes, on long, branching stems, in mid summer. Soft pink. ***Leaves*** Large, with 7–9 jaggedly cut lobes. Dark green.

• NATIVE HABITAT Damp meadows, prairies, E. North America.

• CULTIVATION Grow in moist or wet soils, where it tolerates sun. It will rapidly colonize a boggy garden.

• PROPAGATION By seed in autumn, or by division in autumn or winter.

• OTHER NAMES *F. rubra*.

Z 3–9

HEIGHT 6–8ft (2–2.5m)

SPREAD 4ft (1.2m)

Lamiaceae/Labiatae	

SALVIA INVOLUCRATA

Habit Upright, woody-based, sub-shrubby. ***Flowers*** Large, 2-lipped, borne in dense spikes from late summer to autumn. Rose-crimson with pink bracts. ***Leaves*** Oval, long-pointed, heart-shaped at the base. Rich green.

• NATIVE HABITAT Mexico.

• CULTIVATION Grow in a warm, sunny, sheltered site, in any moderately fertile, well-drained soil.

• PROPAGATION By seed or softwood cuttings in mid summer.

Z 7–9

HEIGHT 4–5ft (1.2–1.5m)

SPREAD 3ft (1m)

Asclepiadaceae	SILK WEED

ASCLEPIAS INCARNATA

Habit Upright, many-branched, tuberous-rooted. ***Flowers*** Small, borne in dense, thick-stemmed clusters, over long periods in summer. Pink to pink-purple, occasionally white. ***Leaves*** Narrowly lance-shaped, slightly fleshy. Blue-green.

• NATIVE HABITAT Marshes, scrub and by pools and lakes, in North America.

• CULTIVATION Grow in fertile, humus-rich, moist but well-drained soil, in a sunny site. Good for an herbaceous border, or for waterside plantings.

• PROPAGATION By seed or division in spring.

Z 3–8

HEIGHT to 5ft (1.5m)

SPREAD 2ft (60cm)

Polygonaceae

RHEUM PALMATUM 'Atrosanguineum'

Habit Clump-forming, with a thick rootstock. ***Flowers*** Tiny, in large, fluffy plumes, borne on long, thick, branching stems in early summer. Crimson. ***Leaves*** Very large, lobed, deeply cut, glossy. Dark red-purple on emergence, later bluish-green.

• NATIVE HABITAT The species occurs in scrub, rocky areas and by streamsides in the mountains of W. China.

• CULTIVATION Grow in deep, fertile, moisture-retentive but well-drained soil, in sun or dappled shade. An annual mulch of organic matter is beneficial. Suitable for planting by streambanks (above water level), for large borders, and a very attractive addition to a woodland garden. It requires a generous allocation of space for best effect. A very handsome plant.

• PROPAGATION By division in spring.

• OTHER NAMES *R. palmatum* 'Atropurpureum'.

Z 5–9

HEIGHT
6ft (2m)

SPREAD
6ft (2m)

Asteraceae/Compositae	

CIRSIUM RIVULARE ATROPURPUREUM

Habit Clump-forming, shortly rhizomatous. ***Flowers*** Small, thistle-like, in clusters on long stems, in mid summer. Deep crimson. ***Leaves*** Narrow, deeply cut, with weak-spined margins, mostly in basal clumps.

- NATIVE HABITAT Species occurs in damp, usually acid meadows, in C. and S.W. Europe.
- CULTIVATION Prefers moist, well-drained, humus-rich, sandy soils. Will not tolerate waterlogged soil.
- PROPAGATION By division in spring, or basal shoots in summer.

Z 4–8

HEIGHT 4ft (1.2m) or more

SPREAD 2ft (60cm)

Campanulaceae	

LOBELIA TUPA

Habit Clump-forming, with a tufted rootstock. ***Flowers*** Large, 2-lipped, with 3 spreading lower lobes, borne in very long spikes in late summer. Bright brick-red. ***Leaves*** Large, lance-shaped, softly hairy, mostly basal. Bright green.

- NATIVE HABITAT Sandy, coastal hills, Chile.
- CULTIVATION Grow in fertile, sandy but humus-rich, very well-drained soil, in sun. Suitable for a warm, sunny border. Dislikes cold, wet conditions in winter.
- PROPAGATION By seed or division in spring.

Z 8–9

HEIGHT 5–6ft (1.5–2m)

SPREAD 3ft (1m)

Papaveraceae	SATIN POPPY

MECONOPSIS NAPAULENSIS

Habit Clump-forming, short-lived perennial or biennial. ***Flowers*** Large, drooping and poppy-like, satiny, borne in branched clusters on long, bristly stems in late spring and early summer. Red, purple or blue. ***Leaves*** Deeply divided. Pale green, clothed in stiff, bronze hairs.

- NATIVE HABITAT Himalayas, C. Nepal to S.W. China.
- CULTIVATION Grow in moist, humus-rich soils, in partial shade or shade, in a cool, sheltered site.
- PROPAGATION By fresh seed in late summer.

pH

Z 6–8

HEIGHT 6ft (2m)

SPREAD 3ft (1m)

Melianthaceae	HONEYBUSH

MELIANTHUS MAJOR

Habit Open-branched evergreen shrub, herbaceous in cool climates. ***Flowers*** Small, tubular, in terminal spikes, in summer. Blood-red. ***Leaves*** Evergreen or deciduous, to 18in (45cm) long, divided into 7–13 toothed, oval leaflets. Glaucous blue.

- NATIVE HABITAT Cape Province, South Africa.
- CULTIVATION Grow in fertile, well-drained soil in sun. Mulch in winter. Cut back top growth in spring. Excellent herbaceous foliage plant in cool climates.
- PROPAGATION Seed in spring or semi-ripe cuttings in summer.

Z 8–10

HEIGHT 6–10ft (2–3m), to 4ft (1.2m) in cool climates

SPREAD 6–10ft (2–3m)

Apiaceae/Umbelliferae	PURPLE FENNEL

FOENICULUM VULGARE 'Purpureum'

Habit Upright, branching. ***Flowers*** Small, in large, flat umbels, in summer. Yellow. ***Leaves*** Aromatic, finely divided into slender filaments. Bronze-purple.

- NATIVE HABITAT Garden origin.
- CULTIVATION Grow in any well-drained soil in sun. Excellent for foliage contrast in a border, especially with silver- or golden-yellow-leaved plants. Deadhead to prevent seeding.
- PROPAGATION By seed in autumn. May self-sow.
- OTHER NAMES *F. vulgare* 'Bronze'.

Z 4–9

HEIGHT to 6ft (2m)

SPREAD 18in (45cm)

Verbenaceae	PURPLE TOP

VERBENA BONARIENSIS

Habit Clump-forming. ***Flowers*** Tiny, in broad, flattened heads on slender, wiry stems, in summer and autumn. Bright blue-purple. ***Leaves*** Lance-shaped, serrated, wrinkled, in basal rosettes. Dark green.

- NATIVE HABITAT Damp grassland, South America.
- CULTIVATION Grow in any fertile soil. May self-sow where conditions suit.
- PROPAGATION By stem cuttings in late summer or autumn, or by seed in autumn or spring.
- OTHER NAMES *V. patagonica*.

Z 7–10

HEIGHT 5ft (1.5m)

SPREAD 20in (50cm)

Melanthiaceae/ Liliaceae	BLACK FALSE HELLEBORE

VERATRUM NIGRUM

Habit Clump-forming, rhizomatous. ***Flowers*** Small, in dense, branched plumes, from late summer onwards. Chocolate-purple. ***Leaves*** Oval to narrowly oval, deeply pleated. Brilliant green.

- NATIVE HABITAT Sub-alpine meadows, S. Europe, Asia and Siberia.
- CULTIVATION Grow in deep, fertile soils in partial-shade, or part-day sun where soils are reliably moist. Provide shelter from wind. The rhizomes are toxic.
- PROPAGATION By division or seed in autumn.

Z 4–9

HEIGHT 6ft (2m)

SPREAD 2ft (60cm)

Asteraceae/Compositae	CARDOON

CYNARA CARDUNCULUS

Habit Clump-forming. ***Flowers*** Large, thistle-like, on thick, gray stems, in late summer. Purple. ***Leaves*** Arching, deeply divided, usually spiny, to 3ft (1m) long. Silver-gray.

- NATIVE HABITAT Rocky slopes, dry grasslands, S.W. Europe.
- CULTIVATION Tolerant of heavy clay soils. Grow in any deep, fertile soil. A stately plant for a large border. The flowers dry well if cut before fully open, and the blanched stems are edible.
- PROPAGATION By seed or division in spring.

Z 7–10

HEIGHT 6ft (2m)

SPREAD 3ft (1m)

Ranunculaceae	MONKSHOOD

ACONITUM 'Spark's Variety'

Habit Upright, tuberous-rooted. ***Flowers*** Large, hooded, with a hemispherical helmet, borne on widely branching, rather flexuous stems in mid to late summer. Rich violet-blue. ***Leaves*** Deeply divided into 3 or 5 narrow, glossy lobes. Dark green.

- NATIVE HABITAT Garden origin.
- CULTIVATION Grow in moist but well-drained, fertile soil, in sun or partial shade. Divide every 2–3 years to maintain vigor. The roots are toxic.
- PROPAGATION By division in autumn.

☼ ◊

Z 3–7

HEIGHT
4ft (1.2m)

SPREAD
20in (50cm)

Lamiaceae/Labiatae	

SALVIA GUARANITICA

Habit Upright, sub-shrubby. ***Flowers*** Tubular, 2-lipped, in branching spikes, in late summer and autumn. Rich deep blue. ***Leaves*** Oval, pointed, heart-shaped at the base. Dark green.

- NATIVE HABITAT Brazil.
- CULTIVATION Grow in a greenhouse in potting soil, or outdoors in full sun in a warm sheltered site, in fertile, well-drained soil. Good for tubs or large pots in a cool sunroom. May be grown as an annual.
- PROPAGATION By seed in spring or softwood cuttings in summer.

☼ ◊

Z 9–11

HEIGHT
5ft (1.5m)

SPREAD
24in (60cm)

Lamiaceae/Labiatae	BOG SAGE

SALVIA ULIGINOSA

Habit Upright, sub-shrubby. ***Flowers*** Tubular, 2-lipped, in long, branching spires, in late summer and autumn. Clear deep blue. ***Leaves*** Oblong to lance-shaped, saw-toothed. Mid-green.

- NATIVE HABITAT Brazil, Uruguay, Argentina.
- CULTIVATION Grow in fertile, moist but well-drained soil, in full sun. Needs a warm, sheltered site. Provide support. May also be grown in tubs or large pots in a cool sunroom.
- PROPAGATION By seed in spring or softwood cuttings in summer.

☼ ◆

Z 8–9

HEIGHT
6ft (2m)

SPREAD
18in (45cm)

Campanulaceae	MILKY BELLFLOWER

CAMPANULA LACTIFLORA 'Prichard's Variety'

Habit Upright, slender-stemmed. ***Flowers*** Large, nodding, bell-shaped, in dense, leafy, branched heads, from early summer to autumn. Violet-blue. ***Leaves*** Narrowly oval, borne along the length of the stem. Mid-green.

• NATIVE HABITAT Garden origin.

• CULTIVATION Tolerates partial shade. Grow in any fertile, moisture-retentive soil. May need staking in windy situations. This is an excellent long-lasting perennial for planting in an herbaceous border or at the edge of a woodland garden in dappled sunshine. It performs a very useful function in providing a contrasting color among the autumnal tints later in the season. Excellent as a cut flower.

• PROPAGATION By basal cuttings in early summer, or division in autumn or spring.

Z 5–7

HEIGHT
30–36in (75cm–1m) or more

SPREAD
24in (60cm)

Asteraceae/Compositae	GLOBE THISTLE

ECHINOPS BANNATICUS

Habit Clump-forming, upright. ***Flowers*** Tiny, in tight, globular heads, borne on branching stems in late summer. Pale to mid-blue. ***Leaves*** Narrow, deeply cut, cobwebbed with fine white hair. Green above, white-downy beneath.

- NATIVE HABITAT Scrub, grasslands, S.E. Europe.
- CULTIVATION Tolerates poor, dry soils. Grow in an open position in well-drained, not-too-fertile soil.
- PROPAGATION By division or seed in autumn, or by root cuttings in winter.
- OTHER NAMES *E. ritro.*

Z 3–8

HEIGHT 6ft (2m)

SPREAD 3ft (1m)

Gunneraceae	GIANT RHUBARB

GUNNERA MANICATA

Habit Slow-growing, massive, clump-forming, rhizomatous. ***Flowers*** Tiny, in conical spikes, in early summer. Light green. ***Leaves*** Rounded, lobed often heart-shaped at base, 5ft (1.5m) across, prickly at the margin, on prickly leaf stalks. Dull green.

- NATIVE HABITAT By streamsides, and among wet, mountain rocks, S. Brazil.
- CULTIVATION Grow in moist, fertile soil and provide shelter from wind. Mulch crowns with dead leaves in winter.
- PROPAGATION By seed in autumn or spring.

Z 7–10

HEIGHT 6ft (2m)

SPREAD 10ft (3m) or more

Leguminosae/ Papilionaceae	

GALEGA × *HARTLANDII* 'Lady Wilson'

Habit Vigorous, upright. ***Flowers*** Small, pea-like, borne in branched spikes above the foliage in summer. Lilac-blue and pinkish-white. ***Leaves*** Divided, with 4–8 pairs of oval leaflets. Mid-green.

- NATIVE HABITAT Garden origin.
- CULTIVATION Grow in an open position, in any well-drained soil. Needs staking.
- PROPAGATION By division in winter.

Z 4–9

HEIGHT 5ft (1.5m)

SPREAD 3ft (1m)

Apiaceae/Umbelliferae	ANGELICA

ANGELICA ARCHANGELICA

Habit Upright, perennial. ***Flowers*** Small, in broad, rounded umbels, in late summer. Greenish-white to cream. ***Leaves*** Aromatic, deeply divided, coarsely toothed. Bright green.

- NATIVE HABITAT Damp habitats throughout N. and E. Europe, to C. Asia.
- CULTIVATION Grow in any well-drained soil in sun or shade. Remove seed heads, otherwise plants may die, although they often self-sow. Stems may be crystallized for culinary use.
- PROPAGATION By seed when ripe.

Z 4–9

HEIGHT 6ft (2m) or more

SPREAD 3ft (1m) or more

Scrophulariaceae	

VERBASCUM OLYMPICUM

Habit Rosette-forming biennial or short-lived perennial. ***Flowers*** Small, on tall, branching, white-felted spires from mid summer onwards. Bright golden-yellow. ***Leaves*** Lance-shaped, covered in white, woolly felt, forming a dense basal clump.
• NATIVE HABITAT Dry, rocky hillsides, Greece and Turkey.
• CULTIVATION Tolerant of dry and alkaline soils. Grow in an open, sunny site in any well-drained soil.
• PROPAGATION By seed in spring or late summer, or by root cuttings in winter. Self-sows easily.

Z 6–9

HEIGHT
6ft (2m)

SPREAD
3ft (1m)

Apiaceae/Umbelliferae	GIANT FENNEL

FERULA COMMUNIS

Habit Robust, upright. ***Flowers*** Small, in rounded umbels, on long, thick, branched stems, from late spring to summer. Yellow. ***Leaves*** Large, finely cut into very slender, linear segments. Rich green.
• NATIVE HABITAT Rough, rocky ground around the Mediterranean.
• CULTIVATION Grow in any well-drained soil. Plants may die after flowering. Not to be confused with culinary fennel, *Foeniculum vulgaris*.
• PROPAGATION By seed when ripe.

Z 6–9

HEIGHT
6–7ft
(2–2.2m)

SPREAD
3–4ft
(1–1.2m)

Dipsacaceae	GIANT SCABIOUS, YELLOW SCABIOUS

CEPHALARIA GIGANTEA

Habit Robust, clump-forming. ***Flowers*** Large, pincushion-like, on upright, wiry stems, in mid summer. Pale primrose-yellow. ***Leaves*** Divided into broadly lance-shaped segments. Dark green.
• NATIVE HABITAT Damp areas, Caucasus to Siberia.
• CULTIVATION Grow in fertile, moist but well-drained soil, in full sun. Good for large borders or for naturalizing in a wild garden.
• PROPAGATION By division in spring, or seed in autumn.
• OTHER NAMES *C. tatarica*.

Z 3–7

HEIGHT
6ft (2m)
or more

SPREAD
4ft (1.2m)

Asteraceae/Compositae

RUDBECKIA 'Goldquelle'

Habit Compact, upright, branching. ***Flowers*** Large, fully double, daisy-like, with many bright yellow petals around a green center, in late summer and autumn. ***Leaves*** Deeply divided, with 3–7 pointed, toothed segments. Green.

- NATIVE HABITAT Garden origin.
- CULTIVATION Tolerates light shade. Grow in any moderately fertile, moisture-retentive but well-drained soil. Flowers are good for cutting.
- PROPAGATION By division in spring.
- OTHER NAMES *R. laciniata* 'Goldquelle'.

Z 3–9

HEIGHT 4–5ft (1.2–1.5m)

SPREAD 3ft (1m)

Asteraceae/Compositae

LIGULARIA STENOCEPHALA

Habit Open, clump-forming. ***Flowers*** Small, daisy-like, in tall spikes, on long, dark purple stems, from mid- to late summer. Orange-yellow. ***Leaves*** Rounded with irregular jagged edges. Dark green.

- NATIVE HABITAT Wet mountains in Japan.
- CULTIVATION Grow in deep, fertile, humus-rich soil. Provide wind shelter and mulch annually with organic matter.
- PROPAGATION By division in spring or by seed in spring or autumn.

Z 4–8

HEIGHT 4ft (1.2m) or more

SPREAD 2ft (60cm)

Asteraceae/Compositae

LIGULARIA PRZEWALSKII

Habit Loosely clump-forming. ***Flowers*** Small, daisy-like, on long, purple-stemmed spikes, from mid- to late summer. Yellow. ***Leaves*** Palmately lobed, with deep, jaggedly cut segments. Dark green.

- NATIVE HABITAT Damp mountains, N. China.
- CULTIVATION Tolerates dappled shade. Grow in deep, humus-rich soil in a sheltered site. Suited to waterside plantings. Leaves prone to slug damage.
- PROPAGATION By division in spring, or by seed in spring or autumn.
- OTHER NAMES *Senecio przewalskii*.

Z 4–8

HEIGHT 4–6ft (1.2–2m)

SPREAD 3ft (1m)

Asphodelaceae/ Liliaceae	

KNIPHOFIA 'Wrexham Buttercup'

Habit Upright, clump-forming. ***Flowers*** Small, narrowly tubular, downward facing, borne in terminal spikes, on sturdy stems in late summer and autumn. Clear lemon-yellow. ***Leaves*** Grass-like, narrowly linear, arching to form basal clumps. Mid-green.

• NATIVE HABITAT Garden origin.

• CULTIVATION Grow in full sun, in moisture-retentive but well-drained soil. Needs ample moisture when in growth. Mulch crowns in cold winter areas. This plant is invaluable for its long flowering period, which is aided by the immediate removal of the dead flower stems. There are many bicolored cultivars of *Kniphofia* (red-hot poker), which are very garden-worthy, but considerably fewer single-colored of which this is an excellent example.

• PROPAGATION By division in spring.

☼ ◊

Z 6–9

HEIGHT
3–4½ ft
(1–1.4m)

SPREAD
2–2½ft
(60–75cm)

Asteraceae/Compositae

INULA MAGNIFICA

Habit Vigorous, clump-forming, upright. ***Flowers*** Large, daisy-like, with very slender petals, borne in clusters on long, leafy stems in late summer. Rich yellow. ***Leaves*** Lance-shaped, toothed, smooth above, hairy beneath. Dark green.

- NATIVE HABITAT In scrub in the E. Caucasus.
- CULTIVATION Tolerates partial shade. Prefers deep, fertile, moisture-retentive soils.
- PROPAGATION By seed or division in spring or autumn.

Z 4–8

HEIGHT
6ft (1.8m)

SPREAD
3ft (1m)

Scrophulariaceae

VERBASCUM 'Cotswold Queen'

Habit Upright, rosette-forming. ***Flowers*** Small, 5-lobed, in tall, branching racemes, throughout summer. Apricot-buff with a darker eye. ***Leaves*** Semi-evergreen, oval, mostly in basal rosettes, but with smaller, narrower stem leaves. Mid-green.

- NATIVE HABITAT Garden origin.
- CULTIVATION Grow in fertile, well-drained soil, in an open, sunny site. Is short-lived, so propagate regularly. A beautiful, long-flowering specimen for herbaceous borders and scree plantings.
- PROPAGATION By root cuttings in winter.

Z 5–9

HEIGHT
3–4ft (1–1.2m) or more

SPREAD
1–2ft (30–60cm)

Asphodelaceae/ Liliaceae — FOXTAIL LILY

EREMURUS ISABELLINUS Shelford Hybrids

Habit Upright, clump-forming, with fleshy roots. ***Flowers*** Small, shallowly cup-shaped, in tall, sturdy spires, in profusion in mid summer. Yellow, orange, pink, buff, or creamy-white. ***Leaves*** Strap-shaped, in basal rosettes. Gray-green.

- NATIVE HABITAT Garden origin.
- CULTIVATION Requires a sheltered site. Protect crowns from frost with straw. Needs staking.
- PROPAGATION By division in spring or early autumn, or by seed in autumn.

Z 5–8

HEIGHT
5ft (1.5m)

SPREAD
2ft (60cm)

Asteraceae/Compositae

HELIOPSIS HELIANTHOIDES var. *SCABRA* 'Light of Loddon'

Habit Upright, clump-forming. ***Flowers*** Double, marguerite-like, in profusion, on strong stems, from late summer to early autumn. Rich golden-yellow. ***Leaves*** Coarse, lance-shaped, serrated. Dark green.

- NATIVE HABITAT Garden origin.
- CULTIVATION Prefers fertile, moist soil, but will tolerate poorer soils. Flowers are good for cutting. Very hardy, long-lived, and easily grown. Lift and divide clumps periodically to maintain vigor.
- PROPAGATION By division in autumn or spring.

Z 4–9

HEIGHT
4–5ft
(1.2–1.5m)

SPREAD
2ft (60cm)

Asteraceae/Compositae

LIGULARIA 'Gregynog Gold'

Habit Clump-forming. ***Flowers*** Small, daisy-like, in tall, pyramidal spires from mid- to late summer. Rich orange-yellow. ***Leaves*** Large, heart-shaped, saw-toothed. Dark green.

- NATIVE HABITAT Garden origin.
- CULTIVATION Grow in a wind-sheltered site, in moist, well-drained soil. Tolerates full sun where soils remain moist. Excellent for damp borders, or waterside plantings with the roots above water level.
- PROPAGATION By division in spring.
- OTHER NAMES *Senecio* 'Gregynog Gold'.

Z 4–8

HEIGHT
6ft (2m)

SPREAD
2ft (60cm)

Zingiberaceae

HEDYCHIUM DENSIFLORUM

Habit Clump-forming, thickly rhizomatous. ***Flowers*** Short-lived, small, fragrant, in dense, upright spikes, in late summer. Orange or yellow. ***Leaves*** Oblong to broadly lance-shaped, conspicuously ribbed, glossy, on reed-like stems. Dark green.

- NATIVE HABITAT Damp forest margins, Himalayas.
- CULTIVATION Grow in rich, moisture-retentive soil in a warm, sheltered border or cool sunroom.
- PROPAGATION By division when growth resumes in spring.

Z 7–9

HEIGHT
4–6ft
(1.2–2m)

SPREAD
2ft (60cm)

Heliconiaceae — PARROT'S FLOWER, PARROT'S PLANTAIN

HELICONIA PSITTACORUM

Habit Tufted, slender-stemmed. ***Flowers*** Cylindrical, in upright clusters (on mature plants only), in summer. Orange, green-tipped, enclosed in large, waxy, orange-red bracts. ***Leaves*** Evergreen, lance-shaped, on long, sometimes scarlet-tinted stalks.

- NATIVE HABITAT Tropical forests of E. Brazil.
- CULTIVATION Grow as a house or greenhouse plant in cooler climates. Water freely when in growth, otherwise water very sparingly.
- PROPAGATION By seed or division in spring.

Min. 64°F
(18°C)

HEIGHT
To 6ft (2m)

SPREAD
3ft (1m)

DELPHINIUMS

Delphiniums are a genus of annuals and perennials grown for their long spikes of cup-shaped, single to fully double flowers, in a range of colors from creamy-whites through lilac-pinks to deep indigo-blue, often with a contrasting "eye" or "bee" formed by the inner sepals. They are well suited to herbaceous borders, and are also grown in beds for cutting.

The delphiniums most usually seen in gardens are hybrids of *D. elatum*, and are clump-forming, fleshy-crowned perennials that flower from early to midsummer. Their leaves are lobed, divided and range from mid- to bright green. Hybrids of *D.* x *belladonna*, are also clump-forming perennials, with more slender, wiry stems bearing branched spikes of spurred flowers.

Delphiniums should be grown in fertile, moist but well-drained soil in full sun with shelter from strong winds. During growth, especially in spring and early summer, they require regular watering and a weekly feed with a balanced liquid fertilizer. To produce good quality blooms, thin out the young shoots when they reach 3in (7cm) tall, leaving 2–3 shoots on young plants, 5–7 on well-established perennials. All but the dwarf cultivars need staking: the lower-growing cultivars with twiggy sticks; the taller ones with stakes, or "grow-through" supports. To avoid damage, insert supports as plants reach 12in (30cm) high, usually by mid-spring. Well-fed and watered plants will produce a second, smaller crop of flowers in late summer. Deadhead flowered spikes, cutting back to the smaller, branching sideshoots. Cut back all growth in autumn.

Both *D. elatum* and *D.* x *belladonna* hybrids can be propagated by taking heeled basal cuttings, 3–4in (7–10cm) long, in early spring. The *D.* x *belladonna* hybrids can also be increased by division.

_D._ 'Butterball'
Flowers Large, semi-double, borne in spikes to 20in (50cm) long. White, overlaid with very pale greenish-yellow, with creamy-yellow eyes.
• HEIGHT 5–5½ft (1.5–1.7m).
• SPREAD 2½ft (75cm).

_D._ 'Butterball'
D. elatum hybrid

Z 2–7

_D._ 'Sandpiper'
Flowers Large, semi-double, borne in spikes to 30in (75cm) long. White with dark creamy-brown eyes.
• HEIGHT 3–4½ft (1–1.35m).
• SPREAD 2½ft (75cm).

_D._ 'Sandpiper'
D. elatum hybrid

Z 2–7

D. 'Olive Poppleton'

Flowers Large, semi-double, borne in spikes to 3ft (1m) long. White with fawn eyes.
- HEIGHT 6–8ft (2–2.5m).
- SPREAD 2½–3ft (75cm–1m).

D. 'Olive Poppleton'
D. elatum hybrid

Z 2–7

D. 'Langdon's Royal Flush'

Flowers Large, semi-double, borne in spikes to 34in (85cm) long. Pinkish-purple, with cream eyes. The petals of the upper flowers are darker than the lower, providing elegant gradation of colour.
- HEIGHT 6ft (2m).
- SPREAD 2½–3ft (75cm–1m).

D. 'Langdon's Royal Flush'
D. elatum hybrid

Z 2–7

D. 'Emily Hawkins'

Flowers Large, semi-double, borne in spikes to 32in (80cm) long. Pale blue, flushed lilac with fawn eyes.
- HEIGHT 6–7ft (2–2.2m).
- SPREAD 2½–3ft (75cm–1m).

D. 'Emily Hawkins'
D. elatum hybrid

Z 2–7

D. 'Fanfare'

Flowers Large, semi-double, borne in spikes to 2–2½ft (60–75cm) long. Pale blue to silvery-mauve, with white and violet eyes.
- HEIGHT 6–7ft (2–2.2m).
- SPREAD 2½–3ft (75cm–1m).

D. 'Fanfare'
D. elatum hybrid

Z 2–7

D. 'Strawberry Fair'

Flowers Large, semi-double, borne in spikes to 31in (78cm) long. Mulberry-pink with white eyes.
- HEIGHT 5½–6ft (1.7–2m).
- SPREAD 2½–3ft (75cm–1m).

***D.* 'Strawberry Fair'**
D. elatum hybrid

Z 2–7

D. 'Mighty Atom'

Flowers Large, semi-double, produced in spikes to 30in (75cm) long. Mid-violet with violet marked, yellowish-brown eyes.
- HEIGHT 5–6ft (1.5–2m).
- SPREAD 2½ft (75cm).

***D.* 'Mighty Atom'**
D. elatum hybrid

Z 2–7

D. 'Bruce'

Flowers Large, semi-double, produced in spikes to 4ft (1.2m) long. Deep violet-purple, flushed silver at the center, with gray-brown eyes.
- HEIGHT 5½–7ft (1.7–2.2m).
- SPREAD 2½–3ft (75cm–1m).

***D.* 'Bruce'**
D. elatum hybrid

Z 2–7

D. 'Gillian Dallas'

Flowers Large, semi-double, produced in spikes to 32in (80cm) long. Pale lilac, growing paler toward the petal margins, with white eyes.
- HEIGHT 6ft (2m).
- SPREAD 2½–3ft (75–1m).

***D.* 'Gillian Dallas'**
D. elatum hybrid

Z 2–7

D. 'Spindrift'

Flowers Large, semi-double, in spikes to 3ft (1m) long. Pink-purple, overlaid with pale blue, and with creamy-white eyes; becoming more intensely blue at the center. On acid soils, the petal color becomes green-tinted.
- HEIGHT 5½–6ft (1.7–2m).
- SPREAD 2½–3ft (75cm–1m).

***D.* 'Spindrift'**
D. elatum hybrid

Z 2–7

D. 'Blue Dawn'

Flowers Large, semi-double, borne in spikes to 4ft (1.2m) long. Pale blue, flushed pink-purple, with dark brown eyes.
- HEIGHT 6–7ft (2–2.2m).
- SPREAD 2½–3ft (75cm–1m).

***D.* 'Blue Dawn'**
D. elatum hybrid

Z 2–7

D. × *BELLADONNA* 'Blue Bees'

Habit Upright, branching.
Flowers Single, occasionally semi-double, to ¾in (2cm) or more across, borne in loose, delicate spikes, to 12in (30cm) long. Sky-blue.
Leaves Palmately divided. Mid- to bright green.
• HEIGHT 3½–5ft (1.1–1.5m).
• SPREAD 2ft (60cm).

***D.* × *belladonna* 'Blue Bees'**

Z 3–7

D. 'Lord Butler'

Flowers Large, semi-double, produced in spikes to 30in (75cm) long. Pale blue flushed pale lilac, with blue-marked, white eyes.
• HEIGHT 5–5½ft (1.5–1.7m).
• SPREAD 2½ft (75cm).

***D.* 'Lord Butler'**
D. elatum hybrid

Z 3–7

D. GRANDIFLORUM 'Blue Butterfly'

Habit Upright, short-lived.
Flowers Single, to 1½in (3.5cm) across, in loose, branching spikes to 6in (15cm) long. Deep blue.
Leaves Palmately divided. Bright green.
• OTHER NAMES *D. chinense* 'Blue Butterfly'.
• HEIGHT 18in (45cm).
• SPREAD 12in (30cm).

***D. grandiflorum* 'Blue Butterfly'**

Z 4–7

D. 'Chelsea Star'

Flowers Large, semi-double, borne in spikes to 3½ft (1.1m) long. Rich deep violet with white eyes.
• HEIGHT 6ft (2m).
• SPREAD 2½–3ft (75cm–1m).

***D.* 'Chelsea Star'**
D. elatum hybrid

Z 2–7

D. 'Loch Leven'

Flowers Large, semi-double, borne in spikes to 3ft (1m) long. Clear blue with white eyes.
• HEIGHT 5½ft (1.7m).
• SPREAD 2½ft (75cm).

***D.* 'Loch Leven'**
D. elatum hybrid

Z 2–7

D. 'Blue Nile'

Flowers Large, semi-double, borne in spikes to 27in (68cm) long. Rich deep blue, with blue-streaked, white eyes.
• HEIGHT 5–5½ft (1.5–1.7m).
• SPREAD 2½ft (75cm).

***D.* 'Blue Nile'**
D. elatum hybrid

Z 2–7

D. 'Sungleam'

Flowers Large, semi-double, 16–30in (40–75cm) long, borne in spikes. White, overlaid with pale yellow, and with yellow eyes.
• HEIGHT 5½–6ft (1.7–2m).
• SPREAD 2½–3ft (75cm–1m).

***D.* 'Sungleam'**
D. elatum hybrid

Z 2–7

Ranunculaceae	RAMCHATKA BUGBANE

CIMICIFUGA SIMPLEX

Habit Upright, rhizomatous. ***Flowers*** Tiny, star-shaped, fragrant, borne in slender, dark-stemmed, arching spikes, in autumn. White. ***Leaves*** Divided into narrowly oval, toothed and irregularly lobed, leaflets. Fresh green.

- NATIVE HABITAT Alpine and sub-alpine meadows, Mongolia, Kamchatka, Japan.
- CULTIVATION Grow in moist, humus-rich soil, in shade or partial shade. Needs staking. Excellent for shady borders and woodland gardens.
- PROPAGATION By fresh seed, or division in spring.

Z 3–8

HEIGHT
4–5ft
(1.2–1.5m)

SPREAD
2ft (60cm)

Ranunculaceae	JAPANESE ANEMONE

ANEMONE × HYBRIDA 'Honorine Jobert'

Habit Vigorous, branching, spreading. ***Flowers*** Single, slightly cupped, with 6–9 pure white petals surrounding a boss of golden stamens, borne on wiry stems, from late summer to early autumn. ***Leaves*** Deeply divided. Dark green.

- NATIVE HABITAT Garden origin.
- CULTIVATION Grow in moderately fertile, well-drained soil, in sun or partial shade. An invaluable, long-flowering specimen for a late summer border.
- PROPAGATION By division in spring or autumn.

Z 4–8

HEIGHT
5ft (1.5m)

SPREAD
2ft (60cm)

Asteraceae/Compositae	

LEUCANTHEMELLA SEROTINA

Habit Erect, bushy. ***Flowers*** Large, single, daisy-like, borne in sprays in late autumn. White with greenish centers. ***Leaves*** Lance-shaped, lobed, toothed. Dark green.

- NATIVE HABITAT Damp habitats in S. E. Europe.
- CULTIVATION Grow in moist but well-drained fertile soil in full sun. The flowers are good for cutting. A statuesque perennial for a large border.
- PROPAGATION By seed or division in spring or autumn.
- OTHER NAMES *Chrysanthemum uliginosum.*

Z 4–9

HEIGHT
7ft (2.2m)

SPREAD
2ft (60cm)

Asteraceae/Compositae	JOE PYE WEED

EUPATORIUM PURPUREUM

Habit Robust, clump-forming, upright. ***Flowers*** Tiny, tubular, in dense, terminal heads, from late summer to autumn. Pink-purple. ***Leaves*** Coarse, finely toothed, lance-shaped to oval, borne in whorls along purple-tinted stems. Mid-green.

• NATIVE HABITAT Damp woodland, E. North America.

• CULTIVATION Grow in moist, fertile, humus-rich soil, in sun or partial shade. Suitable for wild or woodland gardens. Very attractive to butterflies. Difficult to place in a border because of its height. Therefore, careful selection of its companions is required: *Rudbeckia laciniata* and *Macleaya cordata* would be suitable neighbors before descending to tall Michaelmas daisies (*Aster*), *Helenium* and *Persicaria* (*Polygonum*) *amplexicaule*.

• PROPAGATION By seed in spring, or by division in early spring or autumn.

Z 3–9

HEIGHT to 7ft (2.2m)

SPREAD to 3ft (1m)

Ranunculaceae

ANEMONE HUPEHENSIS 'September Charm'

Habit Vigorous, branching, stoloniferous. ***Flowers*** Single, slightly cupped, in wiry-stemmed umbels, from late summer to early autumn. Clear silvery-pink, with a darker petal reverse. ***Leaves*** More or less evergreen, deeply divided. Dark green.

- NATIVE HABITAT Garden origin.
- CULTIVATION Grow in well-drained soil, in sun or partial shade. Excellent in a late summer border.
- PROPAGATION By division in spring or autumn, or by root cuttings.

Z 4–8

HEIGHT 30in (75cm)

SPREAD 20in (50cm)

Ranunculaceae

ANEMONE HUPEHENSIS var. *JAPONICA* 'Bressingham Glow'

Habit Vigorous, branching, clump-forming. ***Flowers*** Semi-double, slightly cupped, borne on wiry stems, from late summer to early autumn. Bright rose-purple. ***Leaves*** Deeply divided. Dark green.

- NATIVE HABITAT Garden origin.
- CULTIVATION Grow in any moderately fertile, well-drained soil, in sun or partial shade. A beautiful long-flowering perennial for a late summer border.
- PROPAGATION By division in spring or autumn.

Z 4–8

HEIGHT 4–5ft (1.2–1.5m)

SPREAD 2ft (60cm)

Lamiaceae/Labiatae

SALVIA INVOLUCRATA 'Bethellii'

Habit Upright, woody-based, sub-shrubby. ***Flowers*** Large, 2-lipped, borne in dense, spike-like heads, from late summer to autumn. Cerise-crimson with pink bracts. ***Leaves*** Oval, heart-shaped at the base. Mid-green.

- NATIVE HABITAT Garden origin.
- CULTIVATION Grow in a warm, sunny site, in any moderately fertile, well-drained soil. Provide good protection from cold wind.
- PROPAGATION By softwood cuttings in mid summer.

Z 7–9

HEIGHT 4–5ft (1.2–1.5m)

SPREAD 3ft (1m)

Phytolaccaceae | RED-INK PLANT, VIRGINIA POKEWEED

PHYTOLACCA AMERICANA

Habit Stout, upright. ***Flowers*** Small, in dense, upright spikes, on thick stems, in late spring or summer. White or pink. ***Fruits*** Globose, shiny, toxic. Black-purple. ***Leaves*** Large, oval to lance-shaped. Bright green, purple in autumn.

- NATIVE HABITAT Grassland, E. North America.
- CULTIVATION Grow in moist but well-drained fertile soil. The berries, although attractive, are toxic. Not suitable for gardens where children play.
- PROPAGATION By seed in autumn or spring.
- OTHER NAMES *P. decandra.*

Z 4–9

HEIGHT 4–5ft (1.2–1.5m)

SPREAD 4–5ft (1.2–1.5m)

Asclepiadaceae	

GOMPHOCARPUS PHYSOCARPUS

Habit Upright, slender, sub-shrubby. ***Flowers*** 5-horned, borne in umbels during summer. Cream or greenish-white. ***Fruits*** Large, inflated, globose seed pods with soft bristles. ***Leaves*** Hairy, lance-shaped. Mid-green.

- NATIVE HABITAT South Africa.
- CULTIVATION Grow in full sun, in humus-rich, well-drained soil. Protect against cold winds in cooler climates.
- PROPAGATION By division or seed in spring.
- OTHER NAMES *Asclepias physocarpa.*

Z 9–10

HEIGHT to 6ft (2m)

SPREAD 2ft (60 cm)

Zingiberaceae	KAHILI GINGER

HEDYCHIUM GARDNERIANUM

Habit Upright, stoutly rhizomatous. ***Flowers*** Short-lived, small, fragrant, borne in dense spikes, from late summer to early autumn. Lemon-yellow, with conspicuous, bright red filaments. ***Leaves*** Lance-shaped, on reed-like stems. Grayish-green.

- NATIVE HABITAT Forests, N. India, Himalayas.
- CULTIVATION Grow in a warm, sunny site in fertile, moist, humus-rich soil. Give protection from cold wind. In cool climates overwinter indoors.
- PROPAGATION By division when growth resumes in spring.

Z 9–10

HEIGHT 5–6ft (1.5–2m)

SPREAD 30in (75cm)

Asphodelaceae/Liliaceae	

KNIPHOFIA 'Ice Queen'

Habit Upright, clump-forming. ***Flowers*** Small, narrowly tubular, borne on thick, upright stems in dense, terminal spikes, in early autumn. Creamy-white, opening from pale green buds. ***Leaves*** Grass-like, arching to form basal clumps. Mid-green.

- NATIVE HABITAT Garden origin.
- CULTIVATION Grow in full sun, in moisture-retentive but well-drained soil. Needs moisture when in growth. Mulch crowns in cold winter areas.
- PROPAGATION By division in spring.

Z 6–9

HEIGHT to 5ft (1.5m)

SPREAD 2ft (60cm)

Asteraceae/Compositae	PERENNIAL SUNFLOWER

HELIANTHUS × *MULTIFLORUS*

Habit Upright, spreading, rhizomatous. ***Flowers*** Large, daisy-like, with ray florets in 2 ranks, from late summer to early autumn. Yellow. ***Leaves*** Coarse, lance-shaped to oval, thin-textured. Mid-green.

- NATIVE HABITAT Garden origin.
- CULTIVATION Grow in any moderately fertile, well-drained soil, in full sun. Needs staking. Where conditions are favorable it may spread rapidly.
- PROPAGATION By division in autumn or spring.

☼ 💧

Z 5–9

HEIGHT to 5ft (1.5m)

SPREAD 2ft (60cm)

Asteraceae/Compositae	

HELIANTHUS 'Capenoch Star'

Habit Upright, clump-forming. ***Flowers*** Large, single, daisy-like, borne at the ends of branching stems, from late summer to early autumn. Lemon-yellow. ***Leaves*** Lance-shaped to oval, toothed. Mid-green.

- NATIVE HABITAT Garden origin.
- CULTIVATION Grow in moderately fertile, well-drained soil. Needs staking. Looks good with blue-flowered plants in a late summer border.
- PROPAGATION By division in autumn or spring.

☼ 💧

Z 5–9

HEIGHT to 4ft (1.2m)

SPREAD 2ft (60cm)

Asteraceae/Compositae	

SOLIDAGO 'Golden Wings'

Habit Vigorous, clump-forming. ***Flowers*** Tiny, mimosa-like, borne in dense, clustered, branching heads on upright stems, in late summer and autumn. Bright golden-yellow. ***Leaves*** Toothed, slightly hairy, lance-shaped. Mid-green.

- NATIVE HABITAT Garden origin.
- CULTIVATION Grow in any well-drained soil, including poor soils, in sun. Good for cutting, the bright flowers are much valued in a late summer border.
- PROPAGATION By division in spring.

☼ 💧

Z 4–9

HEIGHT 5ft (1.5m)

SPREAD 3ft (1m)

Asteraceae/Compositae

HELENIUM 'Sonnenwunder'

Habit Robust, dense, clump-forming. ***Flowers*** Large, daisy-like, with reflexed, rich deep yellow ray florets and a rounded yellow disk, borne over long periods from late summer to autumn. ***Leaves*** Lance-shaped on thick stems. Dark green.

• NATIVE HABITAT Garden origin.

• CULTIVATION Easily grown in almost any soil except waterlogged soil, in full sun. A valuable long-flowering plant for a larger, late summer border. It is important to divide and replant regularly to maintain vigor. A trouble-free perennial for late in the season. This is one of the tallest in a genus that hails from North America. Popularly known as the sneezeweeds, heleniums hybridize freely and now provide cultivars for the entire border, ranging from the yellow-flowered 'The Bishop' at 2ft (60cm) and 'Moerheim Beauty', with reddish-mahogany-colored flowers at 3–4ft (90–120cm). Excellent for cutting provided the lower leaves are removed.

• PROPAGATION By division in spring or autumn.

Z 4–8

HEIGHT to 5ft (1.5m)

SPREAD 3ft (1m)

Asteraceae/Compositae

HELIANTHUS 'Loddon Gold'

Habit Upright, spreading, rhizomatous. ***Flowers*** Large, double, from late summer to early autumn. Bright deep yellow. ***Leaves*** Coarse, lance-shaped to oval, thin-textured. Mid-green.

- NATIVE HABITAT Garden origin.
- CULTIVATION Grow in any moderately fertile, well-drained soil. Needs staking. May spread quickly where conditions suit.
- PROPAGATION By division in autumn or spring.

Z 4–8

HEIGHT 5ft (1.5m)

SPREAD 2ft (60cm)

Asteraceae/Compositae

HELIANTHUS 'Triomphe de Gand'

Habit Upright, clump-forming. ***Flowers*** Large, semi-double, daisy-like, borne at the ends of branching stems, from late summer to early autumn. Rich golden-yellow. ***Leaves*** Lance-shaped and toothed. Mid-green.

- NATIVE HABITAT Garden origin.
- CULTIVATION Grow in moderately fertile, well-drained soil. Needs staking. Looks good planted with blue-flowered plants in a late summer border.
- PROPAGATION By division in autumn or spring.

Z 5–9

HEIGHT 5ft (1.5m)

SPREAD 2½ft (75cm)

Asteraceae/Compositae

HELIANTHUS DECAPETALUS 'Morning Sun'

Habit Upright, clump-forming. ***Flowers*** Large, semi-double, daisy-like, from late summer to early autumn. Bright deep yellow with a yellow disk. ***Leaves*** Coarse, lance-shaped, toothed. Mid-green.

- NATIVE HABITAT Garden origin.
- CULTIVATION Grow in any moderately fertile, well-drained soil. Needs staking. A robust daisy for the large, late summer border.
- PROPAGATION By division in autumn or spring.
- OTHER NAMES *H.* × *laetiflorus* 'Morning Sun'.

Z 5–8

HEIGHT to 6ft (2m)

SPREAD 3ft (1m)

Asteraceae/Compositae

HELIANTHUS 'Monarch'

Habit Upright, spreading. ***Flowers*** Large, to 6in (15cm) across, semi-double, daisy-like, borne on sturdy stems from late summer to early autumn. Bright golden-yellow with a brown-black disk. ***Leaves*** Large, coarse, lance-shaped. Mid-green.

- NATIVE HABITAT Garden origin.
- CULTIVATION Grow in any moderately fertile, well-drained soil. Needs staking. May spread rapidly where conditions suit. A statuesque and robust perennial for the larger herbaceous border.
- PROPAGATION By division in autumn or spring.

Z 5–9

HEIGHT to 7ft (2.2m)

SPREAD 3ft (1m)

Asteraceae/Compositae

HELIANTHUS DECAPETALUS 'Soleil d'Or'

Habit Upright, spreading, rhizomatous. ***Flowers*** Large, double, from late summer to early autumn. The outer ray florets are larger than the inner ones. Bright deep yellow. ***Leaves*** Coarse, lance-shaped to oval, thin-textured. Mid-green.

- NATIVE HABITAT Garden origin.
- CULTIVATION Grow in any moderately fertile, well-drained soil. Needs staking. May spread quickly where conditions suit. A reliable old cultivar for the late summer border.
- PROPAGATION By division in autumn or spring.

Z 5–8

HEIGHT 5ft (1.5m) or more

SPREAD 3ft (1m)

Asteraceae/Compositae

RUDBECKIA 'Herbstsonne'

Habit Robust, upright. ***Flowers*** Large, daisy-like, borne singly on strong, slender stems from late summer to autumn. Rich golden-yellow with a green, cone-shaped center. ***Leaves*** Divided, shallowly lobed. Mid-green.

- NATIVE HABITAT Garden origin.
- CULTIVATION Grow in fertile, moist or well-drained soil, in full sun or light shade. Flowers particularly well during long, hot summers.
- PROPAGATION By division in spring or autumn.
- OTHER NAMES *R.* 'Autumn Sun'.

Z 5–9

HEIGHT 5–7ft (1.5–2.3m)

SPREAD 2–2½ft (60–75cm)

Asteraceae/Compositae

HELENIUM 'Riverton Gem'

Habit Upright, bushy, clump-forming. ***Flowers*** Large, daisy-like, with reflexed, ray florets and a rounded, brown disk, borne over long periods from late summer to autumn. Golden-yellow. ***Leaves*** Lance-shaped, on thick stems. Dark green.

- NATIVE HABITAT Garden origin.
- CULTIVATION Easily grown in almost any soil except waterlogged soil, in full sun. Divide and replant regularly to maintain vigor.
- PROPAGATION By division in spring or autumn.

Z 4–8

HEIGHT 5ft (1.5m)

SPREAD 3ft (1m)

Musaceae	FLOWERING BANANA

MUSA ORNATA

Habit Suckering, palm-like. ***Flowers*** Long, terminal spikes, with single rows of upright, yellow-orange flowers, each almost enclosed by a large, pink bract. ***Fruits*** Yellow-green, inedible bananas, about 2½in (6cm) long. ***Leaves*** Evergreen, paddle-shaped, waxy, to 6ft (2m) long. Bluish-green.
• NATIVE HABITAT Bangladesh, Burma.
• CULTIVATION Grow as a house or greenhouse plant in cooler climates.
• PROPAGATION By division year-round, by suckers after flowering, or by offsets in autumn.

Min. 64°F (18°C)

HEIGHT to 10ft (3m)

SPREAD 7ft (2.2m)

Doryanthaceae/ Liliaceae	

DORYANTHES PALMERI

Habit Rosette-forming. ***Flowers*** Small, borne intermittently in dense panicles. Red-bracted, orange-red and white within. May produce bulbils in place of flowers. ***Leaves*** Evergreen, arching, sword-shaped, fleshy, to 6ft (2m) long. Rich green.
• NATIVE HABITAT Queensland, Australia.
• CULTIVATION Grow as a house or greenhouse plant in cooler climates. Water freely when in growth, and keep just moist in winter.
• PROPAGATION By seed in spring, by mature bulbils, or by suckers after flowering.

Min. 50°F (10°C)

HEIGHT 6–8ft (2–2.5m)

SPREAD 8ft (2.5m)

Strelitziaceae	

STRELITZIA NICOLAI

Habit Thick-trunked, palm-like. ***Flowers*** Short-stemmed, beak-like. White and pale blue, enclosed in a boat-shaped, dark purple bract. Produced intermittently. ***Leaves*** Evergreen, clumped, long-stalked, oval, to 5ft (1.5m) long. Blue-green.
• NATIVE HABITAT Natal, N.E. Cape, South Africa.
• CULTIVATION Grow as a house or greenhouse pla[nt] in cooler climates. Needs fertile, well-drained soil and good light, but shade from hot sun. Water freel[y] when in growth but reduce water in winter.
• PROPAGATION By seed or suckers in spring.

Min. 41–50°F (5–10°C)

HEIGHT to 25ft (8m)

SPREAD 15ft (5m)

Marantaceae

CALATHEA MAJESTICA 'Sanderiana'

Habit Clump-forming. ***Flowers*** Tubular, in short, dense spikes, produced occasionally. White or mauve, with yellow-brown bracts. ***Leaves*** Evergreen, broadly oval, leathery, glossy. Olive-green, striped pink and white, purplish beneath.

- NATIVE HABITAT Garden origin.
- CULTIVATION Grow as a house or greenhouse plant in cooler climates. Water with soft water. Maintain high humidity and constant temperature.
- PROPAGATION By division in spring.
- OTHER NAMES *C. ornata* 'Sanderiana'.

Min. 59°F (15°C)

HEIGHT 4–5ft (1.2–1.5m)

SPREAD 3ft (1m)

Lamiaceae/Labiatae

PYCNOSTACHYS DAWEI

Habit Vigorous, bushy, upright. ***Flowers*** Tubular, 2-lipped, in short, dense, whorled spikes from winter to spring. Brilliant blue. ***Leaves*** Narrowly lance-shaped, serrated, 5–12in (12–30cm) long. Mid-green, red-tinged beneath.

- NATIVE HABITAT Tropical C. Africa.
- CULTIVATION Grow as a house or greenhouse plant in cooler climates. Needs fertile, well-drained soil. Water freely when in full growth.
- PROPAGATION By stem cuttings in early summer.

Min 59°F (15°C)

HEIGHT 4–5ft (1.2–1.5m)

SPREAD 1–3ft (30–90cm)

Agavaceae/Phormiaceae | NEW ZEALAND FLAX

PHORMIUM TENAX Purpureum Group

Habit Upright, clump-forming. ***Flowers*** Tubular, dull in large panicles, to 15ft (5m) high, borne on blue-purple stems in summer. Dark red. ***Leaves*** Evergreen, stiff, sword-shaped, 6ft (2m) or more long, in basal clumps. Red-purple to deep copper.

- NATIVE HABITAT Garden origin.
- CULTIVATION Grow in deep, fertile, humus-rich soil, in a warm, sunny, sheltered site. Excellent for coastal gardens.
- PROPAGATION By division in spring.

Z 9–10

HEIGHT 6–8ft (2–2.5m)

SPREAD 3ft (1m)

Musaceae | JAPANESE BANANA

MUSA BASJOO

Habit Suckering, palm-like. ***Flowers*** In long, terminal spikes, with drooping, pale yellow flowers and brown bracts, in summer. ***Fruits*** Yellow-green, banana-like, 2½in (6cm) long. ***Leaves*** Evergreen, arching, oblong to paddle-shaped, to 3ft (1m) long. Bright green.

- NATIVE HABITAT Ryuku Islands, Japan.
- CULTIVATION Grow in humus-rich soil out of wind or as a house, greenhouse, or sunroom plant.
- PROPAGATION By division year-round, by suckers after flowering, or by offsets in autumn.

Z 9–10

HEIGHT 10–15ft (3–5m)

SPREAD 6–8ft (2–2.5m)

Musaceae	ABYSSINIAN BANANA, ETHIOPIAN BANANA

ENSETE VENTRICOSUM

Habit Palm-like, with a bulbous, trunk-like stem. ***Flowers*** Long, terminal spikes, bearing red-green flowers with red bracts, are produced intermittently. ***Fruits*** Small, dry, banana-like, inedible. ***Leaves*** Evergreen, long, rather pointed, to 20ft (6m) long. Olive-green with a maroon midrib.

- NATIVE HABITAT Tropical Africa.
- CULTIVATION Grow in fertile, humus-rich soil. In cooler climates this plant is only really suitable for a larger heated greenhouse where the temperature does not fall below 50°F (10°C) and the minimum height space is at least 25ft (8m). Can be planted either in a border or a large container. The latter will tend to restrict the growth and could be desirable in a confined space. Container-grown plants will need regular fertilizing.
- PROPAGATION By division year-round, or by seed in spring.
- OTHER NAMES *Musa arnoldiana, M. ensete.*

☼ ◊

Min. 50°F (10°C)

HEIGHT 20ft (6m) or more

SPREAD 10ft (3m) or more

Apiaceae/Umbelliferae

ANTHRISCUS SYLVESTRIS 'Ravenswing'

Habit Clump-forming. ***Flowers*** Tiny, in small umbels, in late spring. Creamy-white, sometimes tinted pink. ***Leaves*** Finely divided fern-like. Green at first, black-purple when mature.

- NATIVE HABITAT Garden origin. Species (cow parsley) occurs in grassy habitats in Europe, N. Africa, to W. Asia.
- CULTIVATION Grow in moist but well-drained soil, in sun. Useful as foliage contrast in herbaceous borders, especially with silver-leaved plants.
- PROPAGATION By division in spring or autumn.

Z 8–10

HEIGHT
3ft (1m)
or more

SPREAD
18in (45cm)

Ranunculaceae

RANUNCULUS ACONITIFOLIUS

Habit Robust, clump-forming. ***Flowers*** Single, shallowly cupped, to 1in (2.5cm) across, in spring and early summer. White, sometimes pink-flushed beneath. ***Leaves*** Divided, 3–5 lobed. Dark green.

- NATIVE HABITAT Sub-alpine meadows, and by streams, from W. to C. Europe.
- CULTIVATION Grow in moist, fertile, humus-rich soil in sun or partial shade. Suitable for a wildflower garden, border, or streamside, above water level.
- PROPAGATION By seed in spring, or division in spring or autumn.

Z 5–9

HEIGHT
3ft (1m)

SPREAD
3ft (1m)

Ranunculaceae | FAIR MAIDS OF FRANCE / KENT

RANUNCULUS ACONITIFOLIUS 'Flore Pleno'

Habit Clump-forming. ***Flowers*** Small, fully double, long-lasting, on sturdy branching stems, from late spring to summer. Pure white. ***Leaves*** Deeply divided, 3–5 lobed. Dark green.

- NATIVE HABITAT Origin uncertain. Species occurs in meadows and by streams, from W. to C. Europe.
- CULTIVATION Grow in moist, fertile, humus-rich soil, in sun or partial shade. Suitable for borders, or stream- and watersides, above water level.
- PROPAGATION By division in spring or autumn.

Z 4–8

HEIGHT
24–30in
(60–75cm)

SPREAD
20in (50cm)

Convallariaceae/Liliaceae | SOLOMON'S SEAL

POLYGONATUM HIRTUM

Habit Upright then arching, rhizomatous. ***Flowers*** Small, pendent, tubular, in clusters of 2–5, on arching stems, in late spring. White, tipped green. ***Leaves*** Alternate, lance-shaped to oval. Fresh green. Finely hairy stems, leaf stalks, and leaves.

- NATIVE HABITAT Woodlands of E.C. and S.E. Europe, W. Russia, N.W. Turkey.
- CULTIVATION Grow in fertile, humus-rich, moisture-retentive but well-drained soil, in shade.
- PROPAGATION By seed or division in early spring.
- OTHER NAMES *P. latifolium*.

Z 4–9

HEIGHT
3ft (1m)

SPREAD
1ft (30cm)

Liliaceae/Liliaceae	FALSE SPIKENARD

SMILACINA RACEMOSA

Habit Arching, clump-forming, rhizomatous. ***Flowers*** Tiny, in dense, feathery sprays, from spring to mid summer. White. ***Fruits*** Small, fleshy, red berries. ***Leaves*** Lance-shaped to oval, with pointed tips. Pale green.

• NATIVE HABITAT Damp woods, North America.

• CULTIVATION Grow in moist, fertile, humus-rich, neutral to acid soil. A beautiful specimen for shady borders and woodland gardens.

• PROPAGATION By division in spring or autumn, or by seed in autumn.

Z 4–9

HEIGHT 36in (90cm) or more

SPREAD 18in (45cm)

Convallariaceae/ Liliaceae	SOLOMON'S SEAL

POLYGONATUM × HYBRIDUM

Habit Arching, rhizomatous. ***Flowers*** Small, pendent, tubular, on arching stems in the leaf axils, in late spring. Greenish-white. ***Leaves*** Stem-clasping, oval. Fresh bright green.

• NATIVE HABITAT Long cultivated, origin uncertain.

• CULTIVATION Grow in any moderately fertile, moisture-retentive but well-drained soil. An elegant specimen for shady borders and woodland gardens. Leaves may be stripped by sawfly larvae.

• PROPAGATION By division in early spring.

Z 4–9

HEIGHT 4ft (1.2m)

SPREAD 3ft (1m)

Saxifragaceae	UMBRELLA PLANT

DARMERA PELTATA

Habit Spreading, rhizomatous. ***Flowers*** Small, in clusters, on sturdy, white-hairy stems, open before the leaves in spring. White or pale pink. ***Leaves*** Round, to 2ft (60cm) across, finely hairy. Mid-green.

• NATIVE HABITAT Mountain streambanks, in forests, N.W. California to S.W. Oregon.

• CULTIVATION Grow in sun or partial shade, in moist soil. Excellent as a marginal water plant.

• PROPAGATION By division in spring, or by seed in autumn or spring.

• OTHER NAMES *Peltiphyllum peltatum.*

Z 5–9

HEIGHT 3–4ft (1–1.2m)

SPREAD 2ft (60cm)

Asteraceae/Compositae

TANACETUM COCCINEUM 'Brenda'

Habit Upright. ***Flowers*** Single, daisy-like, in late spring and summer. Bright magenta-pink, with yellow central disks. ***Leaves*** Faintly aromatic, finely divided. Gray-green.

• NATIVE HABITAT Garden origin.

• CULTIVATION Grow in an open, sunny site, in fertile, well-drained, preferably neutral to slightly acid soil. If cut back after the first flush of flowers, will usually produce a second flush of blooms later in the season. A long-established border plant, invaluable for cutting as the flowers last well in water. It does not do well in a poor, sandy soil, however, more frequent division and feeding will maintain vigor or encourage sturdier growth in a weaker plant.

• PROPAGATION By division in spring.

• OTHER NAMES *Pyrethrum* 'Brenda'.

Z 5–9

HEIGHT
24in (60cm)

SPREAD
18in (45cm) or more

Brassicaceae/Cruciferae

LUNARIA REDIVIVA

Habit Upright, branching. ***Flowers*** Small, scented, 4-petaled, in upright, branching clusters, in spring. White, lilac or purple. ***Fruits*** Elliptical, silvery, translucent. ***Leaves*** Oval-lance-shaped, finely toothed. Mid-green, may be tinted maroon.

• NATIVE HABITAT Sub-alpine woodland and scrub, Europe to eastern Siberia.

• CULTIVATION Grow in fertile, moist, well-drained sun, in partial shade or sun. The seed heads dry well.

• PROPAGATION By seed in autumn or spring, or by division in spring.

Z 6–9

HEIGHT
24–30in (60–75cm)

SPREAD
12in (30cm)

Geraniaceae | MOURNING WIDOW

GERANIUM PHAEUM

Habit Clump-forming, rhizomatous. ***Flowers*** Small, with 5 reflexed petals, borne in loose, clusters from late spring to summer. Deep maroon-purple. ***Leaves*** Divided into 7–9 soft green lobes, sometimes spotted red-purple at base.

• NATIVE HABITAT Woods and sub-alpine meadows, S., C., and W. Europe.

• CULTIVATION Grow in any well-drained soil, in shade or partial shade. Excellent for woodland and wild gardens, or for shady borders.

• PROPAGATION Seed or division in autumn or spring.

Z 4–8

HEIGHT
up to 30in (75cm)

SPREAD
18in (45cm)

NON-BULBOUS IRISES

Grown for their distinctive and colorful flowers, irises form a large genus of perennials, some of which, like the plants featured on the following pages, are rhizomatous, and others bulbous. Each flower has 3 distinctive drooping "falls" which may have beards or crests, and 3 upright horizontal, occasionally drooping "standards." Irises can be grown in rock and woodland gardens, bog gardens, by water, or in an herbaceous border.

Non-bulbous, rhizomatous irises, are divided into three groups: bearded, beardless, and crested. Unless otherwise stated, all have rhizomatous rootstocks and sword-shaped leaves arranged in a basal fan.

Bearded irises flower from early spring to summer and are grouped by size into: Miniature dwarf, to 8in (20cm); Standard dwarf, 8–16in (20–40cm); Intermediate, 16–28in (40–70cm); and tall, 28in (70cm) or more. They should be grown in well-drained, preferably slightly acid soil in full sun. Some tolerate poorer soils and light shade. Onocyclus and Regelia irises are both bearded irises but prefer drier summer conditions and may prove difficult to grow.

Beardless irises need similar conditions to bearded irises, but some prefer heavier, more moisture-retentive soils. They include the Pacific Coast, Spuria, Siberian, and Japanese irises. Many prefer moist waterside conditions, but most may be grown in borders in moist soils, in an open, sunny site.

Crested irises, including the Evansia irises, have ridges or crests instead of beards on the falls. Most thrive in similar conditions to the bearded irises, but a few prefer damp, humus-rich soils. A number in this group are frost tender (min. 41°F/5°C).

Species can be propagated by division of rhizomes or offsets in late summer, or by seed in autumn; cultivars by division only.

I. CONFUSA
Habit Very robust, with aerial rhizomes.
Flowers To 2in (5cm) wide, borne in succession on branching stems, in mid spring. White, yellow-crested falls are spotted yellow and purple.
Leaves Evergreen or semi-evergreen, broad, at the top of bamboo-like stems.
• TIPS Grow in well-drained soil. Best against a warm wall.
• HEIGHT 1–3ft (30cm–1m).
• SPREAD indefinite.

I. confusa
(Evansia)

☼ ◊ Z 9–10

***I.* 'Anniversary'**
Habit Robust, rhizomatous.
Flowers To 4in (10cm) across, borne 1–4 on branched stems from late spring to early summer. White, striped creamy-white at the throat of each fall.
• CULTIVATION Suitable for a bog garden or damp border.
• HEIGHT 2ft (60cm).
• SPREAD indefinite.

***I.* 'Anniversary'**
(Beardless, Siberian)

☼ ◐ Z 3–10

***I.* 'Wisley White'**
Habit Robust, rhizomatous.
Flowers To 4in (10cm) across, borne 2–3 on branched stems in early summer. White standards and white falls stained yellow at the base.
• TIPS Suitable for a bog garden or damp border.
• HEIGHT 3ft (1m).
• SPREAD indefinite.

***I.* 'Wisley White'**
(Beardless, Siberian)

☼ ◐ Z 3–10

I. 'Dreaming Yellow'

Habit Rhizomatous.
Flowers To 4in (10cm) across, borne 1–4 on branched stems from late spring to early summer. White standards, creamy-yellow falls, aging to white.
• TIPS Suitable for a bog garden or damp border.
• HEIGHT 3ft (1m).
• SPREAD indefinite.

I. **'Dreaming Yellow'**
(Beardless, Siberian)

Z 3–10

I. 'Arnold Sunrise'

Habit Rhizomatous.
Flowers 4–5in (10–12cm) across, borne 2–3 on a branched stem in spring. White, tinted lilac with light orange on falls.
• TIPS Prefers moisture-retentive soil. Slow-spreading.
• HEIGHT 10in (25cm).
• SPREAD indefinite.

I. **'Arnold Sunrise'**
(Beardless, Pacific Coast)

Z 3–10

I. KERNERIANA

Habit Rhizomatous.
Flowers To 5in (12cm) wide, borne 2–4 from each pair of bracts on strong, branching stems. Soft lemon- or creamy-yellow. ***Leaves*** Narrow, grass-like. Fresh green.
• TIPS Tolerates partial shade. Needs moist but well-drained soil.
• HEIGHT 6–10in (16–25cm).
• SPREAD indefinite.

I. kerneriana
(Beardless, Spuria)

Z 6–9

I. AFGHANICA

Habit Rhizomatous.
Flowers To 3½in (9cm) across, borne singly on slender stems in spring. Creamy-yellow standards, white falls, heavily veined and blotched purple-brown at the base.
Leaves Curved, linear.
• TIPS Suitable for a rock garden or alpine house. Grow in fertile, sharply drained soil. Provide a period of dry dormancy after flowering.
• HEIGHT 6–12in (15–30cm).
• SPREAD to 12in (30cm).

I. afghanica
(Regelia)

Z 7–9

I. IBERICA

Habit Rhizomatous.
Flowers To 5in (12cm) wide, singly in late spring. Standards white, pale blue or yellow, falls white or pale lilac, spoon-shaped, veined brown-purple.
Leaves Curved, linear. Gray-green.
• TIPS Dry rhizome after flowering. Drain well.
• HEIGHT 6–8in (15–20cm).
• SPREAD indefinite.

I. iberica
(Onocyclus)

Z 6–8

I. 'Geisha Gown'

Habit Robust.
Flowers Double, 6–12in (15–30cm) across, borne 3–5 on branched stems in summer. White standards and falls with rose-purple veining; falls have a yellow blaze and purple styles.
• TIPS For a sunny, open bog or water garden in lime-free soil.
• HEIGHT 32in (80cm).
• SPREAD indefinite.

I. **'Geisha Gown'**
(Beardless, Japanese)

Z 3–10

I. MISSOURIENSIS

Habit Rhizomatous.
Flowers To 3in (8cm) wide, 2–3 per spathe on branched stems, in spring or early summer. Blue, pale lavender, lilac, or white.
Leaves Smooth, grass-like. Pale green.
• TIPS Prefers sun, but tolerates partial shade and shallow water. Resents root disturbance.
• HEIGHT to 30in (75cm).
• SPREAD indefinite.

I. missouriensis
(Beardless, Pacific Coast)

Z 4–9

I. CRISTATA

Habit With branching rhizomes.
Flowers To 1½in (4cm) wide, almost stemless, 1–2 per stem, in early summer. Lilac, blue, lavender or white, with orange-crested falls.
Leaves Narrowly sword-shaped. Yellowish-green.
• TIPS Prefers moist, peaty, acid soil.
• HEIGHT 4in (10cm).
• SPREAD indefinite.

I. cristata
(Evansia)

Z 3–9

I. PALLIDA 'Aurea Variegata'

Habit Rhizomatous.
Flowers Scented, 3–5in (8–12cm) across, on branched stems, late spring to early summer. Pale lilac-blue, with yellow beards.
Leaves Sword-shaped. Green and yellow striped.
• TIPS Likes well-drained, fairly alkaline soil.
• HEIGHT 28–36in (70cm–1m).
• SPREAD indefinite.

***I. pallida* 'Aurea Variegata'**
(Bearded)

Z 4–8

I. 'Joette'

Habit Rhizomatous.
Flowers To 6in (15cm) across, borne on branched stems in late spring and early summer. Standards uniform lavender-blue; falls lavender-blue, with white veining at the base and a golden-yellow beard.
• TIPS Likes well-drained, slightly alkaline soil.
• HEIGHT 18in (45cm).
• SPREAD indefinite.

***I.* 'Joette'**
(Bearded Intermediate)

Z 3–10

I. 'Paradise Bird'

Habit Rhizomatous.
Flowers To 6in (15cm) across, 8–10 borne on well-branched stems, in early summer. Pale magenta standards; falls darker magenta, with a dark golden beard.
• TIPS Grow in fertile, well-drained, slightly alkaline soil, in full sun.
• HEIGHT 34in (85cm).
• SPREAD indefinite.

***I.* 'Paradise Bird'**
(Tall Bearded)

Z 3–10

I. 'Rippling Rose'

Habit Rhizomatous.
Flowers To 6in (15cm) across, 6–10 borne on well-branched stems in early summer. White standards and falls, with rose-purple markings and edges and a lemon-yellow beard,
• TIPS Grow in fertile, well-drained, slightly alkaline soil, in full sun.
• HEIGHT 3ft (1m).
• SPREAD indefinite.

***I.* 'Rippling Rose'**
(Tall Bearded)

Z 3–10

I. TENAX

Habit Rhizomatous.
Flowers 3–5in (8–12cm) wide, 1–2 per spathe, in spring or early summer. Deep purple to lavender-blue, often marked yellow and white on the falls.
Leaves Smooth, grass-like. Dark green, stained pink at the base.
• TIPS Slightly acid soil.
• HEIGHT 6–12in (15–30cm).
• SPREAD indefinite.

I. tenax
(Beardless, Pacific Coast)

Z 7–9

I. VERSICOLOR

Habit Robust.
Flowers 2–4in (5–10cm) wide, borne 3–5 per spathe on branched stems from early to midsummer. Purple-blue, red-purple, lavender or slate-blue, falls usually with purple-veined, white centers.
Leaves Long, curved, or upright. Green, stained purple at the base.
• HEIGHT 2ft (60cm).
• SPREAD indefinite.

I. versicolor
(Beardless)
Blue flag, Wild iris

Z 3–9

I. 'Bold Print'

Habit Rhizomatous.
Flowers Up to 6 flowers, 5in (13cm) across, borne on branched stems in late spring/early summer. Standards white with a purple edge; falls white edged with purple "stitching" and a bronze-tipped, yellow beard.
- TIPS Grow in fertile, well-drained, preferably slightly alkaline soil, in full sun.
- HEIGHT 22in (55cm).
- SPREAD indefinite.

***I.* 'Bold Print'**
(Bearded, Intermediate)

Z 3–10

I. TECTORUM

Habit Rhizomatous.
Flowers ½–3in (1–8cm) across, 2–3 per spathe on sparsely branched stems in early summer. Dark-veined, bright lilac with white-crested falls.
Leaves Ribbed, broadly lance-shaped, in fans.
- TIPS Best in moist soil, by a warm, sheltered wall.
- HEIGHT 10–14in (25–35cm).
- SPREAD indefinite.

I. tectorum
(Evansia)

Z 4–9

I. 'Krasnia'

Habit Rhizomatous.
Flowers 5–7in (13–18cm) across, 8–12 borne on well-branched stems in early summer. Standards purple; falls white, edged purple, with a dark golden-brown beard.
- TIPS Grow in fertile, well-drained, slightly alkaline soil, in full sun.
- HEIGHT 3ft (1m).
- SPREAD indefinite.

***I.* 'Krasnia'**
(Tall Bearded)

Z 3–10

I. UNGUICULARIS 'Mary Barnard'

Habit Rhizomatous.
Flowers 2–3in (5–8cm) wide, long-tubed, almost stemless, scented, borne from late autumn to early spring. Deep violet-blue, with yellow-centered falls. ***Leaves*** Evergreen, tough, narrow.
- TIPS Best in well-drained soil by a wall.
- HEIGHT to 8in (20cm).
- SPREAD indefinite.

***I. unguicularis* 'Mary Barnard'**
(Beardless)

Z 7–9

I. 'Fulvala'

Habit Rhizomatous.
Flowers 2–5in (5–12cm) across, in pairs on zigzag stems in summer. Velvety, deep red-purple standards; falls deep red-purple with a yellow blaze.
- TIPS Suited to a bog garden or damp border.
- OTHER NAMES *I.* × *fulvala.*
- HEIGHT 18in (45cm).
- SPREAD indefinite.

***I.* 'Fulvala'**
(Beardless)

Z 5–10

I. CHRYSOGRAPHES

Habit Rhizomatous.
Flowers 2–4in (5–10cm) across, borne 1–4 on branched stems in late spring to early summer. , Deep red-purple to black-purple standard and falls; falls are gold-etched.
Leaves Linear, to 18in (45cm) long.
• TIPS Good in an acid bog garden.
• HEIGHT 16in (40cm).
• SPREAD indefinite.

I. chrysographes
(Beardless, Siberian)

Z 5–9

I. 'Matinata'

Habit Rhizomatous.
Flowers 6in (15cm) across, 6–9 (up to 12) borne on well-branched stems in early summer. Uniformly dark purple-blue standards and falls, with a dark blue-purple beard.
• TIPS Grow in fertile, well-drained, slightly alkaline soil, in full sun.
• HEIGHT 3ft (1m).
• SPREAD indefinite.

***I.* 'Matinata'**
(Tall Bearded)

Z3–10

I. 'Mary Frances'

Habit Rhizomatous.
Flowers 6in (15cm) across, 6–9 (occasionally 12) borne on well-branched stems in early summer. Uniformly pink. lavender standards and falls, delicately frilled, with a white beard.
• TIPS Grow in fertile, well-drained, slightly alkaline soil, in full sun.
• HEIGHT 3ft (1m).
• SPREAD indefinite.

***I.* 'Mary Frances'**
(Tall Bearded)

Z 3–10

I. DOUGLASIANA

Habit Rhizomatous.
Flowers To 5in (12cm) wide, 1–3 on branched stems in spring to summer. Lavender to purple or white, with central yellowish zone on falls.
Leaves Evergreen, leathery. Dark green, red-purple at the base.
• HEIGHT 10–28in (25–70cm).
• SPREAD indefinite.

I. douglasiana
(Beardless, Pacific Coast)

Z 7–9

I. LACUSTRIS

Habit Rhizomatous.
Flowers To 1½in (4cm) wide, almost stemless, long-tubed, borne 1–2 per stem in early summer. Sky-blue, with a brown-flecked, yellow crest on the falls.
Leaves Linear, upright. Bright green.
• TIPS Needs reliably moist, acid soil.
• HEIGHT 4in (10cm).
• SPREAD indefinite.

I. lacustris
(Evansia)

Z 4–9

I. HOOGIANA

Habit Rhizomatous.
Flowers To 4in (10cm) wide, scented, 2–3 per stem in early summer. Lilac-blue, delicate veined, golden-bearded.
Leaves Linear, slightly arched. Mid-green, often purple-tinted.
• TIPS Suited to a well-drained rock garden.
• HEIGHT 18–32in (45–80cm).
• SPREAD indefinite.

I. hoogiana
(Regelia)

Z 6–9

I. 'Mountain Lake'

Habit Robust, rhizomatous.
Flowers To 4in (10cm) across, borne 1–4 on branched stems from late spring to early summer. Mid-blue standards; falls mid-blue with darker veining
• TIPS Suitable for a bog garden or damp border.
• HEIGHT 3ft (1m).
• SPREAD indefinite.

***I.* 'Mountain Lake'**
(Beardless, Siberian)

Z 3–10

I. LAEVIGATA

Habit Rhizomatous.
Flowers To 5in (12cm) wide, borne 2 to 4 per sparsely branched stem, from early to midsummer. Blue, blue-purple or white.
Leaves Smooth, grass-like. Pale green,
• TIPS Grow in acid soil. Tolerates partial shade and shallow water.
• HEIGHT 2–3ft (60cm–1m).
• SPREAD indefinite.

I. laevigata
(Beardless, Japanese)

Z 4–9

I. SETOSA
Habit Rhizomatous.
Flowers 2–3in (5–8cm) across, 2–13 per spathe, on branched stems, in summer. Small, bristle-like purple-blue standards; falls with paler markings.
Leaves Sword-shaped. Gray-green.
• TIPS Grow in moist soil. Suits a damp border.
• HEIGHT 4in–3ft (10cm–1m).
• SPREAD indefinite.

I. setosa
(Beardless)
Bristle-pointed iris

Z 3–9

I. VARIEGATA
Habit Rhizomatous.
Flowers 2–3in (5–8cm) wide, 1–2 per spathe on branched stems, in early summer. Bright yellow standards; falls white or pale yellow, veined red-brown, appearing striped.
Leaves Ribbed, sickle-shaped. Bright green.
• TIPS For a bog garden.
• HEIGHT 12–20in (30–50cm).
• SPREAD indefinite.

I. variegata
(Bearded)
Variegated iris

Z 5–9

I. 'Early Light'
Habit Rhizomatous.
Flowers To 7in (18cm) across, 8–10 borne on branched stems in early summer. Cream standards, flushed lemon-yellow; falls slightly darker with a yellow beard.
• TIPS Grow in fertile, well-drained, slightly alkaline soil, in full sun.
• HEIGHT 3ft (1m).
• SPREAD indefinite.

I. 'Early Light'
(Tall Bearded)

Z 3–10

I. FORRESTII
Habit Rhizomatous.
Flowers To 2½in (6cm) wide, fragrant, 1–2, in late spring to early summer. Yellow, with black-veined falls, and sometimes brown-flushed standards.
Leaves Linear, glossy. Mid-green.
• TIPS Needs reliably moist, acid soil.
• HEIGHT 6–16in (15–40cm).
• SPREAD indefinite.

I. forrestii
(Beardless, Siberian)

Z 5–9

I. PSEUDACORUS
Habit Robust, rhizomatous.
Flowers 2–5in (5–12cm) across, borne 4–12 on strong branched stems, from early to midsummer. Golden-yellow, usually with brown-violet veining and a darker yellow patch on the lower falls.
Leaves Sword-shaped. Gray-green.
• TIPS Grow in reliably moist soil in partial shade.
• HEIGHT to 6ft (2m).
• SPREAD indefinite.

I. pseudacorus
(Beardless)
Yellow flag

Z 5–9

I. INNOMINATA
Habit Rhizomatous.
Flowers To 3in (7.5cm) wide, 1–2 per stem in late spring to early summer. Cream to orange, or lilac-pink to blue or purple; falls often maroon veined.
Leaves Evergreen, narrow. Purplish at base.
• TIPS Grow in the shelter of a warm, sunny wall.
• HEIGHT 6–10in (16–25cm).
• SPREAD indefinite.

I. innominata
(Beardless, Pacific Coast)

Z 6–9

I. 'Sun Miracle'
Habit Rhizomatous.
Flowers 6–7in (15–18cm) across, 7–10 borne on well-branched stems in early summer. Pure yellow standards and falls, with a dark golden beard.
• TIPS Grow in fertile, well-drained, slightly alkaline soil, in full sun.
• HEIGHT 3ft (1m)
• SPREAD indefinite

***I.* 'Sun Miracle'**
(Tall Bearded)

Z 3–10

I. 'Eyebright'
Habit Rhizomatous.
Flowers To 4in (10cm) across, 2–4 borne on usually unbranched stems in late spring. Standards bright yellow; falls bright yellow, marked dark brown, with a yellow beard.
• TIPS Grow in fertile, well-drained, slightly alkaline soil, in full sun.
• HEIGHT 12in (30cm).
• SPREAD indefinite.

***I.* 'Eyebright'**
(Standard Dwarf Bearded)

Z 3–10

I. 'Shepherd's Delight'
Habit Rhizomatous.
Flowers 6–7in (15–18cm) across, 6–10 on well-branched stems in early summer. Standards and falls clear pink with a yellowish cast, and a dark orange beard.
• TIPS Grow in fertile, well-drained, slightly alkaline soil, in full sun.
• HEIGHT 3ft (1m).
• SPREAD indefinite.

***I.* 'Shepherd's Delight'**
(Tall Bearded)

Z 3–10

I. 'Peach Frost'
Habit Rhizomatous.
Flowers To 6in (15cm) across, 6–10 borne on well-branched stems in early summer. Peach-pink standards; falls white with peach-pink borders and a tangerine beard.
• TIPS Grow in fertile, well-drained, slightly alkaline soil, in full sun.
• HEIGHT 3ft (1m).
• SPREAD indefinite.

***I.* 'Peach Frost'**
(Tall Bearded)

Z 3–10

I. FULVA
Habit Rhizomatous.
Flowers To 3in (7cm) wide, 1–2 in the leaf axils of sparsely branched stems in late spring to early summer. Coppery-orange or orange-red.
Leaves Linear, glossy. Mid-green.
• TIPS Prefers reliably moist soil.
• HEIGHT 18–32in (45–80cm).
• SPREAD indefinite.

I. fulva
(Beardless)

Z 5–9

I. 'Blue-Eyed Brunette'
Habit Rhizomatous.
Flowers To 6in (15cm) across, 7–10 borne on well-branched stems, in early summer. Cigar-brown with a blue blaze and golden-bearded falls.
• TIPS Grow in fertile, well-drained, slightly alkaline soil, in full sun.
• HEIGHT 3ft (1m).
• SPREAD indefinite.

***I.* 'Blue-Eyed Brunette'**
(Tall Bearded)

Z 3–10

I. 'Flamenco'
Habit Rhizomatous.
Flowers To 6in (15cm) across, 6–9 borne on well-branched stems in early summer. Standards gold infused red; falls white to yellow edged red, with a dark golden-brown beard.
• TIPS Grow in fertile, well-drained, slightly alkaline soil, in full sun.
• HEIGHT 3ft (1m)
• SPREAD indefinite

***I.* 'Flamenco'**
(Tall Bearded)

Z 3–10

PEONIES

Herbaceous peonies (*Paeonia* species and cultivars) are valued for their showy flowers, bold foliage, and, in some species, for their ornamental seed pods. The flowers vary from single to double or anemone form (with broad, outer petals and a mass of petaloids in the center) and are often heavily scented.

Peony foliage is also striking, often tinged bronze when young and assuming rich, reddish tints in autumn. Unless otherwise stated, the leaves are large, alternate and divided into oval to lance-shaped linear leaflets.

Besides the wide variety of herbaceous border hybrids and species shown on these pages, there are also a number of tree peonies (cultivars of *P. suffruticosa*), which are open shrubs often over 6ft (2m).

Though they will tolerate a light shady position, peonies are best grown in sun in fertile, humus-rich, moist but well-drained soil. Before planting, prepare the ground by incorporating well-rotted manure or garden compost. Early in the season, provide tall border peonies with grow-through support.

Peonies are long-lived plants that should, if possible, be left undisturbed as they resent transplanting. If it is necessary to split the clumps, lift and divide them in autumn or early spring (p. 325). Species can be increased by seed sown as soon as it is ripe, although it can take as long as three years to germinate.

If shoots wilt, wither, and turn brown, this may be a sign that the plant is affected by peony wilt. This fungus may lie dormant in the soil until conditions are favorable, often in prolonged wet weather, when it starts to form a gray mold on the stems. The best method of control is to cut out the affected shoots to below ground level, and dust with a commercial fungicide.

***P.* EMODI**
Habit Clump-forming.
Flowers Large, fragrant, single, borne singly on tall stems in late spring and early summer. Pure white, with a central boss of golden stamens.
Leaves Divided into glossy leaflets. Mid-green.
• HEIGHT to 4ft (1.2m).
• SPREAD to 3ft (1m).

P. emodi

Z 5–8

***P.* LACTIFLORA**
'Whitleyi Major'
Habit Clump-forming, floriferous.
Flowers Large, well-scented, single, in early to midsummer. Broad, satiny, ivory-white petals, surrounding a boss of clear golden-yellow stamens.
Leaves Very dark green, flushed rich red-brown.
• HEIGHT 34in (85cm).
• SPREAD 34in (85cm).

P. lactiflora
'Whitleyi Major'

Z 4–8

***P.* LACTIFLORA**
'White Wings'
Habit Clump-forming.
Flowers Large, well-scented, single to loosely semi-double, in early to midsummer. Broad white petals, slightly ruffled at the tips, sometimes tinged pale sulphur-yellow, with golden stamens.
Leaves Dark green, provide autumn color.
• HEIGHT 34in (85cm).
• SPREAD 34in (85cm).

P. lactiflora
'White Wings'

Z 4–8

***P.* LACTIFLORA**
'Baroness Schröder'
Habit Vigorous, clump-forming, floriferous.
Flowers Large, fragrant, globe-shaped, double, in early to midsummer. Flesh-pink at first, fading to white, with broad flat outer petals, and incurved, ruffled, tightly packed inner ones. Excellent for cutting.
• HEIGHT 3ft (1m).
• SPREAD 3ft (1m).

P. lactiflora
'Baroness Schröder'

Z 4–8

P. *LACTIFLORA*
'Krinkled White'
Habit Robust, clump-forming.
Flowers Large, single, bowl-shaped, with large petals having slightly ruffled margins, and surrounding a neat boss of golden stamens, in early to midsummer. Milky-white, sometimes flushed very pale pink.
• HEIGHT 32in (80cm).
• SPREAD 32in (80cm).

P. lactiflora
'Krinkled White'

Z 4–8

P. *OFFICINALIS*
'Alba Plena'
Habit Clump-forming.
Flowers Large, double, with many slightly ruffled petals, in early to midsummer. White, often flushed pale pink.
• HEIGHT to 30in (75cm).
• SPREAD to 30in (75cm).

P. officinalis
'Alba Plena'

Z 5–8

P. *LACTIFLORA*
'Alice Harding'
Habit Clump-forming.
Flowers Very large, fragrant, in early to midsummer. Double, creamy white.
• HEIGHT to 3ft (1m).
• SPREAD 3ft (1m).

P. lactiflora
'Alice Harding'

Z 4–8

P. *LACTIFLORA*
'Duchesse de Nemours'
Habit Vigorous, clump-forming, free-flowering.
Flowers Fragrant, double, in early to midsummer. Large, outer petals green-tinted fading to white; narrow, creamy-white inner petals yellow at base.
• OTHER NAMES
P. 'Mrs Gwyn Lewis'.
• HEIGHT to 28in (70cm).
• SPREAD 28in (70cm).

P. lactiflora **'Duchesse de Nemours'**

Z 4–8

P. *LACTIFLORA*
'Cornelia Shaylor'
Habit Erect, clump-forming, floriferous.
Flowers Fragrant, double, with ruffled petals neatly and densely arranged, from early to midsummer. Flushed rose-pink on opening, fading gradually to blush-white.
• HEIGHT to 34in (85cm).
• SPREAD 34in (85cm).

P. lactiflora
'Cornelia Shaylor'

Z 4–8

P. LACTIFLORA
'Shirley Temple'
Habit Clump-forming, floriferous.
Flowers Large, fragrant, fully double, in late spring to early summer. Outer whorls of broad, soft rose-pink petals, fading to soft buff-white, with slightly smaller, loosely arranged inner petals.
• HEIGHT 34in (85cm).
• SPREAD 34in (85cm).

P. lactiflora 'Shirley Temple'

Z 4–8

P. LACTIFLORA
'Mother of Pearl'
Habit Clump-forming.
Flowers Elegant, single, with broad petals, in late spring to early summer. Rose-pink petals, paler at the margins, cupping a boss of golden stamens.
Leaves Bright gray-green.
• HEIGHT 30in (75cm).
• SPREAD 24in (60cm).

P. lactiflora 'Mother of Pearl'

Z 4–8

P. LACTIFLORA
'Kelway's Supreme'
Habit Clump-forming, freely branching, floriferous.
Flowers Large, strongly fragrant, double, borne over long periods from early to midsummer. Broad, incurving, soft blush-pink petals, fading to creamy-white, cupping a boss of golden stamens.
• HEIGHT 3ft (1m).
• SPREAD 3ft (1m).

P. lactiflora 'Kelway's Supreme'

Z 4–8

P. LACTIFLORA
'Avant Garde'
Habit Clump-forming.
Flowers Medium to large, fragrant, single, in mid spring. Pale rose-pink petals with darker veins, and a boss of golden anthers with red filaments. Stiff-stemmed flowers cut well.
Leaves Has particularly luxuriant foliage.
• HEIGHT to 3ft (1m).
• SPREAD to 3ft (1m).

P. lactiflora 'Avant Garde'

Z 4–8

P. LACTIFLORA
'Sarah Bernhardt'
Habit Vigorous, upright, clump-forming, floriferous.
Flowers Very large, fragrant, fully double, with large, slightly ruffled petals, in early to midsummer. Clear rose-pink, fading to soft silvery-pink at the margins.
• HEIGHT to 3ft (1m).
• SPREAD to 3ft (1m).

P. lactiflora 'Sarah Bernhardt'

Z 4–8

P. CAMBESSEDESII
Habit Clump-forming.
Flowers Single, in mid-spring. Deep rose-pink.
Leaves Very dark green, with veins, stalks, and undersides flushed purple-red.
• TIPS Needs a warm, sheltered site, with protection from late spring frost and excessive summer rain. Can be grown in a greenhouse.
• HEIGHT 18in (45cm).
• SPREAD 18in (45cm).

P. cambessedesii
Majorcan peony

☼ ◊ Z 7–8

P. LACTIFLORA 'Ballerina'
Habit Clump-forming.
Flowers Fragrant, double, in spring to early summer. Inner petals are narrower and more densely arranged often with ruffled edges. Soft blush-pink, lilac-tinted at first, fading to white.
Leaves Provide good autumn color.
• HEIGHT 3ft (1m).
• SPREAD 3ft (1m).

***P. lactiflora* 'Ballerina'**

☼ ◊ Z 4–8

P. LACTIFLORA 'Bowl of Beauty'
Habit Clump-forming.
Flowers Very large, anemone-form, in early to midsummer. Broad, outer petals of pale carmine-pink, and numerous narrow, inner petal-like stamens, densely arranged, ivory-white.
• HEIGHT 3ft (1m).
• SPREAD 3ft (1m).

***P. lactiflora* 'Bowl of Beauty'**

☼ ◊ Z 4–8

P. MASCULA
Habit Clump-forming.
Flowers Single. Carmine- or purple-red, or white, around golden stamens with purple filaments.
Fruits Downy, boat-shaped capsules split to reveal purple-black seeds.
Leaves Shiny, leaflets on red stems. Dark green.
• OTHER NAMES *P. corallina.*
• HEIGHT to 3ft (1m).
• SPREAD to 3ft (1m).

P. mascula

☼ ◊ Z 5–8

P. VEITCHII
Habit Clump-forming, spreading.
Flowers Small, single, nodding, borne 2 or more per stem in early summer. Purple-pink.
Leaves Divided into shiny, narrowly oblong to elliptic segments. Bright green.
• HEIGHT to 30in (75cm).
• SPREAD 30in (75cm) or more.

P. veitchii

☼ ◊ Z 5–8

P. *LACTIFLORA*
'Globe of Light'
Habit Clump-forming.
Flowers Large, fragrant, anemone-form, in early to midsummer. Pure pink outer petals with narrow, inner, petal-like stamens, of a clear golden-yellow.
• HEIGHT 3ft (1m).
• SPREAD 3ft (1m).

P. lactiflora
'Globe of Light'

Z 4–8

P. *LACTIFLORA*
'Kelway's Gorgeous'
Habit Clump-forming, floriferous.
Flowers Single, in early summer. Intense carmine, slightly flushed salmon-pink, with a central boss of golden stamens.
• HEIGHT 34in (85cm).
• SPREAD 34in (85cm).

P. lactiflora
'Kelway's Gorgeous'

Z 4–8

P. *LACTIFLORA*
'Silver Flare'
Habit Clump-forming.
Flowers Large, single to loosely semi-double, on dark red-tinted stems in spring to early summer. Golden stamens surrounded by carmine-pink petals, fading to a silvery margin.
Leaves Provide good autumn color.
• HEIGHT to 3ft (1m).
• SPREAD to 3ft (1m).

P. lactiflora
'Silver Flare'

Z 4–8

P. *LACTIFLORA*
'Magic Orb'
Habit Clump-forming.
Flowers Large, fragrant, double, with several whorls of broad ruffles, in early to midsummer. Intense cherry-pink outer petals and pale blush-white inner petals, shaded carmine, surround a central cluster of narrow creamy-white petals.
• HEIGHT 3ft (1m).
• SPREAD 3ft (1m).

P.lactiflora
'Magic Orb'

Z 4–8

P. *OFFICINALIS*
'China Rose'
Habit Clump-forming.
Flowers Large, single, in early to midsummer. Incurved, dark salmon-rose petals, cupping a boss of golden-orange anthers.
• HEIGHT to 18in (45cm).
• SPREAD to 18in (45cm).

P. officinalis
'China Rose'

Z 5–8

P. LACTIFLORA
'Auguste Dessert'
Habit Clump-forming.
Flowers Fragrant, semi-double, in early to midsummer. Carmine-pink, tinted salmon-pink, with ruffled silvery-white petal margins, and a central boss of yellow stamens.
Leaves Color richly in autumn.
- HEIGHT 30in (75cm).
- SPREAD 30in (75cm).

P. lactiflora **'Auguste Dessert'**

☼ ◊ Z 4–8

P. LACTIFLORA
'Instituteur Doriat'
Habit Clump-forming.
Flowers Large, anemone-form, in early summer. Outer petals, carmine-red, inner petal-like stamens paler pinkish-carmine, broader and densely arranged, with ruffled, silvery-white margins.
Leaves Provide good autumn color.
- HEIGHT 3ft (1m).
- SPREAD 3ft (1m).

P. lactiflora **'Instituteur Doriat'**

☼ ◊ Z 4–8

P. LACTIFLORA
'Defender'
Habit Vigorous, clump-forming.
Flowers Strong-stemmed, large, single, in late spring to early summer. Satiny crimson petals, with a central boss of golden stamens.
- HEIGHT 3ft (1m).
- SPREAD 3ft (1m).

P. lactiflora **'Defender'**

☼ ◊ Z 4–8

P. 'Smouthii'
Habit Vigorous, clump-forming, floriferous.
Flowers Large, fragrant, single. Glistening dark crimson, with conspicuous golden-yellow stamens.
Leaves Finely cut. Grayish green, but variable in color.
- OTHER NAMES *P.* x *smouthii*.
- HEIGHT to 18in (45cm).
- SPREAD to 18in (45cm).

P. **'Smouthii'**

☼ ◊ Z 5–8

P. PEREGRINA
'Sunshine'
Habit Clump-forming.
Flowers Large, single, in late spring to early summer. Vermilion, tinged salmon-rose.
Leaves Glossy. Bright green.
- OTHER NAMES *P. peregrina* 'Otto Freubel'.
- HEIGHT to 30in (75cm).
- SPREAD to 30in (75cm).

P. peregrina **'Sunshine'**

☼ ◊ Z 5–8

P. LACTIFLORA
'Knighthood'
Habit Clump-forming.
Flowers Large, very double, with many both broad and rather narrow, densely arranged, ruffled petals in early to midsummer. Intense, deep, rich burgundy-red.
- HEIGHT 30in (75cm).
- SPREAD 30in (75cm).

P. lactiflora 'Knighthood'

Z 4–8

P. TENUIFOLIA
Habit Clump-forming.
Flowers Small, bowl-shaped, single. Dark crimson with a central boss of conspicuous golden yellow stamens.
Leaves Elegant and very finely cut into filament-like segments. Bright green.
- HEIGHT to 18in (45cm).
- SPREAD to 18in (45cm).

P. tenuifolia

Z 5–8

P. LACTIFLORA
'Chocolate Soldier'
Habit Clump-forming.
Flowers Semi-double, in late spring to early summer. Purple-red, with yellow-mottled centers.
Leaves Mid- to dark green, usually tinged bronze-red when young.
- HEIGHT 3ft (1m).
- SPREAD 3ft (1m).

P. lactiflora 'Chocolate Soldier'

Z 4–8

P. LACTIFLORA 'Sir Edward Elgar'
Habit Clump-forming.
Flowers Large, single, in early to midsummer. Solid, rich crimson petals tinted chocolate-brown, arranged loosely around rather lax, lemon-yellow stamens.
Leaves Provide good autumn color.
- HEIGHT 30in (75cm).
- SPREAD 30in (75cm).

P. lactiflora 'Sir Edward Elgar'

Z 4–8

P. OFFICINALIS
'Rubra Plena'
Habit Clump-forming, long-lived.
Flowers Large, double, with many slightly ruffled petals, in early to midsummer. Vivid pink-crimson.
Leaves Distinctively divided into rounded, broadly oval leaflets.
- HEIGHT to 30in (75cm).
- SPREAD to 30in (75cm).

P. officinalis 'Rubra Plena'

Z 5–8

P. WITTMANNIANA
Habit Robust, clump-forming, spreading.
Flowers Large, single, bowl-shaped, in late spring or midsummer. Pale primrose-yellow, with a large central boss of yellow anthers on purple-red filaments.
Leaves Divided into oval segments. Dark green, paler beneath.
- HEIGHT to 3ft (1m).
- SPREAD to 3ft (1m).

P. wittmanniana

Z 5–8

P. LACTIFLORA
'Laura Dessert'
Habit Clump-forming.
Flowers Large, fragrant, double, in late spring to early summer. Creamy-blush-white outer petals, and densely arranged, incurved, inner petals, flushed creamy lemon-yellow, often with cut and slightly ruffled margins.
- HEIGHT 30in (75cm).
- SPREAD 30in (75cm).

P. lactiflora 'Laura Dessert'

Z 4–8

P. MLOKOSEWITSCHII
Habit Clump-forming.
Flowers Large, single, bowl-shaped, in spring. Pale lemon- to creamy-yellow, with a boss of golden stamens.
Leaves Divided into rounded leaflets. Bluish-green sometimes with red-purple edges, strongly suffused red-purple on emergence.
- HEIGHT to 30in (75cm).
- SPREAD to 30in (75cm).

P. mlokosewitschii

Z 4–8

Boraginaceae	

SYMPHYTUM × UPLANDICUM 'Variegatum'

Habit Clump-forming. ***Flowers*** Small, tubular, from late spring to early summer. Pale lilac-blue. ***Leaves*** Large, hairy, lance-shaped. Gray-green with broad cream margins.

• NATIVE HABITAT The green-leaved hybrid occurs in the Caucasus, but is naturalized in N. Europe.

• CULTIVATION Grow in any moist soil, in sun or shade. It produces its best foliage if the flowering stems are removed before they bloom.

• PROPAGATION By division in autumn or spring.

Z 4–9

HEIGHT 3ft (1m)

SPREAD 2ft (60cm)

Boraginaceae	

SYMPHYTUM CAUCASICUM

Habit Robust, clump-forming, rhizomatous. ***Flowers*** Pendent, tubular, in short, paired cymes, from spring to early summer. Azure-blue. ***Leaves*** Coarse, hairy, oval pointed. Mid-green.

• NATIVE HABITAT Scrub and streambanks, Caucasus.

• CULTIVATION Grow in moist soil, in sun or shade. Is invasive, but is well suited to a wild garden, blooming over long periods. Will produce a second flush of bloom if cut back after first flowering.

• PROPAGATION By division in spring or seed in autumn.

Z 4–9

HEIGHT 2–3ft (60–90cm)

SPREAD 2–3ft (60–90cm) or more

Apiaceae/Umbelliferae	GOLDEN SPANIARD

ACIPHYLLA AUREA

Habit Rosette-forming. ***Flowers*** Small, in large, terminal, candelabra-like spikes, about 32in (80cm) tall, from late spring to early summer. Golden-cream. ***Leaves*** Evergreen, rigid, bayonet-like, to 28in (70cm) long. Usually golden-green.

• NATIVE HABITAT Sub-alpine and mountain grassland, South Island, New Zealand.

• CULTIVATION Grow in full sun, in humus-rich, well-drained soil. An excellent architectural shape; especially useful for planting in gravel.

• PROPAGATION By seed sown fresh or in spring.

Z 10–11

HEIGHT 24–30in (60–75cm)

SPREAD 24–30in (60–75cm)

Asteraceae/Compositae	LEOPARD'S BANE

DORONICUM PARDALIANCHES

Habit Clump-forming, tuberous, spreading. ***Flowers*** Small, daisy-like, borne on slender, branching stems in late spring. Rich clear yellow. ***Leaves*** Heart-shaped, softly hairy. Bright green.
- NATIVE HABITAT Woodlands of W. Europe.
- CULTIVATION Grow in any moist, well-drained soil, in shade or partial shade. Is good for naturalizing in wild and woodland gardens.
- PROPAGATION By division in autumn or seed in autumn or spring.
- OTHER NAMES *D. cordatum*.

Z 4–8

HEIGHT
30in (75cm)

SPREAD
24in (60cm)

Asphodelaceae/ Liliaceae	KING'S SPEAR, YELLOW ASPHODEL

ASPHODELINE LUTEA

Habit Clump-forming. ***Flowers*** Small, scented, star-shaped, in dense spikes, on leafy stems, in late spring or summer. Yellow. ***Leaves*** Narrow, linear, to 1ft (30cm) long. Silvery-green to gray-green
- NATIVE HABITAT Rocky slopes, Mediterranean.
- CULTIVATION Grow in a sheltered site, in well-drained soil. In cool climates protect in winter.
- PROPAGATION By seed in autumn or spring, or by careful division in early spring. The fleshy roots are easily damaged.
- OTHER NAMES *Asphodelus lutea*.

Z 6–9

HEIGHT
3ft (1m)

SPREAD
18in (45cm)

Papaveraceae	

CHELIDONIUM MAJUS 'Flore Pleno'

Habit Upright, with a fleshy rootstock. ***Flowers*** Small, cupped, double, about 1in (2.5cm) across, borne on slender, branching stems in late spring and early summer. Bright yellow. ***Leaves*** Deeply cut, with rounded lobes. Bright green.
- NATIVE HABITAT The species occurs in woodland, from Europe to W. Asia.
- CULTIVATION Grow in sun or dappled shade, in any well-drained soil. Suitable for naturalizing in wild and woodland gardens. Seeds freely. Invasive.
- PROPAGATION By seed or division in autumn.

Z 5–8

HEIGHT
2–3ft
(60–90cm)

SPREAD
1ft (30cm)

Ranunculaceae	

TROLLIUS × CULTORUM 'Orange Princess'

Habit Robust, clump-forming. ***Flowers*** Rounded, almost globular, borne on sturdy, slender stems, above the leaves in spring. Golden-orange. ***Leaves*** Deeply divided into jagged-toothed leaflets, mostly in dense, basal clumps. Mid-green.
- NATIVE HABITAT Garden origin.
- CULTIVATION Grow in moist, fertile, humus-rich soil. Larger than most of the genus and good for pool, streamsides, and damp borders.
- PROPAGATION By division in early autumn.

Z 5–8

HEIGHT
30in (75cm)

SPREAD
18in (45cm)

Caryophyllaceae

GYPSOPHILA PANICULATA 'Bristol Fairy'

Habit Mound-forming, with a deep, thick rootstock. ***Flowers*** Tiny, double, in airy panicles, on wiry, very slender, branching stems, in summer. White. ***Leaves*** Slightly fleshy, narrowly lance-shaped. Blue-green.

• NATIVE HABITAT Garden origin.

• CULTIVATION Tolerates light, sandy soils but grows best in deep, moderately fertile, well-drained soil. Resents disturbance. The flowers dry well for winter arrangements. This plant looks charming when allowed to cascade over a low wall. It is excellent for giving a feeling of space and balance in a border, where contrasting colors need a separating foil. The white flowers also emphasize other colors, and so it is important not to exclude them from a mixed border.

• PROPAGATION By grafting in winter.

Z 4–9

HEIGHT
24–30in
(60–75cm)

SPREAD
3ft (1m)

Asteraceae/Compositae

ACHILLEA PTARMICA 'The Pearl'

Habit Upright, creeping, rhizomatous. ***Flowers*** Small, pompon-like, in large, branched heads, in summer. Pure white. ***Leaves*** Narrowly lance-shaped, more or less serrated. Glossy, dark green.

- NATIVE HABITAT Garden origin.
- CULTIVATION Grow in fertile, moist but well-drained soil. May spread rapidly. The flowers are good for air drying, for garlands, and for winter arrangements.
- PROPAGATION By division in spring or autumn.
- OTHER NAMES *A. ptarmica* 'Boule de Neige'.

Z 3–9

HEIGHT to 30in (75cm)

SPREAD 30in (75cm)

Solanaceae — FLOWERING TOBACCO, JASMINE TOBACCO

NICOTIANA ALATA

Habit Rosette-forming, with a thick rootstock. ***Flowers*** Night-scented, tubular, borne in branched clusters, on sticky stems, over long periods in summer. Creamy-white, flushed pale brownish-violet on the outside. ***Leaves*** Soft, spoon-shaped to oval. Mid-green.

- NATIVE HABITAT N.E. Argentina to S. Brazil.
- CULTIVATION Grow in fertile, well-drained soil, in sun or light shade. Best grown as an annual.
- PROPAGATION By seed in spring.
- OTHER NAMES *N. affinis.*

Z 11

HEIGHT 30in (75cm)

SPREAD 12in (30cm)

Asteraceae/Compositae

ACHILLEA AGERATUM 'W. B. Childs'

Habit Upright, spreading. ***Flowers*** Small, in loose, branched heads, borne on lax stems in summer. Pure white, with creamy-white centers. ***Leaves*** Narrow, finely toothed and divided. Dark green.

- NATIVE HABITAT Garden origin.
- CULTIVATION Grow in fertile, moist but well-drained soil. May spread rapidly in good conditions. The flowers are good for air drying, for garlands and winter arrangements.
- PROPAGATION By division in spring or autumn.

Z 7–9

HEIGHT 24–28in (60–70cm)

SPREAD 24in (60cm)

Iridaceae — NEW ZEALAND SATIN FLOWER

LIBERTIA GRANDIFLORA

Habit Loosely clump-forming, rhizomatous. ***Flowers*** Small, iris-like, to ¾in (2cm) across, in branched, spike-like clusters, in early summer. White. ***Leaves*** Rigid, linear, to 24in (60cm) long. Dark green, often turning brown at the tip.

- NATIVE HABITAT By streamsides and in forests in New Zealand.
- CULTIVATION Grow in a warm, sheltered site, in sun or partial shade, in well-drained soil.
- PROPAGATION By division in spring, or by seed in autumn or spring.

Z 9–10

HEIGHT 30in (75cm)

SPREAD 24in (60cm)

Brassicaceae/Cruciferae	DAME'S VIOLET, SWEET ROCKET

HESPERIS MATRONALIS

Habit Upright. ***Flowers*** Small, 4-petaled, in loose, spike-like racemes, in summer. White, lilac or violet. Strongly scented in the evening. ***Leaves*** Lance-shaped to oval, smooth. Mid-green.

• NATIVE HABITAT Mountain woods, scrub and streamsides, from S. Europe to Siberia.

• CULTIVATION Grow in moderately fertile, moist but well-drained soil, in sun or dappled shade. Is often short-lived, so propagate regularly.

• PROPAGATION By basal cuttings in spring, or by seed in autumn or spring.

Z 4–9

HEIGHT
30in (75cm) or more

SPREAD
24in (60cm)

Geraniaceae	

GERANIUM PHAEUM 'Album'

Habit Clump-forming, rhizomatous. ***Flowers*** Larger than the dark-flowered species, with 5 reflexed petals, borne in loose, branched, one-sided clusters from late spring to summer. White. ***Leaves*** Divided into 7–9 soft green lobes.

• NATIVE HABITAT Species occurs in woods and sub-alpine meadows, S., C. and W. Europe.

• CULTIVATION Grow in any well-drained soil, in shade or partial shade. Excellent for woodland and wild gardens, or for shady borders.

• PROPAGATION By division in autumn or spring.

Z 4–8

HEIGHT
30in (75cm)

SPREAD
18in (45cm)

Papaveraceae	WHITE BLEEDING HEART

DICENTRA SPECTABILIS 'Alba'

Habit Clump-forming. ***Flowers*** Pendent, heart-shaped, on fleshy, arching stems, in late spring and early summer. Pure white. ***Leaves*** Fern-like, deeply cut. Light green.

• NATIVE HABITAT Woods and shady valleys, from Siberia to Japan.

• CULTIVATION Grow in humus-rich, moist but well-drained soil, in partial shade. Suitable for a shady border or woodland garden. It has proved hardier than originally thought, although, when planting, it is important to bear in mind that a severe late frost occasionally damages the fresh new growth. It is sometimes difficult to differentiate between this and the pink-flowered species when out of flower, so to avoid disappointment, it is best purchased during the flowering period.

• PROPAGATION By division when dormant in late winter.

Z 3–9

HEIGHT
24–30in (60–75cm)

SPREAD
24in (60cm)

Asphodelaceae/ Liliaceae	WHITE ASPHODEL

ASPHODELUS ALBUS

Habit Upright, clump-forming, with fleshy roots. ***Flowers*** Small, star-shaped, in thick-stemmed, terminal racemes, in late spring and early summer. White. ***Leaves*** Flattened, linear, to 2ft (60cm) long, in basal clumps. Mid-green.

• NATIVE HABITAT Woods, heaths, and rocky places, C. and S. Europe.

• CULTIVATION Grow in a warm, sunny site, in light, well-drained soil.

• PROPAGATION By division in spring, or by seed in autumn.

Z 7–10

HEIGHT
3ft (1m)

SPREAD
18in (45cm)

Lamiaceae/Labiatae	SILVER SAGE

SALVIA ARGENTEA

Habit Rosette-forming. ***Flowers*** Hooded, 2-lipped, sage-like, in branching, candelabra-like clusters, on strong, upright stems, in summer. White. ***Leaves*** Oval, wrinkled, woolly, in a large basal clump. Silver-green.

• NATIVE HABITAT Dry hills in the Mediterranean.

• CULTIVATION Grow in a warm, sunny, sheltered site, in very well-drained soil. Grown for its soft, felty-gray foliage, it is suited to a Mediterranean border, also dry walls and the alpine house.

• PROPAGATION By seed or division in spring.

Z 5–8

HEIGHT
2–3ft
(60cm–1m)

SPREAD
18in (45cm)

Asteraceae/Compositae	PEARL EVERLASTING

ANAPHALIS MARGARITACEA

Habit Bushy, clump-forming. ***Flowers*** Tiny, with papery petals, in clustered heads, on upright stems, in late summer. White. ***Leaves*** Narrowly lance-shaped, white-margined. Silver- or gray-green.

• NATIVE HABITAT On dry, rocky soils, in North America, N. and C. Europe, and N.E. Asia.

• CULTIVATION Grow in any moderately fertile, well-drained, not-too-dry soil. Flowers dry well.

• PROPAGATION By seed in autumn, or by division in late winter or early spring.

• OTHER NAMES *A. yedoensis.*

Z 4–8

HEIGHT
24–30in
(60–75cm)

SPREAD
24in (60cm)

Rutaceae	GAS PLANT

DICTAMNUS ALBUS

Habit Upright, woody-based. ***Flowers*** Fragrant, star-shaped, in erect racemes, in early summer. White, with conspicuous stamens. ***Leaves*** Aromatic, divided into lance-shaped, light green leaflets

• NATIVE HABITAT Dry, rocky sites and open woods, in S.W. Europe, S. and C. Asia, China, and Korea.

• CULTIVATION Grow in a warm, sunny, sheltered site, in fertile, well-drained soil. Resents disturbance. On warm, still evenings, the ripening seedpods give off oils that can be ignited, hence the common name.

• PROPAGATION By seed sown fresh in late summer.

Z 3–8

HEIGHT
to 3ft (1m)

SPREAD
2ft (60cm)

Ranunculaceae	

THALICTRUM AQUILEGIIFOLIUM 'White Cloud'

Habit Dense, clump-forming, slow-growing. ***Flowers*** Tiny, in dense, fluffy, terminal sprays, in early summer. White. ***Leaves*** Smooth, finely divided. Pale grayish-green.
• NATIVE HABITAT Garden origin.
• CULTIVATION Grow in moist but well-drained, fertile soil, in sun or light, dappled shade. Suited to border plantings; especially good in white or silver borders.
• PROPAGATION By division in spring.

☼ ◊

Z 5–9

HEIGHT
3–4ft
(1–1.2m)

SPREAD
1ft (30cm)

Asteraceae/Compositae	SHASTA DAISY

LEUCANTHEMUM × *SUPERBUM* 'Elizabeth'

Habit Robust, clump-forming. ***Flowers*** Large, solitary, semi-double, borne on sturdy stems from mid- to late summer. White, with a yellow central disk. ***Leaves*** Coarse, spoon-shaped, lobed and toothed. Dark green.
• NATIVE HABITAT Garden origin.
• CULTIVATION Grow in any moderately fertile, well-drained soil in full sun. Suitable for cutting.
• PROPAGATION By division in spring or autumn.
• OTHER NAMES *Chrysanthemum* × *superbum* 'Elizabeth'.

☼ ◊

Z 4–9

HEIGHT
3ft (1m)

SPREAD
2ft (60cm)

Asteraceae/Compositae	MARGUERITE, PARIS DAISY

ARGYRANTHEMUM FRUTESCENS

Habit Bushy, woody-based. ***Flowers*** Large, single, daisy-like, produced on strong, slender stems throughout summer. Pure white, pink or yellow. ***Leaves*** Finely divided, fern-like. Blue-green.
• NATIVE HABITAT Canary Islands.
• CULTIVATION Grow in a warm, sunny site, in moderately fertile, well-drained soil.
• PROPAGATION By stem cuttings in autumn, or by seed in spring.
• OTHER NAMES *Chrysanthemum frutescens.*

☼ ◊

Z 11

HEIGHT
3ft (1m)

SPREAD
3ft (1m)

Asteraceae/Compositae	FLEABANE

ERIGERON 'White Quakeress'

Habit Clump-forming. ***Flowers*** Daisy-like, with slender, white ray florets around a greenish-yellow disk, borne in profusion over long periods in summer. ***Leaves*** Lance-shaped to spoon-shaped. Grayish-green.

• NATIVE HABITAT Garden origin.

• CULTIVATION Grow in moderately fertile, well-drained soil in full sun. A charming sport of the pale lilac-pink flowered 'Quakeress', it is noted for its long flowering period. Suitable for the front or middle of a mixed or herbaceous border. Cut back any remnants of the previous year's growth in early spring to maintain a tidy and compact habit. The flowers are good for cutting. The genus includes many garden-worthy plants, offering a range of heights, colors, and flowering seasons.

• PROPAGATION By division in spring or early autumn, or by basal cuttings in early summer.

Z 5–8

HEIGHT
to 32in (80cm)

SPREAD
24in (60cm)

Saxifragaceae	FINGERLEAF RODGERSFLOWER

RODGERSIA AESCULIFOLIA

Habit Vigorous, clump-forming, rhizomatous. ***Flowers*** Fragrant, tiny, in branching, flat-topped clusters, on strong, slender, rusty-hairy stems. Pinkish-white. ***Leaves*** Divided into 7 toothed, crinkled, veined. Bronze-green leaflets.

• NATIVE HABITAT Damp woods and streambanks, in the mountains of W. China.

• CULTIVATION Grow in moist but well-drained, fertile, humus-rich soil, in sun or partial shade. This is a statuesque perennial for damp woodland gardens or pondsides, associating well with similar damp-loving plants. Its horse-chestnut-like leaves have excellent qualities that make it one of the aristocrats of the garden. Best planted alone to give full reign to its architectural features.

• PROPAGATION By division in spring, or seed in autumn.

☼ 💧

Z 5–8

HEIGHT
3ft (1m)

SPREAD
3ft (1m)

Apiaceae/Umbelliferae	SWEET CICELY, GARDEN MYRRH

MYRRHIS ODORATA

Habit Vigorous, with a deep, woody rootstock. ***Flowers*** Tiny, in dense, rounded umbels, in early summer. White. ***Leaves*** Aromatic, softly hairy, finely divided, and fern-like. Fresh bright green.

- NATIVE HABITAT Damp woods, hedges, and streambanks in Europe but widely naturalized.
- CULTIVATION Grow in moist but well-drained, fertile soil, in sun or dappled shade. Grow in an herb garden, or in a border to make an attractive, fresh green foil for more brightly colored perennials.
- PROPAGATION By seed in autumn or spring.

Z 4–8

HEIGHT 2–3ft (60cm–1m)

SPREAD 2ft (60cm)

Saxifragaceae	ELDERLEAF, RODGERSFLOWER

RODGERSIA SAMBUCIFOLIA

Habit Clump-forming, rhizomatous. ***Flowers*** Tiny, in branching, feathery clusters, well above the foliage, in summer. Creamy-white or pale pink. ***Leaves*** Irregularly divided into 8–11 leaflets. Emerald-green, sometimes bronze-flushed.

- NATIVE HABITAT Rocky forest areas in W. China.
- CULTIVATION Grow in moist, fertile humus-rich soil, in sun or partial shade, with shelter from dry winds.
- PROPAGATION By division in spring, or by seed in autumn.

Z 5–8

HEIGHT 3–4ft (1–1.2m)

SPREAD 3ft (1m)

Saxifragaceae	BRONZELEAF RODGERSFLOWER

RODGERSIA PODOPHYLLA

Habit Clump-forming, rhizomatous. ***Flowers*** Tiny, borne in branching clusters above the foliage in summer. Creamy-white. ***Leaves*** Large, divided into 5 shallowly lobed leaflets. Bronze when young; mid-green then coppery in autumn.

- NATIVE HABITAT Damp, mountain woodlands, Japan and Korea.
- CULTIVATION Grow in moist soil, in sun or partial shade, with shelter from dry winds.
- PROPAGATION By division in spring, or by seed in autumn.

Z 5–9

HEIGHT to 4ft (1.2m)

SPREAD 3ft (1m)

Rosaceae	CUTLEAF GOATSBEARD

ARUNCUS DIOICUS 'Kneiffii'

Habit Clump-forming. ***Flowers*** Tiny, star-shaped, in dense plumes, on slender, wiry stems, from mid- to late summer. Creamy-white. ***Leaves*** Feathery, deeply cut into very slender segments. Rich green.

- NATIVE HABITAT Garden origin.
- CULTIVATION Grow in moist but well-drained soil, in sun or partial shade. Plant in a border or by a pond or stream, above water level.
- PROPAGATION By division in spring or autumn.
- OTHER NAMES *A. plumosus* 'Kneiffii', *A. sylvester* 'Kneiffii'.

Z 3–7

HEIGHT 3ft (1m)

SPREAD 20in (50cm)

Papaveraceae

PAPAVER ORIENTALE 'Perry's White'

Habit Clump-forming. ***Flowers*** Large, deeply cupped, with satiny, white petals, each with a dark maroon-purple blotch at the base, borne on strong stems in early summer. ***Leaves*** Divided into hairy, toothed, lance-shaped segments, dying back after flowering. Dark gray-green.

• NATIVE HABITAT Garden origin.

• CULTIVATION Grow in moist, well-drained, fertile soil, in sun. Tends to sprawl and may need support.

• PROPAGATION By root cuttings in winter, or by division in autumn.

Z 4–9

HEIGHT 32in (80cm)

SPREAD 24in (60cm)

Scrophulariaceae — RUSTY FOXGLOVE

DIGITALIS FERRUGINEA

Habit Basal rosette-forming. ***Flowers*** Funnel-shaped, borne in dense, slender spires in mid summer. Pale golden-brown and white.
Leaves Narrowly oval, in basal rosettes, with linear stem leaves. Olive to mid-green.

• NATIVE HABITAT Woodland, scrub, and rocky sites in Turkey.

• CULTIVATION Tolerates dry soils. Grow in any moderately fertile, well-drained soil, in sun or partial shade. Short-lived and best treated as a biennial.

• PROPAGATION By seed in autumn.

Z 4–7

HEIGHT 3–4ft (1–1.2m)

SPREAD 1ft (30cm)

Asteraceae/Compositae

ACHILLEA 'Wesersandstein'

Habit Mound-forming, vigorous. ***Flowers*** Small, in broad, branched heads, throughout summer. Bright salmon-pink, fading to a creamy, sand-yellow. ***Leaves*** Narrowly lance-shaped, feathery, finely divided, finely hairy. Green.

• NATIVE HABITAT Garden origin.

• CULTIVATION Grow in fertile, well-drained soil, in full sun. Divide and replant every third year to maintain vigor. Flower heads dry well.

• PROPAGATION By division in early spring or autumn.

Z 3–9

HEIGHT 18–24in (45–60cm)

SPREAD 24in (60cm)

Primulaceae — GOOSENECK LOOSESTRIFE

LYSIMACHIA CLETHROIDES

Habit Vigorous, clump-forming, rhizomatous.
Flowers Tiny, star-shaped, in dense, slender, spikes that are nodding when in bud, becoming erect when in full bloom. White.
Leaves Lance-shaped. Mid-green, yellow-green when young.

• NATIVE HABITAT Grassy hills in Japan.

• CULTIVATION Grow in moist but well-drained soil, in sun or partial shade.

• PROPAGATION By division in spring, or by seed in autumn.

Z 4–9

HEIGHT 3ft (1m)

SPREAD 2–3ft (60cm–1m)

Campanulaceae

CAMPANULA LACTIFLORA 'Loddon Anna'

Habit Upright, branching, slender-stemmed, with a stout rootstock. ***Flowers*** Large, nodding, broadly bell-shaped, borne in broad, dense, leafy panicles, from mid- to late summer. Soft, dusty lilac-pink. ***Leaves*** Narrowly oval, borne in basal rosettes and scattered up the stems. Mid-green.

• NATIVE HABITAT Garden origin. The species occurs in forests and alpine and sub-alpine meadows in the Caucasus mountains.

• CULTIVATION Prefers fertile, moist but well-drained soil, in full sun but tolerates partial shade. Needs staking especially on windy sites. Excellent for a mixed or herbaceous border. This and other cultivars of the species associate particularly well with old-fashioned roses, since they bear their first flush of flowers at about the same time.

• PROPAGATION By division in spring or autumn.

Z 5–7

HEIGHT
to 4ft
(1.2m)

SPREAD
2ft (60cm)

PHLOX

Border phlox (cultivars of *Phlox maculata* and *P. paniculata*) produce often delicately fragrant, dome-shaped, or conical heads of flowers in late summer in shades of mainly white, pink, and purple. Unless otherwise indicated, the leaves are oval and mid-green.

Phlox thrive in moist but well-drained soil in full sun, or, on drier soils, in light shade. Taller cultivars may need staking. To produce larger flowers, cut back the weakest shoots in spring when the plant is about a third of its eventual height.

Border phlox are particularly prone to nematode infestation; any affected plants should be discarded. Propagate by taking root cuttings from healthy stock. Do not replant in infested soil for at least two years.

P. *PANICULATA*
'Fujiyama'
Habit Upright, clump-forming.
Flowers Tubular, 5-lobed, borne in dense, long, conical heads, on very sturdy stems in late summer. Pure white.
- HEIGHT to 3ft (1m).
- SPREAD 18in (45cm).

P. paniculata **'Fujiyama'**

Z 4–8

P. *PANICULATA*
'Mia Ruys'
Habit Upright, clump-forming.
Flowers Large, tubular, 5-lobed, borne in dense, rounded-conical heads, in late summer. Pure-white.
- HEIGHT 18in (45cm).
- SPREA 18in (45cm).

P. paniculata **'Mia Ruys'**

Z 4–8

P. *MACULATA*
'Omega'
Habit Upright, clump-forming.
Flowers Tubular, 5-lobed, borne in long, cylindrical heads in summer. White with a lilac eye.
- HEIGHT to 3ft (1m).
- SPREAD 18in (45cm).

P. maculata **'Omega'**

Z 3–9

P. *PANICULATA*
'White Admiral'
Habit Upright, open, clump-forming.
Flowers Tubular, 5-lobed, borne in dense, conical heads, in late summer. Pure white.
- HEIGHT 3ft (1m).
- SPREAD 18in (45cm).

P. paniculata **'White Admiral'**

Z 4–8

P. *PANICULATA*
'Mother of Pearl'
Habit Upright, clump-forming.
Flowers Tubular, 5-lobed, borne in dense, rounded-conical heads, in late summer. White, suffused palest pink.
- HEIGHT 4ft (1.2m).
- SPREAD 18in (45cm).

P. paniculata **'Mother of Pearl'**

Z 4–8

P. PANICULATA 'Graf Zeppelin'
Habit Upright, clump-forming.
Flowers Tubular, 5-lobed, borne in dense, rounded-conical heads, in late summer. White with red eyes.
- HEIGHT to 3ft (1m).
- SPREAD 18in (45cm).

P. paniculata 'Graf Zeppelin'

Z 4–8

P. PANICULATA 'Eva Cullum'
Habit Upright, clump-forming.
Flowers Tubular, 5-lobed, borne in open, rounded-conical heads in late summer. Clear pink with magenta eyes.
- HEIGHT to 3ft (1m).
- SPREAD 18in (45cm).

P. paniculata 'Eva Cullum'

Z 4–8

P. PANICULATA 'Balmoral'
Habit Upright, clump-forming.
Flowers Large, tubular, 5-lobed, borne in rounded-conical heads in late summer. Rosy-mauve.
- HEIGHT to 3ft (1m).
- SPREAD 18in (45cm).

P. paniculata 'Balmoral'

Z 4–8

P. MACULATA 'Alpha'
Habit Upright, clump-forming.
Flowers Tubular, 5-lobed, borne in long, cylindrical heads in summer. Rose-pink.
- HEIGHT to 3ft (1m).
- SPREAD 18in (45cm).

P. maculata 'Alpha'

Z 3–

P. PANICULATA 'Sandringham'
Habit Upright, open, clump-forming.
Flowers Tubular, 5-lobed, with widely spaced petals, borne in dense, rounded-conical heads, in late summer. Pink, with a darker pink eye.
- HEIGHT 3ft (1m).
- SPREAD 18in (45cm).

P. paniculata 'Sandringham'

Z 4–8

P. PANICULATA 'Windsor'
Habit Upright, open, clump-forming.
Flowers Tubular, 5-lobed, borne in dense, conical heads, in late summer. Carmine-rose with red eyes.
- HEIGHT 3ft (1m).
- SPREAD 18in (45cm).

P. paniculata 'Windsor'

Z 4–8

P. PANICULATA
'Prince of Orange'
Habit Upright, clump-forming.
Flowers Tubular, 5-lobed, borne in dense, broad, rounded-conical heads, in late summer. Orange-red.
• HEIGHT 3ft (1m).
• SPREAD 18in (45cm).

P. paniculata **'Prince of Orange'**

Z 4–8

P. PANICULATA
'Brigadier'
Habit Upright, clump-forming.
Flowers Tubular, 5-lobed, borne in rounded-conical heads in late summer. Deep orange-red.
• HEIGHT to 3ft (1m).
• SPREAD 18in (45cm).

P. paniculata **'Brigadier'**

Z 4–8

P. PANICULATA
'Harlequin'
Habit Upright, clump-forming.
Flowers Tubular, 5-lobed, borne in dense, rounded-conical heads, in late summer. Red-purple.
Leaves Variegated ivory-white.
• HEIGHT to 3ft (1m).
• SPREAD 18in (45cm).

P. paniculata **'Harlequin'**

Z 4–8

P. PANICULATA
'Aida'
Habit Upright, clump-forming.
Flowers Tubular, 5-lobed, borne in conical heads in late summer. Purple-red with a purple eye.
• HEIGHT to 3ft (1m).
• SPREAD 18in (45cm).

P. paniculata **'Aida'**

Z 4–8

P. *PANICULATA*
'Eventide'
Habit Upright, clump-forming.
Flowers Tubular, 5-lobed, borne in dense, rounded-conical heads in late summer. Lavender-blue.
- HEIGHT to 3ft (1m).
- SPREAD 18in (45cm).

P. paniculata
'Eventide'

☼ ◊ Z 4–8

P. *PANICULATA*
'Le Mahdi'
Habit Upright, clump-forming.
Flowers Tubular, 5-lobed, borne in dense, rounded-conical heads, in late summer. Deep blue-purple, sometimes white-eyed.
- HEIGHT to 3ft (1m).
- SPREAD 18in (45cm).

P. paniculata
'Le Mahdi'

☼ ◊ Z 4–8

P. *PANICULATA*
'Norah Leigh'
Habit Upright, clump-forming.
Flowers Tubular, 5-lobed, borne in dense, rounded-conical heads, in late summer. Pale lilac.
Leaves Variegated ivory-white.
- HEIGHT 3ft (1m).
- SPREAD 18in (45cm).

P. paniculata
'Norah Leigh'

☼ ◊ Z 4–8

P. *PANICULATA*
'Hampton Court'
Habit Upright, clump-forming.
Flowers Tubular, 5-lobed, borne in dense, rounded-conical heads, in late summer. Mauve-blue.
Leaves Very dark green.
- HEIGHT to 3ft (1m).
- SPREAD 18in (45cm).

P. paniculata
'Hampton Court'

☼ ◊ Z 4–8

Morinaceae	WHORLFLOWER

MORINA LONGIFOLIA

Habit Rosette-forming. ***Flowers*** Tubular, hooded, waxy, borne in whorls on sturdy stems, in mid summer. White, pink after fertilization. ***Leaves*** Aromatic, spiny and thistle-like, mostly in a basal rosette. Bright green.
• NATIVE HABITAT Damp, steep slopes, Himalayas.
• CULTIVATION Grow in moist, open, well-drained soil in sun. Shelter from cold, dry winds in spring. Suitable for borders, or as a specimen.
• PROPAGATION By fresh seed in late summer, or by division after flowering.

Z 5–8

HEIGHT
24–30in
(60–75cm)

SPREAD
1ft (30cm)

Rosaceae	BOWMANS ROOT, INDIAN PHYSIC

GILLENIA TRIFOLIATA

Habit Upright, clump-forming. ***Flowers*** Delicate, with 5 slender white petals, on wiry, branching, red stems, in summer. ***Leaves*** Divided into oval-oblong, olive-green leaflets, turning red in autumn.
• NATIVE HABITAT Rocky areas in open woodland, N.E. North America.
• CULTIVATION Grow in sun or partial shade, in any well-drained soil. Can be difficult to establish, but worth the effort. A beautiful and very graceful border plant.
• PROPAGATION By seed in autumn or spring.

Z 4–8

HEIGHT
3–4ft
(1–1.2m)

SPREAD
2ft (60cm)

Scrophulariaceae	WHITE CULVER'S ROOT

VERONICASTRUM VIRGINICUM ALBUM

Habit Upright. ***Flowers*** Small, tubular,borne in slender spires, in late summer. White, with prominent, pale pink stamens. ***Leaves*** Narrow, lance-shaped, in whorls. Dark green.
• NATIVE HABITAT Woods and scrub, E. North America.
• CULTIVATION Grow in moist, well-drained soil.
• PROPAGATION By division in spring or autumn, by seed in autumn, or by softwood or semi-ripe cuttings in summer.
• OTHER NAMES *Veronica virginica* f. *alba*.

Z 4–8

HEIGHT
4ft (1.2m)

SPREAD
18in (45cm)

Valerianaceae	CAT'S VALERIAN, COMMON VALERIAN

VALERIANA OFFICINALIS

Habit Fleshy, clump-forming. ***Flowers*** Tiny, in branched, rounded clusters, in summer. White to pink. ***Leaves*** Divided into toothed or entire, narrow leaflets. Mid-green.

- NATIVE HABITAT Dry or damp meadows and ditches, from Europe to W. Asia.
- CULTIVATION Grow in sun, in moist but well-drained soil. Also tolerates dry soils. Good for wild gardens, herbaceous borders, and sometimes grown in medicinal herb gardens.
- PROPAGATION By seed in spring.

Z 4–9

HEIGHT 3–4ft (1–1.2m)

SPREAD 3ft (1m)

Scrophulariaceae	PURPLE TOADFLAX

LINARIA PURPUREA 'Canon Went'

Habit Upright, clump-forming. ***Flowers*** Small, snapdragon-like, borne in slender spikes, from mid- to late summer. Dusky-pink with orange-tinged throats. ***Leaves*** Linear, smooth, in basal clumps, and along the stems. Gray-green.

- NATIVE HABITAT Garden origin.
- CULTIVATION Grow in any well-drained soil, in sun or light shade. Self-sows freely. Suitable for herbaceous borders and scree plantings. Makes excellent contrasts in a gray or silver border.
- PROPAGATION By seed in autumn or spring.

Z 5–8

HEIGHT 2–3ft (60cm–1m)

SPREAD 2ft (60cm)

Asteraceae/Compositae	

ACHILLEA 'Forncett Candy'

Habit Upright. ***Flowers*** Tiny, uniform in large, flat heads, borne on rigid, leafy stems during summer. Chalky-pink, fading with age. ***Leaves*** Feathery, finely divided. Matte green.

- NATIVE HABITAT Garden origin.
- CULTIVATION Grow in fertile, well-drained soil, in full sun. Divide and replant every third year to maintain vigor. Valued for its clear flower color. The flower heads dry well for winter arrangements.
- PROPAGATION By division in early spring or autumn.

Z 3–9

HEIGHT to 34in (85cm)

SPREAD 24in (60cm) or more

Geraniaceae	

GERANIUM × OXONIANUM 'Winscombe'

Habit Dense, mound-forming. ***Flowers*** Small, cup-shaped, borne in profusion throughout summer. Pale pink, darkening with age. ***Leaves*** Semi-evergreen, with 5 deeply cut, toothed, mid-green lobes, sometimes blotched brown at the base.

- NATIVE HABITAT Garden origin.
- CULTIVATION Grow in any but waterlogged soil, in sun or light shade. Valued as weed-smothering ground cover and for its long flowering season.
- PROPAGATION By division in autumn or spring.

Z 5–8

HEIGHT 24–30in (60–75cm)

SPREAD 18in (45cm)

Malvaceae	MUSK MALLOW, MUSK ROSE

MALVA MOSCHATA

Habit Bushy, branching. ***Flowers*** Saucer-shaped, in spikes, produced in succession from early to late summer. Clear rose-pink. ***Leaves*** Slightly aromatic, deeply divided into 7 narrow, mid-green lobes.

- NATIVE HABITAT Grasslands of Europe to N.W Africa and Turkey.
- CULTIVATION Grow in fertile, well-drained soil, in sun. Ideal for borders and wildflower gardens.
- PROPAGATION By seed in autumn or basal cuttings in summer.

☼ ◊

Z 4–8

HEIGHT
2–3ft
(60cm–1m)

SPREAD
2ft (60cm)

Malvaceae	CHECKERBLOOM, PRAIRIE MALLOW

SIDALCEA MALVIFLORA

Habit Clump-forming. ***Flowers*** Bowl-shaped, borne in erect, terminal racemes in summer. Pink or lilac-pink, with pale-veined, silky petals. ***Leaves*** Divided into 7–9 rounded lobes, mostly basal. Bright green.

- NATIVE HABITAT Grassy slopes and damp hollows in Baja California, California, and Oregon.
- CULTIVATION Grow in moist, well-drained soil, in sun or light shade. Flowers are good for cutting. Ideal for the front of a border; seldom needs staking.
- PROPAGATION By seed or division in spring.

☼ ◊

Z 6–8

HEIGHT
24–32in
(60–80cm)

SPREAD
32in (80cm)

Polygonaceae	

PERSICARIA BISTORTA 'Superba'

Habit Clump-forming, rhizomatous. ***Flowers*** Tiny, in dense, cylindrical spikes, on slender stems, in summer. Soft, clear pink. ***Leaves*** Oval, with triangular stem leaves. Mid-green.

- NATIVE HABITAT Garden origin.
- CULTIVATION Grow in moist, fertile soil. Tolerates drier soils, but flowers less freely. Vigorous and long-flowering specimen for a moist border, but may swamp more delicate plants, so site carefully.
- PROPAGATION By division in spring or autumn.
- OTHER NAMES *Polygonum bistorta superbum.*

☼ ♦

Z 4–8

HEIGHT
24–30in
(60–75cm)

SPREAD
2ft (60cm)
or more

Rutaceae	GAS PLANT

DICTAMNUS ALBUS var. *PURPUREUS*

Habit Upright, woody-based. ***Flowers*** Fragrant, star-shaped, borne in erect racemes in early summer. Pale to deep purplish-pink, with conspicuous stamens. ***Leaves*** Highly aromatic, divided into lance-shaped, leaflets. Light green.

- NATIVE HABITAT Dry rocks and open woods, from S.W. Europe, S. and C. Asia, China, and Korea.
- CULTIVATION Grow in a warm, sunny, sheltered site, in fertile, well-drained soil. Dislikes disturbance.
- PROPAGATION By seed sown fresh in late summer.

Z 3–8

HEIGHT
3ft (1m)

SPREAD
2ft (60cm)

Lamiaceae/Labiatae	BERGAMOT, BEE BALM, OSWEGO TEA

MONARDA 'Croftway Pink'

Habit Clump-forming. ***Flowers*** Small, hooded, in dense, terminal heads, throughout summer. Soft rose-pink. ***Leaves*** Aromatic, toothed, oval, triangular or lance-shaped. Mid-green.

- NATIVE HABITAT Garden origin.
- CULTIVATION Grow in any moist, fertile soil, in sun or light shade. Suitable for herbaceous borders and herb gardens. The flowers attract bees and other insects. Prone to mildew in dry conditions.
- PROPAGATION By division in spring.
- OTHER NAMES *M. didyma* 'Croftway Pink'.

Z 4–8

HEIGHT
3ft (1m)

SPREAD
18in (45cm)

Saxifragaceae	BRIDAL WREATH

FRANCOA SONCHIFOLIA

Habit Clump- or mat-forming. ***Flowers*** Small, cup-shaped, borne in short, dense racemes on slender, upright stems in summer and early autumn. Pink, marked red. ***Leaves*** Evergreen, rounded, deeply lobed, with winged leaf stalks, in dense, basal clumps. Dark green, softly hairy.

- NATIVE HABITAT Rocky, cliffside crevices, Chile.
- CULTIVATION Grow in light, well-drained soil in sun or light shade, in a warm, sheltered site. Good for the front of a border.
- PROPAGATION By seed or division in spring.

Z 7–9

HEIGHT
24–30in
(60–75cm)
or more

SPREAD
18in (45cm)

Geraniaceae	

GERANIUM × *OXONIANUM* 'Southcombe Star'

Habit Dense, mound-forming. ***Flowers*** Small, star-shaped, in profusion through summer. Pink with darker veins. Sometimes produces double flowers with petal-like stamens. ***Leaves*** Semi-evergreen, with 5 deeply cut, toothed lobes. Mid-green, sometimes blotched brown at the base.

- NATIVE HABITAT Garden origin.
- CULTIVATION Grow in any but waterlogged soil, in sun or light shade. Is good for ground cover.
- PROPAGATION By division in autumn or spring.

Z 5–8

HEIGHT
24–30in
(60–75cm)

SPREAD
18in (45cm)

Malvaceae

SIDALCEA 'Jimmy Whittet'

Habit Clump-forming. ***Flowers*** Bowl-shaped, borne in erect, terminal racemes in summer. Purplish-pink, with silky petals. ***Leaves*** Divided into 7–9 rounded lobes, mostly in basal clumps. Bright green.

- NATIVE HABITAT Garden origin.
- CULTIVATION Grow in moist but well-drained soil, in sun or light shade. Provide unobtrusive support. Flowers are good for cutting. A useful perennial for the middle of a border. Its graceful and handsome spikes carry long-lasting flowers. For a second show of flowers cut back after the first flush – this will prolong the season to the autumn. A winter mulch of straw, for example, will help protect during long periods of low temperatures.
- PROPAGATION By division in spring.
- OTHER NAMES *S.* 'Jimmy Whitelet'.

Z 5–8

HEIGHT
3–4ft
(1–1.2m)

SPREAD
3ft (1m)

Asteraceae/Compositae

ARGYRANTHEMUM 'Mary Wootton'

Habit Bushy, woody-based. ***Flowers*** Large, daisy-like, produced on strong, slender stems throughout summer. Pink. ***Leaves*** Finely divided, fern-like. Pale green.

- NATIVE HABITAT Garden origin.
- CULTIVATION Grow in moderately fertile, well-drained soil. Needs a warm, sunny site with protection from cold winds.
- PROPAGATION By stem cuttings in autumn.
- OTHER NAMES *A. frutescens* 'Mary Wootton', *Chrysanthemum frutescens* 'Mary Wootton'.

Z 11

HEIGHT
3ft (1m)

SPREAD
3ft (1m)

Asteraceae/Compositae | KNAPWEED

CENTAUREA PULCHERRIMA

Habit Upright. ***Flowers*** Cornflower-like, borne singly on slender stems in summer. Rose-pink, with paler centers. ***Leaves*** Narrowly lance-shaped, deeply cut, mostly in basal clumps. Silvery-green.

- NATIVE HABITAT Meadows, Caucasus mountains.
- CULTIVATION Grow in open, freely draining, and moderately fertile soil in full sun. Thrives on alkaline soils. Good for herbaceous borders and wildflower gardens.
- PROPAGATION By seed or division in autumn or spring.

Z 4–8

HEIGHT
30in (75cm)

SPREAD
24in (60cm)

Saxifragaceae

ASTILBE 'Venus'

Habit Clump-forming. ***Flowers*** Tiny, in dense feathery plumes, in summer. Pale pink. ***Leaves*** Divided into toothed, oval leaflets. Fresh green.

- NATIVE HABITAT Garden origin.
- CULTIVATION Grow in moist, fertile, humus-rich soil, in sun or partial shade. Mulch in spring. Good for damp borders, bog gardens, or waterside plantings. Flower heads turn brown and dry; will persist into winter unless removed.
- PROPAGATION By division in spring or autumn.
- OTHER NAMES *A.* × *arendsii* 'Venus'.

Z 4–9

HEIGHT
3ft (1m)

SPREAD
3ft (1m)

Saxifragaceae

ASTILBE 'Straussenfeder'

Habit Clump-forming. ***Flowers*** Tiny, in arching, tapering plumes, in summer. Coral-pink. ***Leaves*** Divided into toothed, oval leaflets. Dark green.
• NATIVE HABITAT Garden origin.
• CULTIVATION Grow in moist, fertile, humus-rich soil, in sun or partial shade. Apply an annual spring mulch of organic matter. Good for damp borders, bog gardens, or waterside plantings. Flower heads turn brown and dry, and persist into winter.
• PROPAGATION By division in spring or autumn.
• OTHER NAMES *A.* 'Ostrich Plume'.

Z 4–9

HEIGHT
3ft (1m)

SPREAD
3ft (1m)

Apiaceae/Umbelliferae

CHAEROPHYLLUM HIRSUTUM 'Roseum'

Habit Robust, clump-forming. ***Flowers*** Tiny, borne in small umbels on thick, upright stems in mid summer. Pink, with fringed petals. ***Leaves*** Large, soft, fern-like, divided into overlapping, purple-flushed segments, borne on purplish-green stems.
• NATIVE HABITAT Species occurs in mountain scrub and grassland in Europe.
• CULTIVATION Grow in moist, fertile soil in sun or partial shade. Suitable for borders and wild gardens.
• PROPAGATION By division in early spring.

Z 6–9

HEIGHT
to 4ft
(1.2m)

SPREAD
2ft (60cm)

Scrophulariaceae

DIGITALIS × *MERTONENSIS*

Habit Clump-forming. ***Flowers*** Tubular, to 2½in (6cm) long, borne in open, upright spikes from late spring to early summer. Buff-tinted, strawberry-pink. ***Leaves*** Evergreen, lance-shaped, strongly veined, in basal rosettes. Dark green.
• NATIVE HABITAT Garden origin.
• CULTIVATION Tolerates dry soil and sun, but best in moist, well-drained soil in dappled shade. Ideal for an herbaceous border or woodland garden.
• PROPAGATION By seed in spring or division after flowering.

Z 5–7

HEIGHT
30–36in
(75–90cm)

SPREAD
12in (30cm)

Leguminosae/ Papilionaceae	LUPINE

LUPINUS 'The Chatelaine'

Habit Clump-forming. ***Flowers*** Small, pea-like, in dense, terminal spires, in early summer. Pink and white. ***Leaves*** Palmate, deeply divided into oval-lance-shaped leaflets. Dark bluish-green.

• NATIVE HABITAT Garden origin.

• CULTIVATION Grows best in well-drained, sandy, preferably slightly acid soils. Young foliage is very susceptible to slugs. Deadhead to help maintain vigor.

• PROPAGATION By cuttings of non-flowering sideshoots in spring or early summer.

Z 3–6

HEIGHT 4ft (1.2m)

SPREAD 18in (45cm)

Asteraceae/Compositae	COMMON YARROW, MILLEFOIL

ACHILLEA MILLEFOLIUM 'Cerise Queen'

Habit Upright, vigorous. ***Flowers*** Tiny, in large, flat heads, borne on rigid, leafy stems over long periods in summer. Vivid crimson-pink. ***Leaves*** Feathery, finely divided into lance-shaped segments. Gray-green, finely hairy.

• NATIVE HABITAT Garden origin.

• CULTIVATION Grow in fertile, well-drained soil, in full sun. Excellent for a silver border. Divide and replant every third year to maintain vigor. The flower heads dry well for winter decoration.

• PROPAGATION By division in spring or autumn.

Z 3–9

HEIGHT 3–4ft (1–1.2m)

SPREAD 24in (60cm) or more

Asteraceae/Compositae	PURPLE CONEFLOWER

ECHINACEA PURPUREA 'Robert Bloom'

Habit Upright, vigorous. ***Flowers*** Large, solitary, single, daisy-like, borne on thick stems in summer. Intense cerise-crimson petals surrounding a domed, brown center. ***Leaves*** Lance-shaped. Dark green.

• NATIVE HABITAT Garden origin.

• CULTIVATION Grow in moist, fertile, humus-rich soil, in sun. Contrasts well with softer pink flowers in an herbaceous border. Flowers are good for cutting.

• PROPAGATION By division or root cuttings in spring.

Z 3–8

HEIGHT 4ft (1.2m)

SPREAD 20in (50cm)

Lamiaceae/Labiatae	FALSE DRAGONHEAD

PHYSOSTEGIA VIRGINIANA subsp. *SPECIOSA* 'Variegata'

Habit Upright, rhizomatous. ***Flowers*** Tubular, hooded, in erect spikes, in late summer. Purplish-pink. ***Leaves*** Toothed, elliptic or lance-shaped. Mid-green, edged with white.

- NATIVE HABITAT Garden origin.
- CULTIVATION Grow in moist, humus-rich, fertile soil, in sun. The flowers have hinged stalks, which remain fixed when moved. Suitable for herbaceous borders. The flowers are good for cutting.
- PROPAGATION By division in spring.

Z 4–8

HEIGHT 3–4ft (1–1.2m)

SPREAD 2ft (60cm) or more

Gesneriaceae	

KOHLERIA WARSCEWICZII

Habit Upright, bushy, rhizomatous. ***Flowers*** Tubular, borne in long-stalked clusters in summer and autumn. Pink and white, very hairy, with purple-spotted, green lobes. ***Leaves*** Scalloped. Densely hairy, dark green.

- NATIVE HABITAT Colombia.
- CULTIVATION Grow as a house or greenhouse plant in cooler climates. Plant in moist but well-drained soil, in sun or partial shade.
- PROPAGATION By division or seed in spring.
- OTHER NAMES *K. digitaliflora.*

Min. 59°F (15°C)

HEIGHT 24in (60cm) or more

SPREAD 18in (45cm)

Scrophulariaceae	

REHMANNIA ELATA

Habit Multi-branched, rather straggly. ***Flowers*** Foxglove-like, borne on slender stalks, in the leaf axils from early to mid summer. Bright rose-purple, with yellow throats. ***Leaves*** Hairy, soft, oval, lobed, and sometimes toothed. Bright green.

- NATIVE HABITAT Rocky ground, China.
- CULTIVATION Grow in light, sharply drained soil, in a warm, sunny sheltered site. Dislikes winter moisture, and can be grown in a cold greenhouse.
- PROPAGATION By seed in autumn or spring, or by root cuttings in winter.

Min. 34°F (1°C)

HEIGHT 3ft (1m)

SPREAD 18in (45cm)

Papaveraceae	BLEEDING HEART

DICENTRA SPECTABILIS

Habit Hummock-forming. ***Flowers*** Pendent, heart-shaped, on fleshy, arching stems, in late spring and early summer. Red-pink. ***Leaves*** Fern-like, deeply cut. Mid-green.

- NATIVE HABITAT Woods and shady valleys, from Siberia to Japan.
- CULTIVATION Grow in humus-rich, moist but well-drained soil, in partial shade. A beautiful plant for a shady border or woodland garden.
- PROPAGATION By division when dormant in late winter, or seed in autumn.

Z 3–9

HEIGHT 2ft (60cm)

SPREAD 24–30in (60–75cm)

Lythraceae	

LYTHRUM VIRGATUM 'The Rocket'

Habit Erect, clump-forming. ***Flowers*** Small, 4-petaled, borne on slender, upright spikes, over long periods in summer. Vivid rose-pink. ***Leaves*** Narrowly lance-shaped, all along the stems. Mid-green.

• NATIVE HABITAT Garden origin.

• CULTIVATION Grow in moist, fertile soil, in sun or light shade. Suitable for bog gardens, waterside plantings, and herbaceous borders where soil remains reliably moist.

• PROPAGATION By division in spring or autumn.

Z 4–9

HEIGHT
3ft (1m)

SPREAD
18in (45cm)

Malvaceae	

SIDALCEA 'Elsie Heugh'

Habit Clump-forming. ***Flowers*** Bowl-shaped, borne in erect, terminal racemes in summer. Pale pink, with silky, fringed petals. ***Leaves*** Divided into 7–9 rounded lobes, mostly in basal clumps. Bright green.

• NATIVE HABITAT Garden origin.

• CULTIVATION Grow in any moist but well-drained soil, in sun or light shade. Provide unobtrusive support. Flowers are good for cutting.

• PROPAGATION By division in spring.

Z 5–8

HEIGHT
3–4ft
(1–1.2m)

SPREAD
3ft (1m)

Lythraceae	PURPLE LOOSESTRIFE

LYTHRUM SALICARIA 'Feuerkerze'

Habit Upright, clump-forming. ***Flowers*** Small, 4-petaled, borne in dense, upright spikes from mid- to late summer. Rose-pink. ***Leaves*** Oval to narrowly lance-shaped, opposite or in whorls, all along the stem. Mid-green.

• NATIVE HABITAT Garden origin.

• CULTIVATION Grow in moist, fertile soil, in sun or light shade. Suitable for waterside plantings, bog gardens, and permanently damp herbaceous borders.

• PROPAGATION By division in spring or autumn.

• OTHER NAMES *L. salicaria* 'Firecandle'.

Z 4–9

HEIGHT
3ft (1m)

SPREAD
18in (45cm)

Geraniaceae

GERANIUM PSILOSTEMON

Habit Clump-forming. ***Flowers*** Single, cup-shaped, borne in profusion in mid summer. Bright magenta-pink, with black centers. ***Leaves*** Divided into 7, deeply cut and lobed. Mid-green, túrning red in autumn.

• NATIVE HABITAT Scrub, open forest, and meadows, N.E. Turkey.

• CULTIVATION Grow in fertile, well-drained soil, in full sun. Suitable for wild gardens. A vigorous herbaceous perennial with distinctly colored flowers that need to be carefully placed in a border. While it undoubtedly forms an attractive specimen plant in its own right, it also blends well in mixed company. The early growth has attractive leaf buds tinged with red.

• PROPAGATION By seed or division in autumn or spring.

• OTHER NAMES *G. armenum.*

☼ ♢

Z 4–8

HEIGHT
To 4ft (1.2m)

SPREAD
4ft (1.2m)

Geraniaceae	

GERANIUM × OXONIANUM

Habit Dense, mound-forming. ***Flowers*** Small, funnel-shaped, in abundance through summer. Pink with darker veins, darkening with age. ***Leaves*** Semi-evergreen, with 5 deeply cut, toothed lobes. Mid-green sometimes blotched brown at the base.

- NATIVE HABITAT Garden origin.
- CULTIVATION Tolerant of dry soils. Grow in any but waterlogged soil, in sun or light shade. Good as ground cover, in herbaceous borders, and cottage gardens.
- PROPAGATION By division in autumn or spring.

Z 5–8

HEIGHT
24–30in (60–75cm)

SPREAD
18in (45cm)

Leguminosae/ Papilionaceae	LUPINE

LUPINUS 'Inverewe Red'

Habit Upright, clump-forming. ***Flowers*** Small, pea-like, in dense, erect racemes, in early summer. Rich red. ***Leaves*** Palmate, deeply divided into lance-shaped leaflets. Dark green.

- NATIVE HABITAT Garden origin.
- CULTIVATION Grows best in well-drained, sandy, preferably slightly acid soils. Young foliage is very susceptible to slugs. Deadhead to help maintain vigor. May be short-lived.
- PROPAGATION By cuttings of non-flowering sideshoots in spring or early summer.

Z 3–6

HEIGHT
to 4ft (1.2m)

SPREAD
18in (45cm)

Nyctaginaceae	FOUR O'CLOCK PLANT MARVEL OF PERU

MIRABILIS JALAPA

Habit Bushy, tuberous-rooted. ***Flowers*** Fragrant, trumpet-shaped, opening late on summer afternoons. Crimson, pink, white, or yellow. ***Leaves*** Oval, heart-shaped at the base. Mid-green.

- NATIVE HABITAT Peru.
- CULTIVATION Grow in fertile, well-drained soil, in a sunny, sheltered site. Lift tubers and store over winter in frost-free conditions.
- PROPAGATION By seed or division of tubers in early spring.

Z 10–11

HEIGHT
2–4ft (60cm–1.2 m)

SPREAD
2–2½ft (60–75cm)

Rosaceae	MEADOWSWEET

FILIPENDULA PURPUREA

Habit Upright, rhizomatous. ***Flowers*** Tiny, rich in dense, branched, terminal heads, on slender, purple-tinged stems, in summer. Red-purple. ***Leaves*** Deeply divided into 5–7 finely hairy, serrated lobes. Dark green.

- NATIVE HABITAT Damp habitats in Japan.
- CULTIVATION Grow in moist, humus-rich soil, in partial shade, or in sun where soils remain reliably moist. Good for waterside plantings.
- PROPAGATION By seed in autumn, or by division in autumn or winter.

Z 4–9

HEIGHT
4ft (1.2m)

SPREAD
2ft (60cm) or more

PELARGONIUMS

Pelargoniums, commonly known as geraniums, are a genus of mostly evergreen perennials and sub-shrubs, many of which are treated as annuals. Cultivated primarily for their exuberantly colored flowers, and valued for their long flowering period, pelargoniums are grown as house-plants, as summer bedding, and as container plants, in patio pots, window boxes, and hanging baskets. A number are also grown for their beautifully marked or scented foliage.

Pelargoniums are divided according to type into the following five groups:

Zonal – these have rounded leaves marked with a central darker zone, and fully double, semi-double, or single (5-petaled) flowers.

Regal – shrubby perennials with deeply serrated leaves and brilliantly colored, broadly trumpet-shaped flowers that are prone to rain damage when grown outdoors.

Unique –tall sub-shrubs, with brightly colored flowers, similar to those of the regal types, throughout the season. The variably shaped leaves may be scented.

Ivy-leaved – trailing plants with ivy-shaped, slightly fleshy leaves, and flowers similar to those of zonal pelargoniums.

Scented-leaved and **species** – with small, often irregularly star-shaped flowers.

Grow bedding plants in well-drained soil or compost in full sun, setting out when danger of frost has passed. Deadhead regularly. To overwinter, cut back plants to 5in (12cm) in late autumn/winter, and move into the greenhouse. If grown in the house or sunroom, provide good ventilation and full light, with shade from the hottest summer sun. Fertilize regularly when in growth. Repot, and cut back hard in early spring.

Propagate by softwood cuttings in summer. Sow seed under glass in late winter at 61–64°F (16–18°C).

P. ODORATISSIMUM
Habit Low-growing.
Flowers Tiny, borne in trailing, branched clusters of 5–10, in late spring and summer. White, with red veins on the upper petals.
Leaves Evergreen, rounded, heart-shaped at the base, scalloped, apple-scented. Light green.
• HEIGHT 12–18in (30–45cm).
• SPREAD 12–18in (30–45cm).

P. odoratissimum
(Scented-leaved)
Apple pelargonium
Min. 34°F (1°C)

P. 'Mauritania'
Habit Compact.
Flowers Single, borne in rounded clusters from summer to autumn. White, flushed pale salmon-pink at the base of the petals.
Leaves Rounded. Mid-green with a darker central zone.
• HEIGHT 12in (30cm).
• SPREAD 9in (23cm).

***P.* 'Mauritania'**
(Zonal)
Min. 34°F (1°C)

P. 'Fraicher Beauty'
Habit Compact, upright.
Flowers Double, from early summer to autumn. White petals finely edged with red-pink, becoming deeper in warm, dry conditions.
Leaves Rounded. Mid-green with a darker zone.
• TIPS Excellent pot plant.
• HEIGHT 12in (30cm).
• SPREAD 9in (23cm).

***P.* 'Fraicher Beauty'**
(Zonal)
Min. 34°F (1°C)

P. 'Brookside Primrose'
Habit Compact, bushy.
Flowers Double, borne from summer to autumn. Pale pink.
Leaves With a central, butterfly-shaped mark.
• TIPS Good for window boxes, pots, and bedding.
• HEIGHT 4–5in (10–12cm).
• SPREAD 3–4in (7–10cm).

***P.* 'Brookside Primrose'**
(Dwarf zonal)
Min. 34°F (1°C)

P. 'Golden Lilac Mist'
Habit Bushy.
Flowers Double, in dense heads from summer to autumn. Lavender-pink.
Leaves Evergreen, rounded. Yellow-green, marked bronze.
• TIPS Good for window boxes.
• HEIGHT 10–12in (25–30cm).
• SPREAD 6–8in (15–20cm).

P. 'Golden Lilac Mist'
(Zonal)

Min. 34°F (1°C)

P. 'Fair Ellen'
Habit Shrubby, bushy.
Flowers Small, delicate, irregularly star-shaped, produced in flushes from early summer to autumn. Pale pink, intricately marked red.
Leaves Evergreen, crinkled, 3-lobed, scented. Dark green.
• TIPS Good for pots indoors.
• HEIGHT 15in (38cm).
• SPREAD 12in (30cm).

P. 'Fair Ellen'
(Scented-leaved)

Min. 34°F (1°C)

P. 'Mr. Henry Cox'
Habit Upright.
Flowers Single, borne in small clusters from summer to autumn. Pale pink.
Leaves Evergreen, rounded. Zoned red, yellow, and purple-brown on a mid-green ground.
• TIPS Grown primarily for foliage.
• HEIGHT 12in (30cm).
• SPREAD 6in (15cm).

P. 'Mr. Henry Cox'
(Zonal)

Min. 34°F (1°C)

P. 'The Boar'
Habit Trailing.
Flowers Single, long-stemmed, from summer to autumn. Salmon-pink.
Leaves Evergreen, with 5 notched lobes. Dark green with a central dark brown blotch.
• TIPS Excellent for hanging baskets.
• HEIGHT to 24in (60cm).
• SPREAD to 24in (60cm).

P. 'The Boar'
(Trailing)

Min. 34°F (1°C)

P. 'Bird Dancer'
Habit Dwarf, compact.
Flowers Narrow petaled, star-like, carried high, in ball-headed clusters from summer to autumn. Pale salmon-pink.
Leaves Palmate, lobed. Mid-green with wide, dark green central zone.
• TIPS Good as a house-plant or in a window box.
• HEIGHT 4–5in (10–12cm).
• SPREAD 3–4in (7–10cm).

P. 'Bird Dancer'
(Zonal)

Min. 34°F (1°C)

P. 'Sweet Mimosa'
Habit Vigorous, upright, branching.
Flowers Trumpet-shaped, in small clusters, from summer to autumn. Pink.
Leaves Large, lobed. Mid-green.
• TIPS Good as a specimen plant in a container.
• HEIGHT 20in (50cm).
• SPREAD 12in (30cm).

P. 'Sweet Mimosa'
(Scented-leaved)

Min. 34°F (1°C)

P. 'Apple Blossom Rosebud'
Habit Compact, upright.
Flowers Fully double, resembling miniature rosebuds, from summer to autumn. Pale pinkish-white, with red-flushed petal margins, coloring more strongly in hot, sunny conditions.
Leaves Rounded. Mid-green with a dark center.
• HEIGHT 12in (30cm).
• SPREAD 9in (23cm).

P. 'Apple Blossom Rosebud'
(Zonal)

Min. 34°F (1°C)

P. 'Timothy Clifford'
Habit Compact, miniature, short-jointed.
Flowers Large, fully double, in neat, rounded clusters from summer to autumn. Salmon-pink.
Leaves Very dark green.
• TIPS Good for a sunny windowsill.
• HEIGHT 6–8in (15–20cm).
• SPREAD 4in (10cm).

P. 'Timothy Clifford'
(Zonal)

Min. 34°F (1°C)

P. 'Autumn Festival'
Habit Bushy.
Flowers Large, broadly trumpet-shaped, with waved petals, from summer to autumn. Salmon-pink petals, and a white throat marked with darker salmon-pink veining.
Leaves Oval, deeply serrated. Mid-green.
• HEIGHT 12in (30cm).
• SPREAD 12in (30cm).

P. **'Autumn Festival'**
(Regal)

Min. 34°F (1°C)

P. 'Leslie Judd'
Habit Vigorous, bushy.
Flowers Large, broadly trumpet-shaped, with wavy petals, from summer to autumn. Soft salmon-pink with a red blotch.
Leaves Oval, serrated. Mid-green.
• TIPS Pinch out growing tips before flowering to maintain a dense habit.
• HEIGHT 18–24in (45–60cm).
• SPREAD 12in (30cm).

P. **'Leslie Judd'**
(Regal)

Min. 34°F (1°C)

P. Schöne Helena
Habit Vigorous, floriferous.
Flowers Large, semi-double, borne in dense, rounded clusters from summer to autumn. Salmon-pink.
Leaves Rounded. Mid-green with a darker central zone.
• HEIGHT 12–18in (30–45cm).
• SPREAD 9in (23cm).

P. **Schöne Helena**
(Zonal)

Min. 34°F (1°C)

P. 'Cherry Blossom'
Habit Vigorous, upright.
Flowers Semi-double, from summer to autumn. Mauve-pink with white centers.
Leaves Rounded. Mid-green with a darker central zone.
• TIPS An excellent pot plant for a windowsill.
• HEIGHT to 18in (45cm).
• SPREAD 18in (45cm).

P. **'Cherry Blossom'**
(Zonal)

Min. 34°F (1°C)

P. CUCULLATUM
Habit Upright, sub-shrubby.
Flowers Small, with broad petals, borne in clusters of 5, in spring and summer. Bright purple-pink, with darker veining on the 2 upper petals.
Leaves Evergreen, rounded, to triangular, lobed, cupped. Green with red-tinted margins.
• TIPS Good for home or sunroom.
• HEIGHT to 6ft (2m).
• SPREAD 24in (60cm) or more.

P. cucullatum
(Species)

Min. 34°F (1°C)

P. 'Purple Emperor'
Habit Vigorous.
Flowers Large, broadly trumpet-shaped, profusely from summer, and well into autumn. Pink-mauve, darker at the center.
Leaves Oval, serrated. Mid-green.
• TIPS Excellent for pots in the sunroom or on a patio.
• HEIGHT 18in (45cm) or more.
• SPREAD 12in (30cm).

P. 'Purple Emperor'
(Regal)

Min. 34°F (1°C)

P. 'Alberta'
Habit Upright.
Flowers Small, single, borne in rounded, open clusters from summer to autumn. Crimson and white.
Leaves Rounded. Mid-green with a darker central zone.
• TIPS Good for bedding.
• HEIGHT 18in (45cm).
• SPREAD 12in (30cm).

P. 'Alberta'
(Zonal)

Min. 34°F (1°C)

P. 'Francis Parrett'
Habit Compact, miniature, short-jointed.
Flowers Fully double from early summer to autumn. Purplish-mauve.
Leaves Evergreen, rounded, very small. Mid-green.
• TIPS An excellent pot plant for a sunny windowsill.
• HEIGHT 6–8in (15–20cm).
• SPREAD 4in (10cm).

P. 'Francis Parrett'
(Zonal)

Min. 34°F (1°C)

P. 'Clorinda'
Habit Vigorous, upright.
Flowers Large, single, in flushes from early summer to autumn. Rose-pink.
Leaves Evergreen, crinkled, 3-lobed, cedar-scented.
• TIPS Good in large pots on a patio or in a sunroom.
• HEIGHT 18–24in (45–60cm) or more
• SPREAD 8–10in (20–25cm).

P. 'Clorinda'
(Scented-leaved)

Min. 34°F (1°C)

P. 'Lavender Grand Slam'
Habit Vigorous, bushy.
Flowers Large, broadly trumpet-shaped, with wavy petals, borne from summer to autumn. Silvery-mauve with a light maroon blotch.
Leaves Oval, serrated. Mid-green.
• HEIGHT 18–24in (45–60cm).
• SPREAD 12in (30cm).

P. 'Lavender Grand Slam'
(Regal)

Min. 34°F (1°C)

P. 'Manx Maid'
Habit Compact.
Flowers Relatively small, broadly trumpet-shaped, from summer to autumn. Pink, blotched and veined with burgundy.
Leaves Smaller than most other regals. Bright green.
• TIPS Good for a hanging basket.
• HEIGHT 12–15in (30–38cm).
• SPREAD 10in (25cm).

P. 'Manx Maid'
(Regal)

☼ ◊
Min. 34°F (1°C)

P. 'Paton's Unique'
Habit Vigorous, sub-shrubby.
Flowers Single, in neat clusters, from summer to autumn. Red or pale pink with a white eye.
Leaves Evergreen, lobed, pungent, shiny. Mid-green.
• TIPS Good for pots in a sunroom.
• HEIGHT 15–18in (38–45cm).
• SPREAD 6–8in (15–20cm).

P. 'Paton's Unique'
(Unique)

☼ ◊
Min. 34°F (1°C)

P. 'Amethyst'
Habit Trailing.
Flowers Fully double, from summer to autumn. Mauve-purple.
Leaves Evergreen, fleshy, ivy-shaped with pointed lobes. Fresh green.
• HEIGHT to 5ft (1.5m).
• SPREAD to 5ft (1.5m).

P. 'Amethyst'
(Ivy-leaved)

☼ ◊
Min. 34°F (1°C)

P. 'Tip Top Duet'
Habit Bushy, dainty.
Flowers Broadly trumpet-shaped, from early summer to autumn. White, veined pink, with deep burgundy blotches on uppermost petals.
Leaves Small, oval, serrated. Mid-green.
• TIPS Good for a hanging basket or container.
• HEIGHT 12–15in (30–38cm).
• SPREAD 10in (25cm).

P. 'Tip Top Duet'
(Regal)

☼ ◊
Min. 34°F (1°C)

P. 'Mini Cascade'
Habit Trailing, short-jointed.
Flowers Single, borne in large clusters in profusion from summer to autumn. Pinkish-red.
• TIPS Deadheading is essential for continuous flowering. Excellent for hanging baskets.
• HEIGHT 12–18in (30–45cm).
• SPREAD 12–18in (30–45cm).

P. 'Mini Cascade'
(Ivy-leaved)

☼ ◊
Min. 34°F (1°C)

P. 'Friesdorf'
Habit Compact, dwarf.
Flowers Single, delicate, with narrow petals, borne in open clusters from summer to autumn. Orange-scarlet.
Leaves Rounded. Purple-green with a darker central ring.
• TIPS Good for window boxes, bedding, and border edging.
• HEIGHT 10in (25cm).
• SPREAD 6in (15cm).

P. 'Friesdorf'
(Zonal)

Min. 34°F (1°C)

P. 'Rollisson's Unique'
Habit Vigorous, upright, sub-shrubby.
Flowers Small, single, open, in clusters, from summer to autumn. Wine-red with purple veins.
Leaves Evergreen, oval, notched, pungent.
• TIPS Suitable for large pots in a sunroom.
• HEIGHT 24in (60cm) or more.
• SPREAD 24in (60cm).

P. 'Rollisson's Unique'
(Unique)

Min. 34°F (1°C)

P. 'Rouletta'
Habit Vigorous, trailing.
Flowers Semi-double, from summer to autumn. Red petal edges, fading to white at the center.
Leaves Rounded, lobed. Mid-green.
• TIPS Excellent for hanging baskets. Pinch out growing tips regularly to promote branching.
• HEIGHT 2–3ft (60cm–1m).
• SPREAD to 3ft (1m).

P. 'Rouletta'
(Ivy-leaved)

Min. 34°F (1°C)

P. 'Paul Humphries'
Habit Bushy, compact.
Flowers Fully double, in dense, rounded heads, from summer to autumn. Deep wine-red.
Leaves Rounded. Mid-green with a darker central zone.
• TIPS A good pot plant.
• HEIGHT 12in (30cm).
• SPREAD 9in (23cm).

P. 'Paul Humphries'
(Zonal)

Min. 34°F (1°C)

P. 'Irene'
Habit Bushy, upright.
Flowers Large, semi-double, borne in dense, rounded clusters from summer to autumn. Light crimson.
Leaves Rounded. Mid-green with a darker central zone.
• HEIGHT 18in (45cm).
• SPREAD 9–12in (23–30cm).

P. 'Irene'
(Zonal)

Min. 34°F (1°C)

P. 'Alice Crousse'
Habit Trailing.
Flowers Double, borne in clusters. Cerise rose-pink.
Leaves Green, ivy-shaped.
• TIPS Suited to hanging baskets or window boxes. Take cuttings in autumn or spring.
• HEIGHT 10–12in (25–30cm).
• SPREAD 12–14in (30–35cm).

P. 'Alice Crousse'
(Ivy-leaved)

Min. 34°F (1°C)

P. 'Caligula'
Habit Compact, miniature.
Flowers Small, double, from summer to autumn. Crimson.
Leaves Tiny. Dark green.
• TIPS An excellent pot plant for a windowsill.
• HEIGHT 6–8in (15–20cm).
• SPREAD 4in (10cm).

P. 'Caligula'
(Zonal)

Min. 34°F (1°C)

P. 'Dolly Varden'
Habit Compact.
Flowers Small, single, borne in open clusters from early summer to autumn. Clear bright scarlet.
Leaves Evergreen, rounded. Zoned purple-brown, creamy-white and crimson.
• TIPS Grown primarily for its foliage.
• HEIGHT 12in (30cm).
• SPREAD 9in (23cm).

P. 'Dolly Varden'
(Zonal)

Min. 34°F (1°C)

P. 'Happy Thought'
Habit Vigorous, upright.
Flowers Small, single, in small clusters from summer to autumn. Red.
Leaves Rounded. Mid-green, with paler golden-green central zone.
• TIPS Foliage and flowers suits it to outdoor bedding, tubs and window boxes.
• OTHER NAMES *P.* 'A Happy Thought'.
• HEIGHT 20in (50cm).
• SPREAD 12in (30cm).

***P.* 'Happy Thought'**
(Zonal)

Min. 34°F (1°C)

P. 'Flower of Spring'
Habit Vigorous, upright.
Flowers Small, single, from early summer to autumn. Bright scarlet.
Leaves Evergreen, rounded. Gray-green, edged with white.
• HEIGHT 24in (60cm).
• SPREAD 12in (30cm).

***P.* 'Flower of Spring'**
(Zonal)
Silver-leaved geranium
Min. 34°F (1°C)

P. 'Orange Ricard'
Habit Vigorous, robust.
Flowers Large, semi-double, borne in rounded clusters, in profusion, from summer to autumn. Orange.
Leaves Rounded. Mid-green with darker zone.
• HEIGHT 18–24in (45–60cm).
• SPREAD 12in (30cm).

***P.* 'Orange Ricard'**
(Zonal)

Min. 34°F (1°C)

P. 'Mrs. Pollock'
Habit Upright.
Flowers Small, single, borne in small clusters from summer to autumn. Orange-red.
Leaves Evergreen, rounded. Golden-yellow with a central gray-green, butterfly mark, shot throughout with bronze.
• TIPS Grown primarily for foliage.
• HEIGHT 12in (30cm).
• SPREAD 6in (15cm).

***P.* 'Mrs Pollock'**
(Zonal)

Min. 34°F (1°C)

P. 'Voodoo'
Habit Vigorous, upright, sub-shrubby.
Flowers Small, single, open, borne in open clusters, from early summer to autumn. Pale burgundy, with a purple-black blaze on each petal.
Leaves Evergreen, lobed, aromatic.
• TIPS Suitable for a conservatory or sunroom.
• HEIGHT 20–24in (50–60cm).
• SPREAD 8–10in (20–25cm).

***P.* 'Voodoo'**
(Unique)

Min. 34°F (1°C)

P. 'Bredon'
Habit Upright, vigorous, bushy.
Flowers Large, broadly trumpet-shaped, borne from summer to autumn. Deep maroon.
Leaves Rounded, serrated. Mid-green.
• TIPS Makes a good feature plant in a container for the patio or sunroom.
• HEIGHT 18in (45cm).
• SPREAD 12in (30cm).

***P.* 'Bredon'**
(Regal)

Min. 34°F (1°C)

P. *CAPITATUM*
Habit Erect to arching.
Flowers Small, with slender petals, from summer to autumn. Mauve, with darker veins on the upper 2 petals.
Leaves Evergreen, 3–5 lobed, velvety, with crinkled margins, rose-scented.
• HEIGHT 12–24in (30–60cm).
• SPREAD 12in (30cm).

P. capitatum
(Scented-leaved species)
Rose-scented geranium
Min. 34°F (1°C)

P. 'Lady Plymouth'
Habit Bushy, vigorous.
Flowers Small, with delicate petals, borne in clusters of 5, from early summer to autumn. White to pale pink.
Leaves Evergreen, triangular, deeply lobed, rose-scented. Grayish-green, margined with cream.
• TIPS Excellent in large pots in a warm sunroom.
• HEIGHT 18–24in (45–60cm).
• SPREAD 18in (45cm).

***P.* 'Lady Plymouth'**
(Scented-leaved)

☼ 💧
Min. 34°F (1°C)

P. 'Purple Unique'
Habit Vigorous, upright, sub-shrubby.
Flowers Single, open trumpet-shaped, in small clusters, early summer to autumn. Light purple.
Leaves Evergreen, large-lobed, strongly scented. Mid-green.
• TIPS Train against a sunny wall.
• HEIGHT 3ft (1m) or more.
• SPREAD 3ft (1m).

***P.* 'Purple Unique'**
(Unique)

☼ 💧
Min. 34°F (1°C)

P. 'Mabel Grey'
Habit Vigorous.
Flowers Small, with delicate petals, borne in clusters of 5–10, from early summer to autumn. Mauve.
Leaves Evergreen, diamond-shaped, with 5–7 pointed lobes, lemon-scented. Bright green.
• HEIGHT 18–24in (45–60cm).
• SPREAD 12–18in (30–45cm).

***P.* 'Mabel Grey'**
(Scented-leaved)

☼ 💧
Min. 34°F (1°C)

P. 'Prince of Orange'
Habit Compact.
Flowers Small, single, from early summer to autumn. Pale mauve with maroon veining.
Leaves Evergreen, small, rounded, rough, orange-scented. Light green.
• TIPS Good as a pot plant indoors.
• HEIGHT 10–12in (25–30cm).
• SPREAD 6–8in (15–20cm).

***P.* 'Prince of Orange'**
(Scented-leaved)

☼ 💧
Min. 34°F (1°C)

P. 'L'Elégante'
Habit Trailing.
Flowers Small, single to semi-double, borne in open clusters from early summer to autumn. Pale mauve.
Leaves Evergreen, ivy-shaped. Creamy-white and green, tinted pink in warm, dry conditions.
• TIPS Good for hanging baskets.
• HEIGHT to 24in (60cm).
• SPREAD to 24in (60cm).

***P.* 'L'Elégante'**
(Ivy-leaved)

☼ 💧
Min. 34°F (1°C)

P. 'Old Spice'
Habit Compact, upright.
Flowers Small, single, from early summer. Pale purplish-pink.
Leaves Evergreen, small, rounded, shallowly lobed, softly-hairy, with crisped margins; spice-scented. Gray-green and cream.
• TIPS Good for medium-sized pots indoors.
• HEIGHT to 3ft (1m).
• SPREAD 12–18in (30–45cm).

***P.* 'Old Spice'**
(Scented-leaved)

☼ 💧
Min. 34°F (1°C)

P. CRISPUM 'Variegatum'
Habit Upright, bushy.
Flowers Small, in clusters from early summer to autumn. Pale lilac.
Leaves Evergreen, rough-textured, 3-lobed with crisped margins, lemon-scented. Edged golden-yellow, becoming creamy-white in winter.
• HEIGHT to 3ft (1m).
• SPREAD 12–18in (30–45cm).

***P. crispum* 'Variegatum'**
(Scented-leaved)

☼ 💧
Min. 34°F (1°C)

PENSTEMONS

These elegant and reliable border perennials are increasingly valued by gardeners for their spires of foxglove-like flowers. There are many cultivars available in a wide range of colors including white, pastel and deep pink, warm cherry-red, clear blue, and dusky purple.

Penstemons thrive well in humus-rich, well-drained soil in full sun. Where severe winters are expected, lift the plants after flowering, and overwinter in a cold frame. Deadhead regularly to prolong flowering.

Penstemons are generally not long-lived plants and tend to become woody at the base after a few seasons. Replace regularly with new plants propagated from softwood cuttings of non-flowering shoots taken in mid- to late summer.

P. 'White Bedder'

Habit Vigorous, erect, clump-forming, floriferous.
Flowers Widely tubular, 2-lipped, in long flower heads from midsummer to autumn. Pure white with dark anthers, opening from pink-flushed buds.
Leaves Semi-evergreen, narrowly lance-shaped. Fresh green.
• OTHER NAMES
P. 'Burford White', *P.* 'Royal White', *P.* 'Snow Storm', *P.* 'Snowflake', *P.* 'Bisham Seedling'.
• HEIGHT 28in (70cm).
• SPREAD 2ft (60cm).

P. **'White Bedder'**

☼ ◊ Z 7–8

P. 'Mother of Pearl'

Habit Bushy, clump-forming.
Flowers Small, tubular. 2-lipped, in long, slender spires from midsummer to autumn. Pearly-mauve, tinted pink and white; throat streaked with dark pink.
Leaves Semi-evergreen, linear. Light green.
• HEIGHT to 3ft (1m).
• SPREAD 2ft (60cm).

P. **'Mother of Pearl'**

☼ ◊ Z 7–8

P. 'Beech Park'

Habit Bushy, clump-forming.
Flowers Small, tubular, 2-lipped, in long, slender heads from mid-summer to autumn. Bright pink, with a white throat.
Leaves Semi-evergreen, linear. Light green.
• OTHER NAMES
P. 'Barbara Barker'.
• HEIGHT 2ft (60cm).
• SPREAD 2ft (60cm).

P. **'Beech Park'**

☼ ◊ Z 7–8

P. 'Apple Blossom'

Habit Bushy, clump-forming.
Flowers Small, tubular, 2-lipped, in long, slender heads from mid- to late summer or early autumn. Pale pink, with white throat.
Leaves Semi-evergreen, narrow. Fresh green.
• HEIGHT 2ft (60cm).
• SPREAD 2ft (60cm).

P. **'Apple Blossom'**

☼ ◊ Z 7–8

P. 'Maurice Gibbs'

Habit Bushy, clump-forming.
Flowers Small, tubular, 2-lipped, in long, slender heads from midsummer to autumn. Claret-red with white throats.
Leaves Semi-evergreen, narrowly lance-shaped. Light green.

- HEIGHT 3ft (90cm).
- SPREAD 2ft (60cm).

P. 'Maurice Gibbs'

Z 7–8

P. 'Evelyn'

Habit Erect, bushy, clump-forming, floriferous.
Flowers Small, tubular, 2-lipped, in long, slender heads from midsummer to autumn. Pink.
Leaves Semi-evergreen, narrowly lance-shaped. Mid-green.

- OTHER NAMES
P. 'Phyllis'.
- HEIGHT 18in (45cm).
- SPREAD 18in (45cm).

P. 'Evelyn'

Z 7–8

P. 'Pink Endurance'

Habit Dwarf, bushy, clump-forming.
Flowers Small, tubular, 2-lipped, in short heads in midsummer. Rose-pink.
Leaves Semi-evergreen, linear. Mid-green.

- HEIGHT 12–15in (30–38cm).
- SPREAD 12–15in (30–38cm).

P. 'Pink Endurance'

Z 7–8

P. 'Pennington Gem'

Habit Vigorous, bushy, clump-forming.
Flowers Small, tubular, 2-lipped, in long, slender heads from midsummer to autumn. Pink.
Leaves Semi-evergreen, linear. Fresh green.

- HEIGHT to 3ft (1m).
- SPREAD 2ft (60cm).

P. 'Pennington Gem'

Z 7–8

P. 'Chester Scarlet'

Habit Robust, bushy, clump-forming.
Flowers Large, tubular, 2-lipped, in long, slender heads from midsummer to autumn. Bright red.
Leaves Semi-evergreen, narrowly lance-shaped. Light green.

- OTHER NAMES
P. 'Mrs. Morse'.
- HEIGHT 3ft (90cm).
- SPREAD 3ft (90cm).

P. 'Chester Scarlet'

Z 7–8

P. BARBATUS

Habit Rosette-forming.
Flowers Small, tubular, 2-lipped, well-spaced in long, open heads from midsummer to early autumn. Rose-red.
Leaves Semi-evergreen, oblong to oval, mostly basal, but with linear stem leaves. Mid-green.

- OTHER NAMES
Chelone barbata.
- HEIGHT 3ft (1m).
- SPREAD 1ft (30cm).

P. barbatus

Z 7–8

P. 'Andenken an Friedrich Hahn'

Habit Vigorous, bushy, clump-forming. ***Flowers*** Small, tubular, 2-lipped, in long, slender heads from midsummer to autumn. Deep wine-red.
Leaves Semi-evergreen, narrowly lance-shaped. Fresh green.

- OTHER NAMES
P. 'Garnet'.
- HEIGHT 2–2½ft (60–75cm).
- SPREAD 2ft (60cm).

P. 'Andenken an Friedrich Hahn'

Z 7–8

P. 'King George V'

Habit Bushy, clump-forming.
Flowers Small, funnel-shaped, in long, slender heads from midsummer to autumn. Bright crimson with white throats.
Leaves Semi-evergreen, narrowly oval. Mid-green.
• HEIGHT 30in (75cm).
• SPREAD 18–24in (45–60cm).

P. 'King George V'

Z 7–8

P. 'Prairie Fire'

Habit Vigorous, erect, clump-forming.
Flowers Small, tubular, 2-lipped, well-spaced in long, open, heads from midsummer to autumn. Pinkish-red.
Leaves Semi-evergreen, narrowly lance-shaped, mostly in basal rosettes. Mid-green.
• HEIGHT 5ft (1.5m).
• SPREAD 2ft (60cm).

P. 'Prairie Fire'

Z 7–8

P. 'Burgundy'

Habit Robust, bushy, clump-forming.
Flowers Small, tubular, 2-lipped, in long, slender heads from midsummer to autumn. Purplish-red with dark red-streaked white throats.
Leaves Semi-evergreen, linear. Light green.
• OTHER NAMES *P.* 'Burford Seedling'.
• HEIGHT 4ft (1.2m).
• SPREAD 2ft (60cm).

P. 'Burgundy'

Z 7–8

P. 'Schoenholzeri'

Habit Vigorous, erect, clump-forming, floriferous.
Flowers Large, trumpet-shaped, in long racemes from midsummer to autumn. Brilliant scarlet.
Leaves Semi-evergreen, lance-shaped to narrowly oval. Mid-green.
• HEIGHT 3ft (1m).
• SPREAD 12–18in (30–45cm).

P. 'Schoenholzeri'

Z 7–8

P. 'Rubicundus'

Habit Erect, clump-forming.
Flowers Very large, tubular, 2-lipped, in long, open heads from midsummer to autumn. Bright red with white throats.
Leaves Semi-evergreen, linear. Light green.
• HEIGHT 4ft (1.2m).
• SPREAD 2ft (60cm).

P. 'Rubicundus'

Z 7–8

P. 'Countess of Dalkeith'

Habit Erect, bushy, clump-forming.
Flowers Large, tubular, 2-lipped, in long, slender heads from midsummer to autumn. Deep purple with white throats.
Leaves Semi-evergreen, linear. Light green.
• HEIGHT 3ft (1m).
• SPREAD 2ft (60cm).

P. 'Countess of Dalkeith'

Z 7–8

P. 'Sour Grapes'

Habit Vigorous, erect, clump-forming, floriferous.
Flowers Small, tubular, 2-lipped, in long heads from midsummer to autumn. Deep purple-blue, suffused violet.
Leaves Semi-evergreen, narrowly lance-shaped. Light green.
• HEIGHT 3ft (90cm).
• SPREAD 2ft (60cm).

P. 'Sour Grapes'

Z 7–8

P. 'Alice Hindley'

Habit Upright, clump-forming.
Flowers Small, tubular, 2-lipped, in long heads from mid- to late summer or early autumn. Pale blue-lilac, flushed lilac-pink.
Leaves Semi-evergreen, narrowly lance-shaped, dark green.
• HEIGHT 4ft (1.2m).
• SPREAD 2ft (60cm).

P. 'Alice Hindley'

Z 7–8

Valerianaceae	RED VALERIAN

CENTRANTHUS RUBER

Habit Loosely clump-forming. ***Flowers*** Small, star-shaped, in branching heads, borne above the foliage from late spring to autumn. Deep red-pink. ***Leaves*** Fleshy, oval or lance-shaped. Blue-green.
- NATIVE HABITAT Rocks and coastal shingle, in Mediterranean Europe and N. Africa to Turkey.
- CULTIVATION Grow in full sun in well-drained soil. Thrives in exposed sites, in poor, especially alkaline soils, and in seaside gardens. Excellent for naturalizing in dry walls or gravel.
- PROPAGATION By seed in autumn or spring.

Z 5–8

HEIGHT 2–3ft (60cm–1m)

SPREAD 1½–2ft (45–60cm)

Ranunculaceae	

AQUILEGIA VULGARIS 'Nora Barlow'

Habit Clump-forming. ***Flowers*** Funnel-shaped, double, with short spurs and many narrow, red-pink petals, tipped with pale-green, borne on slender stems in summer. ***Leaves*** Rounded, deeply divided into narrow lobes. Gray-green.
- NATIVE HABITAT Garden origin.
- CULTIVATION Grow in an open, sunny site, in well-drained soil. Long cultivated for its curious flowers, it is suited to borders and cottage gardens.
- PROPAGATION By division when dormant.

Z 3–8

HEIGHT 24–30in (60–75cm)

SPREAD 20in (50cm)

Asteraceae/Compositae	

ACHILLEA 'Lachsschönheit'

Habit Upright. ***Flowers*** Tiny, in flat heads, on rigid, leafy stems, during summer. Pale salmon-red, fading to creamy-yellow. ***Leaves*** Feathery, finely divided into oblong to lance-shaped segments. Gray-green, finely hairy.
- NATIVE HABITAT Garden origin.
- CULTIVATION Grow in fertile, well-drained soil, in full sun. Excellent for a silver border. Divide and replant every third year to maintain vigor.
- PROPAGATION By division in spring or autumn.
- OTHER NAMES *A.* 'Salmon Beauty'.

Z 3–9

HEIGHT up to 4ft (1.2m)

SPREAD 24in (60cm)

Ranunculaceae	CANADIAN COLUMBINE

AQUILEGIA CANADENSIS

Habit Clump-forming. ***Flowers*** Bell-shaped, nodding, yellow, with long, straight, red spurs, borne on slender stems in early to mid summer. ***Leaves*** Rounded, deeply divided into narrow lobes. Dark green.
- NATIVE HABITAT Rocky woods, North America.
- CULTIVATION Grow in well-drained, preferably sandy soil, in dappled shade or sun. Suitable for borders, cottage, or woodland gardens.
- PROPAGATION By seed in autumn or spring, or by division when dormant.

Z 3–8

HEIGHT 24–30in (60–75cm)

SPREAD 20in (50cm)

Saxifragaceae

ASTILBE 'Montgomery'

Habit Clump-forming. ***Flowers*** Tiny, in dense, feathery, branching spires, in summer. Deep salmon-red. ***Leaves*** Divided into toothed, oval, leaflets. Fresh green.
- NATIVE HABITAT Garden origin.
- CULTIVATION Grow in moist, fertile, humus-rich soil, in sun or partial shade. Good for damp borders, bog gardens, or waterside plantings, associating well with *Hosta* and *Rodgersia*. Flower heads turn brown and dry, persisting into winter unless deadheaded.
- PROPAGATION By division in spring or autumn.

◑ 💧

Z 4–9

HEIGHT
3ft (1m)

SPREAD
3ft (1m)

Polygonaceae

PERSICARIA AMPLEXICAULIS 'Firetail'

Habit Clump-forming. ***Flowers*** Tiny, in slender spikes, in late summer and autumn. Bright crimson. ***Leaves*** Pointed, oval-lance-shaped, heart-shaped at the base. Mid-green.
- NATIVE HABITAT Garden origin.
- CULTIVATION Grow in sun or partial shade, in moist but well-drained soil. Suited to an herbaceous border, but may swamp less vigorous species.
- PROPAGATION By division in autumn or spring.
- OTHER NAMES *Polygonum amplexicaule* 'Firetail'.

☼ 💧

Z 4–9

HEIGHT
3–4ft
(1–1.2m)

SPREAD
3–4ft
(1–1.2m)

Dipsacaceae

KNAUTIA MACEDONICA

Habit Upright, clump-forming. ***Flowers*** Double, almost globular, borne on lax, branching stems, in midsummer. Very deep crimson. ***Leaves*** Deeply divided stem leaves. Dark green. Basal leaves wither before flowering.
- NATIVE HABITAT Scrub, open woods, C. Europe.
- CULTIVATION Grow in a warm, sunny, sheltered site, in well-drained soil. May require staking.
- PROPAGATION By basal cuttings in spring, or by seed in autumn.
- OTHER NAMES *Scabiosa rumelica* of gardens.

☼ ◊

Z 4–9

HEIGHT
30in (80cm)

SPREAD
2ft (60cm)

Campanulaceae

LOBELIA 'Cherry Ripe'

Habit Clump-forming. ***Flowers*** 2-lipped, with 3 spreading lower lobes, borne in spikes, from mid- to late summer. Cerise-scarlet. ***Leaves*** Oval. Fresh green, often tinted red-bronze.

- NATIVE HABITAT Garden origin.
- CULTIVATION Grow in moist, fertile, humus-rich soil, in sun or partial shade. Suitable for waterside plantings. In cold areas, pot up over winter, and protect in a cold frame.
- PROPAGATION By division in spring.

☼ ◐

Z 5–9

HEIGHT 3ft (1m)

SPREAD 9in (23cm)

Campanulaceae

LOBELIA 'Queen Victoria'

Habit Clump-forming. ***Flowers*** 2-lipped, with 3 spreading lower lobes, in spikes, from late summer to midautumn. Almost luminous, vivid red. ***Leaves*** Oblong-oval, mostly basal. Deep red-purple.

- NATIVE HABITAT Garden origin.
- CULTIVATION Grow in moist, fertile, humus-rich soil, in sun or partial shade. Suitable for waterside plantings and damp borders. In cold areas, pot up over winter and protect in a cold frame. Dislikes cold, wet conditions in winter.
- PROPAGATION By division in spring.

☼ ◐

Z 5–9

HEIGHT 3ft (1m)

SPREAD 1ft (30cm)

Asteraceae/Compositae — CHOCOLATE COSMOS

COSMOS ATROSANGUINEUS

Habit Upright, tuberous-rooted. ***Flowers*** Single, with an elusive chocolate scent, borne on slender stems, from late summer until first frost. Velvety, maroon-crimson. ***Leaves*** Spoon-shaped, divided. Dark green, sometimes purple-flushed.

- NATIVE HABITAT Mexico.
- CULTIVATION Grow in a warm, sheltered site, in well-drained soil. In winter provide a dry mulch, or lift tubers, and store in a cool, dry, frost-free place.
- PROPAGATION By basal cuttings in spring.
- OTHER NAMES *Bidens atrosanguinea.*

☼ ◐

Z 7–9

HEIGHT 24in (60cm)

SPREAD 18in (45cm)

Acanthaceae

RUELLIA GRAECIZANS

Habit Bushy, sub-shrubby. ***Flowers*** Small, tubular, borne in long-stalked clusters, intermittently throughout the year. Scarlet. ***Leaves*** Evergreen, pointed, narrowly oval. Glossy green.

- NATIVE HABITAT Forest edges, tropical South America.
- CULTIVATION Grow as a house or greenhouse plant in cool climates. Plant in moist, well-drained soil, in partial shade; keep in a humid atmosphere.
- PROPAGATION By stem cuttings or seed in spring.
- OTHER NAMES *R. amoena.*

◑ ◐

Z 9–10

Min. 59°F (15°C)

HEIGHT 2ft (60cm) or more

SPREAD 2ft (60cm) or more

Leguminosae/ Papilionaceae	FRENCH HONEYSUCKLE

HEDYSARUM CORONARIUM

Habit Shrub-like, spreading. ***Flowers*** Small, pea-like, in spikes on sturdy stems, in early summer. Red-purple or carmine-red. ***Leaves*** Divided into 3–5 pairs of elliptic to rounded leaflets. Mid-green.

- NATIVE HABITAT Grasslands of the W. Mediterranean.
- CULTIVATION Grow in a warm, sheltered site, in well-drained soil. Tolerant of poor, rocky soils. Cut back the previous season's growth in spring. Good for Mediterranean borders or scree plantings.
- PROPAGATION By seed in autumn or spring.

Z 4–9

HEIGHT up to 3ft (1m)

SPREAD 3ft (1m)

Gesneriaceae	

COLUMNEA × BANKSII

Habit Trailing. ***Flowers*** Tubular, hooded, to 3in (8cm) long, produced in succession from spring to winter. Brilliant red. ***Leaves*** Evergreen, fleshy, oval, borne on long, pendent stems. Glossy green above, purplish-red beneath.

- NATIVE HABITAT Garden origin.
- CULTIVATION In cool climates, grow as a house or greenhouse plant in moist soil or potting mix with bright, indirect light and moderate humidity. Reduce water in winter. Good for hanging baskets.
- PROPAGATION By tip cuttings after flowering.

Min. 59°F (15°C)

HEIGHT 3ft (90cm)

SPREAD indefinite

Lamiaceae/Labiatae	

MONARDA 'Cambridge Scarlet'

Habit Clump- or mound-forming. ***Flowers*** Small, hooded, in dense, terminal heads, through summer. Rich red. ***Leaves*** Aromatic, hairy, toothed, oval, triangular or lance-shaped. Mid-green.

- NATIVE HABITAT Garden origin.
- CULTIVATION Grow in moist, fertile soil, in sun or light shade. Suitable for herbaceous borders and herb gardens. The flowers attract bees and other insects. Susceptible to mildew in dry conditions.
- PROPAGATION By division in spring.
- OTHER NAMES *M. didyma* 'Cambridge Scarlet'.

Z 4–8

HEIGHT 3ft (1m)

SPREAD 18in (45cm)

Scrophulariaceae	CORAL PLANT, FIRECRACKER PLANT

RUSSELIA EQUISETIFORMIS

Habit Sub-shrubby, weeping. ***Flowers*** Tubular, scarlet, in pendent clusters, in summer and autumn. ***Leaves*** Evergreen, tiny, scale-like, dark green, on slender, green, rush-like stems.

- NATIVE HABITAT Arid areas of Mexico.
- CULTIVATION Grow as a house or greenhouse plant in cool climates. Plant in light, well-drained, potting mix or humus-rich soil, in sun or partial shade. Good for hanging baskets.
- PROPAGATION Stem cuttings or division in spring.
- OTHER NAMES *R. juncea*.

Min. 59°F (15°C)

HEIGHT 3ft (1m) or more

SPREAD 2ft (60cm)

Papaveraceae

PAPAVER ORIENTALE 'Allegro Viva'

Habit Clump-forming. ***Flowers*** Large, deeply cupped, borne on strong stems, in early summer. Satiny, bright scarlet petals, each with a black-purple blotch at the base. ***Leaves*** Divided into hairy, toothed, lance-shaped segments, dying back after flowering. Dark gray-green.

• NATIVE HABITAT Garden origin.

• CULTIVATION Grow in moist but well-drained, fertile soil, in sun. May need support. This cultivar is especially valued for the brilliance of its flowers. The leaves die back after flowering and, as with other oriental poppies, this can leave a gap in the border. Compensate for this by filling in with later-flowering plants to conceal the space. This particular cultivar makes a spectacular display in a completely red border or as a contrast to white-flowered plants.

• PROPAGATION By root cuttings in winter, or by division in autumn.

Z 4–9

HEIGHT
24–30in
(60–75cm)

SPREAD
18in (45cm)

Campanulaceae

LOBELIA × *SPECIOSA* 'Bees' Flame'

Habit Clump-forming. ***Flowers*** 2-lipped, with 3 spreading lower lobes, borne in spikes, from late summer to midautumn. Brilliant scarlet. ***Leaves*** Oblong-oval, mostly basal. Deep bronze-red.
• NATIVE HABITAT Garden origin.
• CULTIVATION Grow in moist, fertile, humus-rich soil, in sun or partial shade. Suitable for waterside plantings and damp borders. In cold areas, pot up over winter and protect in a cold frame. Dislikes cold, wet conditions in winter.
• PROPAGATION By division in spring.

Z 4–8

HEIGHT 3ft (1m)

SPREAD 1ft (30cm)

Haemodoraceae | RED-AND-GREEN KANGAROO PAW

ANIGOZANTHOS MANGLESII

Habit Vigorous, rhizomatous. ***Flowers*** Large, tubular, woolly, on slender stems, in spring and early summer. Red-and-green. ***Leaves*** Linear-lance-shaped, to 16in (40cm) long. Gray-green.
• NATIVE HABITAT W. Australia.
• CULTIVATION Grow in an open, sunny site, in well-drained, peaty or leafy soil. In cool areas, grow in a cool sunroom. Flowers cut and dry well. Ink spot disease may be a problem.
• PROPAGATION By division in spring, or by seed sown fresh in late summer.

Z 10

HEIGHT 3ft (1m)

SPREAD 18in (45cm)

Asteraceae/Compositae

ACHILLEA 'Fanal'

Habit Mound-forming. ***Flowers*** Tiny, in large, flat heads, on stiff, leafy stems in summer. Bright red, fading to yellowish-red. ***Leaves*** Feathery, divided into oblong to lance-shaped segments. Gray-green.
• NATIVE HABITAT Garden origin.
• CULTIVATION Grow in fertile, well-drained soil, in full sun. Divide and replant every third year to maintain vigor. Cut flowers dry well.
• PROPAGATION By division in early spring or autumn and cuttings in summer.
• OTHER NAMES *A.* 'The Beacon'.

Z 3-8

HEIGHT 30in (75cm)

SPREAD 24in (60cm)

Gesneriaceae

KOHLERIA ERIANTHA

Habit Robust, bushy, with scaly rhizomes. ***Flowers*** Tubular, borne in nodding clusters, in summer. Bright orange-red, with yellow-spotted lobes. ***Leaves*** Oval to lance-shaped, borne on hairy stems. Dark green, fringed at the margin with red hairs.
• NATIVE HABITAT Colombia.
• CULTIVATION Grow as a house or greenhouse plant in cool climates. Plant in moist but well-drained potting mix or soil, in sun or partial shade.
• PROPAGATION By division or seed in spring.

Min. 59°F (15°C)

HEIGHT 3ft (1m)

SPREAD 3ft (1m)

Leguminosae/ Papilionaceae	LICORICE

GLYCYRRHIZA GLABRA

Habit Upright, deep-rooted. ***Flowers*** Small, pea-like, in short spikes in the leaf axils, on erect stems, in late summer. Pale purple-blue and white. ***Leaves*** Divided into oval, bluish-green leaflets.

• NATIVE HABITAT Dry scrub and damp ditches from the Mediterranean to S.W. Asia.

• CULTIVATION Grow in deep, fertile, moist but well-drained soil, in full sun. Cultivated commercially for its roots (licorice).

• PROPAGATION By division in spring, or by seed in autumn or spring.

Z 9–10

HEIGHT
4ft (1.2m)

SPREAD
3ft (1m)

Campanulaceae	

LOBELIA × *GERARDII* 'Vedrariensis'

Habit Robust, clump-forming. ***Flowers*** 2-lipped, with 3 spreading lower lobes, borne in spikes, from late summer to midautumn. Rich purple. ***Leaves*** Oval to elliptic, in a basal rosette. Dark green.

• NATIVE HABITAT Garden origin.

• CULTIVATION Grow in moist, fertile, humus-rich soil, in sun or partial shade. Suitable for damp borders but dislikes cold, wet conditions in winter. Provide a deep, dry winter mulch of straw or similar.

• PROPAGATION By division in spring.

Z 4–8

HEIGHT
3ft (1m)

SPREAD
1ft (30cm)

Acanthaceae	

ACANTHUS HUNGARICUS

Habit Densely clump-forming. ***Flowers*** Funnel-shaped, in spikes, 2–5ft (60–150cm) long, in summer. White or pink-flushed, enclosed in spiny, red-purple bracts. ***Leaves*** Lance-shaped in outline, deeply lobed. Glossy, dark green.

• NATIVE HABITAT Woods, scrub, and rocky hills, in the Balkans, Romania, and Greece.

• CULTIVATION Grow in well-drained soil, in full sun.

• PROPAGATION By seed or division in autumn or spring, or by root cuttings in winter.

• OTHER NAMES *A. balcanicus, A. longifolius.*

Z 7–9

HEIGHT
2–3ft
(60cm–1m)

SPREAD
3ft (1m)

Acanthaceae

ACANTHUS SPINOSUS

Habit Densely clump-forming. ***Flowers*** Funnel-shaped, borne freely in spikes, to 5ft (1.5m) long, in summer. White, enclosed in spiny, soft mauve-purple bracts. ***Leaves*** Lance-shaped in outline, deeply dissected, with scattered spines. Glossy, dark green.

- NATIVE HABITAT Scrub and grassland, E. Mediterranean.
- CULTIVATION Grow in any well-drained soil in full sun. This stately perennial requires plenty of space for its undoubted architectural merits. The leaves are attractive in their own right when the plant is not in flower and are sufficiently spectacular to be allocated a corner where they can be seen to their best advantage. The flower spikes may also be air-dried for winter arrangements.
- PROPAGATION By seed or division in autumn or spring, or by root cuttings in winter.

☼ ◊

Z 6–10

HEIGHT
4ft (1.2m)

SPREAD
2ft (60cm) or more

Scrophulariaceae	THREE BIRDS TOADFLAX

LINARIA TRIORNITHOPHORA

Habit Upright, clump-forming. ***Flowers*** Small, snapdragon-like, borne in slender spikes, from mid- to late summer. Purple with yellow throats. ***Leaves*** Lance-shaped, smooth, borne in whorls of 3–4 along the stems. Gray-green.

- NATIVE HABITAT Scrub and hedgerows, Spain and Portugal.
- CULTIVATION Grow in any well-drained soil, in sun or light shade. May self-sow. Suitable for herbaceous borders and scree plantings.
- PROPAGATION By seed in autumn or spring.

Z 7–10

HEIGHT 2–3ft (60cm–1m)

SPREAD 2ft (60cm)

Lamiaceae/Labiatae	

ORIGANUM LAEVIGATUM 'Herrenhausen'

Habit Mat-forming, suckering. ***Flowers*** Tiny, tubular, 2-lipped, in large diffuse, branching sprays, in summer. Lilac-pink. ***Leaves*** Aromatic, basal, oval to elliptic, slightly leathery. Green, flushed purple when young and in winter.

- NATIVE HABITAT Garden origin.
- CULTIVATION Grow in very well-drained soil in a sunny, sheltered site. Suitable for a border front, a Mediterranean-type border or planting in scree.
- PROPAGATION By division in spring.

Z 5–9

HEIGHT 18–28in (45–70cm) in flower

SPREAD 8in (20cm) or more

Brassicaceae/Cruciferae	

ERYSIMUM 'Bowles' Mauve'

Habit Bushy, mound-forming. ***Flowers*** Small, 4-petaled, in dense, rounded, terminal clusters, in spring and summer. Rich mauve. ***Leaves*** Evergreen, narrowly lance-shaped. Gray-green.

- NATIVE HABITAT Garden origin.
- CULTIVATION Grow in any well-drained soil, including poor soils in full sun. Is often short-lived, so propagate regularly. Excellent for a border, valued for its long flowering period.
- PROPAGATION By softwood cuttings in summer.
- OTHER NAMES *Cheiranthus* 'Bowles' Mauve'.

Z 6–9

HEIGHT to 30in (75cm)

SPREAD 18in (45cm) or more

Lamiaceae/Labiatae	

MONARDA 'Beauty of Cobham'

Habit Clump-forming. ***Flowers*** Small, hooded, in dense, terminal heads, throughout summer. Soft, pale lilac-pink, with dark brown-purple bracts beneath. ***Leaves*** Aromatic, toothed, oval, triangular, or lance-shaped. Purple-tinted, green.

- NATIVE HABITAT Garden origin.
- CULTIVATION Grow in any moist, fertile soil, in sun or light shade. Suitable for herbaceous borders and herb gardens. The flowers attract bees and other insects. Susceptible to powdery mildew.
- PROPAGATION By division in spring.

Z 4–8

HEIGHT 3ft (1m)

SPREAD 18in (45cm)

Ranunculaceae

THALICTRUM AQUILEGIIFOLIUM

Habit Dense, clump-forming, slow-growing. ***Flowers*** Tiny, in dense, fluffy, terminal sprays, in summer. Lilac-purple. ***Leaves*** Smooth, finely divided, resembling those of maidenhair fern. Gray-green.

- NATIVE HABITAT Meadows and shady rocks, from Europe to temperate Asia.
- CULTIVATION Grow in moist, well-drained, fertile soil, in sun or light, dappled shade. Provides excellent contrast in a silver border.
- PROPAGATION By seed or division in spring.

Z 5–9

HEIGHT 3–4ft (1–1.2m)

SPREAD 18in (45cm)

Lamiaceae/Labiatae — WILD BERGAMOT

MONARDA FISTULOSA

Habit Clump-forming. ***Flowers*** Small, hooded, downy, borne in loose, terminal heads, throughout summer. Soft lilac-purple. ***Leaves*** Aromatic, toothed, oval to lance-shaped. Gray-green.

- NATIVE HABITAT Woodland margins and dry scrub, in Canada, US, and Mexico.
- CULTIVATION Grow in any moist, fertile soil, in sun or light shade. Suitable for herbaceous borders, herb, and wildflower gardens. The flowers are attractive to bees and other beneficial insects.
- PROPAGATION By seed or division in spring.

Z 3–8

HEIGHT 4ft (1.2m)

SPREAD 18in (45cm)

Geraniaceae

GERANIUM SYLVATICUM 'Mayflower'

Habit Clump-forming, deep-rooted. ***Flowers*** Single, cup-shaped, borne on branching stems, in profusion in early summer. Violet-blue with a white center. ***Leaves*** Mostly basal, divided into 7–9 deeply cut and lobed segments. Mid-green.

- NATIVE HABITAT Garden origin.
- CULTIVATION Grow in fertile, moist but well-drained soil, in partial shade. Suitable for borders and wild or woodland gardens.
- PROPAGATION By division in autumn or spring.

Z 4–8

HEIGHT 3ft (1m)

SPREAD 2ft (60cm)

Campanulaceae — NETTLE-LEAVED BELLFLOWER

CAMPANULA TRACHELIUM

Habit Upright. ***Flowers*** Short-stalked, bell-shaped, widely spaced on erect stems in mid- to late summer. Mid-blue to purple-blue. ***Leaves*** Coarse, serrated, oval, heart-shaped at base. Mid-green.

- NATIVE HABITAT Woodland margins, hedgerows, on alkaline soils, Europe to N. Africa and Siberia.
- CULTIVATION Tolerates dry shade. Grow in any moderately fertile, well-drained soil, in sun or partial shade. Suitable for borders, or for naturalizing in wild and woodland gardens. May self-sow.
- PROPAGATION Seed or division in autumn or spring.

Z 5–8

HEIGHT 2–3ft (60cm–1m)

SPREAD 1ft (30cm)

Ranunculaceae

CLEMATIS INTEGRIFOLIA

Habit Upright or sprawling, sub-shrubby. ***Flowers*** Single, star- to bell-shaped, nodding, borne singly at the stem tips, in midsummer. Dark violet or blue, with creamy-white anthers. ***Leaves*** Entire, lance-shaped, slightly leathery. Mid-green.

- NATIVE HABITAT Grasslands from C. Europe, S.W. Russia, W. and C. Asia.
- CULTIVATION Grow in fertile, moist but well-drained, loamy soil, in sun. Cut old, flower stems back to 2 basal buds in late winter.
- PROPAGATION Seed in autumn or division in spring.

Z 3–7

HEIGHT
30in (75m)

SPREAD
30in (75cm)

Campanulaceae

CAMPANULA GLOMERATA 'Superba'

Habit Vigorous, clump-forming, suckering. ***Flowers*** Large, bell-shaped, borne in dense, rounded, mainly terminal heads, in summer. Rich purplish-blue. ***Leaves*** Oval to lance-shaped, scallop-toothed, in basal rosettes and up the stem. Mid-green.

- NATIVE HABITAT Garden origin.
- CULTIVATION Grow in any fertile, well-drained soil, in sun or light shade. Divide and replant regularly to maintain vigor.
- PROPAGATION By division in spring or autumn.

Z 3–8

HEIGHT
30in (75cm)

SPREAD
3ft (1m)
or more

Scrophulariaceae

VERONICA LONGIFOLIA 'Romiley Purple'

Habit Clump-forming. ***Flowers*** Small, funnel-shaped, borne in long, slender spikes, in profusion in summer. Rich purple. ***Leaves*** Whorled, lance-shaped or narrowly lance-shaped, toothed. Mid-green.

- NATIVE HABITAT Garden origin.
- CULTIVATION Grow in fertile, preferably loamy, well-drained soil, in sun. May need unobtrusive support. A beautiful border perennial; the flowers last quite well when cut.
- PROPAGATION By division in spring or autumn.

Z 4–8

HEIGHT
3–4ft
(1–1.2m)

SPREAD
1–2ft
(30–60cm)

Ranunculaceae

ACONITUM 'Bressingham Spire'

Habit Compact, erect, tuberous-rooted. ***Flowers*** Large, hooded, helmet-shaped, borne in dense, upright, tapering spires, in summer. Deep violet-blue. ***Leaves*** Divided, deeply cut. Glossy, dark green.

- NATIVE HABITAT Garden origin.
- CULTIVATION Grow in moist but well-drained, fertile soil, in sun or partial shade. Divide every 2–3 years to maintain vigor. Excellent as part of an herbaceous border. The roots are toxic.
- PROPAGATION By division in autumn.

Z 3–7

HEIGHT to 3ft (1m)

SPREAD 12in (30cm)

Asteraceae/Compositae

ECHINOPS RITRO 'Veitch's Blue'

Habit Upright, clump-forming. ***Flowers*** Tiny, in tight, globular flower heads, borne on erect, silvery stems, in late summer. Purplish-blue. ***Leaves*** Sharply divided, firm, leathery, spiny. Green above and white-downy beneath.

- NATIVE HABITAT Garden origin.
- CULTIVATION Grow in well-drained, poor or only moderately fertile soil, in sun. Excellent for a silver border. The flowers dry well if cut before fully open.
- PROPAGATION By division in autumn or root cuttings in winter.

Z 3–8

HEIGHT 4ft (1.2m)

SPREAD 30in (75cm)

Commelinaceae

DICHORISANDRA REGINAE

Habit Upright, clump-forming. ***Flowers*** Small, in dense spikes, from summer to autumn. Purple-blue. ***Leaves*** Evergreen, large, elliptic. Glossy green, banded and flecked with silver, purple-red beneath.

- NATIVE HABITAT Tropical areas in Peru.
- CULTIVATION In cool climates, grow as a house or greenhouse plant in fertile, moist, well-drained soil or potting mix, in partial shade. Keep humid and water freely when in growth, otherwise moderately.
- PROPAGATION By division in spring, or by stem cuttings in summer.

Min. 68°F (20°C)

HEIGHT 24–30in (60–75cm)

SPREAD 1ft (30cm)

Campanulaceae

CAMPANULA TRACHELIUM 'Bernice'

Habit Upright. ***Flowers*** Short-stalked, double, narrowly bell-shaped, borne on erect stems in mid- to late summer. Purple-violet. ***Leaves*** Coarse, serrated, oval, heart-shaped at the base. Mid-green.

- NATIVE HABITAT Garden origin.
- CULTIVATION Tolerates dry shade. Grow in any moderately fertile, well-drained soil, in sun or partial shade. Suitable for borders, or wild and woodland gardens.
- PROPAGATION By division in autumn or spring.

Z 5–8

HEIGHT 30in (75cm)

SPREAD 1ft (30cm)

Lamiaceae/Labiatae

SALVIA x *SYLVESTRIS* 'Mainacht'

Habit Neat, clump-forming. ***Flowers*** Small, 2-lipped, borne in dense, upright racemes, in early to midsummer. Rich, dark violet-blue with red-purple bracts. ***Leaves*** Oblong-lance-shaped, heart-shaped at the base, wrinkled. Mid-green.

- NATIVE HABITAT Garden origin.
- CULTIVATION Grow in fertile, well-drained soil in sun. Valued for the fine deep violet-blue of its flowers, this cultivar associates well with old-fashioned roses, and *Paeonia officinalis* and *Papaver orientale* cultivars. It also provides strong contrast when planted with silver-leaved plants. If cut back after the first flush of flowers, it may produce a second, lesser flush later in the season. Its sturdy habit will require little or no staking in the second row of an herbaceous border. It tolerates drought conditions, and the flowers are excellent for cutting, lasting well in water. The plant is pleasantly aromatic and attractive to bees.
- PROPAGATION By division in spring or autumn.
- OTHER NAMES *S.* x *sylvestris* 'May Night'.

Z 5–9

HEIGHT
3ft (1m)

SPREAD
18in (45cm)

Ranunculaceae

ACONITUM × CAMMARUM 'Bicolor'

Habit Erect, tuberous-rooted. ***Flowers*** Large, hooded, helmet-shaped, borne in short, dense, spikes on upright, sparsely branched stems in summer. Violet-blue and white. ***Leaves*** Divided, deeply cut. Glossy dark green.

• NATIVE HABITAT Garden origin.

• CULTIVATION Grow in moist but well-drained, fertile soil, in sun or partial shade. The plant is poisonous.

• PROPAGATION By division in autumn. Divide every 2–3 years to maintain vigor.

Z 3–7

HEIGHT 4ft (1.2m)

SPREAD 20in (50cm)

Leguminosae/ Papilionaceae

GALEGA ORIENTALIS

Habit Vigorous, upright. ***Flowers*** Small, pea-like, borne in slender, upright spikes above the foliage, in summer. Blue-tinged, violet. ***Leaves*** Divided, with 4–10 pairs of oval leaflets. Green, tinted with gray.

• NATIVE HABITAT Meadows, scrub, riversides, in the Caucasus.

• CULTIVATION Grow in an open position, in well-drained soil. Needs staking and may spread freely. Suitable for borders and wildflower meadows.

• PROPAGATION By division in winter.

Z 5–8

HEIGHT 4ft (1.2m)

SPREAD 2ft (60cm)

Leguminosae/ Papilionaceae | BLUE FALSE INDIGO

BAPTISIA AUSTRALIS

Habit Upright, deep-rooted. ***Flowers*** Small, pea-like, in erect, open spikes in early or midsummer. Indigo-blue. ***Leaves*** Divided into 3 oval leaflets. Bright blue-green, borne on gray-green stems.

• NATIVE HABITAT Usually on damp soils, by riverbanks, in eastern US.

• CULTIVATION Grow in deep, fertile, moist but well-drained soil in full sun. Has a long season of interest, being beautiful in both foliage and flower.

• PROPAGATION By seed in autumn, or division in spring.

Z 3–9

HEIGHT 30in (75cm) or more

SPREAD 2ft (60cm)

Plumbaginaceae

LIMONIUM PLATYPHYLLUM

Habit Clump-forming. ***Flowers*** Tiny, borne in diffuse, airy panicles on wiry, branching stems, in late summer. Pale violet. ***Leaves*** Leathery, spoon-shaped to long-elliptic, in basal rosettes. Dark green.

• NATIVE HABITAT Dry grassland, from S.E. and C. Europe to S. Russia.

• CULTIVATION Grow in well-drained, preferably sandy soil, in full sun. Flowers are good for cutting and drying. Cut before fully open, and hang upside down in a cool place with plenty of ventilation. An extremely useful foil in an herbaceous or mixed border where its fluffy flower heads contrast well with more solid neighbors. It also associates well with silver-leaved artemisias. This plant has a general lightening effect and its basal rosette of dark green leaves is distinctive even when it is out of flower.

• PROPAGATION By seed or division in spring or root cuttings in winter.

• OTHER NAMES *L. latifolium*.

Z 4–9

HEIGHT
up to 32in (80cm)

SPREAD
18in (45cm)

Geraniaceae	

GERANIUM PRATENSE 'Mrs. Kendall Clark'

Habit Vigorous, clump-forming. ***Flowers*** Large, saucer-shaped, borne in clusters above the foliage, in summer. Light violet-blue. ***Leaves*** Deeply divided into 7 or 9 narrow, toothed, and divided segments. Dark green.

- NATIVE HABITAT Garden origin.
- CULTIVATION Grow in well-drained, fertile soil, in light shade or full sun. Excellent in cottage gardens and borders where it associates well with old roses.
- PROPAGATION By division in autumn or spring.

☼ ◊

Z 4–8

HEIGHT 24in (60cm) or more

SPREAD 24in (60cm)

Phormiaceae/Liliaceae	FLAX LILY

DIANELLA TASMANICA

Habit Upright, clump-forming, fibrous-rooted. ***Flowers*** Small, nodding, star-shaped, borne in loose, branching panicles, in summer. Bright blue. ***Fruits*** Deep blue berries in autumn. ***Leaves*** Evergreen, stiff, strap-shaped. Dark green.

- NATIVE HABITAT Cool, moist forests of Tasmania and S.E. Australia.
- CULTIVATION Grow in a sheltered site, in cool, moist but well-drained, neutral to acid, peaty soil in partial shade, or in sun where soil is reliably moist.
- PROPAGATION By division or seed in spring.

☼ ◊

Z 9–10

HEIGHT 4ft (1.2m)

SPREAD 20in (50cm)

Apiaceae/Umbelliferae	

ERYNGIUM ALPINUM

Habit Upright, rosette-forming. ***Flowers*** Tiny, in dense, conical heads amidst long, spiny, blue-purple bracts, borne on thick stems in late summer. Purple-blue. ***Leaves*** Deeply toothed, oval to triangular, in basal rosettes, heart-shaped at the base.

- NATIVE HABITAT Sub-alpine meadows, usually on limestone, in the mountains of Europe.
- CULTIVATION Grow in moderately fertile, freely draining soil, in full sun. Flowers dry well.
- PROPAGATION By seed in autumn, by division in spring, or by root cuttings in winter.

☼ ◊

Z 5–8

HEIGHT 30–36in (75cm–1m)

SPREAD 2ft (60cm)

Apiaceae/Umbelliferae	

ERYNGIUM × *TRIPARTITUM*

Habit Upright, rosette-forming. ***Flowers*** Tiny, in dense, rounded-conical heads, with a star of slender bracts beneath, borne on wiry, blue-tinted stems, in late summer and autumn. Metallic-blue. ***Leaves*** Coarsely toothed, in basal rosettes. Gray-green.

- NATIVE HABITAT Dry, rocky habitats, probably around the Mediterranean.
- CULTIVATION Grow in moderately fertile, freely draining soil, in full sun. Flowers dry well.
- PROPAGATION By division in spring, or by root cuttings in winter.

☼ ◊

Z 5–8

HEIGHT 3–4ft (1–1.2m)

SPREAD 20in (50cm)

Apiaceae/Umbelliferae

ERYNGIUM × OLIVERIANUM

Habit Upright. ***Flowers*** Tiny, in large, rounded, cylindrical heads, with spiny, narrow, silvery bracts, in late summer. Steel-blue to lavender-blue. ***Leaves*** Oval, 3-lobed or 5-parted, spiny-toothed, heart-shaped at the base and mostly basal. Mid-green.

• NATIVE HABITAT Garden origin.

• CULTIVATION Grow in moderately fertile, freely draining soil, in full sun. This is one of the most sturdy of the sea hollies for the middle of a mixed or herbaceous border, especially one with a silver- or gray-leaved theme. Site where the attractive basal leaves will not be obscured by neighboring plants. The stiff, silvery ruffs contrast with the large metallic-blue cones to give this plant considerable architectural status. Hang the cut flowers upside down to dry in a cool, airy place.

• PROPAGATION By division in spring, or by root cuttings in winter.

Z 5–8

HEIGHT
2–3ft
(60cm–1m)
or more

SPREAD
18–24in
(45–60cm)

Alliaceae/Liliaceae

AGAPANTHUS 'Blue Giant'

Habit Clump-forming, fleshy-rooted. ***Flowers*** Small, tubular-bell-shaped, in large, rounded, heads, borne on sturdy, upright stems, in late summer. Rich purple-blue. ***Leaves*** Long, narrow, in basal clumps. Green.

- NATIVE HABITAT Garden origin.
- CULTIVATION Grow in moist but well-drained soil, in a warm, sunny site. Mulch the crowns with dry straw or similar in winter.
- PROPAGATION By careful division of established clumps in spring.

Z 8–10

HEIGHT 3ft (1m)

SPREAD 20in (50cm)

Alliaceae/Liliaceae

AGAPANTHUS 'Dorothy Palmer'

Habit Clump-forming, fleshy-rooted. ***Flowers*** Small, tubular-bell-shaped, in large, rounded heads, borne on sturdy, upright stems, in late summer. Rich blue. ***Leaves*** Long, narrow, in basal clumps. Gray-green.

- NATIVE HABITAT Garden origin.
- CULTIVATION Grow in moist but well-drained soil, in a warm, sunny site. Mulch the crowns with dry straw or similar in winter.
- PROPAGATION By careful division of established clumps in spring.

Z 8–10

HEIGHT 3ft (1m)

SPREAD 20in (50cm)

Ranunculaceae

CLEMATIS HERACLEIFOLIA var. *DAVIDIANA* 'Wyevale'

Habit Upright, woody-based. ***Flowers*** Scented, small, tubular, with reflexed petal tips, borne in clusters in summer. Pale sky-blue. ***Leaves*** Divided into irregularly serrated leaflets. Dark green.

- NATIVE HABITAT Garden origin.
- CULTIVATION Grow in fertile, moist, well-drained, loamy soil in sun or dappled shade. Cut flowered stems back to 2 basal buds in late winter. Mulch with well-rotted organic matter.
- PROPAGATION By division in spring.

Z 3–8

HEIGHT 3ft (1m)

SPREAD 30in (75cm)

Campanulaceae

CAMPANULA PERSICIFOLIA 'Telham Beauty'

Habit Upright, rosette-forming. ***Flowers*** Large, nodding, bell-shaped, in slender, upright spikes in summer. Soft, clear blue. ***Leaves*** Lance-shaped to narrowly oval, mostly in basal rosettes, but with scattered, narrow stem leaves. Bright green.

- NATIVE HABITAT Garden origin.
- CULTIVATION Grow in fertile, moist, well-drained soil, in sun. Young leaves are prone to attack by slugs. The cut flowers last reasonably well in water.
- PROPAGATION By division in spring or autumn.

Z 3–8

HEIGHT 3ft (1m)

SPREAD 1ft (30cm)

Asteraceae/Compositae	CHICORY

CICHORIUM INTYBUS

Habit Clump-forming. ***Flowers*** Daisy-like, open in the mornings and closing at midday, borne at the ends of willowy stems, in summer. Bright blue. ***Leaves*** Pinnately lobed to deeply toothed, broadly lance-shaped, mostly basal. Light green.

- NATIVE HABITAT Rough grassland and waste ground, in Europe, W. Asia, N. Africa.
- CULTIVATION Grow in moderately fertile, well-drained, preferably alkaline soil, in full sun. Good for borders and wildflower gardens. May self-sow.
- PROPAGATION By seed in autumn or spring.

Z 4–8

HEIGHT
4ft (1.2m)

SPREAD
18in (45cm)

Papaveraceae	BLUE POPPY

MECONOPSIS BETONICIFOLIA

Habit Erect, clump-forming. ***Flowers*** Large, poppy-like, borne in pendent, few-flowered clusters, on sturdy, leafy stems in early summer. Blue. ***Leaves*** Erect, toothed and hairy, oblong, slightly heart-shaped at the base, mostly basal. Mid-green.

- NATIVE HABITAT Damp, alpine meadows in China.
- CULTIVATION Grow in a cool, shaded, sheltered site, in moist, leafy, acid soil. Tolerates dappled sun in cool, damp climates. Will not thrive in warm, dry climates. Suited to a peat bed or woodland garden.
- PROPAGATION By fresh seed in late summer.

Z 7–8

HEIGHT
3–4ft
(1–1.2m)
or more

SPREAD
12–18in
(30–45cm)

Papaveraceae	

MECONOPSIS GRANDIS 'Branklyn'

Habit Erect, clump-forming. ***Flowers*** Large, pendent, poppy-like, on sturdy stems in early summer. Blue. ***Leaves*** Erect, oblong, slightly toothed and hairy, mostly in basal clumps. Mid-green.

- NATIVE HABITAT Garden origin.
- CULTIVATION Grow in a cool, shaded, sheltered site, in moist, leafy, acid soil. Tolerates dappled sun in cool, damp climates. Will not thrive in warm, dry climates. Suited to a peat bed or woodland garden.
- PROPAGATION By division after flowering.

Z 7–8

HEIGHT
3–4ft
(1–1.2m)
or more

SPREAD
12–18in
(30–45cm)

Lamiaceae/Labiatae	

SALVIA PATENS 'Cambridge Blue'

Habit Upright, branching, compact. ***Flowers*** Hooded, tubular, 2-lipped, borne in whorls in long, spike-like heads, in late summer. Pale blue. ***Leaves*** Sticky-hairy, oval to diamond-shaped. Mid-green.

- NATIVE HABITAT Garden origin.
- CULTIVATION Grow in well-drained soil, in full sun. Excellent for borders, bedding and patio tubs. Overwinter young plants in frost-free conditions.
- PROPAGATION By seed in spring or by softwood cuttings in midsummer.

Z 7–9

HEIGHT
18–24in
(45–60cm)

SPREAD
18in (45cm)

Alliaceae/Liliaceae

AGAPANTHUS PRAECOX subsp. *ORIENTALIS*

Habit Clump-forming. ***Flowers*** Small, tubular-bell-shaped, borne in rounded heads, on sturdy stems, in late summer. Sky-blue. ***Leaves*** Almost evergreen, fleshy, broadly lance-shaped, in basal clumps. Dark green.

- NATIVE HABITAT South Africa.
- CULTIVATION Grow in moist but well-drained soil, in a warm, sunny site. The very striking late-summer flower heads make the entire genus *Agapanthus* extremely useful at a time when borders are beginning to slow down. They require generous provision of moisture. In colder areas, plants can be grown in large pots or tubs and left over winter in a cool greenhouse or sunroom; during the warm summer months they can be moved outdoors again to decorate a courtyard or patio. The seed heads dry well for winter decoration.
- PROPAGATION By careful division of established clumps in spring, or by seed in autumn or spring.
- OTHER NAMES *A. orientalis*.

☼ ♦

Z 9–11

HEIGHT
3ft (1m)

SPREAD
20in (50cm)

Boraginaceae	HIMALAYAN HOUND'S TONGUE

CYNOGLOSSUM NERVOSUM

Habit Clump-forming. ***Flowers*** Small, forget-me-not-like, borne in terminal, branching cymes, in early summer. Bright blue. ***Leaves*** Oval to oblong basal leaves, with narrower stem leaves. Mid-green.

- NATIVE HABITAT Grassy areas in the Himalayas.
- CULTIVATION Grow in sun, in moist but well-drained, not too fertile soil. Plants become lax and leafy in fertile soils.
- PROPAGATION By division in spring, or by seed in autumn or spring.

☼ ◊

Z 4–8

HEIGHT
30in (75cm)

SPREAD
20in (50cm)

Asteraceae/Compositae	

ARTEMISIA ALBA 'Canescens'

Habit Upright, bushy. ***Flowers*** Tiny, insignificant, in narrow spikes, in summer. Grayish-yellow. ***Leaves*** Semi-evergreen, finely divided into slender, delicate, curling segments. Ash-gray.

- NATIVE HABITAT Origin uncertain.
- CULTIVATION Grow in an open, sunny site, in well-drained soil. Cut back in spring for best foliage effects. Indispensable at the front of a silver border and cut stems are attractive in floral arrangements .
- PROPAGATION By division in spring or autumn.

☼ ◊

Z 4–8

HEIGHT
20in (50cm)

SPREAD
12in (30cm)

Boraginaceae	

ANCHUSA AZUREA 'Loddon Royalist'

Habit Upright, clump-forming. ***Flowers*** Small, forget-me-not-like, borne in dense, branching spikes, on upright stems, in early summer. Intense deep blue. ***Leaves*** Hairy, coarse, lance-shaped, mostly basal. Mid-green.

- NATIVE HABITAT Garden origin.
- CULTIVATION Grow in deep, fertile, moist but well-drained soil, in sun. May need unobtrusive staking. Is often short-lived, so propagate regularly. Much-valued for its intense blue flowers.
- PROPAGATION By root cuttings in winter.

☼ ◊

Z 3–8

HEIGHT
4ft (1.2m)

SPREAD
2ft (60cm)

Asteraceae/Compositae	

ARTEMISIA LUDOVICIANA 'Silver Queen'

Habit Upright, bushy, stoloniferous.
Flowers Tiny, in slender plumes, in summer. Grayish-yellow. ***Leaves*** Evergreen, entire, and lance-shaped, sometimes jaggedly toothed, densely hairy. Silvery-white.

- NATIVE HABITAT Garden origin.
- CULTIVATION Grow in an open, sunny site, in well-drained soil. Cut back in spring for best foliage effects. Indispensable in a silver border.
- PROPAGATION By division in spring or autumn.

☼ ◊

Z 4–9

HEIGHT
30–36in (75–90cm)

SPREAD
24in (60cm)

Apiaceae/Umbelliferae

ASTRANTIA MAJOR 'Sunningdale Variegated'

Habit Clump-forming. ***Flowers*** A dome of tiny greenish-pink florets, with a star-shaped collar of papery white, pink, and green bracts beneath, borne throughout summer and autumn. ***Leaves*** Divided into 3–5 coarsely toothed lobes. Mid-green, heavily variegated with pale yellow and cream.
- NATIVE HABITAT Garden origin.
- CULTIVATION Grow in any fertile, well-drained soil in sun. Flowers are good for cutting and drying.
- PROPAGATION By division in spring.

Z 4–7

HEIGHT 24in (60cm)

SPREAD 18in (45cm)

Lamiaceae/Labiatae

NEPETA GOVANIANA

Habit Upright, multi-branched. ***Flowers*** Small, long-tubed, 2-lipped, often paired, borne in open spikes over many weeks from mid- to late summer. Light yellow. ***Leaves*** Aromatic, pointed, oval to elliptic. Gray-green.
- NATIVE HABITAT Open woodland, Himalayas.
- CULTIVATION Grow in moist, well-drained, fertile soil, in a cool position, in sun or dappled shade. A graceful, elegant perennial for herbaceous borders.
- PROPAGATION By division in spring, stem tip cuttings in summer, or seed in autumn.

Z 4–9

HEIGHT 3ft (1m)

SPREAD 2ft (60cm)

Polygonaceae

RHEUM ALEXANDRAE

Habit Clump-forming. ***Flowers*** Small, borne in upright panicles, in early summer. Creamy-white, almost obscured by a large, yellow-green bract. ***Leaves*** Large, oval-oblong, heart-shaped at the base, in neat, basal rosettes. Glossy, dark green.
- NATIVE HABITAT Marshes, streamsides, W. China.
- CULTIVATION Grow in moist but well-drained, fertile soil, in full sun. An unusual, very ornamental perennial for the border, related to edible rhubarb.
- PROPAGATION By division in spring, or by seed in autumn.

Z 6–8

HEIGHT 3ft (1m)

SPREAD 2ft (60cm)

Haemodoraceae | YELLOW KANGAROO PAW

ANIGOZANTHOS FLAVIDUS

Habit Vigorous, rhizomatous. ***Flowers*** Large, tubular, woolly, on sturdy stems, in spring to early summer. Yellow-green, sometimes red-flushed. ***Leaves*** Long, linear-lance-shaped. Mid-green.
- NATIVE HABITAT W. Australia.
- CULTIVATION Grow in an open, sunny site, in well-drained, peaty soil. In cold climates, grow in a cool greenhouse. Flowers are excellent for cutting and drying. Ink-spot disease may be a problem.
- PROPAGATION By division in spring, or by seed sown fresh in late summer.

Z 10

HEIGHT 4ft (1.2m)

SPREAD 18in (45cm)

Dipsacaceae	

SCABIOSA COLUMBARIA var. *OCHROLEUCA*

Habit Clump-forming. ***Flowers*** Borne on strong, wiry stems, in summer. Pale yellow petals around a domed center. ***Leaves*** Lower leaves lance-shaped, toothed stem leaves pinnately divided. Gray-green.
- NATIVE HABITAT Garden origin.
- CULTIVATION Grow in moderately fertile, well-drained soil, in full sun. Excellent for cutting. Suited to herbaceous borders or cottage gardens.
- PROPAGATION By seed or division in spring or autumn.
- OTHER NAMES *S. ochroleuca.*

Z 4–7

HEIGHT
3ft (1m)

SPREAD
3ft (1m)

Scrophulariaceae	YELLOW FOXGLOVE

DIGITALIS GRANDIFLORA

Habit Clump-forming. ***Flowers*** Tubular, 2-lipped, in open, upright spikes from early to midsummer. Pale yellow, veined brown. ***Leaves*** Evergreen, oval-oblong, veined, and in basal rosettes. Mid-green, usually glossy.
- NATIVE HABITAT Woods and by streams, C. Europe.
- CULTIVATION Grows best in moist, well-drained soil in dappled shade but tolerates sun. Excellent for an herbaceous border or woodland garden.
- PROPAGATION By seed in spring.
- OTHER NAMES *D. ambigua.*

Z 3–8

HEIGHT
30–36in
(75–90cm)

SPREAD
12in (30cm)

Scrophulariaceae	

VERBASCUM CHAIXII 'Gainsborough'

Habit Upright, rosette-forming. ***Flowers*** Small, 5-lobed, in tall, branching racemes, throughout summer. Pale sulfur-yellow. ***Leaves*** Semi-evergreen, oval, mostly in basal rosettes, but with smaller, narrower stem leaves. Gray-green.
- NATIVE HABITAT Garden origin.
- CULTIVATION Grow in fertile, well-drained soil, in an open, sunny site. Is short-lived, so propagate regularly. A beautiful, long-flowering specimen for herbaceous borders and scree plantings.
- PROPAGATION By root cuttings in winter.

Z 5–9

HEIGHT
2–4ft
(60cm–1.2 m) or more

SPREAD
1–2ft
(30–60cm)

Ranunculaceae

THALICTRUM LUCIDUM

Habit Dense, clump-forming. ***Flowers*** Tiny, in loose, fluffy, terminal sprays, in summer. Greenish-yellow. ***Leaves*** Finely divided into narrowly oblong leaflets, with linear stem leaves. Smooth, glossy green.

• NATIVE HABITAT Meadows, ditches, and marshy habitats, from Europe to temperate Asia.

• CULTIVATION Grow in moist, but well-drained, fertile soil, in sun or light, dappled shade. Ideal for borders or for a damp site such as by water.

• PROPAGATION By seed or division in spring.

Z 6–9

HEIGHT 1–1.2m (3–4ft)

SPREAD 50cm (20in)

Asteraceae/Compositae

ARGYRANTHEMUM 'Jamaica Primrose'

Habit Bushy, woody-based. ***Flowers*** Large, daisy-like, on slender stems through summer. Soft yellow. ***Leaves*** Evergreen, fern-like. Pale green.

• NATIVE HABITAT Garden origin.

• CULTIVATION Grow in a warm, sunny site, in moderately fertile, well-drained soil.

• PROPAGATION By stem cuttings in early autumn; overwinter young plants under glass, in cool areas.

• OTHER NAMES *A. frutescens* 'Jamaica Primrose', *Chrysanthemum frutescens* 'Jamaica Primrose'.

Z 11

HEIGHT 3ft (1m)

SPREAD 3ft (1m)

Leguminosae/ Papilionaceae

LUPINUS 'Chandelier'

Habit Clump-forming. ***Flowers*** Small, pea-like, in dense, terminal spires in early summer. Yellow. ***Leaves*** Palmate, deeply divided into oval to lance-shaped leaflets. Dark blue-green.

• NATIVE HABITAT Garden origin.

• CULTIVATION Grows best in well-drained, sandy, preferably slightly acid soils. Young foliage is very susceptible to slugs. Deadhead to help maintain vigor.

• PROPAGATION By cuttings of non-flowering sideshoots in spring or early summer.

Z 3–6

HEIGHT 4ft (1.2m)

SPREAD 18in (45cm)

Ranunculaceae	WOLF'S BANE

ACONITUM LYCOCTONUM subsp. *VULPARIA*

Habit Erect, fibrous-rooted. ***Flowers*** Narrow, hooded, in short spikes on upright, sparsely branched stems in summer. Pale buff-yellow. ***Leaves*** Divided, deeply cut. Glossy, dark green.

- NATIVE HABITAT Meadows in Europe and E. Asia.
- CULTIVATION Grow in moist, but well-drained, fertile soil, in partial shade. Needs staking. Plants are toxic. Divide every 2–3 years to maintain vigor.
- PROPAGATION By seed or division in autumn.
- OTHER NAMES *A. vulparia.*

Z 5–8

HEIGHT 3–4ft (1–1.2m)

SPREAD 1–2ft (30–60cm)

Gentianaceae	GREAT YELLOW GENTIAN

GENTIANA LUTEA

Habit Upright. ***Flowers*** Small, short-tubed, star-shaped, borne in summer in the upper leaf axils in dense, whorled clusters with cupped, green bracts beneath. Yellow. ***Leaves*** Large, lance-shaped to elliptic; upper leaves clasp the stem. Bluish-green.

- NATIVE HABITAT Alpine meadows and woodland margins in the mountains of Europe.
- CULTIVATION Grow in deep, fertile, moist but well-drained soil, in sun. A stately perennial for herbaceous borders.
- PROPAGATION Division in spring; seed in autumn.

Z 7–8

HEIGHT 3–4ft (1–1.2m)

SPREAD 2ft (60cm)

Asteraceae/Compositae	

ANTHEMIS TINCTORIA 'E. C. Buxton'

Habit Clump-forming. ***Flowers*** Large, single, daisy-like, borne singly on slender, sturdy stems, and produced in profusion during summer. Pale lemon-yellow. ***Leaves*** Fern-like, finely divided into narrow segments. Dark green.

- NATIVE HABITAT Garden origin.
- CULTIVATION Grow in well-drained soil, in full sun. Cut flowers last well in water. Cut back hard immediately after flowering to maintain vigor.
- PROPAGATION By basal cuttings in spring or late summer.

Z 3–7

HEIGHT 3ft (1m)

SPREAD 3ft (1m)

Primulaceae	GARDEN LOOSESTRIFE

LYSIMACHIA PUNCTATA

Habit Upright, rhizomatous. ***Flowers*** Small, star-shaped, borne in whorls at the ends of upright stems, over long periods in summer. Bright yellow. ***Leaves*** Lance-shaped to elliptic, opposite or in whorls of 3–4. Mid-green.

• NATIVE HABITAT Ditches, marshes, and riversides, from S.E. and C. Europe to Turkey.

• CULTIVATION Grow in moist, fertile soil in partial shade. *L. punctata* is a long-lived perennial that is valued for its strongly upright habit and long flowering season. It can be invasive, since it spreads widely by means of rhizomes. It is ideal for plantings in broad drifts to give strong color in damp areas of the wild garden or in informal plantings by the sides of pools or streams. In a damp border, if necessary, control spread by digging out excess growth from the margins of the clumps.

• PROPAGATION By seed or division in spring or autumn.

☼ ◑

Z 4–8

HEIGHT
2½–3ft
(75cm–1m)

SPREAD
2ft (60cm)

Euphorbiaceae

EUPHORBIA SIKKIMENSIS

Habit Clump-forming, rhizomatous. ***Flowers*** Small, surrounded by large, rounded, yellow bracts, in terminal clusters, in early or midsummer. ***Leaves*** Lance-shaped, smooth. Green, deep pink at base and margins, with white, pink-tinted midrib, on reddish stems.

- NATIVE HABITAT Woodland clearings, Himalayas.
- CULTIVATION Grow in fertile, humus-rich, moist or wet soil, in sun or light dappled shade.
- PROPAGATION By seed or division in spring or early autumn, or by basal cuttings in spring or summer.

Z 6–9

HEIGHT 4ft (1.2m) or more

SPREAD 18in (45cm)

Euphorbiaceae

EUPHORBIA PALUSTRIS

Habit Upright, bushy, rhizomatous. ***Flowers*** Small, but surrounded by bright lime-yellow bracts, borne in terminal clusters from spring to late summer. ***Leaves*** Smooth, oblong to lance-shaped. Yellowish-green, yellow, and orange in autumn.

- NATIVE HABITAT Damp areas, Europe, Caucasus.
- CULTIVATION Grow in fertile, humus-rich, moist or wet soil, in sun or dappled shade. Good for damp borders, waterside plantings, or woodland gardens.
- PROPAGATION By seed or division in spring or early autumn; by basal cuttings in spring or summer.

Z 5–8

HEIGHT 3ft (1m) or more

SPREAD 3ft (1m)

Asteraceae/Compositae

SOLIDAGO 'Goldenmosa'

Habit Vigorous, clump-forming. ***Flowers*** Tiny, acacia-like, borne in dense, clustered, branching heads, on upright stems, in late summer and autumn. Bright golden-yellow. ***Leaves*** Toothed, hairy, lance-shaped. Yellowish-green.

- NATIVE HABITAT Garden origin.
- CULTIVATION Grow in any well-drained soil, including poor soils, in sun. Good for cutting, the bright flowers are much valued in a late summer border.
- PROPAGATION By division in spring

Z 4–9

HEIGHT 3ft (1m)

SPREAD 2ft (60cm)

Lamiaceae/Labiatae

PHLOMIS RUSSELIANA

Habit Mound-forming. ***Flowers*** Hooded, tubular, 2-lipped, borne in whorls, on thick stems in summer. Pale creamy-yellow. ***Leaves*** Evergreen, coarse, hairy, broadly oval, and heart-shaped at the base. Sage-green.

- NATIVE HABITAT Scrub and woodland in Turkey.
- CULTIVATION Grow in any moderately fertile, well-drained soil, in sun. Makes excellent, weed-smothering ground cover. The dried flower stems are persistent and attractive in winter. May self-sow.
- PROPAGATION Seed in autumn; division in spring.

Z 4–9

HEIGHT
3ft (1m)

SPREAD
2ft (60cm)
or more

Asteraceae/Compositae

INULA HOOKERI

Habit Clump-forming. ***Flowers*** Slightly scented, daisy-like, with very slender, greenish-yellow ray florets and a golden-yellow disk, borne on strong, slender, leafy stems, in late summer. ***Leaves*** Coarse, hairy, elliptic to lance-shaped. Mid-green.

- NATIVE HABITAT Mountain scrub, Himalayas.
- CULTIVATION Grow in moist but well-drained soil, in sun or light shade. May spread rapidly. Suitable for borders and wild or woodland gardens.
- PROPAGATION By seed or division in spring or autumn.

Z 4–8

HEIGHT
30in (75cm)

SPREAD
18in (45cm)

Leguminosae/
Papilionaceae

THERMOPSIS MONTANA

Habit Upright, rhizomatous, clump-forming. ***Flowers*** Small, pea-like, in erect, open, lupine-like spikes, during summer. Bright or pale yellow. ***Leaves*** Divided into 3 broadly oval to lance-shaped leaflets. Dark green.

- NATIVE HABITAT Rockies, North America.
- CULTIVATION Grow in light, well-drained, fertile soil, in sun or dappled shade. May spread rapidly.
- PROPAGATION By seed in autumn; division in spring.
- OTHER NAMES *T. rhombifolia.*

Z 3–8

HEIGHT
2–3ft
(60cm–1m)

SPREAD
2ft (60cm)
or more

Asteraceae/Compositae

CENTAUREA MACROCEPHALA

Habit Robust, clump-forming. ***Flowers*** Large, thistle-like, on leafy stems, in summer. Bright yellow, enclosed in silvery-brown bracts. ***Leaves*** Stalkless, lance-shaped, slightly hairy. Mid-green.

- NATIVE HABITAT Sub-alpine meadows in the Caucasus and N.E. Turkey.
- CULTIVATION Grow in fertile, moist, well-drained soil in full sun. Excellent for a summer border or cottage garden.
- PROPAGATION By seed or division in spring or autumn.

Z 3–7

HEIGHT
3ft (1m)

SPREAD
2ft (60cm)

Asteraceae/Compositae

RUDBECKIA FULGIDA var. *SULLIVANTII* 'Goldsturm'

Habit Upright, clump-forming. ***Flowers*** Large, daisy-like, with narrow, rich golden-yellow ray florets and a conical black center, borne singly on strong stems, in late summer and autumn. ***Leaves*** Coarse, rough-textured, oval to lance-shaped. Mid-green.

- NATIVE HABITAT Garden origin.
- CULTIVATION Grow in any moist but well-drained soil, in sun or light shade. Valued for its strongly upright form and the prolific production of brilliantly colored flowers that are borne well above the substantial clumps of foliage. It has a long flowering period and is an invaluable addition to the late summer border, especially when planted in bold drifts. The cut flowers last reasonably well in water.
- PROPAGATION By division in spring.
- OTHER NAMES *R. fulgida* 'Goldsturm'.

Z 4–9

HEIGHT
30in (75cm)

SPREAD
12in (30cm) or more

Scrophulariaceae	DARK MULLEIN

VERBASCUM NIGRUM

Habit Upright, clump-forming. ***Flowers*** Small, 5-lobed, in narrow spikes, from summer to autumn. Golden-yellow, purple-centered. ***Leaves*** Semi-evergreen, oblong. Gray-green, downy beneath.

- NATIVE HABITAT Grassland and rocky places, W. Europe to the Caucasus and Siberia.
- CULTIVATION Grow in fertile, well-drained soil, in an open, sunny site. Suitable for borders, scree plantings, and wildflower gardens.
- PROPAGATION By seed in spring or late summer, or by root cuttings in winter.

Z 6–8

HEIGHT
2–3ft (60cm–1m) or more

SPREAD
2ft (60cm)

Asteraceae/Compositae	

SOLIDAGO 'Laurin'

Habit Compact, clump-forming. ***Flowers*** Tiny, acacia-like, borne in dense, clustered, branching spikes, at the ends of upright stems, in late summer and autumn. Bright golden-yellow. ***Leaves*** Toothed, lance-shaped. Mid-green, hairy.

- NATIVE HABITAT Garden origin.
- CULTIVATION Grow in any well-drained soil, including poor soils, in sun. A compact plant suitable for smaller herbaceous borders. Good for cutting, the bright flowers are valuable in late summer borders.
- PROPAGATION By division in spring.

Z 4–9

HEIGHT
24–30in (60–75cm)

SPREAD
18in (45cm)

Asteraceae/Compositae	

HELIOPSIS HELIANTHOIDES var. *SCABRA* 'Sommersonne'

Habit Upright, clump-forming. ***Flowers*** Large, single, daisy-like, in profusion in late summer. Rich yellow with a deep orange-yellow center. ***Leaves*** Coarse, serrated, oval to lance-shaped. Dark green.

- NATIVE HABITAT Garden origin.
- CULTIVATION Easy to grow in fertile, well-drained soil, in full sun. A useful long-flowering plant for an autumn border. The cut flowers last well in water.
- PROPAGATION By division in autumn or spring.
- OTHER NAMES *H.* 'Summer Sun'.

Z 4–9

HEIGHT
3–4ft (1–1.2m)

SPREAD
2ft (60cm)

Asteraceae/Compositae

HELENIUM 'Butterpat'

Habit Dense, branching, clump-forming. ***Flowers*** Large, daisy-like, with reflexed ray florets and a rounded disk, borne over long periods in late summer. Rich deep yellow. ***Leaves*** Lance-shaped, on thick stems. Dark green.

• NATIVE HABITAT Garden origin.

• CULTIVATION Easy to grow in any soil unless waterlogged, in full sun. Divide and replant regularly to maintain vigor. The flowers are produced in great profusion and need an unobtrusive, grow-through support to carry their weight. A valuable long-flowering plant for a late summer border. The rich, deep yellow flowers associate particularly well with copper or bronze foliage plants and with the deep mahogany-red or bronze-marked flowers of *H.* 'Wyndley' or *H.* 'Moerheim Beauty'. The flowers last well in water when cut.

• PROPAGATION By division in spring or autumn.

Z 4–8

HEIGHT
3ft (1m)

SPREAD
2ft (60cm)

DAYLILIES

Daylilies belong to the genus of perennials called *Hemerocallis*. As their name might suggest, they belong to the lily family; however, they are not true lilies, and their common name comes from the short-lived lily-like flowers, which usually last only a day.

Some daylilies are evergreen. They range in size from small, compact plants of just 12–15in (30–38cm) tall, to considerably larger plants of up to 5ft (1.5m). There is a wide range of modern cultivars available in a variety of colors from pale creamy-white through to yellow, vivid orange and red, pink, and purple.

The flowers have a delicate appearance and some have colored bands or streaks on the petals. Most daylilies produce flowers, in succession, over a period of two to six weeks, during the summer months. The taller cultivars make elegant additions to a more formal herbaceous border. Some daylily species and a few cultivars have a rich, strong fragrance.

Daylilies will thrive in most soils, but for the best results, they should be planted in fertile, humus-rich soil that is moist but well-drained. Although they will tolerate some shade, the best blooms are produced by plants that receive direct sunlight for at least half the day. Protect the plants from slugs and snails, especially in spring.

The plants may be propagated by division in autumn or spring. Species come true from seed if they are grown in isolation. The seeds should be sown as soon as they are ripe. Young plants should be overwintered in frost-free conditions under glass.

Any abnormally swollen buds that appear in late spring or early summer should be picked off and discarded, since this may be an indication that the plant is infected by *Hemerocallis* gall midges.

H. 'Gentle Shepherd'
Habit Clump-forming.
Flowers From early to midsummer. White with green throats and ruffled petals.
Leaves Semi-evergreen, strap-shaped. Light green.
- HEIGHT 28in (70cm).
- SPREAD 24in (60cm).

H. 'Gentle Shepherd'

☼ 💧 Z 3–9

H. 'Siloam Virginia Henson'
Habit Low-growing, clump-forming.
Flowers Rounded, in early summer. Creamy-pink, ruffled petals, with rose-pink banding and green throats.
Leaves Broadly strap-shaped. Mid-green.
- HEIGHT 18in (45cm).
- SPREAD 26in (65cm).

H. 'Siloam Virginia Henson'

☼ 💧 Z 3–9

H. 'Lullaby Baby'
Habit Vigorous, clump-forming.
Flowers Large, from early spring to mid-summer. Very pale pink petals with ruffled edges and green throats.
Leaves Semi-evergreen, strap-shaped. Mid-green.
- HEIGHT 20in (50cm).
- SPREAD 20in (50cm)).

H. 'Lullaby Baby'

☼ 💧 Z 3–9

H. 'Scarlet Orbit'
Habit Low-growing, clump-forming.
Flowers Produced in midsummer. Rich deep scarlet, revealing gold-flushed green throats as they open flat.
Leaves Semi-evergreen, luxuriant, strap-shaped. Mid-green.
- HEIGHT 20in (50cm).
- SPREAD 26in (65cm).

H. 'Scarlet Orbit'

☼ 💧 Z 3–9

***H.* 'Whisky on Ice'**
Habit Clump-forming.
Flowers Rounded, from early to mid-summer. Very distinctive combination of amber, lemon, and paler creamy-yellow with green throats.
Leaves Semi-evergreen, luxuriant, strap-shaped. Bluish-green.
• HEIGHT 20in (50cm).
• SPREAD 20in (50cm).

***H.* 'Whisky on Ice'**

Z 3–9

***H.* 'Jolyene Nichole'**
Habit Clump-forming.
Flowers Rounded in summer. Rose-pink with ruffled petal margins.
Leaves Semi-evergreen, luxuriant, strap-shaped. Blue-green.
• HEIGHT 20in (50cm).
• SPREAD 20in (50cm).

***H.* 'Jolyene Nichole'**

Z 3–9

***H.* 'Frank Gladney'**
Habit Robust, clump-forming.
Flowers Very large, rounded, in summer. Vivid coral-pink, with golden throats and black anthers.
Leaves Semi-evergreen, broadly strap-shaped. Mid-green.
• HEIGHT 24in (60cm).
• SPREAD 24in (60cm).

***H.* 'Frank Gladney'**

Z 3–9

***H.* 'Stafford'**
Habit Vigorous, clump-forming.
Flowers Trumpet-shaped, in succession from mid- to late summer. Glowing, rich crimson with maroon and yellow throats, each petal with a narrow yellow midrib.
Leaves Broadly strap-shaped. Mid-green.
• HEIGHT 30in (75cm).
• SPREAD 24in (60cm).

***H.* 'Stafford'**

Z 3–9

***H.* 'Prairie Blue Eyes'**
Habit Clump-forming.
Flowers Produced in midsummer. Maroon-purple, with green throats.
Leaves Semi-evergreen, slender, strap-shaped.. Mid-green.
• HEIGHT 32in (80cm).
• SPREAD 3ft (90cm).

***H.* 'Prairie Blue Eyes'**

Z 3–9

***H.* 'Little Grapette'**
Habit Vigorous, clump-forming.
Flowers From early spring to midsummer. Large, rich grape-purple, with ruffled petal margins, green throats, and darker purple eyes.
Leaves Semi-evergreen, slender, strap-shaped. Mid-green.
• HEIGHT 12–20in (30–50cm).
• SPREAD 24in (60cm).

***H.* 'Little Grapette'**

Z 3–9

H. 'Super Purple'

Habit Vigorous, clump-forming.
Flowers Rounded, velvety petals with ruffled margins, produced in midsummer. Red-purple, with lime-green throats.
Leaves Strap-shaped. Light green.
• HEIGHT 27in (68cm).
• SPREAD 26in (65cm).

H. 'Super Purple'

Z 3–9

H. 'Marion Vaughan'

Habit Clump-forming.
Flowers Large, fragrant, trumpet-shaped, in succession, in midsummer. Lemon-yellow petals, each with a raised, white central stripe. ***Leaves*** Strap-shaped. Mid-green.
• HEIGHT 3ft (1m).
• SPREAD 24in (60cm).

H. 'Marion Vaughan'

Z 3–9

H. LILIOASPHODELUS

Habit Robust, clump-forming, spreading.
Flowers Delicate, trumpet-shaped, very fragrant, each lasting 1–2 days, and borne in late spring and early summer. Lemon- to chrome-yellow.
Leaves Strap-shaped. Mid-green.
• OTHER NAMES *H. flava*.
• HEIGHT 24in (60cm) or more.
• SPREAD 24in (60cm).

H. lilioasphodelus
Lemon lily

Z 3–9

H. 'Brocaded Gown'

Habit Clump-forming.
Flowers Rounded, borne in summer. Creamy-white with ruffled petal margins.
Leaves Semi-evergreen, broadly strap-shaped. Mid-green.
• HEIGHT to 2ft (60cm).
• SPREAD to 2ft (60cm).

H. 'Brocaded Gown'

Z 3–9

H. CITRINA

Habit Vigorous, clump-forming. ***Flowers*** Large, very fragrant, trumpet-shaped, opening at night in midsummer and, each lasting a day. Rich lemon-yellow.
Leaves Strap-shaped. Dark green.
• HEIGHT 30in (75cm).
• SPREAD 30in (75cm).

H. citrina

Z 3–9

H. 'Corky'

Habit Clump-forming.
Flowers Trumpet-shaped, opening in late spring and early summer. Lemon-yellow with a brown petal reverse.
Leaves Slender, strap-shaped. Mid-green.
• HEIGHT 18in (45cm).
• SPREAD 18in (45cm).

H. 'Corky'

Z 3–9

H. 'Cartwheels'

Habit Clump-forming.
Flowers Large, simple, produced in summer, opening widely at maturity. Rich, light golden-orange petals, slightly ruffled at the margin.
Leaves Strap-shaped. Mid-green.
• HEIGHT 30in (75cm).
• SPREAD 30in (75cm).

H. 'Cartwheels'

Z 3–9

H. 'Hyperion'

Habit Clump-forming.
Flowers Very fragrant, lily-like, in midsummer. Slender, pale lemon yellow petals.
Leaves Narrow, strap-shaped. Mid green.
• HEIGHT 3ft (90cm).
• SPREAD 3ft (90cm).

H. 'Hyperion'

Z 3–9

H. 'Golden Chimes'

Habit Clump-forming, graceful.
Flowers Small, delicate, trumpet-shaped, each lasting a day but borne in succession from early to midsummer. Golden-yellow with a brown petal reverse.
Leaves Narrow, strap-shaped. Mid green.
• HEIGHT 30in (75cm).
• SPREAD 24in (60cm).

H. 'Golden Chimes'

Z 3–9

H. 'Betty Woods'

Habit Robust, spreading, clump-forming.
Flowers Large, double, peony-like, borne in mid- and late summer. Yellow.
Leaves Evergreen, arching, strap-shaped. Mid-green.
• HEIGHT 26in (65cm).
• SPREAD 24in (60cm).

H. 'Betty Woods'

Z 3–9

H. 'Ruffled Apricot'

Habit Slow-growing, clump-forming.
Flowers Large, in midsummer. Deep apricot, with ruffled petals, each with a lavender-pink midrib.
Leaves Stiff, strap-shaped. Mid-green.
• HEIGHT 20in (50cm).
• SPREAD 26in (65cm).

H. 'Ruffled Apricot'

Z 3–9

H. FULVA 'Kwanso'

Habit Vigorous, clump- or mound-forming.
Flowers Large, double, trumpet-shaped, in mid- to late summer. Rich tawny-orange.
Leaves Strap-shaped. Light green.
• OTHER NAMES *H.* 'Kwanzo Flore Pleno'.
• HEIGHT 3ft (1m).
• SPREAD 30in (75cm).

H. fulva 'Kwanso'

Z 3–9

Asteraceae/Compositae	

ACHILLEA 'Coronation Gold'

Habit Upright. ***Flowers*** Tiny, in large, flat heads, on slender, rigid stems during summer. Golden-yellow. ***Leaves*** Feathery, finely divided into oblong to lance-shaped segments. Silvery gray-green, hairy.

• NATIVE HABITAT Garden origin.

• CULTIVATION Grow in fertile, moisture-retentive, well-drained soil, in full sun. Divide and replant every third year to maintain vigor. The flowerheads dry well and retain their herbal fragrance.

• PROPAGATION By division in early spring or autumn.

Z 3–9

HEIGHT 3ft (1m)

SPREAD 2ft (60cm)

Acanthaceae	ZEBRA PLANT, SAFFRON SPIKE

APHELANDRA SQUARROSA 'Louisae'

Habit Erect. ***Flowers*** Tubular, 2-lipped, in dense spikes from the axils of yellow bracts, in late summer to autumn. Golden-yellow. ***Leaves*** Evergreen, oval, slightly wrinkled. Glossy, dark green with white veins and midrib.

• NATIVE HABITAT Mountains of tropical Americas.

• CULTIVATION Grow as a house or sunroom plant in cool climates, in humus-rich, well-drained soil in bright light, out of direct sun and drafts. Apply liquid fertilizer as flowers form.

• PROPAGATION By tip cuttings in spring.

Min. 55°F (13°C)

HEIGHT To 3ft (1m)

SPREAD 2ft (60cm)

Asteraceae/Compositae	

BERKHEYA MACROCEPHALA

Habit Upright, sparsely branched. ***Flowers*** Daisy-like, with a spiny calyx beneath, borne on branching, spiny-leaved stems, throughout summer. Bright yellow with an orange-yellow center. ***Leaves*** Narrowly oblong, deeply and irregularly lobed, spiny. Dark green.

• NATIVE HABITAT Damp, rocky grasslands in the Drakensberg Mountains, Natal.

• CULTIVATION Grow in fertile, moist but well-drained soil, in a warm, sunny, sheltered site.

• PROPAGATION By seed or division in spring.

Z 9–10

HEIGHT 3ft (1m)

SPREAD 3ft (1m)

Asteraceae/Compositae

HELIOPSIS 'Ballet Dancer'

Habit Upright, clump-forming. ***Flowers*** Large, double, daisy-like, with toothed petals, borne in profusion in late summer. Rich yellow with a deep orange-yellow center. ***Leaves*** Coarse, serrated, oval to lance-shaped. Dark green.

• NATIVE HABITAT Garden origin.

• CULTIVATION Grow in any moderately fertile, well-drained soil in full sun. Will tolerate dry soils, but performs best on soils that do not become too dry in summer. A notably hardy, long-lived, undemanding, and easily grown perennial. For best results lift and divide periodically, and incorporate organic matter into the soil before replanting. This robust cultivar makes a valuable, long-flowering addition to the late summer and autumn border, where it associates particularly well with orange- and red-flowered plants. The cut flowers last moderately well in water.

• PROPAGATION By division in autumn or spring.

Z 4–9

HEIGHT
3–4ft
(1–1.2m)

SPREAD
2ft (60cm)

Asteraceae/Compositae

ACHILLEA FILIPENDULINA 'Gold Plate'

Habit Upright. ***Flowers*** Tiny, in large, flat heads, borne on rigid, leafy stems during summer. Deep yellow. ***Leaves*** Feathery, finely divided into oblong to lance-shaped segments. Grayish-green, densely hairy.

- NATIVE HABITAT Garden origin.
- CULTIVATION Grow in fertile, moisture-retentive, well-drained soil, in full sun. Divide and replant every third year to maintain vigor. The flowerheads dry well and retain their color and fragrance.
- PROPAGATION Division in early spring or autumn.

Z 3–9

HEIGHT 4ft (1.2m) or more

SPREAD 2ft (60cm)

Malvaceae | DESERT MALLOW

SPHAERALCEA AMBIGUA

Habit Shrubby, multi-branched. ***Flowers*** Mallow-like, broadly funnel-shaped, with 5 broad petals, produced singly in the leaf axils, from summer to first frost. Coral-orange. ***Leaves*** Rounded, 3-lobed, soft, and hairy. Gray-green.

- NATIVE HABITAT Dry, open habitats, from Utah to California.
- CULTIVATION Grow in a warm, sunny, sheltered site, in fertile, well-drained soil.
- PROPAGATION By seed or division in spring.

Z 9–10

HEIGHT 30in (75cm)

SPREAD 30in (75cm)

Asphodelaceae/Liliaceae

KNIPHOFIA 'Royal Standard'

Habit Upright, clump-forming. ***Flowers*** Small, narrowly tubular, borne on thick, upright stems in dense, terminal spikes, in late summer. Bright lemon-yellow, opening from scarlet-vermilion buds. ***Leaves*** Tough, narrow, linear, arching to form dense basal clumps. Mid-green.

- NATIVE HABITAT Garden origin.
- CULTIVATION Grow in full sun, in damp but well-drained soil. Needs ample moisture when in growth. Protect crowns in cold winter areas.
- PROPAGATION By division in spring.

Z 5–9

HEIGHT 3–4ft (1–1.2m)

SPREAD 2ft (60cm)

Asphodelaceae/Liliaceae

KNIPHOFIA THOMSONII var. *SNOWDENII*

Habit Upright, clump-forming. ***Flowers*** Small, pendent, narrowly tubular, borne on upright stems in open, terminal spikes, from midsummer to first frosts. Coral-pink, yellowish on the inside. ***Leaves*** Tough, linear, forming basal clumps. Mid-green.

- NATIVE HABITAT Damp, mountain grasslands in C. Africa.
- CULTIVATION Grow in damp but well-drained soil, in full sun. Needs ample moisture during growth. Protect crowns in winter in cold areas.
- PROPAGATION By seed or division in spring.

Z 6–9

HEIGHT 3ft (1m)

SPREAD 20in (50cm)

Alstroemeriaceae/ Liliaceae	PERUVIAN LILY

ALSTROEMERIA Ligtu Hybrids

Habit Upright to slightly arching. ***Flowers*** Widely funnel-shaped, in summer. A range of rich and subtle pinks, yellows, and orange, usually streaked and/or spotted with contrasting shades. ***Leaves*** Linear to narrowly lance-shaped, slightly fleshy, twisted. Mid-green.

- NATIVE HABITAT Garden origin.
- CULTIVATION Grow in fertile, moist, well-drained soil, in a warm, sunny site. Excellent for cutting. Provide a winter mulch of leaf mold or similar.
- PROPAGATION By division in early spring.

Z 7–10

HEIGHT 18–24in (45–60cm)

SPREAD 2–3ft (60cm–1m)

Asclepiadaceae	BUTTERFLY WEED

ASCLEPIAS TUBEROSA

Habit Upright, tuberous-rooted. ***Flowers*** Small, 5-horned, borne in dense, flat-topped clusters, over a long period in summer. Bright orange. ***Leaves*** Variable, usually lance-shaped and slightly fleshy. Light green.

- NATIVE HABITAT Dry grasslands, E. and S. North America.
- CULTIVATION Grow in deep, sandy, humus-rich and well-drained soil, in a warm, sunny site. It may take some time to become established.
- PROPAGATION By seed or division in spring.

Z 4–9

HEIGHT to 30in (75cm)

SPREAD 18in (45cm)

Euphorbiaceae	

EUPHORBIA GRIFFITHII 'Fireglow'

Habit Upright, bushy, rhizomatous. ***Flowers*** Small, but surrounded by conspicuous, bright orange-red bracts, borne in terminal clusters in early summer. ***Leaves*** Smooth, linear to lance-shaped. Mid-green, with pale red-pink midribs.

- NATIVE HABITAT Garden origin.
- CULTIVATION Grow in fertile, humus-rich, moist but well-drained soil, in sun or light dappled shade. Good for borders and woodland gardens.
- PROPAGATION By division in spring or early autumn, or by basal cuttings in spring or summer.

Z 4–9

HEIGHT to 3ft (1m)

SPREAD 20in (50cm)

Caryophyllaceae	JERUSALEM CROSS, MALTESE CROSS

LYCHNIS CHALCEDONICA

Habit Upright, clump-forming. ***Flowers*** Small, cross-shaped, borne in dense, flat heads, at the ends of sturdy stems, in early summer. Brilliant vermilion. ***Leaves*** Oval, borne along the length of the flowering stem. Mid-green.

- NATIVE HABITAT Scrub and woodland, W. Russia.
- CULTIVATION Grow in fertile, moist but well-drained soil, in sun or light shade, sheltered from the wind. May need staking. Looks good alongside yellow-flowered and bronze-foliaged plants.
- PROPAGATION Seed or division in autumn or spring.

Z 4–8

HEIGHT 3–4ft (1–1.2m)

SPREAD 12–18in (30–45cm)

Ranunculaceae	DOLL'S EYES, WHITE BANEBERRY

ACTAEA ALBA

Habit Compact, clump-forming. ***Flowers*** Small, borne in fluffy, rounded heads, on slender stems, in early summer. White. ***Fruits*** Small, globose, toxic, white berries in late summer. ***Leaves*** Long-stalked, toothed, lobed. Fresh green.

- NATIVE HABITAT Woodlands of E. North America.
- CULTIVATION Grow in moist, leafy, humus-rich soil, in shade or partial shade. Good for shady borders and woodland gardens.
- PROPAGATION Division in spring; seed in autumn.
- OTHER NAMES *A. pachypoda.*

Z 4–9

HEIGHT
3ft (1m)

SPREAD
20in (50cm)

Polygonaceae	

PERSICARIA CAMPANULATA

Habit Compact, creeping, stoloniferous. ***Flowers*** Tiny, bell-shaped, in branching, nodding heads, on slender stems, from midsummer to autumn. Pink or white. ***Leaves*** Oval, ribbed. Dark green and hairy, white to brownish-pink beneath.

- NATIVE HABITAT Damp forests, Himalayas.
- CULTIVATION Grow in cool, moist, fertile soil, in shade or partial shade. An elegant perennial for damp borders and woodland gardens.
- PROPAGATION Seed or division in autumn or spring.
- OTHER NAMES *Polygonum campanulatum.*

Z 5–9

HEIGHT
3ft (1m)

SPREAD
3ft (1m)

Scrophulariaceae	TURTLE-HEAD

CHELONE OBLIQUA

Habit Stiffly upright. ***Flowers*** Hooded, borne in stiff, erect, terminal spikes, in late summer and autumn. Lilac-pink. ***Leaves*** Lance-shaped, sharply toothed. Dark green.

- NATIVE HABITAT Damp woods and swamps, from Tennessee to Florida and Mississippi, US.
- CULTIVATION Easy to grow in moist, well-drained, humus-rich soil, in sun or partial shade. A weather-resistant plant for a late summer border.
- PROPAGATION By soft tip cuttings in summer, or by seed or division in autumn or spring.

Z 6–9

HEIGHT
3ft (1m)

SPREAD
20in (50cm)

Ranunculaceae

ANEMONE HUPEHENSIS

Habit Vigorous, branching, stoloniferous. ***Flowers*** Single, slightly cupped, borne in wiry-stemmed sprays from late summer to early autumn. White, soft pink or purplish-pink, darker on the reverse of the petals. ***Leaves*** More or less evergreen, deeply divided, with toothed leaflets. Dark green.

- NATIVE HABITAT Shady rocks and scrub, C. China.
- CULTIVATION Grow in any moderately fertile, well-drained soil, in sun or partial shade. An excellent perennial for a late summer border.
- PROPAGATION Seed or division in spring or autumn.

Z 4–8

HEIGHT
24–30in (60–75cm)

SPREAD
18in (45cm)

Convallariaceae/ Liliaceae | TOAD LILY

TRICYRTIS FORMOSANA

Habit Upright, rhizomatous. ***Flowers*** Spurred, lily-like, borne in open clusters, in early autumn. Yellow-throated, white to pink, heavily spotted with deep pinkish-mauve. ***Leaves*** Broadly lance-shaped, clasping stem. Glossy, deep green, dark-spotted.

- NATIVE HABITAT Damp forest, Taiwan.
- CULTIVATION Grow in moist, humus-rich soil, in a sheltered site, or in warm areas, in partial shade. An unusual plant for borders or woodland gardens.
- PROPAGATION Division in spring; seed in autumn.
- OTHER NAMES *T. stolonifera.*

Z 5–9

HEIGHT
2–3ft (60cm–1m)

SPREAD
18in (45cm)

Asteraceae/Compositae

CHRYSANTHEMUM 'Clara Curtis'

Habit Bushy, free-flowering. ***Flowers*** Large, flat, daisy-like, borne in profusion from summer to autumn. Clear pink, with yellow centers. ***Leaves*** Triangular-oval, divided into toothed and lobed segments. Dark bluish-green.

- NATIVE HABITAT Garden origin.
- CULTIVATION Grow in well-drained soil, in sun. Divide plants regularly to maintain vigor.
- PROPAGATION By division in spring.
- OTHER NAMES *C. rubellum* 'Clara Curtis', *Dendranthema zawadskii* 'Clara Curtis'.

Z 4–9

HEIGHT
30in (75cm)

SPREAD
18in (45cm)

Florists' Chrysanthemums

Florists' chrysanthemums, which are now botanically classified under the genus *Dendranthema*, make up the vast majority of chrysanthemums cultivated today. They are widely grown for their attractive and colorful flower heads that make them popular for borders, cutting, and exhibition.

Florists' chrysanthemums are grouped according to flowering season (early, mid- or late autumn), flower size and shape, and habit. They are further divided into disbudded and non-disbudded types.

Disbudded types – single, anemone-centered, incurved, intermediate, and reflexed – have all but the crown bud removed. Exhibition plants are generally disbudded to leave about half the number of blooms per plant than garden plants.

Non-disbudded types – cushions, pompon and spray types – produce several flowers per stem. **Cushions** are rounded, dwarf plants with hundreds of star-shaped, single flowers. **Cascades** are similar but are trained into a variety of shapes. **Pompons** are also dwarf and bear 50 or more flower heads. **Sprays** are allowed to develop 4–5 stems, with at least 5 flowers per stem.

Most florists' chrysanthemums are not reliably hardy and should be lifted in autumn and overwintered in frost-free conditions. Some earlies are hardier and may not need lifting if kept dry. The lates need heat to flower and should be grown under cover at a minimum of 50°F (10°C). Grow in well-drained, neutral to slightly acid soil, enriched with well-rotted organic matter, in full sun. Insert supporting stakes for tall cultivars at planting time and tie the stems in to the supports as growth proceeds. Water well during the growing season, and apply a balanced liquid fertilizer every 7–10 days.

Propagate by basal softwood cuttings in spring. Spray to control aphids, miners, spider mites, mildew, and rust.

INCURVED
Fully double, spherical flowers with incurved petals closing tightly over the crown.

FULLY REFLEXED
Fully double, almost spherical, with curved, pointed petals reflexing outward and downward to touch the stem.

REFLEXED
Similar to fully reflexed, but with less strongly reflexed petals forming an umbrella-like or spiky outline.

INTERMEDIATE
Fully double, roughly spherical, with loosely incurving petals, either enclosing the crown or reflexing in the bottom half of the flower.

ANEMONE-CENTERED
Single, with a dome-shaped disk, up to half the diameter of the bloom, and an outer ring of up to 5 rows of flat, occasionally spoon-shaped petals at 90° to the stem.

SINGLE
Single, daisy-like flowers with a golden- or green-centered disk, and up to 5 rows of flat petals held at right angles to the stem, sometimes incurving or reflexing at their tips.

POMPON
Fully double, spherical or occasionally hemispherical, with tubular petals having flat, rounded tips.

SPOON-TYPE
Similar to single types, but with tubular petals expanding at their tips to form a spoon shape.

C. 'Pavilion'
Habit Upright.
Flowers Fully double, spherical, to 7in (18cm) across, with loosely incurved petals, produced in early autumn. White.
• TIPS More suitable for exhibition than for garden use.
• HEIGHT 4½ft (1.35m).
• SPREAD 2–2½ft (60–75cm).

C. 'Pavilion'
(Intermediate, Early)

C. 'Cloudbank'
Habit Upright.
Flowers Single, anemone-centered, 3–3½in (8–9cm) across, with about 5 rows of flat petals, produced in late autumn. White.
• HEIGHT 4ft (1.2m)
• SPREAD 2½ft (75cm).

C. 'Cloudbank'
(Anemone-centered, Spray, Late)

C. 'Michael Fish'
Habit Upright.
Flowers Fully double, spherical, to 6in (15cm) across, with fairly tightly incurved petals, produced in early autumn. White.
• TIPS Suitable for exhibition.
• HEIGHT 4ft (1.2m).
• SPREAD 2–2½ft (60–75cm).

C. 'Michael Fish'
(Intermediate, Early)

C. 'Dawn Mist'
Habit Upright.
Flowers Single, 3–3½in (8–9cm) across, produced in early autumn. About 5 rows of flat, very pale pink petals, arranged around a golden-yellow disk.
• TIPS May not need lifting if kept dry.
• HEIGHT 4ft (1.2m).
• SPREAD 2½–3ft (75cm–1m).

C. 'Dawn Mist'
(Single, Spray, Early)

C. 'Pennine Oriel'
Habit Upright.
Flowers Single, 3½in (9cm) across, produced in early autumn. Creamy-white anemone-center, surrounded by about 5 rows of white petals with slightly incurved margins.
• TIPS May not need lifting if kept dry. Good for exhibition.
• HEIGHT 4ft (1.2m).
• SPREAD 2–2½ft (60–75cm).

C. 'Pennine Oriel'
(Anemone-centered, Spray, Early)

C. 'Alison Kirk'
Habit Upright.
Flowers Fully double, spherical, 5–6in (12–15cm) across, with incurved petals, in early autumn. Pure white.
• TIPS More suitable for exhibition than for garden use.
• HEIGHT 4ft (1.2m).
• SPREAD 1–2ft (30–60cm).

C. 'Alison Kirk'
(Incurved, Early)

C. 'Duke of Kent'
Habit Upright.
Flowers Fully double, to 10in (25cm) across, with almost fully reflexed petals, produced in late autumn. White.
• TIPS Suitable only for exhibition. Grow under cover. Needs warmth to flower.
• HEIGHT 5ft (1.5m).
• SPREAD 1ft (30cm).

C. 'Duke of Kent'
(Reflexed, Late)

Min. 50°F (10°C)

C. 'Salmon Fairweather'
Habit Upright.
Flowers Fully double, spherical, 5½–6in (14–15cm) across, with incurved petals, in late autumn. Pale salmon-pink.
• TIPS Suitable for exhibition. Grow under cover. Needs warmth to flower.
• HEIGHT 3–3½ft (1–1.1m).
• SPREAD to 2½ft (75cm).

C. 'Salmon Fairweather'
(Incurved, Late)

Min. 50°F (10°C)

C. 'Roblush'

Habit Upright. ***Flowers*** Fully double, to 3in (8cm) across, produced in late autumn. Pale pink, reflexed, petals with green-tinted centers.
- TIPS Good for exhibition. Grow under cover. Needs warmth to flower.
- HEIGHT 5ft (1.5m).
- SPREAD 2½–3ft (75–1m).

C. 'Roblush'
(Reflexed, Spray, Late)

Min. 50°F (10°C)

C. 'Marian Gosling'

Habit Upright. ***Flowers*** Fully double, to 5½in (14cm) across, with fully reflexed petals, produced in early autumn. Pale pink.
- TIPS Good for exhibition.
- HEIGHT 4–4½ft (1.2–1.35m).
- SPREAD 2ft (60cm).

C. 'Marian Gosling'
(Reflexed, Early)

C. 'Dorridge Dream'

Habit Upright. ***Flowers*** Fully double, spherical, 5in (12cm) across, with incurved petals, produced in early autumn. Rose-pink.
- TIPS Excellent for exhibition. Grow under cover. Needs warmth to flower.
- HEIGHT 4ft (1.2m).
- SPREAD 2ft (60cm).

C. 'Dorridge Dream'
(Incurved, Early)

Min. 50°F (10°C)

C. 'Madeleine'

Habit Upright. ***Flowers*** Fully double, 3in (8cm) across, with reflexed petals, produced in early autumn. Pink
- TIPS Good for exhibition. May not need lifting if kept dry.
- HEIGHT 4ft (1.2m).
- SPREAD 2½–3ft (75cm–1m).

C. 'Madeleine'
(Reflexed, Spray, Early)

C. 'Ringdove'

Habit Dome-forming. ***Flowers*** Single, to 1in (2.5cm) across, produced in late autumn. Deep pink petals, arranged around a greenish yellow disk.
- TIPS Excellent for exhibition. Grow under cover. Needs warmth to flower.
- HEIGHT 3ft (1m).
- SPREAD 3ft (1m).

C. 'Ringdove'
(Single, Cushion, Late)

Min. 50°F (10°C)

C. 'Brietner'

Habit Upright.
Flowers Fully double to 5in (12cm) across, produced in early autumn. Pink, reflexed petals giving a spiky outline.
• HEIGHT 3½–4ft (1.1–1.2m).
• SPREAD to 2½ft (75cm).

C. 'Brietner'
(Reflexed, Early)

C. 'Pennine Flute'

Habit Upright.
Flowers Fully double, 2½–3in (6–8cm) across in early autumn. Pink, very narrowly spoon-shaped petals around a greenish-yellow center. Similar to *C.* 'Pennine Jewel'
• TIPS May not need lifting if kept dry. Good for exhibition.
• HEIGHT 4ft (1.2m).
• SPREAD 2–2½ft (60–75cm).

C. 'Pennine Flute'
(Spoon-type, Spray, Early)

C. 'Talbot Jo'

Habit Upright.
Flowers Single, to 3in (8cm) across, Produced in early autumn. About 5 rows of flat, rich pink petals surrounding the greenish-gold disk.
• TIPS Good for exhibition. May not need lifting if kept dry.
• HEIGHT 5ft (1.5m).
• SPREAD 2½–3ft (75cm–1m).

C. 'Talbot Jo'
(Single, Spray, Early)

C. 'Chippendale'

Habit Upright.
Flowers Fully double, to 7in (18cm) across, with fully reflexed petals, produced in midautumn. Pink with paler reverse.
• TIPS Better suited to exhibition than for garden use.
• HEIGHT 4ft (1.2m).
• SPREAD 1½ft (45cm).

C. 'Chippendale'
(Reflexed, Mid-season)

C. 'Skater's Waltz'

Habit Upright.
Flowers Fully double, spherical, 6–7in (15–18cm) across, with loosely incurved petals, produced in early autumn. Deep pink with a paler reverse.
• TIPS Grow under cover. Needs warmth to flower.
• HEIGHT 5ft (1. 5m).
• SPREAD 2–2½ft (60–75cm).

C. 'Skater's Waltz'
(Intermediate, Early)

Min. 50°F (10°C)

C. 'Yvonne Arnaud'

Habit Upright.
Flowers Fully double, to 5in (12cm) across, with reflexed petals, produced in early autumn. Deep pinkish-purple.
• HEIGHT 4ft (1.2m).
• SPREAD 2–2½ft (60–75cm).

C. 'Yvonne Arnaud'
(Reflexed, Early)

C. 'Purple Pennine Wine'

Habit Upright.
Flowers Fully double, to 3in (8cm) across, with reflexed petals, produced in early autumn. Rich red-purple.
• TIPS Very good for exhibition. May not need lifting if kept dry.
• HEIGHT 4ft (1.2m).
• SPREAD 2–2½ft (60–75cm).

C. 'Purple Pennine Wine'
(Reflexed, Spray, Early)

C. 'Maria'

Habit Upright, compact.
Flowers Small, fully double, spherical, 1½in (4cm) across, with densely arranged, tubular petals that are flat at the tip, produced in early autumn. Pink.
• TIPS May not need lifting if kept dry.
• HEIGHT 1½ft (45cm).
• SPREAD 1–2ft (30–60cm).

C. 'Maria'
(Pompon, Early)

C. 'Cherry Chintz'
Habit Upright.
Flowers Fully double, to 6in (15cm) across, with fully reflexed petals, produced in early autumn. Red.
• TIPS Excellent for exhibition.
• HEIGHT 4ft (1.2m).
• SPREAD 1½ft (45cm).

C. 'Cherry Chintz'
(Reflexed, Early)

C. 'Rose Yvonne Arnaud'
Habit Upright.
Flowers Fully double, to 5in (12cm) across, with reflexed petals, produced in early autumn. Deep rose-pink. A sport of *C.* 'Yvonne Arnaud'.
• HEIGHT 4ft (1.2m).
• SPREAD 2–2½ft (60–75cm).

C. 'Rose Yvonne Arnaud'
(Reflexed, Early)

C. 'Sentry'
Habit Upright.
Flowers Fully double, to 5in (12cm) across, with fully reflexed petals, produced in early autumn. Red.
• TIPS Excellent for exhibition.
• HEIGHT 4–4½ft (1.2–1.35m).
• SPREAD 2–2½ft (0–75cm).

C. 'Sentry'
(Reflexed, Early)

C. 'George Griffiths'
Habit Upright.
Flowers Fully double, to 5½in (14cm) across, with fully reflexed petals, produced in early autumn. Dark red.
• TIPS Excellent for exhibition.
• HEIGHT 4–4½ft (1.2–1.35m).
• SPREAD 2½ft (75cm).

C. 'George Griffiths'
(Reflexed, Early)

C. 'Redwing'
Habit Upright.
Flowers Single, to 3in (8cm) across, produced in early autumn. About 5 rows of flat red petals, arranged around a golden yellow disk.
• TIPS Suitable for exhibition.
• HEIGHT 4–4½ft (1.2–1.35m).
• SPREAD 2ft (60cm).

C. 'Redwing'
(Single, Spray, Early)

C. 'Green Satin'
Habit Upright.
Flowers Fully double, loosely spherical, 5in (12cm) across, with loosely incurved petals, in late autumn. Green.
• TIPS Grow under cover. Needs warmth to flower.
• HEIGHT 4ft (1.2m).
• SPREAD 2ft (60cm).

C. 'Green Satin'
(Intermediate, Late)

Min. 50°F (10°C)

C. 'Marion'
Habit Upright.
Flowers Fully double, 3in (8cm) across, with reflexed petals, produced from late summer. Pale yellow.
• TIPS May not need lifting if kept dry.
• HEIGHT 4ft (1.2m).
• SPREAD 2½ft (75cm).

C. 'Marion'
(Reflexed, Spray, Early)

C. 'Discovery'
Habit Upright.
Flowers Fully double, loosely spherical, 4–5in (10–12cm) across, with loosely incurved petals, in early autumn. Pale yellow.
• HEIGHT 4ft (1.2m).
• SPREAD 2½ft (75cm).

C. 'Discovery'
(Intermediate, Early)

C. 'Marlene Jones'
Habit Upright.
Flowers Fully double, loosely spherical, to 5–5½in (12–14cm) across, with loosely incurved petals, in early autumn. Pale yellow.
• TIPS Good for exhibition. May not need lifting if kept dry.
• PROPAGATION
• HEIGHT 3ft (1m).
• SPREAD 2ft (60cm).

C. 'Marlene Jones'
(Intermediate, Early)

C. 'Yellow John Hughes'
Habit Upright.
Flowers Fully double, spherical, 5–5½in (12–14cm) across, with incurved petals, in late autumn. Yellow.
• TIPS Excellent for exhibition. Grow under cover. Needs warmth to flower.
• HEIGHT 4ft (1.2m).
• SPREAD 2–2½ft (60–75cm).

C. 'Yellow John Hughes'
(Incurved, Late)

Min. 50°F (10°C)

C. 'Primrose West Bromwich'
Habit Upright.
Flowers Fully double, to 7in (18cm) or more across, with fully reflexed petals, produced in midautumn. Pale yellow.
• TIPS Suitable only for exhibition.
• HEIGHT 7ft (2.2m)
• SPREAD 1½–2ft (45–60cm).

C. 'Primrose West Bromwich'
(Reflexed, Mid-season)

C. 'Edwin Painter'
Habit Upright.
Flowers Single, 5½in (14cm) across, produced in late autumn. About 5 rows of narrow, pointed, yellow petals, arranged around a central green disk.
• TIPS Grow under cover. Needs warmth to flower.
• HEIGHT 4½–5ft (1.35–1.5m).
• SPREAD 2½–3ft (75cm–1m).

C. 'Edwin Painter'
(Single, Late)

Min. 50°F (10°C)

C. 'Pennine Jewel'
Habit Upright.
Flowers Fully double 2½–3in (6–8cm) across, with narrowly spoon-shaped petals, produced in early autumn. Pale bronze petals arranged around a golden-bronze center.
• TIPS Suitable for exhibition. May not need lifting if kept dry.
• HEIGHT 4ft (1.2m).
• SPREAD 2–2½ft (60–75cm).

C. 'Pennine Jewel'
(Spoon-type, Spray Early)

C. 'Yellow Brietner'
Habit Upright.
Flowers Fully double, to 5in (12cm) across, with reflexed pètals giving a spiky outline, produced in early autumn. Yellow. A sport of *C.* 'Brietner'.
• HEIGHT 3½–4ft (1.1–1.2m).
• SPREAD 2½ft (75cm).

C. 'Yellow Brietner'
(Reflexed, Early)

C. 'Pennine Alfie'
Habit Upright.
Flowers Fully double, 2½–3in (6–8cm) across, in early autumn. Pale bronze, spoon-shaped, petals, darker at the base, arranged around a golden-bronze center.
• TIPS May not need lifting if kept dry.
• HEIGHT 4ft (1.2m).
• SPREAD 2–2½ft (60–75cm).

C. 'Pennine Alfie'
(Spoon-type, Spray, Early)

C. 'Golden Woolman's Glory'
Habit Upright.
Flowers Single, 7in (18cm) across, in late autumn. About 5 rows of narrow, pointed, deep golden-yellow petals, around a green disk.
• TIPS Excellent for exhibition. Grow under cover. Needs warmth to flower.
• HEIGHT 5ft (1.5m).
• SPREAD 3ft (1m).

C. 'Golden Woolman's Glory'
(Single, Late)

Min. 50°F (10°C)

C. 'Wendy'
Habit Upright.
Flowers Fully double, to 3in (8cm) across, produced in early autumn. Pale bronze, reflexed petals, darker towards the center.
• TIPS May not need lifting if kept dry.
• HEIGHT 4ft (1.2m).
• SPREAD 2–2½ft (60–75cm).

C. 'Wendy'
(Reflexed, Spray, Early)

C. 'Sally Ball'
Habit Upright.
Flowers Single, 3½in (9cm) across, produced in early autumn. About 5 rows of flattish bronze petals around a yellow-bronze anemone-center.
• TIPS Suitable for exhibition. May not need lifting if kept dry.
• HEIGHT 4ft (1.2m).
• SPREAD 2½ft (75cm).

C. 'Sally Ball'
(Anemone-centered, Spray, Early)

C. 'Bronze Fairie'
Habit Upright, compact. ***Flowers*** Small, fully double, spherical, 1½in (4cm) across, with densely arranged, tubular petals that are flat at the tip, produced in early autumn. Bronze.
• TIPS May not need lifting if kept dry.
• HEIGHT 2–2ft (30–60cm).
• SPREAD 2ft (60cm).

C. 'Bronze Fairie'
(Pompon, Early)

C. 'Bronze Yvonne Arnaud'
Habit Upright.
Flowers Fully double, to 5in (12cm) across, with reflexed petals, produced in early autumn. Bronze. A sport of *C.* 'Yvonne Arnaud'.
• HEIGHT 4ft (1.2m).
• SPREAD 2–2½ft (60–75cm).

C. 'Bronze Yvonne Arnaud'
(Reflexed, Early)

C. 'Salmon Fairie'
Habit Upright, compact.
Flowers Small, fully double, spherical, 1½in (4cm) across, with densely arranged, tubular petals that are flat at the tip, in early autumn. Salmon-orange. Similar to *C.* 'Bronze Fairie'.
• TIPS Grow under cover. Needs warmth to flower.
• HEIGHT 1–2ft (30–60cm).
• SPREAD 2ft (60cm).

C. 'Salmon Fairie'
(Pompon, Early)

Min. 50°F (10°C)

C. 'Rytorch'
Habit Upright.
Flowers Single, to 3in (8cm) across, in late autumn. About 5 rows of flat, bronze-red petals, with a ring of yellow surrounding the greenish-gold central disk.
• TIPS Good for exhibition. Grow under cover. Needs warmth to flower.
• HEIGHT 5ft (1.5m).
• SPREAD 2½–3ft (75cm–1m).

C. 'Rytorch'
(Single, Spray, Late)

Min. 50°F (10°C)

C. 'Bronze Hedgerow'
Habit Upright, robust.
Flowers Single, to 5in (12cm) across, produced in late autumn. Bronze, reflexed petals around a green central disk.
• TIPS Grow under cover. Needs warmth to flower.
• HEIGHT 5ft (1.5m).
• SPREAD 2½–3ft (75cm–1m).

C. 'Bronze Hedgerow'
(Single, Late)

Min. 50°F (10°C)

C. 'Peach Margaret'
Habit Upright.
Flowers Fully double, 3–3½in (8–9cm) across, with reflexed petals, produced in early autumn. Pale salmon-pink.
• TIPS Excellent for exhibition. May not need lifting if kept dry.
• HEIGHT 4ft (1.2m).
• SPREAD to 2½ft (75cm).

C. 'Peach Margaret'
(Reflexed, Spray, Early)

C. 'Peach Brietner'
Habit Upright.
Flowers Fully double, to 5in (12cm) across, with fully reflexed petals, giving a spiky outline, produced in early autumn. Peach-pink. A sport of C. 'Brietner'.
• HEIGHT 3½–4ft (1.1–1.2m).
• SPREAD to 2½ft (75cm).

C. 'Peach Brietner'
(Reflexed, Early)

C. 'Salmon Margaret'
Habit Upright.
Flowers Fully double, 3–3½in (8–9cm) across, with reflexed petals, produced in early autumn. Salmon. Similar form to C. 'Peach Margaret'.
• TIPS May not need lifting if kept dry.
• HEIGHT 4ft (2m).
• SPREAD to 2½ft (75cm).

C. 'Salmon Margaret'
(Reflexed, Spray, Early)

C. 'Autumn Days'
Habit Upright.
Flowers Fully double, loosely spherical, to 5in (12cm) across, with loosely incurved petals, in early autumn. Bronze.
• HEIGHT 3½–4ft (1.1–1.2m).
• SPREAD to 2½ft (75cm).

C. 'Autumn Days'
(Intermediate, Early)

C. 'Oracle'
Habit Upright.
Flowers Fully double, spherical, to 5in (12cm) across, with loosely incurved petals, produced in early autumn. Pale bronze
• TIPS Good for exhibition.
• HEIGHT 4ft (1.2m).
• SPREAD 2–2½ft (60–75cm).

C. 'Oracle'
(Intermediate, Early)

C. 'Buff Margaret'
Habit Upright.
Flowers Fully double, 3–3½in (8–9cm) across, with reflexed petals, produced in early autumn. Pale bronze. Similar form to C. 'Peach Margaret'.
• TIPS May not need lifting if kept dry.
• HEIGHT 4ft (1.2m).
• SPREAD to 2½ft (75cm).

C. 'Buff Margaret'
(Reflexed, Spray, Early)

ASTERS

Asters are invaluable late-flowering border plants, grown for their profusion of daisy-like flower heads. They provide a useful source of color in a late-summer or autumn display, and are generally good for cutting.

Grow in full sun or light shade in fertile, humus-rich, well-drained soil that remains reliably moist in summer. Provide twiggy or grow-through support for tall plants. Deadhead early-flowering cultivars.

Propagate by softwood cuttings in spring, or by division in spring or autumn. Some Asters, particularly modern cultivars of *A. novi-belgii*, are susceptible to powdery mildew. Where this is a problem treat the plants regularly with a fungicide, or choose resistant cultivars.

A. ERICOIDES
'White Heather'
Habit Bushy.
Flowers Very small, daisy-like, long-lasting, borne in branching, wiry-stemmed sprays in late autumn. White ray florets surrounding a yellow disk.
Leaves Small, lance-shaped. Fresh green.
- TIPS Needs unobtrusive staking.
- HEIGHT 30in (75cm).
- SPREAD 20in (50cm).

***A. ericoides* 'White Heather'**

Z 5–8

A. LATERIFLORUS
'Delight'
Habit Spreading.
Flowers Tiny, daisy-like, borne in dense sprays in autumn. White ray florets surrounding a central golden disk.
Leaves Small, narrowly lance-shaped. Dark green.
- TIPS Needs staking.
- HEIGHT 4ft (1.2m).
- SPREAD 3ft (1m).

***A. lateriflorus* 'Delight'**

Z 4–8

A. NOVAE-ANGLIAE
'Herbstschnee'
Habit Vigorous, upright.
Flowers Daisy-like, single, borne in clusters in autumn. White with yellow centers.
Leaves Rough, lance-shaped. Dull green.
- TIPS May need staking.
- OTHER NAMES *A.* 'Autumn Snow'.
- HEIGHT 2½–3½ft (75cm–1.1m).
- SPREAD to 2ft (60cm).

***A. novae-angliae* 'Herbstschnee'**

Z 4–8

A. NOVI-BELGII
'White Swan'
Habit Vigorous, spreading.
Flowers Large, daisy-like, double, borne in dense sprays in autumn. Pure white ray florets.
Leaves Lance-shaped. Mid-green.
- TIPS May need staking.
- HEIGHT 4ft (1.2m).
- SPREAD 24in (60cm).

***A. novi-belgii* 'White Swan'**

Z 4–8

A. CORDIFOLIUS
'Silver Spray'
Habit Lax, bushy, upright.
Flowers Small, daisy-like, borne in airy sprays in autumn. Pink-tinged white ray florets, around a yellow disk.
Leaves Lance-shaped. Mid-green.
• TIPS Needs staking.
• HEIGHT 4ft (1.2m).
• SPREAD 3ft (1m).

A. cordifolius **'Silver Spray'**

☼ ◊ Z 5

A. LATERIFLORUS
'Horizontalis'
Habit Freely branching.
Flowers Tiny, borne in branching sprays in autumn. White, sometimes pink-tinted, ray florets surrounding a darker pink disk.
Leaves Small, lance-shaped. Dark green.
• HEIGHT 24in (60cm).
• SPREAD 20in (50cm).

A. lateriflorus **'Horizontalis'**

☼ ◊ Z 4–8

A. NOVI-BELGII
'Apple Blossom'
Habit Vigorous, spreading.
Flowers Daisy-like, single, borne in dense heads in autumn. Soft pale pink ray florets around a tiny yellow disk.
Leaves Lance-shaped. Mid-green.
• HEIGHT 3ft (90cm)
• SPREAD 24–30in (60–75cm).

A. novi-belgii **'Apple Blossom'**

☼ ◊ Z 4–8

A. NOVAE-ANGLIAE
'Harrington's Pink'
Habit Vigorous, upright.
Flowers Daisy-like, single, borne in profuse clusters in autumn. Bright, clear pink ray florets around a yellow disk.
Leaves Rough-textured, lance-shaped. Mid-green.
• TIPS May need staking.
• HEIGHT 4–5ft (1.2–1.5m).
• SPREAD 24in (60cm).

A. novae-angliae **'Harrington's Pink'**

☼ ◊ Z 4–8

A. NOVI-BELGII
'Lassie'
Habit Vigorous, spreading.
Flowers Large, daisy-like, single, borne in dense clusters in autumn. Clear pink ray florets, surrounding a golden central disk.
Leaves Lance-shaped. Mid-green.
• TIPS May need staking.
• HEIGHT 4ft (1.2m).
• SPREAD 30in (75cm).

A. novi-belgii **'Lassie'**

☼ ◊ Z 4–8

A. NOVAE-ANGLIAE
'Barr's Pink'
Habit Vigorous, upright.
Flowers Daisy-like, semi-double, borne in profuse clusters in late summer and autumn. Bright, rose-pink ray florets around a dark pinkish-yellow disk.
Leaves Rough-textured, lance-shaped. Mid-green.
• TIPS May need staking.
• HEIGHT 30in (75cm).
• SPREAD 24in (60cm).

A. novae-angliae **'Barr's Pink'**

☼ ◊ Z 4–8

A. NOVI-BELGII
'Carnival'
Habit Vigorous, spreading.
Flowers Daisy-like, double, borne in dense clusters in autumn. Cerise-red ray florets obscure the central disk.
Leaves Lance-shaped. Dark green.
• HEIGHT 30in (75cm).
• SPREAD to 18in (45cm).

A. novi-belgii **'Carnival'**

☼ ◊ Z 4–8

A. NOVI-BELGII 'Royal Ruby'

Habit Vigorous, low-growing.
Flowers Large, daisy-like, semi-double, borne in dense clusters in autumn. Rich red ray florets, surrounding a yellow disk.
Leaves Lance-shaped. Mid-green.
- HEIGHT 18in (45cm).
- SPREAD 18in (45cm).

A. novi-belgii 'Royal Ruby'

Z 4–8

A. NOVI-BELGII 'Freda Ballard'

Habit Vigorous, spreading.
Flowers Daisy-like, semi-double, borne in dense clusters in autumn. Rich rose-red ray florets, surrounding a golden central disk.
Leaves Lance-shaped. Mid-green.
- TIPS May need staking.
- HEIGHT 4ft (1.2m).
- SPREAD 20in (50cm).

A. novi-belgii 'Freda Ballard'

Z 4–8

A. × *FRIKARTII* 'Mönch'

Habit Bushy.
Flowers Daisy-like, single, produced in profusion from late summer to autumn. Soft lavender-blue ray florets surrounding a greenish-yellow central disk.
Leaves Rough-textured, oblong. Dark green.
- HEIGHT 30in (75cm).
- SPREAD 18in (45cm).

A. × *frikartii* 'Mönch'

Z 5–8

A. NOVI-BELGII 'Fellowship'

Habit Vigorous, spreading.
Flowers Large, daisy-like, double, borne in dense clusters in autumn. Clear deep pink ray florets.
Leaves Lance-shaped. Mid-green.
- TIPS May need staking.
- HEIGHT 4ft (1.2m).
- SPREAD 20in (50cm).

A. novi-belgii 'Fellowship'

Z 4–8

A. NOVI-BELGII 'Patricia Ballard'

Habit Vigorous, spreading.
Flowers Large, daisy-like, semi-double, borne in dense heads in autumn. Pink ray florets, surrounding a small golden disk.
Leaves Lance-shaped. Mid-green.
- TIPS May need staking.
- HEIGHT 4ft (1.2m).
- SPREAD 30in (75cm).

A. novi-belgii 'Patricia Ballard'

Z 4–8

A. NOVI-BELGII 'Orlando'

Habit Vigorous, spreading.
Flowers Large, daisy-like, single, borne in dense clusters in autumn. Bright pink ray florets, surrounding a golden central disk.
Leaves Lance-shaped. Dark green.
- HEIGHT to 3ft (1m).
- SPREAD to 18in (45cm).

A. novi-belgii 'Orlando'

Z 4–8

A. NOVAE-ANGLIAE 'Andenken an Alma Pötschke'

Habit Vigorous, upright.
Flowers Single, daisy-like, in clusters, in autumn. Bright cerise ray florets around a yellow disk.
Leaves Rough-textured, lance-shaped. Mid-green.
- OTHER NAMES *A.* 'Alma Potschke'.
- TIPS May need staking.
- HEIGHT 30in (75cm).
- SPREAD 24in (60cm).

A. novae-angliae 'Andenken an Alma Pötschke'

Z 4–8

A. NOVI-BELGII 'Jenny'

Habit Vigorous, spreading.
Flowers Daisy-like, double, borne in dense clusters, in autumn. Red ray florets, surrounding a dark red central disk.
Leaves Lance-shaped. Mid-green.
- HEIGHT 18in (45cm).
- SPREAD 12in (30cm).

A. novi-belgii 'Jenny'

Z 4–8

A. THOMSONII 'Nanus'

Habit Compact, upright.
Flowers Single, with slender, pointed ray florets. Pale lilac with a central yellow disk.
Leaves Oval, coarsely toothed. Mid-green.
• TIPS Suitable for a border front or large rock garden.
• HEIGHT 18in (45cm).
• SPREAD 9in (23cm)

A. thomsonii 'Nanus'

Z 4–9

A. NOVI-BELGII 'Marie Ballard'

Habit Vigorous, spreading.
Flowers Large, daisy-like, single, borne in dense clusters in autumn. Clear pink ray florets surrounding a golden central disk.
Leaves Lance-shaped. Mid-green.
• HEIGHT to 3ft (1m).
• SPREAD to 18in (45cm).

A. novi-belgii 'Marie Ballard'

Z 4–8

A. TURBINELLUS

Habit Upright.
Flowers Small, single, daisy-like, produced in autumn. Pale violet ray florets surrounding a central yellow disk.
Leaves Narrowly lance-shaped. Mid-green.
• TIPS Disease-resistant and easy to grow.
• HEIGHT 4ft (1.2m).
• SPREAD 2ft (60cm).

A. turbinellus

Z 4–8

A. × FRIKARTII 'Wunder von Stäfa'

Habit Bushy.
Flowers Daisy-like, single, produced in profusion from late summer to autumn. Lavender ray florets, surrounding a greenish-yellow central disk.
Leaves Rough-textured, oblong, dark green.
• HEIGHT 30in (75cm).
• SPREAD 18in (45cm).

A. × frikartii 'Wunder von Stäfa'

Z 5–8

A. NOVI-BELGII 'Professor Anton Kippenburg'

Habit Bushy, compact.
Flowers Daisy-like, borne in large clusters in autumn. Yellow disk florets surrounded by clear blue ray florets.
Leaves Narrowly lance-shaped. Mid-green.
• HEIGHT 12in (30cm).
• SPREAD 18in (45cm).

A. novi-belgii 'Professor Anton Kippenburg'

Z 4–8

A. AMELLUS
'King George'
Habit Bushy.
Flowers Large, terminal, daisy-like, produced in autumn. Deep violet-blue ray florets around a central golden disk.
Leaves Rough, hairy, lance-shaped to oval. Mid-green.
• HEIGHT 20in (50cm).
• SPREAD 20in (50cm).

A. amellus 'King George'

Z 5–8

A. NOVI-BELGII
'Royal Velvet'
Habit Vigorous, spreading. ***Flowers*** Large, daisy-like, single-double, borne in dense clusters in autumn. Rich deep violet ray florets, surrounding a yellow disk.
Leaves Lance-shaped. Mid-green.
• TIPS May need staking.
• HEIGHT 4ft (1.2m).
• SPREAD 30in (75cm).

A. novi-belgii 'Royal Velvet'

Z 4–8

A. NOVI-BELGII
'Peace'
Habit Vigorous, spreading.
Flowers Large, daisy-like, single, borne in dense clusters in autumn. Mauve ray florets, surrounding a golden disk.
Leaves Lance-shaped. Mid-green.
• TIPS May need staking.
• HEIGHT 4ft (1.2m).
• SPREAD 30in (75cm).

A. novi-belgii 'Peace'

Z 4–8

A. NOVI-BELGII
'Chequers'
Habit Vigorous, spreading.
Flowers Daisy-like, single, borne in dense clusters in autumn. Purple ray florets around a golden-yellow disk.
Leaves Lance-shaped. Mid-green.
• HEIGHT 3ft (90cm).
• SPREAD 24–30in (60–75cm).

A. novi-belgii 'Chequers'

Z 4–8

A. LINOSYRIS
Habit Upright, with unbranched stems.
Flowers Small, in wiry-stemmed clusters, in late summer and autumn. Golden-yellow. An unusual aster with the disk florets forming the flowers rather than the ray florets.
Leaves Narrowly lance-shaped. Mid-green.
• OTHER NAMES *A. linosyris* 'Goldilocks'.
• HEIGHT 24in (60cm).
• SPREAD 12in (30cm).

A. linosyris 'Goldilocks'

Z 4–8

Acanthaceae	

STROBILANTHES ATROPURPUREUS

Habit Upright, clump-forming. ***Flowers*** Curved, tubular, borne in many-flowered spikes, on branching stems, from summer to autumn. Dark violet-blue to purple. ***Leaves*** Soft, serrated, oval, long-stalked. Mid-green or yellowish-green.

• NATIVE HABITAT Scrub and forests, Himalayas.

• CULTIVATION Grow in fertile, moist but well-drained soil, in partial shade, or in sun where soils remain reliably moist. Shelter from strong winds.

• PROPAGATION By seed, basal stem cuttings, or division in spring.

Z 11

HEIGHT to 4ft (1.2m)

SPREAD to 2ft (60cm)

Gentianaceae	WILLOW GENTIAN

GENTIANA ASCLEPIADEA

Habit Arching, clump-forming. ***Flowers*** Trumpet-shaped, borne in pairs in the leaf axils, towards the ends of arching stems, in late summer and autumn. Dark blue, spotted and striped on the inside. ***Leaves*** Lance-shaped. Fresh green.

• NATIVE HABITAT Woods and mountain meadows, from Europe to Turkey.

• CULTIVATION Grow in fertile, reliably moist, humus-rich, soil, in sun or partial shade.

• PROPAGATION By division in spring, or seed in autumn.

Z 6–9

HEIGHT to 3ft (90cm)

SPREAD to 2ft (60cm)

Asphodelaceae/Liliaceae	

KNIPHOFIA 'Percy's Pride'

Habit Upright, clump-forming. ***Flowers*** Small, narrowly tubular, borne on thick, upright stems in dense, narrow, terminal spikes, in autumn. Cream, tinted green or yellow. ***Leaves*** Tough, narrow, linear, arching to form dense basal clumps. Mid-green.

• NATIVE HABITAT Garden origin.

• CULTIVATION Grow in full sun, in damp, but well-drained soil. Needs ample moisture when in growth. Protect crowns in winter in cold areas.

• PROPAGATION By division in spring.

Z 6–9

HEIGHT 3ft (1m)

SPREAD 20in (50cm)

Hydrangeaceae

KIRENGESHOMA PALMATA

Habit Upright, clump-forming, rhizomatous. ***Flowers*** Narrowly funnel-shaped, with fleshy petals, borne in slender-stalked clusters in the upper leaf axils, in late summer and autumn. Creamy-yellow. ***Leaves*** Divided into shallow, irregular, pointed lobes. Bright green.

- NATIVE HABITAT Mountain woodlands, Japan.
- CULTIVATION Grow in moist, humus-rich soil in partial shade. An exceptionally graceful plant for an herbaceous or mixed border, or woodland garden.
- PROPAGATION Seed or division in autumn or spring.

Z 5–8

HEIGHT 3ft (1m)

SPREAD 2ft (60cm)

Asphodelaceae/Liliaceae

KNIPHOFIA CAULESCENS

Habit Upright, clump-forming. ***Flowers*** Small, narrowly tubular, borne on upright stems in dense, terminal spikes, in autumn. Yellow, opening from salmon-red buds. ***Leaves*** Evergreen, tough, linear, forming basal clumps. Blue-green.

- NATIVE HABITAT In peaty niches among damp rocks, in the mountains of South Africa.
- CULTIVATION Grow in full sun, in damp but well-drained soil. Needs ample moisture when in growth. Protect crowns in winter in cold areas.
- PROPAGATION By seed or division in spring.

Z 6–9

HEIGHT 4ft (1.2m)

SPREAD 2ft (60cm)

Asteraceae/Compositae

HELENIUM 'Wyndley'

Habit Bushy, branching, clump-forming. ***Flowers*** Large, daisy-like, produced over long periods in late summer and autumn. Reflexed, red-streaked, coppery-yellow ray florets around a rounded, brown disk. ***Leaves*** Lance-shaped. Dark green.

- NATIVE HABITAT Garden origin.
- CULTIVATION Easily grown in almost any but waterlogged soil, in full sun. A valuable long-flowering plant for the late summer border. Divide and replant regularly to maintain vigor.
- PROPAGATION By division in spring or autumn.

Z 4–8

HEIGHT 24–30in (60–75cm)

SPREAD 20in (50cm)

Asphodelaceae/Liliaceae

KNIPHOFIA 'Atlanta'

Habit Upright, clump-forming. ***Flowers*** Small, tubular, borne on thick, upright stems in dense, terminal spikes, in early autumn. Deep orange-red and pale yellow. ***Leaves*** Grass-like, linear, arching to form basal clumps. Mid-green.

- NATIVE HABITAT Garden origin.
- CULTIVATION Grow in full sun, in damp but well-drained soil. Needs ample moisture when in growth. Protect crowns in cold winter areas. Well-suited to coastal gardens.
- PROPAGATION By division in spring.

Z 6–9

HEIGHT to 3ft (1m)

SPREAD 18in (45cm)

Asphodelaceae/Liliaceae

KNIPHOFIA TRIANGULARIS

Habit Upright, clump-forming. ***Flowers*** Small, narrowly tubular, borne on upright stems in short terminal spikes, in autumn. Coral-orange. ***Leaves*** Narrow, linear, forming basal clumps. Mid-green.

- NATIVE HABITAT Damp, peaty grasslands in the mountains of South Africa.
- CULTIVATION Grow in full sun, in damp but well-drained soil. Needs ample moisture when in growth. Protect crowns in winter in cold areas.
- PROPAGATION By seed or division in spring.
- OTHER NAMES *K. galpinii* of gardens.

Z 6–9

HEIGHT
4ft (1.2m)

SPREAD
2ft (60cm)

Lamiaceae/Labiatae

SALVIA CONFERTIFLORA

Habit Upright, woody-based. ***Flowers*** Tubular, 2-lipped, downy, in long, simple racemes, in late summer and autumn. Rich orange-vermilion. ***Leaves*** Large, oval, pointed. Bright green, clothed in tawny down beneath.

- NATIVE HABITAT Brazil.
- CULTIVATION Grow under glass in well-drained potting mix, or in full sun outdoors in a warm, sheltered site. Good for tubs in a cool sunroom.
- PROPAGATION By seed in spring or softwood cuttings in summer.

Z 9–11

HEIGHT
to 5ft (1.5m)

SPREAD
2ft (60cm)

Asteraceae/Compositae

HELENIUM 'Moerheim Beauty'

Habit Upright, clump-forming. ***Flowers*** Large, daisy-like, borne on strong stems, in early autumn. Rich, dark orange-red ray florets surrounding a rounded, brown disk. ***Leaves*** Lance-shaped. Dark green.

- NATIVE HABITAT Garden origin.
- CULTIVATION Easily grown in almost any soil unless waterlogged, in full sun. A valuable long-flowering plant for a late summer border. Divide and replant regularly to maintain vigor.
- PROPAGATION By division in spring or autumn.

Z 4–8

HEIGHT
3ft (1m)

SPREAD
2ft (60cm)

Marantaceae	NEVER-NEVER PLANT

CTENANTHE OPPENHEIMIANA 'Tricolor'

Habit Vigorous, bushy. ***Flowers*** Small, 3-petaled, borne in spikes, produced intermittently. White. ***Leaves*** Evergreen, leathery, lance-shaped. Green, irregularly blotched with creamy-white.

• NATIVE HABITAT Garden origin.

• CULTIVATION Grow as a house or greenhouse plant in cool climates in moist, humus-rich, well-drained soil. Keep soil mix moist with tepid, soft water. Maintain even temperatures and humidity.

• PROPAGATION By division in spring.

Min. 59°F (15°C)

HEIGHT 3ft (1m)

SPREAD 3ft (1m)

Araceae	CRYSTAL ANTHURIUM

ANTHURIUM CRYSTALLINUM

Habit Erect, tufted. ***Flowers*** Long-lasting, intermittent. Red-purple spathes, with a green spadix. ***Leaves*** Evergreen, to 18in (45cm) long and 12in (30cm) wide, heart-shaped at the base. Velvety, dark green, with white or pale green veins.

• NATIVE HABITAT Tropical forest, Panama to Peru.

• CULTIVATION Grow as a house or greenhouse plant in cool climates, in well-drained, peaty soil. Give bright light in winter; indirect sun in summer. Water freely in growth and maintain high humidity.

• PROPAGATION By division in spring.

Min. 59°F (15°C)

HEIGHT 30in (75cm)

SPREAD 24in (60cm)

Lamiaceae/Labiatae	

PLECTRANTHUS FORSTERI 'Marginatus'

Habit Bushy, or semi-trailing. ***Flowers*** Small, tubular, borne irregularly. White to pale mauve. ***Leaves*** Aromatic, oval, 2½in (6 cm) long. Gray-green with scalloped, creamy-white margins.

• NATIVE HABITAT Garden origin.

• CULTIVATION Grow as a house or greenhouse plant in cool climates, in moist soil, in sun or partial shade. Water and fertilize regularly in growth.

• PROPAGATION By stem cuttings or division in spring or summer.

• OTHER NAMES *P. coleoides* 'Marginatus'.

Min. 50°F (10°C)

HEIGHT 2ft (60cm)

SPREAD 2ft (60cm)

Acanthaceae	FRECKLE FACE, POLKA-DOT PLANT

HYPOESTES PHYLLOSTACHYA

Habit Bushy, sub-shrubby. ***Flowers*** Small, tubular, intermittent. Lavender. ***Leaves*** Evergreen, oval, softly downy. Dark green, with irregular pink spots.

• NATIVE HABITAT South Africa, Madagascar, S.E. Asia.

• CULTIVATION Grow as a house or greenhouse plant in cool climates, in fertile, well-drained soil in bright light. Water freely when in full growth.

• PROPAGATION By seed in spring or stem cuttings in spring or summer.

• OTHER NAMES *H. sanguinolenta* of gardens.

Min. 50°F (10°C)

HEIGHT 30in (75cm)

SPREAD 30in (75cm)

Araceae	

CALADIUM BICOLOR 'Pink Beauty'

Habit Tufted, tuberous-rooted. ***Flowers*** Tubular white spathes are produced in summer. ***Leaves*** Long-stalked, triangular. Dark green, mottled pink, with darker pink veins.

• NATIVE HABITAT Garden origin.

• CULTIVATION Grow as a house or greenhouse plant in cool climates, in moist, humus-rich soil. Give bright light in winter; indirect sun in summer. Water freely in growth and maintain humidity. When leaves die, store tubers in a dark, frost-free place.

• PROPAGATION By tubers when repotting in spring.

Min. 66°F (19°C)

HEIGHT 3ft (90cm)

SPREAD 3ft (90cm)

Araceae	FLAMINGO FLOWER, TAIL FLOWER

ANTHURIUM ANDREANUM

Habit Erect. ***Flowers*** Long-lasting, produced intermittently. Bright red spathes with a red-tipped, yellow spadix. ***Leaves*** Evergreen, long-stalked, broadly oval, heart-shaped at the base. Dark green.

• NATIVE HABITAT Forest, Colombia, Ecuador.

• CULTIVATION Grow as a house or greenhouse plant in cool climates, in moist, well-drained, peaty soil. Provide bright light in winter and indirect sun in summer. Water freely when in growth and maintain high humidity.

• PROPAGATION By division in spring.

Min. 59°F (15°C)

HEIGHT 24–30in (60–75cm)

SPREAD 20in (50cm)

Lamiaceae/Labiatae	

SALVIA ELEGANS

Habit Upright, woody-based. ***Flowers*** Tubular, 2-lipped, in loose, branched racemes, in winter and spring. Scarlet. ***Leaves*** Oval to diamond-shaped, smooth or slightly downy. Mid-green.

• NATIVE HABITAT Mexico, Guatemala.

• CULTIVATION Grow in fertile, well-drained potting mix, under glass, or in similar soils outdoors, in full sun. Needs a warm, sheltered site. Good for tubs in a cool sunroom.

• PROPAGATION By seed in spring or softwood cuttings in summer.

Z 11

HEIGHT 5ft (1.5m) or more

SPREAD 2ft (60cm)

Nepenthaceae	

NEPENTHES × *HOOKERIANA*

Habit Epiphytic, insectivorous. ***Flowers*** Pendent, pitcher-shaped, to 5in (13cm) long, with a spurred lid, long-lasting. Pale green, marked red-purple. ***Leaves*** Evergreen, lance-shaped. Dark green.

• NATIVE HABITAT Tropical forest, S.E. Asia.

• CULTIVATION Grow as a house or greenhouse plant in cool climates in lattice pots,in a damp mix of bark, perlite and peat moss. Maintain humidity.

• PROPAGATION By seed in spring, or stem cuttings in spring or summer.

• OTHER NAMES *N. rafflesiana* × *ampullaria*.

Min. 64°F (18°C)

HEIGHT 24–30in (60–75cm)

SPREAD 24–30in (60–75cm)

Agavaceae

PHORMIUM 'Dazzler'

Habit Upright, clump-forming. ***Flowers*** Tubular, in large panicles, to 15ft (5m) high, in summer. Dark red, borne on blue-purple stems. ***Leaves*** Evergreen, stiff, sword-shaped, to 6ft (2m) long, in basal clumps. Striped yellow, salmon-pink, orange-red, and bronze.

• NATIVE HABITAT Garden origin.

• CULTIVATION Grow in deep, fertile, humus-rich soil, in a warm, sunny, sheltered site. Excellent for coastal gardens and scree plantings. This cultivar combines a strongly architectural outline with brilliantly colored foliage. It is invaluable as an accent plant in an herbaceous or mixed border, providing strong contrasts of form against other more softly rounded shapes. It is also useful as a free-standing specimen plant in a courtyard or similar situation. Provide a dry winter mulch in very cold areas.

• PROPAGATION By division in spring.

☼ 💧

Z 9–10

HEIGHT
6–8ft
(2–2.5m)

SPREAD
3ft (1m)

Solanaceae	BUSH VIOLET

BROWALLIA SPECIOSA

Habit Bushy. ***Flowers*** Five-lobed, borne in profusion in summer or winter. Violet-blue with white eyes. ***Leaves*** Oval, pointed. Bright green.
• NATIVE HABITAT Tropical South America.
• CULTIVATION Grow as a house or greenhouse plant in cool climates, in well-drained soil mix or soil, in sun or partial shade. Keep moist and feed when in flower. Encourage bushiness by pinching out young shoots. Often grown as a bedding annual.
• PROPAGATION By seed in spring or, for winter flowers, in late summer.

Min. 50–59°F (10–15°C)

HEIGHT 24–30in (60–75cm)

SPREAD 18in (45cm)

Araceae	TANNIA

XANTHOSOMA SAGITTIFOLIUM

Habit Spreading, tufted, tuberous-rooted. ***Flowers*** Green spathes, to 8in (20cm) long, are produced intermittently. ***Leaves*** Broadly arrow-shaped, to 2ft (60cm) long. Glaucous, grayish-green.
• NATIVE HABITAT Cultivated for edible tubers in New World tropics, but natural range unknown.
• CULTIVATION Grow as a house or greenhouse plant in cool climates in moist, well-drained soil or potting mix, in partial shade. Maintain humidity.
• PROPAGATION By division or stem cuttings in spring or summer.

Min. 59°F (15°C)

HEIGHT to 6ft (2m) in flower

SPREAD 6ft (2m) or more

Araceae	

ALOCASIA CUPREA

Habit Upright, tufted, rhizomatous. ***Flowers*** Purple spathes produced intermittently. ***Leaves*** Oval, 12in (30cm) long, heart-shaped at base. Metallic, purple-green above, purple beneath.
• NATIVE HABITAT Tropical forest, Malaysia, Borneo.
• CULTIVATION Grow as a house or greenhouse plant in cool climates, in partial shade, with high humidity, in a mix of ground bark, soil, sharp sand, and charcoal.
• PROPAGATION By seed, stem cuttings, or division of the rhizomes in spring.

Min. 59°F (15°C)

HEIGHT to 3ft (1m)

SPREAD to 3ft (1m)

Asteraceae/Compositae	SILVER KING

ARTEMISIA LUDOVICIANA var. *ALBULA*

Habit Upright, bushy, stoloniferous. ***Flowers*** Tiny, in slender plumes, in summer. Gray-white. ***Leaves*** Evergreen, variable: entire and lance-shaped, or jaggedly toothed and broadly oval to elliptic. Silvery-white, densely hairy.
• NATIVE HABITAT Dry grassland, or light woodland, California, US.
• CULTIVATION Grow in an open, sunny site, in well-drained soil. Cut back in spring for best foliage effects. Indispensable in a silver border.
• PROPAGATION By division in spring or autumn.

Z 4–9

HEIGHT 4ft (1.2m)

SPREAD 2ft (60cm)

Gesneriaceae

COLUMNEA MICROPHYLLA VARIEGATA

Habit Trailing. ***Flowers*** Tubular, hooded, borne singly in the leaf axils, in winter and spring. Scarlet, with yellow throats. ***Leaves*** Evergreen, oval to rounded. Gray-green, edged cream, often red-flushed beneath.

• NATIVE HABITAT Garden origin.

• CULTIVATION In cool climates, grow as a house or greenhouse plant in moist, well-drained soil or potting mix. Needs humidity and bright, indirect light. Keep drier in winter. Good in hanging baskets.

• PROPAGATION By tip cuttings after flowering.

Min. 59°F (15°C)

HEIGHT 3ft (1m) or more

SPREAD indefinite

Apiaceae/Umbelliferae | BAYONET PLANT, COMMON SPANIARD

ACIPHYLLA SQUARROSA

Habit Rosette-forming. ***Flowers*** Small, scented, in large, branching, candelabra-like spikes, to 6ft (2m) tall, in early summer. Yellow. ***Leaves*** Evergreen, rigid, bayonet-like, to 28in (70cm) long. Green or golden-green.

• NATIVE HABITAT Sub-alpine and mountain grassland, North and South Island, New Zealand.

• CULTIVATION Grow in full sun, in humus-rich, well-drained soil. Excellent architectural form, especially useful for planting in scree.

• PROPAGATION By seed sown fresh, or in spring.

Z 10

HEIGHT 3–4ft (1–1.2m)

SPREAD 3–4ft (1–1.2m)

Asparagaceae/Liliaceae

ASPARAGUS DENSIFLORUS 'Sprengeri'

Habit Trailing, tuberous-rooted. ***Flowers*** Inconspicuous, borne in clusters in the leaf axils, in summer. Pink-tinted, white. ***Fruits*** Small, bright red berries, to ½in (1cm) across. ***Leaves*** Evergreen, small, flat, linear, leaf-like stems. Bright green.

• NATIVE HABITAT South Africa.

• CULTIVATION Grow as a house or greenhouse plant in cool climates, in fertile, moist but well-drained soil or potting mix. Position in partial shade, or in bright, indirect light.

• PROPAGATION By seed or division in spring.

Min. 50°F (10°C)

HEIGHT to 3ft (1m)

SPREAD 20in (50cm)

Asparagaceae/Liliaceae	

ASPARAGUS DENSIFLORUS 'Myers'

Habit Upright, tuberous-rooted. ***Flowers*** Inconspicuous, borne in axillary clusters in summer. Pink-tinted, white. ***Fruits*** Small, bright red berries, to ½in (1cm) across. ***Leaves*** Evergreen, needle-like, borne in dense, cylindrical spikes. Dark green.

• NATIVE HABITAT Garden origin.

• CULTIVATION Grow as a house or greenhouse plant in cool climates. Place in fertile, moist but well-drained soil or potting mix. Position in partial shade, or in bright, indirect light.

• PROPAGATION By seed or division in spring.

Min. 50°F (10°C)

HEIGHT to 3ft (1m)

SPREAD 20in (50cm)

Acanthaceae	MARBLE LEAF

PERISTROPHE HYSSOPIFOLIA 'Aureovariegata'

Habit Bushy, sub-shrubby. ***Flowers*** Small, long-tubed, 2-lipped, in clusters, in winter. Rose-pink. ***Leaves*** Evergreen, lance-shaped, pointed. Dark green with a central, creamy-yellow blotch.

• NATIVE HABITAT Garden origin.

• CULTIVATION Grow as a house or greenhouse plant in cool climates, in well-drained soil or potting mix. Place in sun or partial shade. Water freely in growth, less in winter. Attractive foliage plant.

• PROPAGATION Stem cuttings in spring or summer.

Min. 59°F (15°C)

HEIGHT to 2ft (60cm) or more

SPREAD 4ft (1.2m)

Zingiberaceae	

GLOBBA WINITII

Habit Clump-forming, rhizomatous. ***Flowers*** Small, tubular, in pendent sprays, intermittently. Yellow, with large, reflexed, red-purple bracts. ***Leaves*** Evergreen, lance-shaped, heart-shaped at the base. Mid-green and slightly hairy beneath.

• NATIVE HABITAT Thailand.

• CULTIVATION Grow as a house or greenhouse plant in cool climates, in moist, well-drained, humus-rich soil or potting mix. Maintain humidity; water freely in growth, less when dormant in winter.

• PROPAGATION By division or seed in spring.

Min. 64°F (18°C)

HEIGHT 3ft (1m)

SPREAD 1ft (30cm)

Strelitziaceae	BIRD-OF-PARADISE FLOWER

STRELITZIA REGINAE

Habit Clump-forming, palm-like. ***Flowers*** Short-stemmed, beak-like, borne mainly in spring. Orange and blue, enclosed in a boat-shaped, red-edged bract. ***Leaves*** Evergreen, long-stalked, oblong, to 28in (70cm) long. Bluish-green.

• NATIVE HABITAT South Africa.

• CULTIVATION Grow as a greenhouse or house plant in cool climates, in fertile, well-drained soil or potting mix. Place in good light, but shade from hot sun. Water freely in growth, sparingly in winter.

• PROPAGATION By seed or suckers in spring.

Min. 41–50°F (5–10°C)

HEIGHT 3ft (1m) or more

SPREAD 30in (75cm)

Berberidaceae

EPIMEDIUM x *YOUNGIANUM* 'Niveum'

Habit Compact, clump-forming. ***Flowers*** Small, cup-shaped, with or without spurs, borne in loose, branched clusters of 4–12, in late spring. White. ***Leaves*** Divided into 2–9 heart-shaped, serrated leaflets. Bright green, bronze on emergence.

- NATIVE HABITAT Garden origin.
- CULTIVATION Grow in moist but well-drained, humus-rich soil, in partial shade. Provides good ground cover in a damp, shady border. Cut away old foliage in late winter.
- PROPAGATION By division in spring or autumn.

Z 5–8

HEIGHT 6–12in (15–30cm)

SPREAD 12in (30cm)

Boraginaceae

PULMONARIA OFFICINALIS 'Sissinghurst White'

Habit Neat, clump-forming. ***Flowers*** Funnel-shaped, borne in terminal clusters in spring. Pure white. ***Leaves*** Semi-evergreen, long, elliptic. Mid-green with paler spotting.

- NATIVE HABITAT Garden origin.
- CULTIVATION Grow in fertile, humus-rich, moist but well-drained soil, in shade or partial shade. Excellent for a woodland garden or shady border, especially beneath shrubs or trees.
- PROPAGATION By division in spring or autumn.

Z 4–8

HEIGHT 12in (30cm)

SPREAD 18–24in (45–60cm)

Lamiaceae/Labiatae

LAMIUM MACULATUM 'White Nancy'

Habit Mat-forming. ***Flowers*** Small, hooded, 2-lipped, in dense, terminal, spike-like clusters, from late spring to summer. Pure white. ***Leaves*** Semi-evergreen, oval. Variegated silver-white.

- NATIVE HABITAT Garden origin.
- CULTIVATION Grow in cool, moist but well-drained soil, in full or partial shade. Good ground cover, but dislikes excessive winter moisture.
- PROPAGATION By division in autumn or early spring, or by stem tip cuttings of non-flowering shoots in midsummer.

Z 4–8

HEIGHT 6in (15cm)

SPREAD 3ft (1m)

Brassicaceae/Cruciferae

PACHYPHRAGMA MACROPHYLLUM

Habit Spreading, rhizomatous. ***Flowers*** Small, 4-petaled, borne in dense, terminal clusters in spring. White. ***Leaves*** Large, oval, heart-shaped at the base, held on long stalks. Glossy, dark green.

- NATIVE HABITAT Moist, deciduous woodland, in the Caucasus, and N.E. Turkey.
- CULTIVATION Grow in moist, humus-rich soils in shade or partial shade. Provides good ground cover.
- PROPAGATION By division or stem cuttings in late spring, or by seed in autumn.
- OTHER NAMES *Thlaspi macrophyllum*.

Z 5–9

HEIGHT to 12in (30cm)

SPREAD indefinite

Trilliaceae/Liliaceae	

TRILLIUM CERNUUM f. *ALBUM*

Habit Clump-forming. ***Flowers*** Nodding, 3-petaled, borne in spring, beneath the leaves. White, with maroon centers. ***Leaves*** Short-stalked, rhombic, borne in terminal whorls of three, on slender stems. Mid-green.

• NATIVE HABITAT Moist woods, E. North America.

• CULTIVATION Grow in moist, leafy, neutral to acid soils, in full or partial shade. Excellent for a woodland garden.

• PROPAGATION By division, after foliage dies back in summer, or by seed in autumn.

Z 4–9

HEIGHT
12–18in (30–45cm)

SPREAD
12in (30cm)

Convallariaceae/ Liliaceae	LILY-OF-THE-VALLEY

CONVALLARIA MAJALIS

Habit Creeping, rhizomatous. ***Flowers*** Small, very fragrant, pendent, bell-shaped, on arching stems in late spring or early summer. Waxy white. ***Leaves*** Narrowly oval. Mid- to dark green.

• NATIVE HABITAT Woodland, scrub and meadows, in the mountains of northern temperate regions.

• CULTIVATION Grows best in moist, leafy soil, in shade or partial shade. Excellent for naturalizing in a woodland garden or shady border.

• PROPAGATION By division after flowering or in autumn.

Z 2–7

HEIGHT
6in (15cm)

SPREAD
indefinite

Lamiaceae/Labiatae	

LAMIUM MACULATUM ALBUM

Habit Mat-forming. ***Flowers*** Small, hooded, 2-lipped, borne in terminal, spike-like clusters, in late spring and summer. Pure white. ***Leaves*** Semi-evergreen, oval. Green with a silvery-white blotch.

• NATIVE HABITAT Garden origin.

• CULTIVATION Grow in cool, moist but well-drained soil, in full or partial shade. Excellent ground cover, but dislikes excessive winter moisture.

• PROPAGATION By division in autumn or early spring, or by stem tip cuttings of non-flowering shoots in midsummer.

Z 4–8

HEIGHT
8in (20cm)

SPREAD
3ft (1m)

Convallariaceae/ Liliaceae	FAIRY LANTERNS

DISPORUM SMITHII

Habit Spreading, clump-forming, rhizomatous. ***Flowers*** Small, pendent, tubular-bell-shaped, singly or in terminal clusters of 2–6, in spring. White, tipped green. ***Fruits*** Oval, orange-red berries, from late summer. ***Leaves*** Oval to lance-shaped, heart-shaped at the base. Mid-green.

• NATIVE HABITAT Evergreen forests, coastal mountains of W. North America.

• CULTIVATION Grow in cool, moist, humus-rich soil in partial shade. Good for woodland gardens.

• PROPAGATION Seed in autumn; division in spring.

Z 7–9

HEIGHT
12–24in (30–60cm)

SPREAD
24in (60cm) or more

Trilliaceae/Liliaceae	WAKE-ROBIN

TRILLIUM GRANDIFLORUM

Habit Clump-forming. ***Flowers*** Large, 3-petaled, borne above the leaves in spring. Pure white, flushed pink with age. ***Leaves*** Large, oval to almost circular, borne in terminal whorls of 3, on slender stems. Mid-green.

• NATIVE HABITAT Moist woodlands and thickets, in E. North America.

• CULTIVATION Grow in moist, leafy, neutral to acid soils in full or partial shade. Excellent for a peat terrace. This is the hardiest and most rewarding of all the trilliums. In its double form, it is spectacular. For the most impressive springtime display, do not overcrowd the plants with other vigorous subjects, but allow them enough space to spread. This perennial does particularly well in the company of hostas, whose foliage matures later in the season.

• PROPAGATION By division, after foliage dies back in summer, or by seed in autumn.

Z 4–9

HEIGHT
15in (38cm)

SPREAD
12in (30cm)

Trilliaceae/Liliaceae	

TRILLIUM OVATUM

Habit Clump-forming. ***Flowers*** Musk-scented, 3-petaled, borne above the leaves in spring. Pure white, fading to pink. ***Leaves*** Diamond-shaped, borne in terminal whorls of 3. Dark green, on slender red stems.

• NATIVE HABITAT Forest, W. North America.

• CULTIVATION Grow in moist, leafy, neutral to acid soils, in full or partial shade. Excellent for woodland gardens.

• PROPAGATION By division, after foliage dies back in summer, or by seed in autumn.

Z 5–9

HEIGHT 10–15in (25–38cm)

SPREAD 8in (20cm)

Ranunculaceae	

ADONIS BREVISTYLA

Habit Clump-forming, with thick, branching roots. ***Flowers*** Small, buttercup-like, borne singly at the ends of slender stems, in early spring. White, tinted blue on the petal reverse. ***Leaves*** Finely divided into flattened, pointed, lobes. Mid-green.

• NATIVE HABITAT Damp forest, scrub, and rocky ravines, in Bhutan and W. China.

• CULTIVATION Grow in moist, humus-rich soil, in shade or partial shade; shelter from cold, dry winds.

• PROPAGATION By fresh seed in late summer or by division after flowering.

Z 4–9

HEIGHT 6–9in (15–23cm)

SPREAD 6–9in (15–23cm)

Berberidaceae	HIMALAYAN MAY APPLE

PODOPHYLLUM HEXANDRUM

Habit Clump-forming. ***Flowers*** Flattish, with 6 petals, borne singly at the ends of sturdy stems, in spring. White or pale pink. ***Fruits*** Fleshy, oval red berries, in summer. ***Leaves*** Divided into 3 lobes, unfurling fully after flowering. Dark green, mottled with brown.

• NATIVE HABITAT Scrub, forest, and meadows, in the Himalayas and W. China.

• CULTIVATION Grow in moist, humus-rich soil.

• PROPAGATION Division in spring; seed in autumn.

• OTHER NAMES *P. emodi.*

Z 5–8

HEIGHT 12–18in (30–45cm)

SPREAD 12in (30cm)

Ranunculaceae	SNOWDROP, WINDFLOWER

ANEMONE SYLVESTRIS

Habit Carpeting, rhizomatous. ***Flowers*** Fragrant, semi-pendent, cupped, borne singly or in pairs, on slender stems in spring and early summer. White, with yellow anthers. ***Leaves*** Divided and lobed. Mid-green, hairy beneath.

• NATIVE HABITAT Woods and rocky hills, C. and E. Europe to the Caucasus.

• CULTIVATION Grow in humus-rich, moist, well-drained soil. May be invasive where conditions suit.

• PROPAGATION By division in spring, by fresh seed in late summer, or by root cuttings in winter.

Z 4–9

HEIGHT 12in (30cm)

SPREAD 12in (30cm)

Trilliaceae/Liliaceae

TRILLIUM CHLOROPETALUM

Habit Clump-forming. ***Flowers*** Fragrant, with 3 upright or incurved petals, borne above the leaves in spring. Purplish-pink to greenish-white. ***Leaves*** Diamond-shaped, borne in terminal whorls of 3, on red-green stems. Dark green, gray-marbled.

- NATIVE HABITAT Damp forests in California, US.
- CULTIVATION Grow in moist, leafy, neutral to acid soils, in full or partial shade. Excellent for peat banks, woodland gardens, or shady borders.
- PROPAGATION By division, after foliage dies back in summer, or by seed in autumn.

Z 5–9

HEIGHT 12–18in (30–45cm)

SPREAD 12–18in (30–45cm)

Saxifragaceae

BERGENIA 'Silberlicht'

Habit Clump-forming. ***Flowers*** Small, open cup-shaped, borne in dense clusters, on sturdy stems in spring. White, often flushed pink. ***Leaves*** Evergreen, leathery, oval to rounded, toothed margins, in basal rosettes. Mid-green.

- NATIVE HABITAT Garden origin.
- CULTIVATION Grow in sun or partial shade, in any well-drained soil. Best with some shelter from cold, dry winds to avoid foliage scorch.
- PROPAGATION Division in spring, after flowering.
- OTHER NAMES *B.* 'Silverlight'.

Z 3–8

HEIGHT 12in (30cm)

SPREAD 20in (50cm)

Berberidaceae

EPIMEDIUM PUBIGERUM

Habit Dense, carpeting. ***Flowers*** Small, cup-shaped, borne in loose clusters of 12–35, in late spring. Yellow petals with creamy-white or pink inner sepals. ***Leaves*** Evergreen, divided into smooth, heart-shaped leaflets. Glossy, dark green.

- NATIVE HABITAT Woodland, Turkey, S.E. Europe.
- CULTIVATION Grow in moist, well-drained, humus-rich soil, in partial shade. Provides good ground cover in a shady border. May be damaged by late frosts. Cut away old foliage in late winter.
- PROPAGATION By division in spring or autumn.

Z 5–9

HEIGHT 18in (45cm)

SPREAD 18in (45cm)

Geraniaceae

GERANIUM MACRORRHIZUM 'Ingwersen's Variety'

Habit Compact, carpeting, rhizomatous. ***Flowers*** Small, in pairs or umbels, in late spring and early summer. Soft rose-pink. ***Leaves*** Aromatic, semi-evergreen, divided into 5–7 deeply cut lobes. Mid-green, tinted red and bronze in winter.

- NATIVE HABITAT Mount Koprovnik, Montenegro.
- CULTIVATION Grow in almost any soil, in sun or partial shade. Good weed-smothering ground cover.
- PROPAGATION By division in autumn or spring or by semi-ripe cuttings in summer.

Z 4–8

HEIGHT 12in (30cm)

SPREAD 24in (60cm)

Saxifragaceae

BERGENIA CILIATA

Habit Clump-forming. ***Flowers*** Small, open cup-shaped, in dense clusters, in early spring. White, fading to pink. ***Leaves*** Evergreen, large, leathery, rounded, toothed, heart-shaped at the base, fringed with bristles. Dark green, turning red in autumn.

• NATIVE HABITAT Woods and rocky places, in the Himalayas, from Afghanistan to S.E. Tibet.

• CULTIVATION Grow in sun or partial shade, in a cool position, in any well-drained soil. The best results will be achieved if some shelter is given from cold and wind. This perennial is not hardy everywhere, and the leaves may be cut back by severe cold, although they will recover speedily. A good idea is to plant in the proximity of a small shrub by way of permanent protection.

• PROPAGATION By division in spring, after flowering.

Z 5–8

HEIGHT
12in (30cm)

SPREAD
20in (50cm)

Saxifragaceae

BERGENIA 'Ballawley'

Habit Clump-forming. ***Flowers*** Small, open cup-shaped, borne in dense clusters, on sturdy, red stems, in spring. Bright crimson. ***Leaves*** Evergreen, leathery, oval to rounded, toothed, in basal rosettes. Mid-green, turning red in winter.

- NATIVE HABITAT Garden origin.
- CULTIVATION Grow in sun or partial shade, in any well-drained soil. Best with some shelter from cold, dry winds to avoid foliage scorch.
- PROPAGATION By division in spring, after flowering.

☼ ◊

Z 3–8

HEIGHT to 24in (60cm)

SPREAD 24in (60cm)

Saxifragaceae

BERGENIA CORDIFOLIA 'Purpurea'

Habit Clump-forming. ***Flowers*** Small, bell-shaped, borne in dense clusters, on sturdy red stems, from late winter to early spring. Rose-pink. ***Leaves*** Evergreen, leathery, rounded, with wavy margins. Dark green, tinted purple, especially in winter.

- NATIVE HABITAT Garden origin.
- CULTIVATION Grow in sun or partial shade, in any well-drained soil. This and its parent species are among the most cold- and heat-tolerant of bergenias. Good for ground cover.
- PROPAGATION Division in spring, after flowering.

☼ ◊

Z 3–8

HEIGHT 20in (50cm)

SPREAD 20in (50cm)

Melanthiaceae/Liliaceae

HELONIOPSIS ORIENTALIS

Habit Rosette-forming, rhizomatous. ***Flowers*** Small, narrow petaled, in nodding clusters, in late spring or early summer. Rose-pink. ***Leaves*** Evergreen, lance-shaped, in basal rosettes. Mid-green.

- NATIVE HABITAT Mountain woodland, scrub, and meadows in Japan, Korea, and Sakhalin Island.
- CULTIVATION Grow in moist but well-drained, humus-rich soil, in a cool, shady position.
- PROPAGATION By division in autumn, or by seed in autumn or spring.
- OTHER NAMES *H. japonica.*

◑ ♦

Z 4–8

HEIGHT 12in (30cm)

SPREAD 12in (30cm)

Leguminosae/ Papilionaceae

LATHYRUS VERNUS 'Alboroseus'

Habit Bushy, clump-forming. ***Flowers*** Small, pea-like, borne in 3–15 flowered sprays, in spring. White and deep pink. ***Leaves*** Fern-like, divided into 2–4 pairs of pointed, oval leaflets. Mid-green.

- NATIVE HABITAT Species occurs in European scrub and woodland.
- CULTIVATION Grow in any well-drained soil, including poor rocky soils, in sun or light shade. Dislikes root disturbance and may be slow to establish after transplanting.
- PROPAGATION By careful division in spring.

☼ ◊

Z 5–9

HEIGHT 12in (30cm)

SPREAD 12in (30cm)

Berberidaceae

EPIMEDIUM GRANDIFLORUM 'Rose Queen'

Habit Dense, clump-forming. ***Flowers*** Small, cup-shaped, spurred, on branching, wiry stems in spring. Deep pink. ***Leaves*** Divided into 2–3 smooth, thin, heart-shaped leaflets. Copper-tinted dark green.

• NATIVE HABITAT Garden origin.

• CULTIVATION Grow in moist but well-drained, humus-rich soil, in partial shade. Provides good ground cover in a shady border. May be damaged by wind and late frost. Cut back old leaves in winter.

• PROPAGATION By division in spring or autumn.

Z 5–8

HEIGHT 12in (30cm)

SPREAD 12in (30cm)

Berberidaceae

EPIMEDIUM × RUBRUM

Habit Compact, carpeting, rhizomatous. ***Flowers*** Small, cup-shaped, in loose, branched clusters in spring. Crimson, with yellow spurs. ***Leaves*** Divided into heart-shaped, serrated leaflets. Mid-green, bronze-red on emergence and in autumn.

• NATIVE HABITAT Garden origin.

• CULTIVATION Grow in moist, well-drained, humus-rich soil, in partial shade. Cut back old foliage in late winter. Excellent ground cover in a damp, shady border, or woodland garden.

• PROPAGATION By division in spring or autumn.

Z 4–8

HEIGHT 12in (30cm)

SPREAD 8in (20cm)

Lamiaceae/Labiatae

LAMIUM MACULATUM

Habit Mat-forming, stoloniferous. ***Flowers*** Small, hooded, 2-lipped, borne in terminal, spike-like clusters, in midspring. Mauve-pink. ***Leaves*** Semi-evergreen, oval, with a central, silver-white stripe.

• NATIVE HABITAT Woodland and meadows, from Europe and N. Africa to W. Asia.

• CULTIVATION Grow in moist but well-drained soil, in full or partial shade. Excellent ground cover.

• PROPAGATION By division in autumn or early spring, or by stem tip cuttings of non-flowering shoots in midsummer.

Z 4–8

HEIGHT 8in (20cm)

SPREAD 3ft (1m)

Trilliaceae/Liliaceae — BIRTHROOT, SQUAWROOT

TRILLIUM ERECTUM

Habit Clump-forming. ***Flowers*** Ill-scented, semi-nodding, with 3 petals, borne above the leaves in late spring. Maroon-purple. ***Leaves*** Broadly oval, in terminal whorls of 3. Mid-green.

• NATIVE HABITAT Damp woodlands, E. North America.

• CULTIVATION Grow in moist, leafy, neutral to acid soils in full or partial shade. Excellent for peat banks, woodland gardens, or borders.

• PROPAGATION By division, after foliage dies back in summer, or by seed in autumn.

Z 4–9

HEIGHT 12–18in (30–45cm)

SPREAD 12in (30cm)

Berberidaceae

EPIMEDIUM GRANDIFLORUM 'Crimson Beauty'

Habit Dense, clump-forming. ***Flowers*** Small, cup-shaped, spurred, borne on wiry stems in spring. Crimson. ***Leaves*** Divided into 2–3 smooth, thin, heart-shaped leaflets. Copper-tinted dark green.
- NATIVE HABITAT Garden origin.
- CULTIVATION Grow in moist but well-drained, humus-rich soil, in partial shade. Provides good ground cover in a shady border. May be damaged by wind and late frost. Cut back old foliage in winter.
- PROPAGATION By division in spring or autumn.

Z 5–8

HEIGHT
12in (30cm)

SPREAD
12in (30cm)

Berberidaceae

EPIMEDIUM GRANDIFLORUM 'Lilafee'

Habit Dense, clump-forming. ***Flowers*** Small, cup-shaped, spurred, borne on branching, wiry stems in spring. Lavender-violet. ***Leaves*** Divided into 2–3 smooth, thin-textured, heart-shaped leaflets. Copper-tinted dark green.
- NATIVE HABITAT Garden origin.
- CULTIVATION Grow in moist but well-drained, humus-rich soil, in partial shade. Provides good ground cover in a shady border. May be damaged by wind and late frosts. Cut back old foliage in winter.
- PROPAGATION By division in spring or autumn.

Z 5–8

HEIGHT
12in (30cm)

SPREAD
12in (30cm)

Trilliaceae/Liliaceae | TOADSHADE, WAKE-ROBIN

TRILLIUM SESSILE

Habit Clump-forming. ***Flowers*** Musk-scented, borne above the leaves in late spring. Has 3 maroon-brown petals and 3 brown-red sepals. ***Leaves*** Stemless, rounded, in terminal whorls of 3. Dark green, marked white, pale green, or bronze.
- NATIVE HABITAT Woodland, E. North America.
- CULTIVATION Easily grown in moist, humus-rich, neutral to acid soils, in full or partial shade. Good for peat banks, woodland gardens, or borders.
- PROPAGATION By division, after foliage dies back in summer, or by seed in autumn.

Z 5–9

HEIGHT
12–15in (30–38cm)

SPREAD
12–18in (30–45cm)

Berberidaceae

EPIMEDIUM ACUMINATUM

Habit Tufted, creeping, clump-forming. ***Flowers*** Small, cup-shaped, with curved spurs, borne on branching, wiry stems, in spring or early summer. Pale violet-rose, yellow, or white. ***Leaves*** Divided into 3 lance-shaped, long-pointed, spiny-toothed leaflets. Mid-green, tinted deep pink on emergence.
- NATIVE HABITAT Mountains of W. and C. China.
- CULTIVATION Grow in moist, well-drained, soil, in a shady border. Cut back old foliage in late winter.
- PROPAGATION By seed or division in spring or autumn.

Z 7–9

HEIGHT
10–20in (25–50cm)

SPREAD
12in (30cm)

Ranunculaceae

ANEMONE NEMOROSA 'Robinsoniana'

Habit Carpeting, rhizomatous. ***Flowers*** Large, single, cup-shaped at first, opening flat, borne on red-tinted stems, in profusion in spring. Petals are pale lavender-blue with a creamy-gray petal reverse. ***Leaves*** Deeply divided into lance-shaped, toothed segments, dying down in midsummer. Dark green.

• NATIVE HABITAT Garden origin.

• CULTIVATION Like all wood anemones, this perennial is excellent for a wild or woodland garden. It will naturalize with considerable ease in loose, moist, humus-rich soil in partial shade or dappled sunlight. It is also very attractive if planted at the foot of shrubs in a shrub border. The extended flowering period in early spring makes *A. nemorosa* 'Robinsoniana' one of the choicest of all the anemone cultivars.

• PROPAGATION By division in late summer.

Z 4–8

HEIGHT
6in (15cm)

SPREAD
12in (30cm) or more

Ranunculaceae

ANEMONE NEMOROSA 'Allenii'

Habit Carpeting, rhizomatous. ***Flowers*** Large, single, cup-shaped, borne in profusion in spring. Pale lavender-blue, rich lilac on the reverse of the petals. ***Leaves*** Deeply divided into slender, toothed segments, dying down in midsummer. Mid-green.

- NATIVE HABITAT Garden origin.
- CULTIVATION Grow in moist, humus-rich soil, in partial shade or dappled sunlight. Excellent for naturalizing in a woodland garden or shrub border.
- PROPAGATION By division in late summer.

Z 4–8

HEIGHT 6in (15cm)

SPREAD 12in (30cm) or more

Paeoniaceae

GLAUCIDIUM PALMATUM

Habit Leafy, sparse-stemmed, thick-rooted. ***Flowers*** Large, cup-shaped, delicate, borne singly on slender stems, in late spring. Pale mauve. ***Leaves*** Paired, with 7–11 irregularly toothed lobes, borne at the ends of upright stems. Bright green.

- NATIVE HABITAT Mountain woodland, Japan.
- CULTIVATION Grow in moist but well-drained, humus-rich soil, in partial shade or dappled sunlight, in a cool position with shelter from wind. Good for a woodland garden or cool, shady border.
- PROPAGATION By seed in autumn.

Z 6–9

HEIGHT 20in (50cm)

SPREAD 20in (50cm)

Geraniaceae

GERANIUM NODOSUM

Habit Clump-forming, rhizomatous. ***Flowers*** Upright, funnel-shaped, borne in loose, open clusters throughout summer. Lilac or lilac-pink petals with dark-veins. ***Leaves*** Shiny, with 3–5 shallow, unevenly toothed lobes. Dark green.

- NATIVE HABITAT Woodland, in hills and mountains, from C. France to the Balkans.
- CULTIVATION Thrives in deep shade, even in poor, dry soils, but grows best in fertile, humus-rich soils. Suitable for a wild or woodland garden.
- PROPAGATION Seed or division in autumn or spring

Z 5–8

HEIGHT 18in (45cm)

SPREAD 18in (45cm)

Leguminosae/ Papilionaceae — SPRING VETCH

LATHYRUS VERNUS

Habit Bushy, clump-forming. ***Flowers*** Small, pea-like, borne in 3–15 flowered clusters in spring. Bright purple and blue with red veins. ***Leaves*** Fern-like, divided into 2–4 pairs of pointed, oval leaflets. Mid-green.

- NATIVE HABITAT Scrub and woodland in Europe.
- CULTIVATION Grow in well-drained soil, including poor rocky soils, in sun or light shade. Dislikes root disturbance and takes time to become established.
- PROPAGATION By seed in autumn or careful division in spring.

Z 5–9

HEIGHT 12in (30cm)

SPREAD 12in (30cm)

Brassicaceae/Cruciferae

CARDAMINE PENTAPHYLLOS

Habit Upright, spreading, rhizomatous. ***Flowers*** Small, funnel-shaped, borne in clusters above the leaves, in spring. White or pale purple. ***Leaves*** Divided into 3–5 toothed, smooth leaflets. Dark green.

• NATIVE HABITAT Mountain woodland, W. and C. Europe.

• CULTIVATION Grow in moist but freely draining, preferably sandy, humus-rich soil, in cool conditions. Excellent for a woodland garden or damp, shady border. It grows particularly well in dappled shade beneath deciduous trees in more naturalistic areas of the garden, but is equally well-placed at the front of a border in more formal plantings. It is valued for its early flowering period, and associates well with spring-flowering bulbs.

• PROPAGATION By seed or division in autumn.

• OTHER NAMES *Dentaria digitata, D. pentaphylla.*

Z 5–9

HEIGHT
12–24in
(30–60cm)

SPREAD
18–24in
(45–60cm)

Boraginaceae

PULMONARIA SACCHARATA

Habit Clump-forming. ***Flowers*** Funnel-shaped, borne in terminal heads in spring. Pink then blue to blue-purple. ***Leaves*** Semi-evergreen, long, elliptic. Mid-green, variably spotted with white, and covered in fine hairs.

- NATIVE HABITAT Scrub and woodland, Europe.
- CULTIVATION Grow in fertile, humus-rich, moist but well-drained soil, in shade or partial shade. Excellent for a woodland garden or shady border, especially beneath shrubs or trees.
- PROPAGATION Seed or division in spring or autumn.

Z 4–8

HEIGHT 12in (30cm)

SPREAD 24in (60cm)

Lamiaceae/Labiatae

LAMIUM ORVALA

Habit Mound-forming, stoloniferous. ***Flowers*** Small, hooded, 2-lipped, in leafy, terminal, spike-like clusters, in late spring and early summer. Pink or purple-pink. ***Leaves*** Oval to diamond-shaped. Mid-green, sometimes with a central white stripe.

- NATIVE HABITAT Woodland margins, S.C. Europe.
- CULTIVATION Grow in well-drained soil, in partial shade.
- PROPAGATION By seed or division in autumn or early spring, or by stem tip cuttings of non-flowering shoots in midsummer.

Z 4–8

HEIGHT 12in (30cm) or more

SPREAD 12in (30cm)

Polemoniaceae

POLEMONIUM REPTANS 'Lambrook Mauve'

Habit Mound-forming, with a short rootstock. ***Flowers*** Funnel-shaped, to ¾in (2cm) long, borne in loose, terminal clusters, in late spring and early summer. Lilac-blue. ***Leaves*** Finely divided into 7–19 elliptic to lance-shaped leaflets. Mid-green.

- NATIVE HABITAT Garden origin.
- CULTIVATION Grow in reasonably fertile, humus-rich, well-drained soil. Although not generally recommended for a sunny situation, this plant is in fact quite accommodating and will tolerate woodland conditions in dappled sunlight or partial shade. The leaves are generally evergreen and remain attractive for the greater part of the year. Excellent for herbaceous borders and cottage gardens.
- PROPAGATION By division in spring.
- OTHER NAMES *P. reptans* 'Lambrook Manor'.

Z 4–8

HEIGHT 12–18in (30–45cm)

SPREAD 12–18in (30–45cm)

Solanaceae

SCOPOLIA CARNIOLICA

Habit Clump-forming, rhizomatous. ***Flowers*** Tubular to bell-shaped, variable, borne singly in the leaf axils, in early spring. Pale yellow to brownish-purple and yellow within. ***Leaves*** Coarse, oval to oblong, pointed. Mid-green.

• NATIVE HABITAT Beech woods, in mountains, from C. and S.E. Europe to Russia.

• CULTIVATION Grow in fertile, very well-drained soil, in shade or partial shade. Good for a woodland garden or beneath shrubs in a border.

• PROPAGATION Division in spring; seed in autumn.

Z 5–8

HEIGHT 24in (60cm)

SPREAD 24in (60cm)

Scrophulariaceae | TOOTHWORT

LATHRAEA CLANDESTINA

Habit Spreading, rhizomatous, parasitic on willow or poplar roots. ***Flowers*** Hooded, tubular, 2-lipped, borne in short heads that emerge from soil level, in late winter and early spring. Purple. ***Leaves*** Reduced to pale, fleshy scales on the rhizomes.

• NATIVE HABITAT Damp woods and streamside meadows, S.W. Europe.

• CULTIVATION Grow in moist soil, in shade or dappled shade, at the roots of willow or poplar trees.

• PROPAGATION By fresh seed sown in moist soil, at the host tree roots, in late summer.

Z 5–9

HEIGHT 4in (10cm)

SPREAD indefinite

Ranunculaceae

HELLEBORUS PURPURASCENS

Habit Neat, clump-forming. ***Flowers*** Large, nodding, cup-shaped, in clusters of 2–4, in early spring. Deep purple-violet to maroon outside, sometimes green within. ***Leaves*** Deciduous, divided into 2–6 lance-shaped, coarsely toothed segments. Dark green.

• NATIVE HABITAT Mountain woodland, open grassland, often on sandy soils, in eastern C. Europe.

• CULTIVATION Grow in deep, fertile, moist but well-drained, humus-rich soil, in partial shade.

• PROPAGATION By fresh seed or division in autumn.

Z 5–8

HEIGHT 12in (30cm)

SPREAD 12in (30cm)

Boraginaceae

PULMONARIA ANGUSTIFOLIA 'Mawson's Variety'

Habit Clump- or mat-forming, rhizomatous. ***Flowers*** Funnel-shaped, borne in terminal clusters, in early spring. Intense clear blue, tinted red with age. ***Leaves*** Long, narrowly lance-shaped, finely hairy. Dark green and without spots.

• NATIVE HABITAT Garden origin.

• CULTIVATION Grow in fertile, humus-rich, moist, well-drained soil, in shade or partial shade. Excellent for a woodland garden or shady border.

• PROPAGATION Seed or division in spring or autumn.

Z 3–8

HEIGHT 9in (23cm)

SPREAD 9in (23cm) often more

Boraginaceae	BLUE BELLS, VIRGINIA COWSLIP

MERTENSIA PULMONARIOIDES

Habit Clump-forming, summer-dormant. ***Flowers*** Pendent, tubular-bell-shaped, in hanging clusters in the leaf axils, in spring. Rich blue. ***Leaves*** Oval, dying down by midsummer. Soft blue-green.
• NATIVE HABITAT Wet meadows and streambanks, North America.
• CULTIVATION Grow in moist, but well-drained, humus-rich soil, in shade, partial shade, or in sun in reliably moist soil. Prone to slug damage.
• PROPAGATION Division in spring; seed in autumn.
• OTHER NAMES *M. virginica.*

Z 6–9

HEIGHT 12–24in (30–60cm)

SPREAD 12–18in (30–45cm)

Boraginaceae	

PULMONARIA SACCHARATA 'Frühlingshimmel'

Habit Clump-forming. ***Flowers*** Funnel-shaped, borne in terminal clusters, in spring. Pale sky blue with purple calyces. ***Leaves*** Semi-evergreen, long, elliptic. Mid-green spotted with white, finely hairy.
• NATIVE HABITAT Scrub and woodland, Europe.
• CULTIVATION Grow in fertile, humus-rich, moist but well-drained soil, in shade or partial shade. Excellent for a woodland garden or shady border.
• PROPAGATION By division in spring or autumn.
• OTHER NAMES *P. saccharata* 'Spring Beauty'.

Z 4–8

HEIGHT 12in (30cm)

SPREAD 24in (60cm)

Boraginaceae	

BRUNNERA MACROPHYLLA 'Dawson's White'

Habit Clump-forming, rhizomatous. ***Flowers*** Small, in delicate panicles in spring. Bright blue, forget-me-not-like. ***Leaves*** Heart-shaped. Mid-green, irregularly edged with creamy-white.
• NATIVE HABITAT Garden origin.
• CULTIVATION Grow in moist, well-drained, humus-rich soil; shelter from wind to avoid leaf scorch. Good ground cover.
• PROPAGATION By division in spring or autumn.
• OTHER NAMES *B. macrophylla* 'Variegata'.

Z 3–7

HEIGHT 18in (45cm)

SPREAD 24in (60cm)

Papaveraceae	HAREBELL POPPY

MECONOPSIS QUINTUPLINERVIA

Habit Mat-forming. ***Flowers*** Nodding, poppy-like, borne singly on strong, slender stems in late spring and early summer. Lavender-blue, darker at the base. ***Leaves*** Lance-shaped, in basal rosettes. Mid-green, clothed in rusty or golden hairs.
• NATIVE HABITAT Alpine meadows, Tibet, China.
• CULTIVATION Grow in moist, leafy soil, in a cool, sheltered site in dappled shade. Excellent for woodland or a peat bed. Dislikes warm conditions.
• PROPAGATION By fresh seed in late summer or by division after flowering.

pH

Z 7–8

HEIGHT 12–18in (30–45cm)

SPREAD 12in (30cm)

Boraginaceae

BUGLOSSOIDES PURPUROCAERULEA

Habit Ascending, spreading, rhizomatous. ***Flowers*** Small, funnel-shaped, 5-lobed, in terminal clusters, in early spring and early summer. Red-purple at first, later turning deep blue. ***Leaves*** Lance-shaped. Mid-green.

• NATIVE HABITAT Scrub, woodland edge, usually on limestone, from W. Europe to Iran.

• CULTIVATION Grown in fertile, well-drained soil in partial shade or sun. This plant is ideally suitable for a border or woodland garden. It is a robust perennial of charming and delicate appearance that associates well with smaller species, and particularly with cultivars of *Narcissus*. Where conditions suit, it will spread to form colonies.

• PROPAGATION By seed or division in autumn or spring.

• OTHER NAMES *Lithospermum purpureocaeruleum*.

Z 6–8

HEIGHT
24in (60cm)

SPREAD
24in (60cm)

PRIMROSES

Primroses belong to the genus *Primula,* which are hardy to frost-tender annuals, biennials, and perennials, some of which are evergreen. All have basal rosettes of leaves and tubular, bell-shaped, or flat (primrose-like) flowers. There are primroses to suit almost every garden situation, from rock garden, peat bed, and alpine house to herbaceous border, waterside and bog garden; a number are also grown as houseplants. Nearly all thrive best in climates with cool, moist summers.

Primroses are classified into a number of groups, of which the following are the most widely known and cultivated.

Candelabra primroses have tubular, flat-faced flowers in tiered whorls up the stem.

Polyanthus primroses have large clusters of flowers on thick stems and are often treated as biennials.

Auricula primroses include alpine, border, and show auriculas. Their flattish flowers, which are borne in clusters above the leaves, often have a bright central ring or "paste." Show auriculas and some border auriculas have a waxy powder or "farina" on the leaves.

For ease of reference, their cultivation requirements may be grouped as follows.

1 full sun and constantly moist soil
2 full sun or partial shade and moist, well-drained soil
3 partial shade and moist,well-drained soil
4 partial shade and well-drained, gritty soil
5 full sun or partial shade and alkaline soil
6 partial shade and gritty alkaline soil
7 full or partial shade and moist, peaty soil
8 full sun and gritty, peaty soil
9 partial shade and gritty, peaty soil.

Propagate species by seed when fresh or in spring. Increase selected forms when dormant, either by division or root cuttings. Protect border perennials from slugs and snails, especially in damp situations.

***P.* VULGARIS**
'Gigha White'
Habit Neat, clump-forming, floriferous.
Flowers Flat, singly amid the foliage in early spring. White, yellow-eyed.
Leaves Lance-shaped to oval, crinkled, toothed or scalloped. Fresh green.
• CULTIVATION 1or 3.
• HEIGHT 6–8in (15–20cm).
• SPREAD 6–8in (15–20cm).

P. vulgaris
'Gigha White'

Z 3–8

***P.* 'Craddock White'**
Habit Clump-forming.
Flowers Fragrant, flat, upward-facing, in short-stemmed clusters in spring. Creamy-white.
Leaves Oval-oblong. Dark green with red veins.
• CULTIVATION 1 or 3.
• HEIGHT 3in (8cm).
• SPREAD 5in (13cm).

***P.* 'Craddock White'**
(Polyanthus Primrose)

Z 5–7

***P.* DENTICULATA ALBA**
Habit Vigorous, upright, clump-forming.
Flowers Small, flat, in rounded heads, on strong stems in early to mid-spring. Yellow-eyed white.
Leaves Spoon-shaped, toothed. Bright green.
• CULTIVATION 1 or 3.
• HEIGHT 12–24in (30–60cm).
• SPREAD 12–18in (30–45cm).

P. denticulata alba

Z 6–8

***P.* JAPONICA**
'Postford White'
Habit Clump-forming.
Flowers Small, tubular, in tiered whorls in early summer. White, spreading petal lobes, pink-eyed.
Leaves Oval or broadly spoon-shaped. Pale green.
• CULTIVATION 1 or 7. Good for a bog garden.
• HEIGHT 12–24in (30–60cm).
• SPREAD 12–18in (30–45cm).

P. japonica
'Postford White'
(Candelabra Primrose)

Z 6–8

P. *PULVERULENTA* Bartley Hybrids
Habit Clump-forming.
Flowers Tubular, on white farinose stems, in tiered whorls in early summer. Pale pink with a dark red-pink eye.
Leaves Lance-shaped to oval, toothed. Mid-green.
• CULTIVATION 1 or 7.
• HEIGHT 2–3ft (60cm–1m).
• SPREAD 12–18in (30–45cm).

P. pulverulenta **Bartley Hybrids**
(Candelabra Primrose)

Z 5–7

P. 'Iris Mainwaring'
Habit Neat, clump-forming.
Flowers Small, primrose-like, on short stems in early spring. Pale mauve, flushed red.
Leaves Oval to lance-shaped, toothed. Bright green.
• CULTIVATION 1 or 3.
• HEIGHT 6–8in (15–20cm).
• SPREAD 6–8in (15–20cm).

***P.* 'Iris Mainwaring'**

Z 5–7

P. *FARINOSA*
Habit Compact, clump-forming.
Flowers Small, tubular on short, sturdy stems in spring. White-eyed, with spreading, pink, occasionally white, petals.
Leaves Lance-shaped to oval, toothed. Mid-green, densely farinose.
• CULTIVATION 8.
• HEIGHT 6–12in (15–30cm).
• SPREAD 6in (15cm).

P. farinosa
Bird's eye primrose

Z 5–7

P. *VULGARIS* subsp. *SIBTHORPII*
Habit Neat, clump-forming, floriferous.
Flowers Flat, singly, amid the foliage in early spring. Pink or purplish-pink with a yellowish-green eye.
Leaves Lance-shaped to oval, toothed. Fresh green.
• CULTIVATION 1 or 3.
• HEIGHT 6–8in (15–20cm).
• SPREAD 6–8in (15–20cm).

P. vulgaris **subsp. *sibthorpii***

Z 3–8

P. *ALLIONII*
Habit Cushion- or rosette-forming.
Flowers Tubular, but flat-faced, on short stems from late winter to spring. Rose-pink, mauve or white.
Leaves Fleshy, lance-shaped to almost round, downy. Mid-green.
• CULTIVATION 5. Best in an alpine house.
• HEIGHT 3in (8cm).
• SPREAD 3–6in (8–15cm).

P. allionii

Z 7–8

P. *MALACOIDES*
Habit Clump-forming.
Flowers Small, single or double, in dense, tiered whorls in winter and early spring. Pink, purplish-pink or white.
Leaves Broadly oval, with shallow, toothed lobes, softly hairy. Pale green.
• CULTIVATION 4.
• HEIGHT 8–12in (20–30cm).
• SPREAD 8–12in (20–30cm).

P. malacoides
Fairy primrose

Min. 41°F (5°C) Z 11

P. *ROSEA*
Habit Clump-forming.
Flowers Flat, with heart-shaped, cleft petals, borne in short-stemmed clusters in spring. Glowing rose-pink with a yellow eye.
Leaves Lance-shaped to oval, toothed. Mid-green.
• CULTIVATION 1 or 7.
• HEIGHT 4–6in (10–15cm).
• SPREAD 6–8in (15–20cm).

P. rosea

Z 4–8

P. *WARSHENEWSKIANA*
Habit Very compact, clump-forming.
Flowers Tiny, flat, with spreading petal lobes, borne in small umbels in early spring. Bright pink, white-eyed.
Leaves Small, spoon-shaped. Dark green.
• CULTIVATION 8. Best in an alpine house.
• HEIGHT 1in (2.5cm).
• SPREAD 1½–2in (3.5–5cm).

P. warshenewskiana

Z 5–7

P. CLUSIANA

Habit Compact, clump-forming.
Flowers Tubular with spreading, heart-shaped deeply cleft petal lobes, borne in small clusters in spring. Pink, white-eyed.
Leaves Oval, leathery. Mid-green, gray-green beneath.

- CULTIVATION 8.
- HEIGHT 6–9in (15–23cm).
- SPREAD 6in (15cm).

P. clusiana

Z 5–7

P. SIEBOLDII

Habit Spreading, clump-forming.
Flowers Flat, in heads above foliage in early summer. White-eyed pink, purple, or white.
Leaves Oval to oblong with toothed lobes, soft, downy. Pale green.

- CULTIVATION 7.
- HEIGHT 6–8in (15–20cm).
- SPREAD 6–8in (15–20cm).

P. sieboldii

Z 5–8

P. PULVERULENTA

Habit Upright, clump-forming.
Flowers Tubular, with spreading petal lobes, on white-farinose stems, in tiered whorls in early summer. Deep red with a dark purplish-red eye.
Leaves Oval to lance-shaped, toothed. Mid-green.

- CULTIVATION 1 or 7. Excellent for streamsides.
- HEIGHT 2–3ft (60cm–1m).
- SPREAD 12–18in (30–45cm).

P. pulverulenta
(Candelabra Primrose)

Z 6–8

P. SECUNDIFLORA

Habit Clump-forming.
Flowers Pendent, funnel-shaped, in small clusters on long, farinose stems in summer. Reddish-purple.
Leaves Oblong to oval or lance-shaped, toothed. Mid-green.

- CULTIVATION 1 or 7. Good for a damp border.
- HEIGHT 12–18in (30–45cm).
- SPREAD 12in (30cm).

P. secundiflora

Z 6–8

P. JAPONICA 'Miller's Crimson'

Habit Clump-forming.
Flowers Small, tubular, with spreading petal lobes, in tiered whorls in early summer. Crimson.
Leaves Oval, or broadly spoon-shaped. Pale green.

- CULTIVATION 1 or 7. Good for a bog garden.
- HEIGHT 12–24in (30–60cm).
- SPREAD 12–18in (30–45cm).

P. japonica 'Miller's Crimson'
(Candelabra Primrose)

Z 6–8

P. VIALII

Habit Clump-forming.
Flowers Small, tubular, borne in slender, conical spikes in late spring. Red in bud, opening purple.
Leaves Broadly lance-shaped to oblong, toothed. Soft, mid-green.

- CULTIVATION 1 or 3. Excellent for stream and pond side, and damp borders. Short-lived.
- HEIGHT 12–18in (30–45cm).
- SPREAD 8–12in (20–30cm).

P. vialii

Z 6–8

P. Cowichan
Habit Vigorous, rosette-forming.
Flowers Primrose-like, in long-stemmed, clusters in early spring. Red, blue, violet, or yellow.
Leaves Oval, crinkled. Bright to dark green.
• CULTIVATION 2.
• HEIGHT 4in (10cm).
• SPREAD 6–8in (15–20cm).

***P.* Cowichan**
(Polyanthus Primrose)

Z 5–7

P. NANA
Habit Rosette-forming.
Flowers Flat, singly on short stems in spring. Pale blue to pale mauve with a white eye.
Leaves Spoon-shaped irregularly toothed or lobed. Pale green.
• CULTIVATION 8.
• OTHER NAMES *P. edgeworthii.*
• HEIGHT 2–4in (5–10cm).
• SPREAD 4–6in (10–15cm).

P. nana

Z 5–7

P. SONCHIFOLIA
Habit Rosette-forming.
Flowers Tubular, borne in dense umbels in spring. Spreading, blue-purple petal lobes edged with yellow.
Leaves Oval, serrated, lobed. Mid-green.
• CULTIVATION 8. Best in an alpine house.
• HEIGHT 8–12in (20–30cm).
• SPREAD 8–12in (20–30cm).

P. sonchifolia

Z 5–7

P. PETIOLARIS
Habit Rosette-forming.
Flowers Tubular, borne in spring. Yellow-eyed, with spreading, toothed, satiny, purplish-pink petal lobes.
Leaves Small, oval, toothed. Mid-green.
• CULTIVATION 8. Best in an alpine house.
• HEIGHT 2–4in (5–10cm).
• SPREAD 4–6in (10–15cm).

P. petiolaris

Z 5–7

P. MODESTA* var. *FAURIEAE
Habit Clump-forming.
Flowers Tubular, with heart-shaped petal lobes, borne in short-stemmed umbels in spring. Pinkish-purple, with a yellow-eye.
Leaves Elliptic to spoon-shaped, wavy, toothed. Mid-green, very farinose.
• CULTIVATION 8. Best in an alpine house.
• HEIGHT 2in (5cm).
• SPREAD 2in (5cm).

P. modesta* var. *faurieae

Z 4–7

***P. AURICULA* 'Mark'**
Habit Rosette-forming.
Flowers Flat, with rounded petals, produced in spring. Intense wine-purple, fading to pink at the margins, and with a pale creamy center.
Leaves Oval, smooth. Vibrant green.
• CULTIVATION 2.
• HEIGHT 9–11in (23–28cm).
• SPREAD 6–9in (15–23cm).

***P. auricula* 'Mark'**
(Alpine Auricula Primrose)

Z 5–7

***P. AURICULA* 'Adrian'**
Habit Rosette-forming.
Flowers Flat, with rounded petals, borne from mid- to late spring. Light to dark purplish-blue, with a white center.
Leaves Oval. Mid-green.
• CULTIVATION 2. Good for exhibition. Needs sharp drainage.
• HEIGHT 9–10in (22–25cm).
• SPREAD 6–8in (15–20cm).

***P. auricula* 'Adrian'**
(Alpine Auricula Primrose)

Z 5–7

P. DENTICULATA
Habit Vigorous, upright, clump-forming.
Flowers Small, flat, in rounded heads, on strong stems in early to mid-spring. Lilac, pink, or white, with a yellow eye.
Leaves Oval, toothed. Bright green.
• CULTIVATION 1 or 3.
• HEIGHT 12–24in (30–60cm).
• SPREAD 12–18in (30–45cm).

P. denticulata
Drumstick primrose

Z 6–8

P. FLACCIDA
Habit Lax, clump-forming.
Flowers Small, pendent, broadly funnel-shaped, farinose, in conical heads in early summer. Lavender or violet.
Leaves Oval, toothed. Pale to mid-green.
• CULTIVATION 7 or 8.
• HEIGHT 6–2in (15–30cm).
• SPREAD 6–9in (15–23cm).

P. flaccida

Z 5–7

P. MARGINATA
Habit Neat, clump-forming.
Flowers Small, funnel-shaped, in clusters in early spring. Blue-lilac, with a tiny white eye.
Leaves Oval to oblong, toothed, slightly fleshy, farinose. Mid-green.
• CULTIVATION 5.
• HEIGHT 4–6in (10–15cm).
• SPREAD 4–8in (10–20cm).

P. marginata

Z 4–7

P. MARGINATA
'Linda Pope'
Habit Rosette-forming.
Flowers Flat, borne in short-stemmed, umbel-like clusters in spring. White-eyed mauve-blue.
Leaves Narrowly oval, toothed. Pale green, covered with white farina.
• CULTIVATION 5. Needs sharp drainage.
• HEIGHT 4–6in (10–15cm).
• SPREAD 6–9in (15–23cm).

***P. marginata* 'Linda Pope'**
(Auricula Primrose)

Z 5–7

P. WHITEI
'Sherriff's Variety'
Habit Clump-forming.
Flowers Tubular, in neat heads in spring. White- or creamy-eyed pale purplish-blue.
Leaves Small, oval, toothed. Mid-green.
• CULTIVATION 8.
• OTHER NAMES *P. bhutanica*.
• HEIGHT 6in (15cm).
• SPREAD 6–9in (15–23cm).

***P. whitei* 'Sherriff's Variety'**

Z 5–7

P. AURICULA
'Margaret Martin'
Habit Rosette-forming.
Flowers Flat, borne in mid- to late spring. Gray-edged petals, flushed black at the base, and with a white central ring.
Leaves Spoon-shaped. Gray-green, farinose.
• CULTIVATION 2. Excellent for exhibition. Needs sharp drainage.
• HEIGHT 8in (20cm).
• SPREAD 6in (15cm).

***P. auricula* 'Margaret Martin'**
Show auricula

Z 5–7

P. ALPICOLA
var. *LUNA*
Habit Clump-forming.
Flowers Pendent, bell-shaped, on long, slender stems in early summer. Soft sulfur-yellow.
Leaves Oval to lance-shaped. Mid-green.
• CULTIVATION 7.
• HEIGHT 6–25in (15–60cm).
• SPREAD 6–12in (15–30cm).

P. alpicola* var. *luna

Z 6–8

P. FLORINDAE
Habit Clump-forming.
Flowers Sweetly fragrant, pendent, bell-shaped, in large, long-stemmed heads in early summer. Sulphur yellow.
Leaves Broadly oval, toothed, shining. Mid-green.
• CULTIVATION 1 or 7. Good for a pondside, damp border or bog garden.
• HEIGHT 2–3ft (60cm–1m).
• SPREAD 1–2ft (30–60cm).

P. florindae
Giant Himalayan Cowslip

Z 6–8

P. VULGARIS
Habit Neat, clump-forming.
Flowers Flat, fragrant, borne singly amid the foliage in early spring. Soft yellow.
Leaves Lance-shaped to oval, toothed. Fresh green.
• CULTIVATION 1 or 3. Good for a wild garden.
• HEIGHT 6–8in (15–20cm).
• SPREAD 6–8in (15–20cm).

P. vulgaris
English Primrose

Z 3–8

P. AURICULA 'Moonstone'
Habit Rosette-forming.
Flowers Rounded, double, produced in profusion in spring. Pale greenish-yellow.
Leaves Oval. Mid-green.
• CULTIVATION 2. Best in an alpine house. Needs good drainage.
• HEIGHT 9–10in (23–25cm).
• SPREAD 6–8in (15–20cm).

***P. auricula* 'Moonstone'**
(Border Auricula Primrose)

Z 5–7

P. PROLIFERA
Habit Upright, clump-forming.
Flowers Fragrant, nodding, bell-shaped, borne in tiered whorls in summer. Yellow.
Leaves Oval, toothed. Pale green.
• CULTIVATION 1 or 7.
• OTHER NAMES *P. helodoxa*.
• HEIGHT 2–3ft (60cm–1m).
• SPREAD 12–18in (30–45cm).

P. prolifera
(Candelabra Primrose)

Z 6–8

P. SIKKIMENSIS
Habit Upright, clump-forming.
Flowers Pendent, funnel-shaped, borne in long-stemmed clusters in summer. Pale yellow.
Leaves Rounded to oval, toothed. Pale green.
• CULTIVATION 1 or 7. Good for a damp border.
• HEIGHT 18–30in (45–75cm).
• SPREAD 12–18in (30–45cm).

P. sikkimensis

Z 5–8

P. ELATIOR
Habit Clump-forming.
Flowers Small, fragrant, tubular with spreading, heart-shaped petal lobes, borne in umbels in spring. Yellow.
Leaves Oval to elliptic, scalloped or irregularly toothed. Bright green.
• CULTIVATION 1, 7, or 9. Good in light woodland.
• HEIGHT 6–12in (15–30cm).
• SPREAD 6in (15cm).

P. elatior
Oxlip

Z 3–7

P. AURICULA 'Blairside Yellow'
Habit Rosette-forming.
Flowers Small, slightly funnel-shaped, borne in short-stemmed clusters in early spring. Golden-yellow.
Leaves Tiny, rounded to oval, in a dense basal rosette. Pale green.
• CULTIVATION 2. Needs sharp drainage.
• HEIGHT 1in (2.5cm).
• SPREAD 6in (15cm).

***P. auricula* 'Blairside Yellow'**
(Alpine Auricula Primrose)

Z 5–7

P. KEWENSIS
Habit Upright, clump-forming.
Flowers Scented, tubular, with heart-shaped petal lobes, in whorls in late winter and early spring. Bright yellow.
Leaves Oval, toothed. Pale green, white-farinose.
• CULTIVATION 4. Best in a cool greenhouse.
• HEIGHT 12in (30cm).
• SPREAD 6–12in (15–30cm).

P. kewensis

Min. 41°F (5°C) Z 11

P. VERTICILLATA
Habit Clump-forming.
Flowers Fragrant, bell-shaped, in tiered whorls in spring. Yellow.
Leaves Oval to lance-shaped, sharply serrated. Mid-green, farinose beneath.
• CULTIVATION 4. Best in a cold greenhouse.
• HEIGHT 8–10in (20–25cm).
• SPREAD 6–8in (15–20cm).

P. verticillata

Z 8–9

P. FORRESTII
Habit Clump-forming, with woody rhizomes.
Flowers Flat, in dense heads in late spring or early summer. Yellow with orange eyes.
Leaves Oval, wrinkled, toothed. Dark green.
• CULTIVATION 8. Needs sharp drainage.
• HEIGHT 6–9in (15–23cm).
• SPREAD 6–12in (15–30cm).

P. forrestii

Z 7–8

P. VERIS
Habit Clump-forming.
Flowers Small, fragrant, funnel-shaped, in dense, thick-stemmed clusters in spring. Yellow.
Leaves Oval to lance-shaped, crinkled, toothed. Fresh green.
• CULTIVATION 1 or 3. Good to grow through turf.
• HEIGHT 6–8in (15–20cm).
• SPREAD 6–8in (15–20cm).

P. veris
Cowslip

Z 7–8

P. CHUNGENSIS
Habit Clump-forming.
Flowers Tubular with spreading petal lobes, borne in tiered whorls in early summer. Orange.
Leaves Elliptic to oblong, toothed and shallowly lobed. Mid-green.
• CULTIVATION 1 or 7.
• HEIGHT 24in (60cm).
• SPREAD 12in (30cm).

P. chungensis
(Candelabra Primrose)

Z 6–8

P. BULLEYANA
Habit Upright, clump-forming.
Flowers Tubular with spreading petal lobes, borne in tiered whorls in early summer. Deep orange.
Leaves Oval to lance-shaped, toothed. Dark green.
• CULTIVATION 1 or 7.
• HEIGHT 24in (60cm).
• SPREAD 12in (30cm).

P. bulleyana
(Candelabra Primrose)

Z 6–8

P. AURICULA 'Janie Hill'
Habit Rosette-forming.
Flowers Flat, borne in mid- to late spring. Dark to golden brown. with a golden center.
Leaves Oval. Mid-green.
• CULTIVATION 2. Good for exhibition. Needs sharp drainage.
• HEIGHT 9–10in (23–25cm).
• SPREAD 6–8in (15–20cm).

***P. auricula* 'Janie Hill'**
(Alpine Auricula Primrose)

Z 5–7

P. 'Inverewe'
Habit Vigorous, upright, clump-forming.
Flowers Tubular with spreading lobes, borne in tiered whorls on long, floury stems in summer. Bright orange-red.
Leaves Coarse, oval to lance-shaped. Mid-green.
• CULTIVATION 1 or 7.
• HEIGHT 18–30in (45–75cm).
• SPREAD 12–18in (30–45cm).

***P.* 'Inverewe'**
(Candelabra Primrose)

Z 5–7

P. Gold-Laced Group
Habit Rosette-forming.
Flowers Small, flat, in heads from mid- to late spring. Dark red to almost black petals with a fine golden edge, yellow-centered.
Leaves Oval, wrinkled. Mid- to pale green.
• CULTIVATION 2 or 3.
• PROPAGATION By seed or division every year.
• HEIGHT 8in (20cm).
• SPREAD 10in (25cm).

***P.* Gold-Laced Group**
(Polyanthus Primrose)

Z 6–8

Convallariaceae/ Liliaceae

DISPORUM SESSILE 'Variegatum'

Habit Spreading, clump-forming, rhizomatous. ***Flowers*** Small, pendent, tubular-bell-shaped, borne singly or in clusters of 2–3 at ends of stems in spring. White, tipped green. ***Leaves*** Oval-lance-shaped, pleated. Striped green and white.

• NATIVE HABITAT Garden origin. Species occurs in wooded hills in Japan.

• CULTIVATION Grow in cool, moist, humus-rich soil, in partial shade. Excellent for shady borders and woodland gardens.

• PROPAGATION By division in spring.

Z 4–9

HEIGHT 18in (45cm)

SPREAD 12in (30cm) or more

Ranunculaceae

HELLEBORUS CYCLOPHYLLUS

Habit Clump-forming. ***Flowers*** Small, nodding, cup-shaped, borne in clusters of up to 7, in early spring. Greenish-yellow with prominent creamy-white stamens. ***Leaves*** Deciduous, palmately divided into 5–9 lance-shaped leaflets. Bright green.

• NATIVE HABITAT Woods, scrub, and grassy hills, in Greece, S. Balkans, S. Bulgaria, and Albania.

• CULTIVATION Grow in fertile, moist but well-drained soil, in sun or partial shade.

• PROPAGATION By fresh seed or division in autumn.

Z 6–9

HEIGHT to 24in (60cm)

SPREAD 24in (60cm)

Euphorbiaceae

EUPHORBIA CYPARISSIAS

Habit Bushy, spreading, rhizomatous. ***Flowers*** Tiny, borne in rounded umbels, in late spring. Yellowish-green with conspicuous lime-green bracts. ***Leaves*** Linear, smooth. Gray-green, sometimes flushed orange on poor soils.

• NATIVE HABITAT Dunes and dry, rocky meadows, in W. C. and S. Europe.

• CULTIVATION Grow in a warm, dry position in almost any well-drained soil. May be invasive.

• PROPAGATION By division or seed in spring or early autumn; by basal cuttings in spring or summer.

Z 4–9

HEIGHT 12in (30cm)

SPREAD 12in (30cm) or more

Euphorbiaceae

EUPHORBIA AMYGDALOIDES var. *ROBBIAE*

Habit Creeping, rhizomatous. ***Flowers*** Tiny, in rounded, branching heads in spring. Yellowish-green with conspicuous yellow-green bracts. ***Leaves*** Spoon-shaped, in rosettes. Dark green.

- NATIVE HABITAT Woodland in Turkey.
- CULTIVATION Best in damp, well-drained soil, in sun or partial shade. Good ground cover. Avoid contact with the irritant sap.
- PROPAGATION By division or seed in spring or early autumn; by basal cuttings in spring or summer.

Z 6–9

HEIGHT 18–24in (45–60cm)

SPREAD 24in (60cm)

Euphorbiaceae

EUPHORBIA SEGUIERIANA

Habit Bushy, clump-forming. ***Flowers*** Tiny, borne in large, terminal clusters over long periods, from late spring. Yellowish-green, with conspicuous, sulfurous yellow-green bracts. ***Leaves*** Narrow, lance-shaped, smooth. Bluish-green.

- NATIVE HABITAT Dry scrub, rocky hillsides, C. and W. Europe, east to the Caucasus and Siberia.
- CULTIVATION Grow in a warm, dry position in almost any well-drained soil.
- PROPAGATION By division or seed in spring or early autumn; by basal cuttings in spring or summer.

Z 8–10

HEIGHT 18in (45cm)

SPREAD 18in (45cm)

Saxifragaceae

TELLIMA GRANDIFLORA

Habit Spreading, clump-forming. ***Flowers*** Small, bell-shaped, with fringed petals, borne in erect sprays, in late spring. Greenish-white or cream. ***Leaves*** Semi-evergreen, hairy, 3- to 7-lobed, kidney-shaped, heart-shaped at the base. Dark green, flushed purple.

- NATIVE HABITAT Coniferous woods of W. North America.
- CULTIVATION Grow in moist but well-drained soil in shade or partial shade.
- PROPAGATION Seed or division in spring or autumn

Z 4–9

HEIGHT 24in (60cm)

SPREAD 24in (60cm)

Valerianaceae

VALERIANA PHU 'Aurea'

Habit Clump-forming, rhizomatous. ***Flowers*** Small, tubular, insignificant, borne in clusters in summer. White. ***Leaves*** Lance-shaped, some divided into leaflets. Bright golden-yellow in spring, turning lime-green and then mid-green by midsummer.

- NATIVE HABITAT Species occurs on rocky hill-sides, in Europe and the Caucasus. Garden origin.
- CULTIVATION Grow in any moderately fertile soil in sun.
- PROPAGATION By division in autumn.

Z 5–8

HEIGHT 15in (38cm)

SPREAD 12–15in (30–38cm)

Ranunculaceae	GLOBE FLOWER

TROLLIUS × *CULTORUM* 'Alabaster'

Habit Clump-forming. ***Flowers*** Rounded, almost globular, borne on sturdy, slender stems, above the leaves in late spring. Creamy-yellow, tinted pale green. ***Leaves*** Deeply divided into jagged-toothed leaflets, mostly in dense, basal clumps. Fresh green.

- NATIVE HABITAT Garden origin.
- CULTIVATION Grow in moist, fertile, humus-rich soil in sun or partial shade. The native globe flower of Europe, *T. europaeus*, has long been in cultivation as a first-class border and pondside plant. A number of named cultivars have been introduced in recent years, usually of darker orange hues, so that *T.* × *cultorum* 'Alabaster' is an important introduction taking the color down the other side of the spectrum into the paler shades. It plays a very useful role as a foil to other colors in the garden.
- PROPAGATION By division in early autumn.

Z 5–8

HEIGHT
24in (60cm)

SPREAD
18in (45cm)

Asteraceae/Compositae	GIANT BUTTERBURR

PETASITES JAPONICUS

Habit Spreading, rhizomatous. ***Flowers*** Tiny, daisy-like, in dense, rounded heads in early spring. Yellowish-white, cupped by pale green bracts. ***Leaves*** Coarse, rounded, 32in (80cm) or more across, emerging after the flowers. Light green.

- NATIVE HABITAT Streambanks in woodland, Japan, Korea, China.
- CULTIVATION Grow in moist, humus-rich soil in sun or shade. Very invasive, but makes good ground cover by streambanks in large wild gardens.
- PROPAGATION By division in spring or autumn.

Z 5–9

HEIGHT 24in (60cm)

SPREAD 5ft (1.5m) or more

Brassicaceae/Cruciferae	

CARDAMINE ENNEAPHYLLOS

Habit Upright, spreading, rhizomatous. ***Flowers*** Funnel-shaped, borne in nodding clusters above the leaves, in spring. Creamy-yellow. ***Leaves*** Divided into 2–6 pairs of coarsely toothed leaflets. Fresh green, bronzed when young.

- NATIVE HABITAT Mountain woodland in the eastern Alps and Carpathians to S. Italy.
- CULTIVATION Grow in moist but freely draining, preferably sandy, humus-rich soil, in cool conditions.
- PROPAGATION By seed or division in autumn.
- OTHER NAMES *Dentaria enneaphylla.*

Z 5–8

HEIGHT 12–24in (30–60cm)

SPREAD 18–24in (45–60cm)

Ranunculaceae	

ANEMONE × *LIPSIENSIS*

Habit Prostrate, carpeting, rhizomatous. ***Flowers*** Large, single, cup-shaped, borne in profusion in spring. Pale yellow. ***Leaves*** Deeply divided into slender, toothed segments. Mid-green.

- NATIVE HABITAT Natural hybrid (*A. nemorosa* × *A. ranunculoides*) occurring in European woodland.
- CULTIVATION Grow in moist, humus-rich soil, in partial shade or dappled sunlight.
- PROPAGATION By division in late summer.
- OTHER NAMES *A.* × *seemannii.*

Z 5–8

HEIGHT 6in (15cm)

SPREAD 12in (30cm) or more

Ranunculaceae	

ANEMONE RANUNCULOIDES

Habit Spreading, rhizomatous. ***Flowers*** Large, single, buttercup-like, borne in profusion in spring. Deep yellow. ***Leaves*** Short-stalked, deeply divided into slender, toothed segments. Fresh green.

- NATIVE HABITAT Damp, deciduous woods and heathland, from N. Europe to W. Asia.
- CULTIVATION Grow in moist, humus-rich soil, in partial shade or dappled sunlight. Excellent for naturalizing in woodland gardens.
- PROPAGATION By division or fresh seed in late summer.

Z 4–8

HEIGHT 8in (20cm)

SPREAD 8in (20cm) or more

Berberidaceae	

EPIMEDIUM DAVIDII

Habit Tufted, slowly creeping, clump-forming. ***Flowers*** Small, cup-shaped, with curved spurs, borne on branching, wiry stems, from spring to early summer. Pale yellow. ***Leaves*** Divided into oval, pointed leaflets. Mid-green, bluish-green beneath.
- NATIVE HABITAT Scrub and woodlands in the mountains of W. Sichuan, China.
- CULTIVATION Grow in moist, humus-rich soil; shelter from cold winds. For shady borders and woodland gardens. Remove old leaves in late winter.
- PROPAGATION Seed or division in spring or autumn.

Z 7–9

HEIGHT
12–20in
(30–50cm)

SPREAD
12in (30cm)

Berberidaceae	

EPIMEDIUM PERRALDERIANUM

Habit Dense, carpeting. ***Flowers*** Small, pendent, cupped, borne in loose, upright clusters, in spring. Pale yellow with short brown spurs. ***Leaves*** Evergreen or semi-evergreen, divided into oval to rounded, sharply toothed leaflets. Glossy, dark green, bronze when young.
- NATIVE HABITAT Scrub and oak woodland in the mountains of Algeria.
- CULTIVATION Grow in moist, well-drained soil in a sheltered site. Remove old leaves in late winter.
- PROPAGATION By division in spring or autumn.

Z 5–8

HEIGHT
12in (30cm)

SPREAD
18in (45cm)

Berberidaceae	

EPIMEDIUM × *VERSICOLOR* 'Neosulphureum'

Habit Compact, mound-forming. ***Flowers*** Small, cup-shaped, short-spurred, borne in loose clusters on branching stems, in spring. Pale yellow. ***Leaves*** Divided into 3 heart-shaped, serrated leaflets. Bright green, tinted red-purple on emergence.
- NATIVE HABITAT Garden origin.
- CULTIVATION Grow in moist, well-drained, humus-rich soil, in partial shade. Provides good ground cover in a shady border. Remove old leaves in late winter.
- PROPAGATION By division in spring or autumn.

Z 5–9

HEIGHT
12in (30cm)

SPREAD
12in (30cm)

Convallariaceae/ Liliaceae	BELLWORT, MERRY-BELLS

UVULARIA GRANDIFLORA

Habit Upright, clump-forming. ***Flowers*** Pendulous, narrowly bell-shaped, borne on slender stems in late spring or early summer. Yellow. ***Leaves*** Lance-shaped, encircling the stem. Bluish-green.
- NATIVE HABITAT Woodland, E. North America.
- CULTIVATION Grow in moist, well-drained, humus-rich soil in dappled shade. Protect young growth from slugs.
- PROPAGATION By division in early spring, before flowering.

Z 5–9

HEIGHT
18–24in
(45–60cm)

SPREAD
12in (30cm)

Ranunculaceae	GLOBEFLOWER

TROLLIUS EUROPAEUS

Habit Clump-forming. ***Flowers*** Rounded, almost globular, borne on sturdy, slender stems, above the leaves in late spring. Lemon- to mid-yellow. ***Leaves*** Deeply divided into jagged-toothed leaflets, mostly in dense, basal clumps. Mid-green.

- NATIVE HABITAT Woodland streamsides and wet, shady meadows in Europe, Russia, North America.
- CULTIVATION Grow in moist, fertile, humus-rich soil, in sun or partial shade. Ideal if planted by water.
- PROPAGATION By seed in summer or autumn or by division in early autumn.

Z 5–8

HEIGHT
24in (60cm)

SPREAD
18in (45cm)

Ranunculaceae	

TROLLIUS × *CULTORUM* 'Earliest of All'

Habit Clump-forming. ***Flowers*** Rounded, almost globular, borne singly on sturdy, slender stems, above the leaves, in early spring. Butter-yellow. ***Leaves*** Deeply divided into jagged-toothed leaflets, mostly in dense, basal clumps. Fresh green.

- NATIVE HABITAT Garden origin.
- CULTIVATION Grow in moist, fertile, humus-rich soil in sun or partial shade. Excellent for pool- and streamsides and for damp borders.
- PROPAGATION By division in early autumn.

Z 5–8

HEIGHT
24in (60cm)

SPREAD
18in (45cm)

Euphorbiaceae	SPURGE

EUPHORBIA POLYCHROMA

Habit Rounded, clump-forming. ***Flowers*** Tiny, borne in terminal, flattened heads over long periods in spring. Yellowish-green, with conspicuous bright yellow bracts. ***Leaves*** Oval, softly hairy. Mid-green.

- NATIVE HABITAT Scrub and woodland, from C. and S.E. Europe to Turkey.
- CULTIVATION Grow in fertile, moist but well-drained soil, in sun or partial shade.
- PROPAGATION By division or seed in spring or early autumn; by basal cuttings in spring or summer.
- OTHER NAMES *E. epithymoides*.

Z 4–9

HEIGHT
18–24in (45–60cm)

SPREAD
24in (60cm)

Ranunculaceae	

ADONIS VERNALIS

Habit Clump-forming. ***Flowers*** Buttercup-like, borne singly at the ends of slender stems, in early spring. Shining yellow. ***Leaves*** Finely divided into slender, linear lobes. Mid-green.

- NATIVE HABITAT Dry, rocky scrub and grassland, from Europe to Russia and Finland.
- CULTIVATION Grow in moist but very well-drained, humus-rich, preferably alkaline soil, in sun or partial shade.
- PROPAGATION By fresh seed in late summer or by division after flowering.

Z 4–7

HEIGHT
9–12in (23–30cm)

SPREAD
9–12in (23–30cm)

Asteraceae/Compositae

DORONICUM 'Miss Mason'

Habit Low-growing, clump-forming, rhizomatous. ***Flowers*** Solitary, daisy-like, borne well above the foliage in mid- to late spring. Slender, bright yellow ray florets surrounding a golden-yellow disk. ***Leaves*** Heart-shaped, toothed. Dark green.

- NATIVE HABITAT Garden origin.
- CULTIVATION Grows best in moist but well-drained humus-rich soil, although it will do well in most soils. It needs a light, shady position and is particularly useful for woodland gardens. It is also suitable for the front of a shady border, and the flowers are good for cutting. This is an excellent plant for early in the year, when a generous show of yellow daisies heralds the spring. Once established in favorable conditions, it will spread steadily.
- PROPAGATION By division in early autumn.

Z 4–7

HEIGHT
18in (45cm)

SPREAD
24in (60cm)

Ranunculaceae

ADONIS AMURENSIS

Habit Clump-forming. ***Flowers*** Buttercup-like, borne singly in late winter and early spring. Shining yellow, with a bronze-tinted petal reverse. ***Leaves*** Finely divided into narrowly lance-shaped, toothed lobes. Mid-green.

- NATIVE HABITAT Mountain meadows, Manchuria, Japan, Korea.
- CULTIVATION Grow in moist but very well-drained, humus-rich soil in sun or partial shade.
- PROPAGATION By fresh seed in late summer or by division after flowering.

Z 4–7

HEIGHT
12in (30cm)

SPREAD
9–12in
(23–30cm)

Ranunculaceae — KING CUP, MARSH MARIGOLD

CALTHA PALUSTRIS

Habit Marginal aquatic, clump-forming. ***Flowers*** Cup-shaped, 1½in (4cm) across, in long-stalked clusters in spring. Waxy, bright golden-yellow. ***Leaves*** Kidney-shaped, toothed, to 4in (10cm) across. Glossy dark green.

- NATIVE HABITAT Marshes and streamsides, throughout most of the Northern Hemisphere.
- CULTIVATION Grow in full sun in wet soil by pond edges, or in shallow water to a depth of 9in (23cm).
- PROPAGATION By seed in autumn; by division in autumn or early spring.

Z 4–9

HEIGHT
2ft (60cm)

SPREAD
18in (45cm)

Papaveraceae	WELSH POPPY

MECONOPSIS CAMBRICA

Habit Spreading. ***Flowers*** Poppy-like, with delicate petals, borne singly in spring and summer. Lemon-yellow, golden-yellow, or rich orange. ***Leaves*** Fern-like, deeply divided into irregular lobes, mostly in basal clumps. Fresh green.
• NATIVE HABITAT Woodlands, mountain rocks, and old walls in W. Europe.
• CULTIVATION Grow in moist soil in sun, partial shade, or shade. Will naturalize in wild gardens.
• PROPAGATION By fresh seed in late summer, or division after flowering. Self-sows freely.

Z 6–8

HEIGHT
12–18in (30–45cm)

SPREAD
12in (30cm)

Berberidaceae	

EPIMEDIUM x *WARLEYENSE*

Habit Clump- or mound-forming. ***Flowers*** Small, cup-shaped, borne in loose clusters on wiry stems, in spring. Coppery-orange and yellow. ***Leaves*** Evergreen, oval, pointed, with few spiny teeth. Light green, tinted red-purple on emergence.
• NATIVE HABITAT Garden origin.
• CULTIVATION Grow in moist, well-drained, humus-rich soil, in partial shade. Provides good ground cover in a shady border. Cut away old foliage in late winter.
• PROPAGATION By division in spring or autumn.

Z 5–9

HEIGHT
12in (30cm)

SPREAD
12in (30cm)

Campanulaceae	

CAMPANULA ALLIARIIFOLIA

Habit Mound-forming. ***Flowers*** Nodding, bell-shaped, borne in one-sided clusters throughout summer. Creamy-white. ***Leaves*** Triangular, heart-shaped at the base, roughly hairy. Mid-green.
• NATIVE HABITAT Damp cliffs, scrub, and conifer forests in the Caucasus and N. Turkey.
• CULTIVATION Grow in moist but well-drained soil in sun or partial shade. Excellent for herbaceous and mixed borders.
• PROPAGATION By basal cuttings in early summer; by seed or division in spring or autumn.

Z 3–7

HEIGHT
24in (60cm)

SPREAD
20in (50cm)

Rubiaceae	SWEET WOODRUFF, WOODRUFF

GALIUM ODORATUM

Habit Carpeting, rhizomatous. ***Flowers*** Tiny, 4-petaled, star-shaped, in terminal, clusters in early to midsummer. White. ***Leaves*** Small, elliptic, in whorls of 6 up the stems. Glossy, bright green. Aromatic when dried.

- NATIVE HABITAT Deciduous woods and hedgebanks in Europe and N. Africa.
- CULTIVATION Grow in moist, well-drained soil, in partial shade or sun. Good ground cover.
- PROPAGATION Division in early spring or autumn.
- OTHER NAMES *Asperula odoratum.*

Z 5–8

HEIGHT
6in (15cm)

SPREAD
12in (30cm) often more

Ranunculaceae	

ANEMONE NARCISSIFLORA

Habit Clump-forming. ***Flowers*** Single, cup-shaped, borne in stiff-stemmed sprays in late spring and early summer. Widely spreading white petals, stained blue or pink on the reverse. ***Leaves*** Deeply divided into toothed, cut lobes. Dark green.

- NATIVE HABITAT Damp, mountain meadows in Europe, Turkey, Russia, Japan, and North America.
- CULTIVATION Grow in humus-rich, moist but well-drained soil, in sun or partial shade.
- PROPAGATION By seed in late summer; by careful division in spring. A difficult plant to propagate.

Z 5–8

HEIGHT
24in (60cm)

SPREAD
20in (50cm)

Ranunculaceae	

ANEMONE RIVULARIS

Habit Clump-forming. ***Flowers*** Delicate, cup-shaped, borne on stiff, free-branching stems in summer. White, with a metallic-blue tinge to the petal reverse and blue anthers. ***Leaves*** Deeply divided into toothed, cut lobes. Dark green.

- NATIVE HABITAT Damp, mountain meadows, and woodland clearings, from N. India to S.W. China.
- CULTIVATION Grow in humus-rich, moist but well-drained soil, in sun or partial shade.
- PROPAGATION By seed in late summer or by careful division in spring.

Z 6–8

HEIGHT
24in (60cm)

SPREAD
12in (30cm)

Asteraceae/Compositae	

LEUCANTHEMUM × *SUPERBUM* 'Esther Read'

Habit Robust, clump-forming. ***Flowers*** Large, solitary, double, borne singly in summer. White. ***Leaves*** Coarse, lobed, and toothed. Dark green.

- NATIVE HABITAT Garden origin.
- CULTIVATION Grow in moderately fertile, well-drained soil, in full sun. Suitable for cutting. Divide and replant every two years to maintain vigor.
- PROPAGATION By division in spring or autumn.
- OTHER NAMES *Chrysanthemum* × *superbum* 'Esther Read'.

Z 4–9

HEIGHT
18in (45cm)

SPREAD
18in (45cm)

Anthericaceae/Liliaceae	ST BERNARD'S LILY

ANTHERICUM LILIAGO

Habit Upright, fleshy-rooted. ***Flowers*** Small, trumpet-shaped, borne in long, spike-like heads, in early summer. White. ***Leaves*** Long, narrow, grass-like. Gray-green.

- NATIVE HABITAT Sunny meadows and scrub in mountains from S. Europe to S. Turkey.
- CULTIVATION Grow in fertile, well-drained soil, in full sun. Good for herbaceous borders and for cutting. May self-sow where conditions suit.
- PROPAGATION By division in spring or seed in autumn.

☼ ◊

Z 5–9

HEIGHT
18–24in (45–60cm)

SPREAD
12in (30cm)

Asteraceae/Compositae	

ANTHEMIS PUNCTATA subsp. *CUPANIANA*

Habit Carpeting, sub-shrubby. ***Flowers*** Small, single, daisy-like, borne singly on short stems in early summer. White with a yellow disk. ***Leaves*** Evergreen, finely cut. Silvery, turn green in winter.

- NATIVE HABITAT Cliffs and rocky places, Sicily.
- CULTIVATION Grow in well-drained soil, in a warm, sheltered site in full sun. Excellent for border edges. Cut back after flowering to maintain vigor.
- PROPAGATION By division in spring; basal cuttings in late summer, autumn, or spring.

☼ ◊

Z 6–9

HEIGHT
12in (30cm)

SPREAD
12in (30cm) or more

Asteraceae/Compositae	

ANAPHALIS TRIPLINERVIS var. *INTERMEDIA*

Habit Lax, spreading, clump-forming. ***Flowers*** Tiny, with papery petals, in dense clusters, in late summer and early autumn. White. ***Leaves*** Lance-shaped, densely hairy. Silvery gray-green.

- NATIVE HABITAT Woodland clearings, Himalayas.
- CULTIVATION Grow in any moderately fertile, well-drained, not too dry soil. Flowers dry well.
- PROPAGATION By seed in autumn, or by division in late winter or early spring.
- OTHER NAMES *A. nepalensis.*

☼ ◊

Z 3–8

HEIGHT
8–12in (20–30cm)

SPREAD
12in (30cm)

Asteraceae/Compositae	

ANAPHALIS NEPALENSIS var. *MONOCEPHALA*

Habit Compact, tuft-forming. ***Flowers*** Tiny, with papery petals, in dense, terminal, short-stemmed clusters, in late summer. White. ***Leaves*** Lance-shaped, densely hairy. Silver- or gray-green.

- NATIVE HABITAT Open habitats, Himalayas.
- CULTIVATION Grow in any moderately fertile, well-drained, not too dry soil. Flowers dry well.
- PROPAGATION By seed in autumn, or by division in late winter or early spring.
- OTHER NAMES *A. nubigena*

Z 6–8

HEIGHT 8–12in (20–30cm)

SPREAD 6in (15cm)

Brassicaceae/Cruciferae	SEA KALE

CRAMBE MARITIMA

Habit Robust, mound-forming, with a woody rootstock. ***Flowers*** Small, sweetly scented, borne in large, rounded, branching heads, above the foliage in summer. White. ***Leaves*** Large, fleshy, with curled, wavy-margined lobes. Blue-green.

- NATIVE HABITAT Seaside gravel, on the coasts of N. Europe, the Baltic, and the Black Sea.
- CULTIVATION Grow in well-drained, preferably sandy soil, in full sun. Excellent for coastal gardens.
- PROPAGATION By seed in autumn or spring; by root cuttings in winter.

Z 6–9

HEIGHT 2ft (60cm)

SPREAD 2ft (60cm)

Lamaceae/Labiatae	VARIEGATED APPLE MINT

MENTHA SUAVEOLENS 'Variegata'

Habit Dense, spreading, rhizomatous. ***Flowers*** Small, tubular, 2-lipped, seldom produced. White or pale pink. ***Leaves*** Apple-scented, rounded, wrinkled, softly woolly. Mid-green, heavily splashed with creamy-white.

- NATIVE HABITAT Garden origin.
- CULTIVATION Grow in any soil unless water-logged, in full sun or light shade. Less invasive than most mints and provides good foliage contrast in an herbaceous border. Leaves dry well for potpourri.
- PROPAGATION By division in spring or autumn.

Z 5–9

HEIGHT 12–18in (30–45cm)

SPREAD 24in (60cm)

Apiaceae/Umbelliferae	VARIEGATED GROUND ELDER

AEGOPODIUM PODAGRARIA 'Variegatum'

Habit Vigorous, spreading. ***Flowers*** Tiny, insignificant, in small umbels in summer. White. ***Leaves*** Aromatic, divided into 3–9 oval, pointed, toothed leaflets. Grayish-green, variegated creamy-white.

- NATIVE HABITAT Garden origin.
- CULTIVATION Grow in any soil unless water-logged, in sun or light shade. Good ground cover, but may be invasive, though less so than the green-leaved species. Deadhead to prevent seeding.
- PROPAGATION By division in spring or autumn.

Z 4–9

HEIGHT 4–6in (10–15cm)

SPREAD indefinite

Saxifragaceae

ASTILBE 'Irrlicht'

Habit Clump-forming. ***Flowers*** Tiny, in dense, feathery, tapering spires, in summer. White. ***Leaves*** Divided into toothed, oval leaflets. Dark green.

• NATIVE HABITAT Garden origin.

• CULTIVATION Grow in moist, fertile, humus-rich soil, in sun or partial shade. Good for damp borders, bog gardens or waterside plantings, associating well with *Hosta* and *Rodgersia*. Flowerheads turn brown and die, persisting into winter unless deadheaded.

• PROPAGATION By division in spring or autumn.

Z 4–9

HEIGHT 18–24in (45–60cm)

SPREAD to 3ft (1m)

Saxifragaceae

ASTILBE 'Deutschland'

Habit Clump-forming. ***Flowers*** Tiny, in dense, feathery sprays, on strong stems, in summer. Creamy-white. ***Leaves*** Divided into toothed, oval leaflets. Dark green.

• NATIVE HABITAT Garden origin.

• CULTIVATION Grow in moist, fertile, humus-rich soil, in sun or partial shade. Good for damp borders, bog gardens, or waterside plantings. The flowerheads turn brown and die, persisting into winter unless deadheaded.

• PROPAGATION By division in spring or autumn.

Z 4–9

HEIGHT to 2ft (60cm)

SPREAD to 3ft (1m)

Saxifragaceae

HEUCHERA CYLINDRICA 'Greenfinch'

Habit Dense, clump- or carpet-forming. ***Flowers*** Tiny, bell-shaped, borne in graceful spikes on long, slender, hairy stems, in summer. Pale green. ***Leaves*** Evergreen, rounded, lobed, wavy-edged, in dense basal rosettes. Dark green.

• NATIVE HABITAT Garden origin.

• CULTIVATION Grow in moist but well-drained soil, in sun or partial shade. Good ground cover in an herbaceous border or woodland garden.

• PROPAGATION By division in autumn or spring, using young, outer portions of the crown.

Z 4–8

HEIGHT 18–24in (45–60cm)

SPREAD 20in (50cm)

Saxifragaceae

TIARELLA TRIFOLIATA

Habit Spreading, clump-forming. ***Flowers*** Tiny, star-shaped, borne in slender, open spires on upright stems, from early to midsummer. White to pale pink. ***Leaves*** Semi-evergreen, 3-lobed, each lobe further divided and toothed. Dark green.

• NATIVE HABITAT Streambanks in damp woods in W. North America.

• CULTIVATION Grow in moist but well-drained soil in shade or partial shade.

• PROPAGATION By seed or division in spring or autumn.

Z 5–8

HEIGHT 12in (30cm)

SPREAD 12in (30cm)

Commelinaceae

TRADESCANTIA × *ANDERSONIANA* 'Osprey'

Habit Clump-forming. ***Flowers*** 3-petaled, borne in succession throughout summer. Pure white, with blue-purple stamens, surrounded by two leaf-like, green bracts. ***Leaves*** Slightly fleshy, narrowly lance-shaped, borne on jointed stems. Mid-green.

• NATIVE HABITAT Garden origin.

• CULTIVATION Grow in moist, well-drained soil, in sun or light shade. A long-flowering plant for an herbaceous border. Protect young growth from slugs.

• PROPAGATION By division in spring or autumn.

☼ ◐

Z 5–9

HEIGHT
to 24in (60cm)

SPREAD
18in (45cm)

Caryophyllaceae

GYPSOPHILA 'Rosenschleier'

Habit Mound-forming, with trailing stems. ***Flowers*** Tiny, double, in airy sprays, in summer. White then very pale pink. ***Leaves*** Slightly fleshy, narrowly lance-shaped. Blue-green.

• NATIVE HABITAT Garden origin (*G. paniculata* × *G. repens* 'Rosea').

• CULTIVATION Grows best in deep, moderately fertile, well-drained soil. Resents disturbance. The flowers dry well for winter arrangements.

• PROPAGATION By grafting in winter.

• OTHER NAMES *G.* 'Veil of Roses', *G.* 'Rosy Veil'.

☼ ○

Z 3–9

HEIGHT
12in (30cm)

SPREAD
to 3ft (1m)

Geraniaceae

GERANIUM CLARKEI 'Kashmir White'

Habit Clump- or carpet-forming, rhizomatous. ***Flowers*** Cup-shaped, borne in open clusters throughout summer. White, with lilac or lilac-pink veined petals. ***Leaves*** Deeply cut into 7 dissected, lobes. Dark green.

• NATIVE HABITAT A selection of the species which occurs in alpine meadows in Kashmir.

• CULTIVATION Grow in fertile, humus-rich, moist but well-drained soils, in sun or light shade.

• PROPAGATION By division in autumn or spring.

• OTHER NAMES *G. pratense* 'Kashmir White'.

☼ ○

Z 4–8

HEIGHT
18–24in (45–60cm)

SPREAD
18–24in (45–60cm)

Gesneriaceae

STREPTOCARPUS CAULESCENS

Habit Upright, clump-forming. ***Flowers*** Small, tubular, intermittently on long stalks in the leaf axils, through the year. White or violet, with violet stripes. ***Leaves*** Fleshy, narrowly oval. Dark green.

• NATIVE HABITAT Tanzania, Kenya.

• CULTIVATION Grow as a house or greenhouse plant in cool climates, in moist, humus-rich soil or potting mix. Requires bright indirect light and high humidity. Avoid wetting the leaves when watering.

• PROPAGATION By seed in spring, division after flowering, or by tip cuttings in spring or summer.

◑ ◐

Min. 50–59°F (10–15°C)

HEIGHT
to 18in (45cm) or more

SPREAD
to 18in (45cm) or more

Geraniaceae

GERANIUM RENARDII

Habit Compact, mound-forming. ***Flowers*** Single, borne in open clusters above the foliage in early to midsummer. White or blue-tinted, with maroon-purple veins. ***Leaves*** Rounded, wrinkled and softly hairy, with 5–7 toothed, shallow lobes. Sage-green.

• NATIVE HABITAT Cliffs and rocky meadows in the Caucasus mountains.

• CULTIVATION Grow in well-drained soil in full sun. This perennial can play a valuable double role in the border. Its attractively marked flowers provide summer interest, while its neat form and foliage act as a subtle foil for other more vibrant colored herbaceous plants at the front of the border. The leaves also look good in a silver- or gray-leaved border.

• PROPAGATION By seed or division in autumn or spring.

Z 6–8

HEIGHT
12in (30cm)

SPREAD
12in (30cm)

Acanthaceae

RUELLIA DEVOSIANA

Habit Bushy, sub-shrubby. ***Flowers*** Tubular, borne singly in the leaf axils, in spring and summer. White, tinged and striped mauve. ***Leaves*** Evergreen, broadly lance-shaped. Dark green and pale-veined above, purple beneath.

• NATIVE HABITAT Forest margins, Brazil.

• CULTIVATION Grow as a house or greenhouse plant in cool climates, in moist but well-drained soil or potting mix. Site in partial shade and maintain high humidity.

• PROPAGATION By stem cuttings or seed in spring.

Min. 59°F (15°C)

HEIGHT 18in (45cm) or more

SPREAD 18in (45cm) or more

Asteraceae/Compositae

OSTEOSPERMUM 'Whirligig'

Habit Clump-forming, woody-based. ***Flowers*** Large, single, daisy-like, with spoon-shaped petals, during summer. White above, powder-blue to chalky-gray beneath, with dark blue-gray central disks. ***Leaves*** Evergreen, aromatic, long, narrow, toothed, and serrated. Dark gray-green.

• NATIVE HABITAT Garden origin.

• CULTIVATION Grow in well-drained soil in full sun. Overwinter young plants in frost-free conditions.

• PROPAGATION By cuttings of non-flowering shoots in midsummer.

Z 9–10

HEIGHT 24in (60cm)

SPREAD 12–18in (30–45cm)

Iridaceae

DIPLARRHENA MOLRAEA

Habit Clump-forming, tufted, rhizomatous. ***Flowers*** Small, scented, iris-like, borne on wiry stems in early summer. Has 3 rounded, white petals, and yellow and purple centers. ***Leaves*** Long, narrow, strap-shaped, Mid-green.

• NATIVE HABITAT Damp, mountain grassland in Tasmania and S.E. Australia.

• CULTIVATION Grow in a warm, sunny, sheltered site, in humus-rich, sandy, well-drained soil that remains moist during summer. Protect from frost.

• PROPAGATION By seed or division in spring.

Z 9–10

HEIGHT 18in (45cm)

SPREAD 9in (23cm)

Saxifragaceae

HEUCHERA MICRANTHA var. *DIVERSIFOLIA* 'Palace Purple'

Habit Dense, clump- or carpet-forming. ***Flowers*** Tiny, bell-shaped, borne in graceful, open sprays, on slender, dark-purple stems in summer. White. ***Leaves*** Evergreen, with toothed and cut lobes, in dense basal clumps. Metallic, dark purple-red.

• NATIVE HABITAT Garden origin.

• CULTIVATION Grow in moist, well-drained soil, in sun or partial shade. Provides good ground cover.

• PROPAGATION By division in autumn or spring, using young, outer portions of the crown.

Z 4–8

HEIGHT 18–24in (45–60cm)

SPREAD 20in (50cm)

Lamiaceae/Labiatae	BASTARD BALM

MELITTIS MELISSOPHYLLUM

Habit Upright, clump-forming. ***Flowers*** Tubular, 2-lipped, borne in whorls in the axils of leafy spikes, in summer. White, purple, or pink, with a purple lower lip. ***Leaves*** Aromatic, oval, finely scalloped, and hairy. Mid- to bright green.
• NATIVE HABITAT Mountain woodland and scrub, from W.C. and S. Europe to the Ukraine.
• CULTIVATION Grow in fertile, well-drained soil, in light shade. Suitable for a wildflower border.
• PROPAGATION By seed in autumn, or by division in spring or autumn.

Z 6–9

HEIGHT
12in (30cm)

SPREAD
12in (30cm)

Asteraceae/Compositae	DUSTY MILLER, SILVER LACE

TANACETUM PTARMICIFLORUM

Habit Shrubby, clump-forming. ***Flowers*** Small, daisy-like, to 1in (2.5cm) across, borne in dense heads in summer. White. ***Leaves*** Very finely divided and downy. Silver-gray.
• NATIVE HABITAT Canary Islands.
• CULTIVATION Grow in full sun, in any moderately fertile, well-drained soil. Good for a border front, as edging, in scree plantings, and for containers. Excellent as a filler in a silver border. May be grown as an annual.
• PROPAGATION By seed or stem cuttings in spring.

Z 9–11

HEIGHT
To 20in (50cm)

SPREAD
20in (50cm)

Apiaceae/Umbelliferae	

ASTRANTIA MAJOR subsp. *INVOLUCRATA*

Habit Clump-forming. ***Flowers*** A dome of tiny, greenish-pink florets, surrounded by long, papery, white and pink, green-tipped bracts, borne in summer and autumn. ***Leaves*** Divided into 3–5 coarsely toothed lobes. Dark green.
• NATIVE HABITAT Meadows and woodland in the mountains of C. and E. Europe.
• CULTIVATION Grow in any fertile, well-drained soil in sun. Flowers are good for cutting and drying.
• PROPAGATION By division in spring or fresh seed in late summer.

Z 4–7

HEIGHT
24in (60cm)

SPREAD
18in (45cm)

Apiaceae/Umbelliferae	

ASTRANTIA MAJOR

Habit Clump-forming. ***Flowers*** A dome of tiny, greenish-pink florets, with a star-shaped collar of papery white, pink, and green bracts beneath, borne throughout summer and autumn. ***Leaves*** Divided into 3–5 coarsely toothed lobes. Mid-green.
• NATIVE HABITAT Meadows and woodland in the mountains of C. and E. Europe.
• CULTIVATION Grow in any fertile, well-drained soil in sun. Flowers are good for cutting and drying.
• PROPAGATION By division in spring or fresh seed in late summer.

Z 4–7

HEIGHT
24in (60cm)

SPREAD
18in (45cm)

Scrophulariaceae

MIMULUS 'Andean Nymph'

Habit Spreading, mat-forming. ***Flowers*** Snapdragon-like, tubular with spreading lobes, freely produced throughout summer. Rose-pink, tipped creamy-yellow, and spotted deep pink at the throat. ***Leaves*** Broadly oval, toothed. Bright green.

• NATIVE HABITAT Garden origin, Chile.

• CULTIVATION Grow in moist soil in full sun. In cold areas, overwinter young plants in frost-free conditions as insurance against winter losses. Although it has a tendency to be rather short-lived, this is an extremely useful and colorful plant for the edge of a pond or stream where it can be mixed with complementary water plants. In particular, the pink flowers match perfectly the pink tones in the leaves of the variegated *Houttuynia cordata* 'Chameleon'.

• PROPAGATION By division in spring or softwood cuttings in late summer.

☼ ◐

Z 9–10

HEIGHT
9in (23cm)

SPREAD
10in (25cm)

Saxifragaceae

x *HEUCHERELLA TIARELLOIDES*

Habit Dense, carpet-forming, stoloniferous. ***Flowers*** Tiny, bell-shaped, borne in feathery, long-stemmed sprays in early summer. Pink. ***Leaves*** Evergreen, rounded, with a lobed, toothed, and scalloped margin, in dense basal clumps. Mid-green.

- NATIVE HABITAT Garden origin.
- CULTIVATION Grow in moist but well-drained soil, in sun or partial shade. Good for ground cover at the front of an herbaceous border.
- PROPAGATION By division in autumn or spring, using young, outer portions of the crown.

Z 4–8

HEIGHT 18in (45cm)

SPREAD 18in (45cm)

Saxifragaceae

x *HEUCHERELLA ALBA* 'Bridget Bloom'

Habit Dense, clump-forming, stoloniferous. ***Flowers*** Tiny, bell-shaped, in feathery, long-stemmed sprays, intermittently from early summer until autumn. Soft rose-pink. ***Leaves*** Evergreen, lobed, in dense basal clumps. Mid-green.

- NATIVE HABITAT Garden origin.
- CULTIVATION Grow in moist well-drained soil, in sun or partial shade. Good ground cover at the front of an herbaceous border.
- PROPAGATION By division in autumn or spring, using young, outer portions of the crown.

Z 4–8

HEIGHT 18in (45cm)

SPREAD 12in (30cm)

Apiaceae/Umbelliferae

ASTRANTIA MAXIMA

Habit Mat- or clump-forming. ***Flowers*** A dome of tiny, rose-pink florets with a star-shaped collar of papery, greenish-pink bracts beneath, borne during summer and autumn. ***Leaves*** Divided into 3 coarsely toothed lobes. Mid-green.

- NATIVE HABITAT Woods and damp meadows, from S. Europe to the Caucasus.
- CULTIVATION Grow in any fertile, well-drained soil in sun. Flowers are good for cutting and drying.
- PROPAGATION By division in spring or fresh seed in late summer.

Z 5–8

HEIGHT 24in (60cm)

SPREAD 12in (30cm)

Asteraceae/Compositae

ERIGERON 'Charity'

Habit Robust, clump-forming. ***Flowers*** Daisy-like, borne in profusion over long periods in summer. Slender, pale lilac-pink ray florets around a greenish-yellow disk. ***Leaves*** Lance-shaped to spoon-shaped. Mid-green.

- NATIVE HABITAT Garden origin.
- CULTIVATION Grow in moderately fertile, well-drained soil in sun. A valuable addition to the summer border, noted for its long flowering period.
- PROPAGATION By division in spring or early autumn, or by softwood cuttings in early summer.

Z 5–8

HEIGHT 24in (60cm)

SPREAD 24in (60cm)

Papaveraceae

DICENTRA 'Spring Morning'

Habit Hummock-forming. ***Flowers*** Small, pendent, narrowly heart-shaped, borne on fleshy, arching stems, in late spring and summer. Pink. ***Leaves*** Fern-like, deeply cut. Bright grayish-green.

• NATIVE HABITAT Garden origin.

• CULTIVATION Grow in humus-rich, moist but well-drained soil, in partial shade. A beautiful plant for a shady herbaceous border or woodland garden. Thrives best and flowers for longer periods in cool shaded conditions, but will tolerate part-day sun where soil remains reliably moist during the growing season. Valued for the neat hummocks of finely divided foliage and elegant sprays of flowers, it associates well with ferns and makes an attractive feature when planted with other dicentras with darker flowers, such as *D.* 'Bacchanal'.

• PROPAGATION By division when dormant in late winter.

Z 3–9

HEIGHT
12in (30cm)

SPREAD
12in (30cm)

Geraniaceae

GERANIUM ENDRESSII

Habit Compact, carpeting, rhizomatous. ***Flowers*** Single, cup-shaped, borne in profusion throughout summer. Rose-pink. ***Leaves*** Semi-evergreen, with 5 broadly toothed, deeply cut lobes. Mid- to bright green.

- NATIVE HABITAT Damp habitats in the Pyrenees.
- CULTIVATION Grow in moist, well-drained soil, in full sun. Excellent for herbaceous borders, cottage gardens, and with old-fashioned roses.
- PROPAGATION By seed or division in autumn or spring.

☼ ◊

Z 4–8

HEIGHT
18in (45cm)

SPREAD
24in (60cm)

Geraniaceae

GERANIUM × *OXONIANUM* 'Wargrave Pink'

Habit Dense, carpeting. ***Flowers*** Small, cup-shaped, borne in profusion throughout summer. Bright salmon-pink. ***Leaves*** Semi-evergreen, with 5 deeply cut, toothed lobes. Mid-green.

- NATIVE HABITAT Garden origin.
- CULTIVATION Grow in any soil unless waterlogged, in sun or light shade. Excellent weed-smothering ground cover. Also suitable for the front of herbaceous borders and for cottage gardens.
- PROPAGATION By division in autumn or spring.

☼ ◊

Z 4–8

HEIGHT
18in (45cm)

SPREAD
24in (60cm)

Geraniaceae

GERANIUM ASPHODELOIDES

Habit Mound-forming. ***Flowers*** Small, delicate, star-shaped, on very slender stems, throughout summer. White, or pale to dark pink, with darker veins. ***Leaves*** Mostly basal, divided into 5 or 7 lobes. Mid-green.

- NATIVE HABITAT Woods and meadows, from S. Europe to Turkey and N. Iran.
- CULTIVATION Grow in moderately fertile, well-drained soil, in sun or light shade. Suitable for borders, or a cottage or wildflower garden.
- PROPAGATION Seed or division in spring or autumn.

☼ ◊

Z 8–10

HEIGHT
to 24in (60cm)

SPREAD
24in (60cm)

Rosaceae | JAPANESE BURNET

SANGUISORBA OBTUSA

Habit Clump-forming, rhizomatous. ***Flowers*** Tiny, in dense, slightly arching, bottle-brush spikes, borne above the foliage in midsummer. Rose-crimson. ***Leaves*** Divided, with 13–17 oval or elliptic leaflets. Gray-green, blue-green beneath.

- NATIVE HABITAT Alpine meadows, Japan.
- CULTIVATION Tolerates partial shade. Grow in fertile, moist, but well-drained soil. Good for damp borders, woodland gardens, and waterside plantings.
- PROPAGATION By division in spring or seed in autumn.

☼ ◐

Z 4–8

HEIGHT
3–4ft (1–1.2m)

SPREAD
2ft (60cm)

Scrophulariaceae

DIASCIA RIGESCENS

Habit Trailing, mat-forming. ***Flowers*** Spurred, flat-faced, in dense, upright spikes throughout summer. Salmon-pink. ***Leaves*** Heart-shaped, toothed. Mid-green.

- NATIVE HABITAT Damp forest margins and grassland in South Africa.
- CULTIVATION Grow in fertile, humus-rich, moist but well-drained soil, in full sun. Excellent for a rock garden, border front, or raised bed.
- PROPAGATION By fresh seed or softwood cuttings in spring, or semi-ripe cuttings in summer.

Z 7–9

HEIGHT
9in (23cm)

SPREAD
to 12in (30cm)

Scrophulariaceae

DIASCIA VIGILIS

Habit Prostrate. ***Flowers*** Flat, outward-facing, short-spurred, in loose, upright spires throughout summer. Clear pink. ***Leaves*** Narrowly oval, toothed. Pale green.

- NATIVE HABITAT Damp, rocky places and scrub in the Drakensberg mountains and W. Lesotho.
- CULTIVATION Grow in fertile, humus-rich, moist but well-drained soil, in full sun. Is excellent for a border front or raised bed.
- PROPAGATION By fresh seed or softwood cuttings in spring, or semi-ripe cuttings in summer.

Z 7–9

HEIGHT
12–16in (30–40cm)

SPREAD
24in (60cm)

Caryophyllaceae | FLOWER OF JOVE

LYCHNIS FLOS-JOVIS

Habit Upright, clump-forming. ***Flowers*** Variable, borne in terminal, rounded clusters, in midsummer. Soft rose-pink, purplish-pink, or scarlet. ***Leaves*** Lance- to spoon-shaped. Gray-green, white-hairy.

- NATIVE HABITAT Dry, sub-alpine slopes in the European Alps.
- CULTIVATION Grow in well-drained, not too fertile soil, in full sun. Suitable for the front of an herbaceous border or for cottage gardens.
- PROPAGATION By division or seed in autumn or spring.

Z 5–9

HEIGHT
18in (45cm)

SPREAD
18in (45cm)

Caryophyllaceae | ALPINE CATCHFLY

LYCHNIS VISCARIA

Habit Upright, clump-forming. ***Flowers*** Small, sticky, star-shaped, borne in dense, upright, spike-like heads, in early summer. Bright reddish-purple. ***Leaves*** Oval to lance-shaped, sticky-hairy beneath. Mid-green.

- NATIVE HABITAT Dry, rocky hills and cliffs, from Europe to W. Asia.
- CULTIVATION Grow in well-drained, not too fertile soil, in full sun. Suitable for the front of an herbaceous border and for cottage gardens.
- PROPAGATION Seed or division in autumn or spring.

Z 4–8

HEIGHT
12in (30cm) or more

SPREAD
12–18in (30–45cm)

Geraniaceae

GERANIUM MACRORRHIZUM

Habit Compact, carpeting, rhizomatous. ***Flowers*** Small, in pairs or clusters, in early summer. Magenta-pink, soft rose-pink, or white. ***Leaves*** Aromatic, semi-evergreen, divided into 5–7 deeply cut lobes. Mid-green, tinted red and bronze in autumn.

• NATIVE HABITAT Scrub, woodland and screes in the mountains of S. Europe.

• CULTIVATION Grow in moist or dry soil, in sun or partial shade. Provides good ground cover.

• PROPAGATION By seed or division in autumn or spring, or by semi-ripe cuttings in summer.

Z 4–8

HEIGHT 12–15in (30–38cm)

SPREAD 24in (60cm) or more

Asteraceae/Compositae

OSTEOSPERMUM JUCUNDUM

Habit Clump-forming, woody-based. ***Flowers*** Large, single, daisy-like, borne in profusion in late summer. Soft pink, dark-eyed. ***Leaves*** Evergreen, lance-shaped, toothed, and serrated. Mid-green.

• NATIVE HABITAT Mountain rocks and damp grassland, often at high altitudes, in South Africa.

• CULTIVATION Grow in well-drained soil in sun.

• PROPAGATION By seed in spring or by cuttings of non-flowering shoots in midsummer.

• OTHER NAMES *O. barberiae, Dimorphotheca barberiae.*

Z 9–10

HEIGHT 12in (30cm)

SPREAD 12in (30cm)

Polygonaceae

PERSICARIA MACROPHYLLA

Habit Clump-forming, spreading, rhizomatous. ***Flowers*** Tiny, borne in dense, sometimes nodding, cylindrical spikes, on strong, slender stems, in midsummer. Rich rose-pink. ***Leaves*** Lance-shaped. Blue-green.

• NATIVE HABITAT Alpine meadows, Himalayas.

• CULTIVATION Grow in moist, fertile soil. Vigorous and long-flowering specimen for a moist border.

• PROPAGATION Seed or division in spring or autumn.

• OTHER NAMES *P. sphaerostachya, Polygonum macrophyllum, Polygonum sphaerostachyum.*

Z 4–9

HEIGHT 18–24in (45–60cm)

SPREAD 12in (30cm) often more

Asteraceae/Compositae

CENTAUREA HYPOLEUCA 'John Coutts'

Habit Upright, clump-forming. ***Flowers*** Large, cornflower-like, borne on branching stems from early to midsummer. Deep bright pink with paler centers. ***Leaves*** Deeply divided into lobed and cut, slightly hairy segments. Green, densely white-hairy beneath.

• NATIVE HABITAT Garden origin.

• CULTIVATION Grow in any well-drained soil, including poor soils, in full sun. Good for the front of an herbaceous border and for cottage gardens.

• PROPAGATION By division in spring or autumn.

Z 4–7

HEIGHT 24in (60cm)

SPREAD 18in (45cm)

Lamiaceae/Labiatae

PHYSOSTEGIA VIRGINIANA 'Vivid'

Habit Upright, rhizomatous. ***Flowers*** Tubular, hooded, 2-lipped, in erect spikes, in late summer. Dark lilac-pink. ***Leaves*** Toothed, elliptic or lance-shaped. Mid-green.

• NATIVE HABITAT Garden origin.

• CULTIVATION Grow in moist, humus-rich, fertile soil, in sun. The flowers have hinged stalks that stay fixed when moved, hence the common name of obedient plant. Suitable for herbaceous borders. The flowers are good for cutting.

• PROPAGATION By division in spring.

Z 4–8

HEIGHT
12–24in (30–60cm)

SPREAD
12–24in (30–60cm)

Geraniaceae | STORKSBILL

ERODIUM MANESCAVII

Habit Mound-forming. ***Flowers*** Geranium-like, in loose clusters of 5–20, throughout summer. Deep magenta-pink with darker blotches. ***Leaves*** Divided into deeply cut, toothed leaflets. Blue-green.

• NATIVE HABITAT Alpine meadows, Pyrenees.

• CULTIVATION Grow in moist but well-drained soil, in a warm, sunny site. Good for the front of an herbaceous border and for scree plantings.

• PROPAGATION By semi-ripe cuttings in summer, or by seed in autumn or spring.

Z 6–8

HEIGHT
18in (45cm)

SPREAD
24in (60cm)

Melastomataceae | SPANISH-SHAWL

HETEROCENTRON ELEGANS

Habit Mat-forming, dense, creeping. ***Flowers*** Small, 4-petaled, profusely in summer and autumn. Magenta to mauve. ***Leaves*** Evergreen, small, oval to oblong, bristly to downy. Mid-green.

• NATIVE HABITAT Mexico, Guatemala, Honduras.

• CULTIVATION Grow as a house or conservatory plant in cool climates, in well-drained soil or potting mix in full sun. Suitable for inside borders and pots, or for sunny banks outside in frost-free areas.

• PROPAGATION By softwood or stem tip cuttings in late winter or early spring.

Z 11

Min. 41°F (5°C)

HEIGHT
2in (5cm)

SPREAD
indefinite

Bignoniaceae

INCARVILLEA MAIREI

Habit Compact, clump-forming. ***Flowers*** Trumpet-shaped, on short stems in early summer; stems elongate after flowering. Purplish-pink, gray-white or yellow within. ***Leaves*** Divided into pairs of oval to oblong leaflets. Mid- to dark green.

• NATIVE HABITAT Dry, rocky slopes, Himalayas.

• CULTIVATION Grow in deep, sandy, very well-drained soil, in full sun. Protect young growth from slugs. Mulch crowns with dry straw or similar in winter.

• PROPAGATION By seed in autumn or spring.

Z 7–8

HEIGHT
12in (30cm)

SPREAD
12in (30cm)

Asteraceae/Compositae | BUTTON SNAKEWORT

LIATRIS SPICATA

Habit Upright, clump-forming. ***Flowers*** Small, in dense, upright, cylindrical spikes, borne on stiff stems in late summer. Bright purplish-pink. ***Leaves*** Narrow, grass-like, borne in basal tufts. Mid-green.

• NATIVE HABITAT Damp meadows and marshes, E. North America.

• CULTIVATION Grow in fertile, moist, well-drained soil, in full sun. Cut flowers last well in water.

• PROPAGATION By division in spring.

• OTHER NAMES *L. callilepis.*

Z 4–9

HEIGHT
24in (60cm)

SPREAD
12in (30cm)

Saxifragaceae

BOYKINIA JAMESII

Habit Rhizomatous, mound-forming. ***Flowers*** Open, bell-shaped, 1in (2.5cm) across, borne in long-stalked sprays in early summer. Spoon-shaped, cherry-carmine petals with a green eye. ***Leaves*** Kidney-shaped, 1in (2.5cm) wide, leathery, in basal rosettes. Bright green.

• NATIVE HABITAT Moist, shady mountain habitats in northwest US.

• CULTIVATION Needs moist but well-drained, humus-rich, neutral to acid soil. Suits a shady niche in a rock garden. It is also an excellent plant for the alpine house, and responds well to generous applications of liquid fertilizer. It rarely sets seed in cultivation.

• PROPAGATION Division in spring, or seed in autumn.

• OTHER NAMES *Telesonix jamesii.*

pH

Z 5–9

HEIGHT
24in (60cm)

SPREAD
12in (30cm)

Geraniaceae

GERANIUM 'Ann Folkard'

Habit Clump-forming, with a short, creeping rootstock. ***Flowers*** Single, cup-shaped, borne in great profusion in midsummer. Bright magenta-pink, with dark veins and black centers. ***Leaves*** Rounded, divided into 7 deeply cut lobes. Bright yellowish-green leaves turning red in autumn.
• NATIVE HABITAT Garden origin.
• CULTIVATION This geranium is easily grown in any moderately fertile, well-drained soil, in full sun or partial shade. It is well-suited for inclusion in an herbaceous border and makes a very attractive addition to an informal cottage-style garden. This is one of the most reliable and attractive of the more recently introduced hardy geraniums and is widely available.
• PROPAGATION Many geraniums are easily propagated by division, but each plant of *G.* 'Ann Folkard' forms just one rootstock that defies division. It is therefore best propagated by cuttings taken of side shoots in summer.

Z 5–8

HEIGHT
20in (50cm)

SPREAD
36in (1m)

Gesneriaceae

ACHIMENES 'Little Beauty'

Habit Bushy. ***Flowers*** Large, funnel-shaped, in summer. Deep pink with a yellow eye. ***Leaves*** Oval, toothed. Glossy, bluish-green.
• NATIVE HABITAT Garden origin.
• CULTIVATION Grow as a house or greenhouse plant in cool climates in well-drained, humus-rich potting soil. Site in bright, indirect light. Water freely when in growth. Dry out after flowering, and store rhizomes above freezing point over winter.
• PROPAGATION By division of rhizomes in spring, or by stem cuttings in summer.

Min. 50°F (10°C)

HEIGHT
10in (25cm)

SPREAD
12in (30cm)

Scrophulariaceae

MIMULUS LEWISII

Habit Creeping, upright. ***Flowers*** Snapdragon-like, tubular with spreading lobes, borne singly in the leaf axils, in summer. Deep rose-pink, paler and spotted deep pink at the throat. ***Leaves*** Lance-shaped with wavy-toothed margins. Mid-green.
• NATIVE HABITAT By streamsides in the mountains of W. North America.
• CULTIVATION Tolerates dry soils, but best in moist or wet soil, in full sun. Good for a bog garden.
• PROPAGATION By seed or division in spring or softwood cuttings in late summer.

Z 6–9

HEIGHT
24in (60cm)

SPREAD
18in (45cm)

CARNATIONS AND PINKS

Carnations and pinks belong to the genus *Dianthus.* They are widely grown both for their attractive, often spicy-scented flowers, and their silvery, gray- or blue-green leaves.

The single, double, or semi-double flowers, which come in almost every color except blue and green, may be "selfs," all of one color; "fancies" with contrasting stripes, flakes, or spots; "picotee" with petals edged in a contrasting color to the usually white or yellow ground; or "laced" in which the center of each petal has a zone of a contrasting color.

Carnations and pinks are divided here into the following groups:

Border carnations have an upright habit and flower prolifically once in midsummer. Each stem bears 5 or more, often scented flowers. Grow in a border, or for cutting and exhibition.

Perpetual-flowering carnations are grown under glass for cutting and exhibition. They bloom all year, and are usually disbudded to leave one terminal bud per stem. Spray forms have the central bud removed to leave 4–5 flowers per stem.

Old-fashioned pinks are grown in borders for their clove-scented flowers, produced in midsummer.

Modern pinks have clove-scented flowers, produced in flushes in summer. They are excellent for borders or cutting.

Carnations and pinks need an open position in full sun, and humus-rich, well-drained, neutral and alkaline soil. All except the perpetual-flowering carnations are hardy.

Carnations and pinks can be propagated from cuttings of non-flowering shoots in summer for hardy perennials, and in late winter under glass for half-hardy perennials. Propagate border carnations after flowering by layering. This involves wounding and pinning down the stems of non-flowering sideshoots to encourage new roots to form.

D. 'Mrs. Sinkins'

Habit Clump-forming.
Flowers Heavily scented, fully-double, with fringed petals, borne in profusion in midsummer. White.
Leaves Evergreen, linear. Gray-green.
• TIPS A sturdy and reliable old cultivar.
• HEIGHT 12in (30cm).
• SPREAD 9–12in (23–30cm).

D. 'Mrs. Sinkins'
(Old-fashioned pink)

Z 5–9

D. 'Haytor'

Habit Clump-forming.
Flowers Clove-scented, semi-double with fringed petals, in clusters of 4–6, in several flushes through summer. White.
Leaves Evergreen, linear, Gray-green.
• CULTIVATION Excellent for cutting.
• HEIGHT 12–18in (30–45cm).
• SPREAD 9–12in (23–30cm).

D. 'Haytor'
(Modern pink)

Z 5–9

D. 'Musgrave's Pink'

Habit Clump-forming.
Flowers Scented, single, profusely, in midsummer. White with a green eye.
Leaves Evergreen, linear. Gray-green.
• TIPS A very old and reliable cultivar.
• OTHER NAMES *D.* 'Charles Musgrave', *D.* 'Green Eyes'.
• HEIGHT 12in (30cm).
• SPREAD 9–12in (23–30cm).

D. 'Musgrave's Pink'
(Old-fashioned pink)

Z 5–9

D. 'White Ladies'

Habit Clump-forming.
Flowers Very fragrant, fully double, borne in profusion in midsummer. Fringed white petals flushed green at the base.
Leaves Evergreen, linear. Gray-green.
• HEIGHT 12–18in (30–45cm).
• SPREAD 9–12in (23–30cm).

D. 'White Ladies'
(Old-fashioned pink)

Z 5–9

D. 'Nives'
Habit Neat.
Flowers Fully double, to 4in (10cm) across, produced throughout the year but mainly in summer. White.
Leaves Evergreen, linear. Blue-green.
• TIPS Needs staking.
• HEIGHT 3–5ft (1–1.5m).
• SPREAD 1ft (30cm).

D. 'Nives'
(Perpetual-flowering carnation)

D. 'Fair Folly'
Habit Clump-forming.
Flowers Clove-scented, single, in clusters of 4–5, in midsummer only. Dusky pink to purple, each petal with 2 white splashes.
Leaves Evergreen, linear. Gray-green.
• OTHER NAMES *D.* 'Constance Finnis'.
• HEIGHT 12–18in (30–45cm).
• SPREAD 9–12in (23–30cm).

D. 'Fair Folly'
(Old-fashioned pink)

Z 5–9

D. 'Eva Humphries'
Habit Clump-forming.
Flowers Scented, semi-double, to 3in (8cm) across, in clusters of up to 5, in mid-summer. White petals finely edged with purple.
Leaves Evergreen, linear. Blue-green.
• HEIGHT 2½ft (75cm).
• SPREAD 1ft (30cm).

D. 'Eva Humphries'
(Border carnation)

Z 5–9

D. 'Gran's Favourite'
Habit Clump-forming.
Flowers Scented, semi-double, borne in profusion in mid-summer. White with deep raspberry-pink lacing.
Leaves Evergreen, linear. Grey-green.
• HEIGHT 12–18in (30–45cm).
• SPREAD 9–12in (23–30cm).

D. 'Gran's Favourite'
(Modern laced pink)

Z 5–10

D. 'Dad's Favourite'
Habit Clump-forming.
Flowers Scented, semi-double, borne in profusion in midsummer. White with red and chocolate-brown lacing.
Leaves Evergreen, linear. Gray-green.
• OTHER NAMES *D.* 'A.J. Macsel'.
• HEIGHT 12–18in (30–45cm).
• SPREAD 9–12in (23–30cm).

D. 'Dad's Favourite'
(Old-fashioned pink)

Z 4–9

D. 'Alice'

Habit Clump-forming. ***Flowers*** Clove-scented, semi-double, borne in clusters of 4–6, in several flushes throughout summer. Ivory-white petals with a bold crimson eye. ***Leaves*** Evergreen, linear. Gray-green.
- HEIGHT 12–18in (30–45cm).
- SPREAD 9–12in (23–30cm).

D. 'Alice'
(Modern pink)

Z 5–9

D. 'Prudence'

Habit Clump-forming, spreading. ***Flowers*** Well-scented, semi-double, borne in profusion in midsummer. Palest pink, laced with red-purple. ***Leaves*** Evergreen, linear. Gray-green.
- HEIGHT 12in (30cm).
- SPREAD 9–12in (23–30cm) or more.

D. 'Prudence'
(Old-fashioned pink)

Z 5–9

D. 'London Brocade'

Habit Clump-forming. ***Flowers*** Clove-scented, fully double, in clusters of 4–5, in profusion in midsummer. Crimson-laced, pink petals. ***Leaves*** Evergreen, linear. Gray-green.
- TIPS Excellent for cutting.
- HEIGHT 12–18in (30–45cm).
- SPREAD 9–12in (23–30cm).

D. 'London Brocade'
(Old-fashioned pink)

Z 5–9

D. 'Forest Treasure'

Habit Clump-forming. ***Flowers*** Scented, double, to 3in (8cm).across, in clusters of up to 5, in midsummer. White petals splashed with reddish-purple. ***Leaves*** Evergreen, linear. Blue-green.
- HEIGHT 2½ft (75cm).
- SPREAD 1ft (30cm).

D. 'Forest Treasure'
(Border carnation)

Z 5–9

D. 'London Delight'

Habit Clump-forming. ***Flowers*** Scented, semi-double, borne in profusion in midsummer. Lavender petals laced with purple. ***Leaves*** Evergreen, linear. Gray-green.
- HEIGHT 12in (30cm).
- SPREAD 9–12in (23–30cm).

D. 'London Delight'
(Old-fashioned pink)

Z 5–9

D. 'Pierrot'

Habit Neat – needs support.
Flowers Fully double, to 4in (10cm) across, all year but mainly in summer. Pale rose-lavender petals finely edged with purple.
Leaves Evergreen, linear. Blue-green.

- OTHER NAMES *D.* 'Pink Calypso'.
- HEIGHT 3–5ft (1–1.5m).
- SPREAD 1ft (30cm).

D. 'Pierrot'
(Perpetual-flowering carnation)

D. 'Emile Paré'

Habit Clump-forming.
Flowers Small, scented semi-double, borne in dense clusters in midsummer. Salmon-pink.
Leaves Evergreen, linear. Mid-green.

- HEIGHT 12–18in (30–45cm).
- SPREAD 9–12in (23–30cm).

D. 'Emile Paré'
(Old-fashioned pink)

Z 5–10

D. 'Doris'

Habit Clump-forming.
Flowers Clove-scented fully double, in clusters of 4–6, in profuse flushes throughout summer. Pale pink with a darker salmon-pink ring at the center.
Leaves Evergreen, linear, gray-green.

- HEIGHT 12–18in (30–45cm).
- SPREAD 9–12in (23–30cm).

D. 'Doris'
(Modern pink)

Z 5–10

D. 'Monica Wyatt'

Habit Clump-forming.
Flowers Strongly clove-scented, fully double, in clusters of 4–6, in several flushes through summer. Cyclamen-pink with a magenta eye.
Leaves Evergreen, linear. Gray-green.

- HEIGHT 12–18in (30–45cm).
- SPREAD 9–12in (23–30cm).

D. 'Monica Wyatt'
(Modern pink)

Z 5–10

D. 'Pink Calypso'

Habit Neat – needs support.
Flowers Fully double, to 4in (10cm) across, produced all year round but mainly in summer. Strong, clear pink petals.
Leaves Evergreen, linear. Blue-green.

- OTHER NAMES *D.* 'Truly Yours'.
- HEIGHT 3–5ft (1–1.5m).
- SPREAD 1ft (30cm).

D. 'Pink Calypso'
(Perpetual-flowering carnation)

D. 'Valda Wyatt'

Habit Clump-forming.
Flowers Strongly clove-scented, fully double, borne in clusters of 4–6, in several flushes throughout summer. Rose-lavender.
Leaves Evergreen, linear. Gray-green.

- HEIGHT 12–18in (30–45cm).
- SPREAD 9–12in (23–30cm).

D. 'Valda Wyatt'
(Modern pink)

Z 5–10

D. 'Becky Robinson'

Habit Clump-forming.
Flowers Clove-scented, semi-double, borne in clusters of 4–6, in several flushes throughout summer. Rose-pink petals laced with ruby-red.
Leaves Evergreen, linear. Gray-green.

- TIPS Good for exhibition.
- HEIGHT 12–18in (30–45cm).
- SPREAD 9–12in (23–30cm).

D. 'Becky Robinson'
(Modern laced pink)

Z 5–9

D. 'Pink Jewel'

Habit Clump-forming.
Flowers Clove-scented, semi-double, in several flushes throughout summer. Pink.
Leaves Evergreen, linear, Gray-green.
• TIPS Very floriferous and excellent for rock gardens.
• HEIGHT 4–6in (10–15cm).
• SPREAD 9–12in (23–30cm).

D. 'Pink Jewel'
(Modern pink)

Z 3–8

D. 'Joy'

Habit Clump-forming.
Flowers Clove-scented, fully double, borne in clusters of 4–6, in several flushes throughout summer. Rich pink.
Leaves Evergreen, linear. Gray-green.
• TIPS Excellent for cutting.
• HEIGHT 12–18in (30–45cm).
• SPREAD 9–12in (23–30cm).

D. 'Joy'
(Modern pink)

Z 5–9

D. 'Houndspool Ruby'

Habit Clump-forming.
Flowers Clove-scented, fully double, in clusters of 4–6, in profuse flushes in summer. Ruby-pink, with a darker ring at the center.
Leaves Evergreen, linear. Gray-green.
• OTHER NAMES *D.* 'Ruby', *D.* 'Ruby Doris'.
• HEIGHT 12–18in (30–45cm).
• SPREAD 9–12in (23–30cm).

D. 'Houndspool Ruby'
(Modern pink)

Z 5–9

D. 'Christopher'

Habit Clump-forming.
Flowers Lightly clove-scented, fully double, borne in clusters of 4–6, in several flushes in summer. Bright salmon-red.
Leaves Evergreen, linear. Gray-green.
• TIPS Excellent for cutting.
• HEIGHT 12–18in (30–45cm).
• SPREAD 9–12in (23–30cm).

D. 'Christopher'
(Modern pink)

Z 5–9

D. 'Bovey Belle'

Habit Clump-forming.
Flowers Clove-scented, fully double, borne in clusters of 4–6, in several flushes throughout summer. Bright purplish-pink.
Leaves Evergreen, linear. Gray-green.
• TIPS Good for cutting.
• HEIGHT 12–18in (30–45cm).
• SPREAD 9–12in (23–30cm).

D. 'Bovey Belle'
(Modern pink)

Z 5–9

D. 'Laced Monarch'

Habit Clump-forming.
Flowers Fully double, to 2in (5cm) across, in profusion, in midsummer. Pink, with maroon-red lacing.
Leaves Evergreen, linear. Blue-green.
• HEIGHT 12–18 in (30–45cm).
• SPREAD 9–12in (23–30cm).

D. 'Laced Monarch'
(Modern laced pink)

Z 5–9

D. 'Astor'

Habit Neat.
Flowers Scented, fully double, to 4in (10cm) across, produced throughout the year but mainly in summer. Scarlet.
Leaves Evergreen, linear. Blue-green.
• TIPS Needs staking.
• HEIGHT 3–5ft (1–1.5m).
• SPREAD 1ft (30cm).

D. 'Astor'
(Perpetual-flowering carnation)

D. 'Nina'

Habit Neat.
Flowers Fully double, to 4in (10cm) across, produced throughout the year but mainly in summer. Crimson, with neatly arranged, smooth-edged petals.
Leaves Evergreen, linear. Blue-green.

- TIPS Needs staking.
- HEIGHT 3–5ft (1–1.5m).
- SPREAD 1ft (30cm).

D. 'Nina'
(Perpetual-flowering carnation)

D. 'Bookham Perfume'

Habit Clump-forming.
Flowers Scented, semi-double, to 3in (8cm) across, borne on short, stiff stems in clusters of up to 5, in midsummer. Crimson.
Leaves Evergreen, linear. Blue-green.

- HEIGHT 2½ft (75cm).
- SPREAD 1ft (30cm).

D. 'Bookham Perfume'
(Border carnation)

Z 5–9

D. 'Brympton Red'

Habit Clump-forming.
Flowers Single, in profusion in midsummer. Bright crimson with darker shading.
Leaves Evergreen, linear. Gray-green.

- HEIGHT 12in (30cm).
- SPREAD 9–12in (23–30cm).

D. 'Brympton Red'
(Old-fashioned pink)

Z 5–9

D. 'Lavender Clove'

Habit Vigorous, clump-forming. ***Flowers*** Scented, semi-double, to 3in (8cm) across, borne on long stems in clusters of up to 5, in midsummer. Dusky lavender-gray.
Leaves Evergreen, linear. Blue-green.

- HEIGHT 2½ft (75cm).
- SPREAD 1ft (30cm).

D. 'Lavender Clove'
(Border carnation)

Z 5–9

D. 'Bookham Fancy'

Habit Clump-forming.
Flowers Scented, semi-double, to 3in (8cm) across, borne on short, stiff stems in clusters of up to 5, in midsummer. Bright yellow, edged and flecked carmine-purple.
Leaves Evergreen, linear. Blue-green.

- HEIGHT 2½ft (75cm).
- SPREAD 1ft (30cm).

D. 'Bookham Fancy'
(Border carnation)

Z 5–9

D. 'Happiness'

Habit Clump-forming.
Flowers Scented, semi-double, to 3in (8cm) across, in clusters of up to 5, in midsummer. Yellow petals, striped scarlet-orange.
Leaves Evergreen, linear. Blue-green.

- HEIGHT 2½ft (75cm).
- SPREAD 1ft (30cm).

D. 'Happiness'
(Border carnation)

Z 5–9

D. 'Clara'

Habit Neat – needs support.
Flowers Fully double, to 4in (10cm). across, produced throughout the year but mainly in summer. Yellow; flecked with salmon-red.
Leaves Evergreen, linear. Blue-green.

- HEIGHT 3–5ft (1–1.5m).
- SPREAD 1ft (30cm).

D. 'Clara'
(Perpetual-flowering carnation)

D. 'Crompton Princess'

Habit Neat.
Flowers Fully double, to 4in (10cm) across, produced throughout the year but mainly in summer. Pure white.
Leaves Evergreen, linear. Blue-green.

- TIPS Needs staking.
- HEIGHT 3–5ft (1–1.5m).
- SPREAD 1ft (30cm).

D. 'Crompton Princess'
(Perpetual-flowering carnation)

D. 'Cream Sue'

Habit Neat.
Flowers Fully double, to 4in (10cm) across, produced throughout the year but mainly in summer. Rich cream.
Leaves Evergreen, linear. Blue-green.

- TIPS Needs staking.
- HEIGHT 3–5ft (1–1.5m).
- SPREAD 1ft (30cm).

***D.* 'Cream Sue'**
(Perpetual-flowering carnation)

D. 'Borello'

Habit Neat.
Flowers Fully double, to 4in (10cm) across, produced throughout the year but mainly in summer. Yellow.
Leaves Evergreen, linear. Blue-green.

- TIPS Needs staking.
- HEIGHT 3–5ft (1–1.5m).
- SPREAD 1ft (30cm).

***D.* 'Borello'**
(Perpetual-flowering carnation)

D. 'Golden Cross'

Habit Clump-forming.
Flowers Scented, double, to 3in (8cm) across, in clusters of up to 5, in midsummer. Yellow.
Leaves Evergreen, linear. Blue-green.

- HEIGHT 2½ft (75cm).
- SPREAD 1ft (30cm).

***D.* 'Golden Cross'**
(Border carnation)

Z 5–9

D. 'Aldridge Yellow'

Habit Clump-forming.
Flowers Semi-double, to 3in (8cm) across, borne in clusters of up to 5, in midsummer. Clear yellow.
Leaves Evergreen, linear. Blue-green.

- HEIGHT 2½–3½ft (75–110cm).
- SPREAD 1ft (30cm).

***D.* 'Aldridge Yellow'**
(Border carnation)

Z 5–9

D. 'Valencia'

Habit Neat.
Flowers Fully double, to 4in (10cm) across, produced throughout the year but mainly in summer. Golden-orange petals.
Leaves Evergreen, linear. Blue-green.

- TIPS Needs staking.
- HEIGHT 3–5ft (1–1.5m).
- SPREAD 1ft (30cm).

***D.* 'Valencia'**
(Perpetual-flowering carnation)

D. 'Raggio di Sole'

Habit Neat.
Flowers Fully double, to 4in (10cm) across, produced throughout the year but mainly in summer. Bright orange petals.
Leaves Evergreen, linear. Blue-green.

- TIPS Needs staking.
- HEIGHT 3–5ft (1–1.5m).
- SPREAD 1ft (30cm).

***D.* 'Raggio di Sole'**
(Perpetual-flowering carnation)

D. 'Christine Hough'

Habit Clump-forming.
Flowers Scented, semi-double, to 3in (8cm) across, in clusters of up to 5, in midsummer. Apricot petals overlaid and streaked with dark pink.
Leaves Evergreen, linear. Blue-green.

- HEIGHT 2½ft (75cm).
- SPREAD 1ft (30cm).

***D.* 'Christine Hough'**
(Border carnation)

Z 5–9

D. 'Albisola'

Habit Neat.
Flowers Fully double, to 4in (10cm) across, produced throughout the year but mainly in summer. Clear tangerine-orange.
Leaves Evergreen, linear. Blue-green.

- TIPS Needs staking.
- HEIGHT 3–5ft (1–1.5m).
- SPREAD 1ft (30cm).

***D.* 'Albisola'**
(Perpetual-flowering carnation)

Gesneriaceae

SINNINGIA 'Red Flicker'

Habit Low-growing, tuberous-rooted. ***Flowers*** Large, fleshy, funnel-shaped, borne on short stems, in summer. Pinkish-red. ***Leaves*** Large, oval, in basal rosettes. Bluish-green.

• NATIVE HABITAT Garden origin.

• CULTIVATION In cool climates, grow as a house or greenhouse plant in moist, peaty soil or potting mix. Site in bright light, water freely, and keep humid. Overwinter dried tubers in frost-free conditions.

• PROPAGATION By division of tubers or by stem cuttings in late spring or summer.

Min. 59°F (15°C)

HEIGHT to 12in (30cm)

SPREAD 18in (45cm)

Bignoniaceae

INCARVILLEA DELAVAYI

Habit Clump-forming. ***Flowers*** Trumpet-shaped, borne in few-flowered clusters at the ends of sturdy stems, in early summer. Pinkish-red. ***Leaves*** Divided into pairs of oval to oblong segments, in basal clumps. Mid- to dark green.

• NATIVE HABITAT Scrub and grassland, in the mountains of S.W. China.

• CULTIVATION Grow in deep, sandy, moist, well-drained soil, in full sun. Protect young growth from slugs. Mulch crowns with dry straw in winter.

• PROPAGATION By seed in autumn or spring.

Z 7–8

HEIGHT 18–24in (45–60cm)

SPREAD 12in (30cm)

Verbenaceae

VERBENA 'Sissinghurst'

Habit Mat-forming. ***Flowers*** Small, brilliant, borne in rounded heads on lax stems, throughout summer. Magenta-pink. ***Leaves*** Oval to lance-shaped, cut, and toothed. Mid-green.

• NATIVE HABITAT Garden origin.

• CULTIVATION Grow in fertile, well-drained soil, in full sun. Overwinter young plants in frost-free conditions. The low, mat-forming habit suits the front of a mixed or herbaceous border, or edging for paths and borders. *V.* 'Sissinghurst' is also excellent for planting in hanging baskets, large window boxes or tubs for patio decoration. The brilliant magenta-pink flowers associate well with deep blue and purple flowers and are especially beautiful in combinations with gray- or silver-leaved plants. The cut flowers last well in water.

• PROPAGATION By stem cuttings in late summer or autumn.

Z 6–9

HEIGHT 6–8in (15–20cm)

SPREAD 18in (45cm)

Rosaceae

POTENTILLA NEPALENSIS 'Miss Willmott'

Habit Clump-forming. ***Flowers*** Open cup-shaped, on slender, branching stems, throughout summer. Pink, with cherry-red centers. ***Leaves*** Palmately divided into 5 toothed leaflets. Mid-green.

• NATIVE HABITAT Garden origin.

• CULTIVATION Grow in moderately fertile, well-drained soil, in sun or light shade. Good for the front of an herbaceous border and for cottage gardens.

• PROPAGATION By division in spring or autumn. Seed comes reasonably true; sow in autumn.

Z 5–8

HEIGHT 20in (50cm)

SPREAD 24in (60cm)

Caryophyllaceae

LYCHNIS VISCARIA 'Splendens Plena'

Habit Upright, clump-forming. ***Flowers*** Small, double, borne in dense, spike-like heads, in early summer. Bright magenta-pink. ***Leaves*** Oval to lance-shaped, sticky-hairy beneath. Mid-green.

• NATIVE HABITAT The species occurs on dry, rocky hills and cliffs, from Europe to W. Asia.

• CULTIVATION Grow in well-drained, not too fertile soil, in full sun. Suitable for the front of an herbaceous border and for cottage gardens.

• PROPAGATION By division in autumn or spring.

• OTHER NAMES *L. viscaria* 'Flore Pleno'.

Z 4–8

HEIGHT 18in (45cm)

SPREAD 18in (45cm)

Commelinaceae

TRADESCANTIA × *ANDERSONIANA* 'Purewell Giant'

Habit Clump-forming. ***Flowers*** 3-petaled, borne in succession throughout summer. Red-purple, surrounded by two leaf-like, green bracts. ***Leaves*** Slightly fleshy, narrowly lance-shaped, borne on jointed stems. Mid-green.

• NATIVE HABITAT Garden origin.

• CULTIVATION Grow in fertile, moist but well-drained soil, in sun or light shade. Protect young growth from slugs.

• PROPAGATION By division in spring or autumn.

Z 6–9

HEIGHT to 24in (60cm)

SPREAD 18in (45cm)

Papaveraceae

DICENTRA 'Stuart Boothman'

Habit Tufted, clump-forming. ***Flowers*** Small, pendent, narrowly heart-shaped, borne on arching stems, over long periods in late spring and summer. Carmine-pink. ***Leaves*** Fern-like, very finely cut. Dark gray-green.

• NATIVE HABITAT Garden origin.

• CULTIVATION Grow in humus-rich, moist, well-drained soil, in partial shade. Suitable for a shady herbaceous border or woodland garden.

• PROPAGATION By division in late winter.

• OTHER NAMES *D.* 'Boothman's Variety'.

Z 3–9

HEIGHT 18in (45cm)

SPREAD 12in (30cm)

Crassulaceae

SEDUM 'Ruby Glow'

Habit Clump-forming. ***Flowers*** Small, borne in dense, flattened heads on leafy stems, in profusion from late summer to autumn. Rich ruby-red. ***Leaves*** Fleshy, oval. Purple-gray.

- NATIVE HABITAT Garden origin.
- CULTIVATION Grow in fertile, well-drained soil, with adequate moisture during summer, in full sun. The nectar-rich flowers are very attractive to bees, butterflies, and other beneficial insects. This perennial's handsome leaves and flowers and informal habit make it an excellent choice for softening the front of a mixed or herbaceous border; associates especially well with gray- or silver-leaved plants. It is also suitable for a raised bed, or the top of a wall or terrace, where it is given room to sprawl over the edge.
- PROPAGATION By division in spring.
- OTHER NAMES *Hylotelephium* 'Ruby Glow'.

Z 4–9

HEIGHT
12–18 in
(30–45 cm)

SPREAD
12–18 in
(30–45 cm)

Caryophyllaceae

LYCHNIS CORONARIA

Habit Upright, clump-forming, often short-lived. ***Flowers*** Small, profuse, in open, gray-stemmed sprays, throughout summer. Bright magenta-pink to rose-crimson. ***Leaves*** Oval to lance-shaped, densely hairy, mostly in basal clumps. Silver-gray.
• NATIVE HABITAT Scrub, woodland, rocky slopes, from S.E. Europe to Iran and Turkestan.
• CULTIVATION Grow in well-drained soil, in full sun. Suitable for an herbaceous, especially silver border or a cottage garden. Self-sowing may pose a problem.
• PROPAGATION Seed or division in spring.

Z 4–8

HEIGHT
18–24in (45–60cm)

SPREAD
18in (45cm)

Euphorbiaceae

EUPHORBIA DULCIS 'Chameleon'

Habit Upright, rhizomatous. ***Flowers*** Tiny, borne in branching, slender-stemmed heads in early summer. Yellowish-green, with conspicuous purple-flushed, yellow-green bracts. ***Leaves*** Oblong to lance-shaped. Dark purple, tinted red in autumn.
• NATIVE HABITAT Garden origin.
• CULTIVATION Grow in moist, well-drained soil, in partial shade or sun. Avoid contact with irritant sap.
• PROPAGATION By division in spring or early autumn, or by basal cuttings in spring or summer.

Z 4–9

HEIGHT
18–24in (45–60cm)

SPREAD
24in (60cm)

Leguminosae/ Papilionaceae — CORAL GEM, PARROTS BEAK

LOTUS BERTHELOTII

Habit Trailing. ***Flowers*** Large, beak- or claw-like, in clusters, in summer. Orange-red to scarlet or purple. ***Leaves*** Finely divided into linear or thread-like segments, on silvery stems. Silver-hairy.
• NATIVE HABITAT Canary Islands, Cape Verde Islands, Tenerife.
• CULTIVATION In cooler climates, grow as a house or greenhouse plant in freely draining, sandy potting mix. Site in full sun. Excellent in a hanging basket.
• PROPAGATION By scarified seed in spring, or by semi-ripe cuttings in summer.

Z 11

Min. 41°F (5°C)

HEIGHT
12in (30cm)

SPREAD
indefinite

Saxifragaceae

ASTILBE 'Fanal'

Habit Clump-forming. ***Flowers*** Tiny, deep in neat, feathery, tapering spires, on strong stems, in summer. Crimson-red. ***Leaves*** Divided into toothed, oval, leaflets. Dark green.
• NATIVE HABITAT Garden origin.
• CULTIVATION Grow in moist, fertile, humus-rich soil, in sun or partial shade. Good for damp borders, bog gardens, or waterside plantings. The flower heads dry and turn brown, persisting into winter unless deadheaded.
• PROPAGATION By division in spring or autumn.

Z 4–9

HEIGHT
2ft (60cm)

SPREAD
to 3ft (1m)

Gesneriaceae

SINNINGIA 'Switzerland'

Habit Low-growing, tuberous-rooted. ***Flowers*** Large, fleshy, funnel-shaped, in summer. Scarlet, with ruffled, white-rimmed petals. ***Leaves*** Large, oval, velvety, in basal rosettes. Dark green.
• NATIVE HABITAT Garden origin.
• CULTIVATION In cool climates, grow as a house or greenhouse plant in moist, peaty soil or potting mix. Site in bright light, water freely and keep humid. Overwinter dried tubers in frost-free conditions.
• PROPAGATION By division of tubers or by stem cuttings in late spring or summer.

Min. 59°F (15°C)

HEIGHT
to 12in (30cm)

SPREAD
18in (45cm)

Papaveraceae

DICENTRA 'Bacchanal'

Habit Spreading, rhizomatous. ***Flowers*** Small, pendent, narrowly heart-shaped, on fleshy, arching stems, in late spring and summer. Very dark red. ***Leaves*** Fern-like, deeply cut. Fresh green.
• NATIVE HABITAT Garden origin.
• CULTIVATION Grow in humus-rich, moist but well-drained soil, in partial shade. An exceptionally dark-flowered cultivar and a beautiful plant for a shady herbaceous border or woodland garden.
• PROPAGATION By division when dormant in late winter.

Z 3–9

HEIGHT
12–18in (30–45cm)

SPREAD
18in (45cm) or more

Saxifragaceae

HEUCHERA 'Red Spangles'

Habit Dense, clump-forming. ***Flowers*** Small, bell-shaped, in open spikes on slender, dark red stems, in early summer and again in late summer. Crimson-scarlet. ***Leaves*** Evergreen, heart-shaped, with toothed, rounded, lobes. Purplish-green.
• NATIVE HABITAT Garden origin.
• CULTIVATION Grow in moist, well-drained soil, in sun or partial shade. Provides good ground cover.
• PROPAGATION By division in autumn or spring, using young, outer portions of the crown.

Z 4–8

HEIGHT
12in (30cm)

SPREAD
12in (30cm)

Gesneriaceae

SMITHIANTHA 'Orange King'

Habit Bushy, upright, with tuber-like rhizomes. ***Flowers*** Pendent, tubular, borne in summer and autumn. Orange-red, spotted red within and with yellow lips. ***Leaves*** Large, oval, and heart-shaped at the base, scalloped, velvety. Emerald green, veined dark reddish-purple.

• NATIVE HABITAT Garden origin.

• CULTIVATION Grow as a house or greenhouse plant in cool climates and place in bright, indirect light. The plant benefits from space where air can circulate freely. Feed and water generously when in growth, gradually reducing water after flowering and, in winter, kept almost dry until the spring repotting takes place. Suitable for an herbaceous border in tropical gardens, in well-drained, humus-rich soil.

• PROPAGATION By division of rhizomes in early spring.

Min. 59°F (15°C)

HEIGHT to 24in (60cm)

SPREAD to 24in (60cm)

Caryophyllaceae

LYCHNIS x *ARKWRIGHTII* 'Vesuvius'

Habit Upright, clump-forming. ***Flowers*** Small, cross-shaped, in flat heads at the ends of sturdy stems, in early summer. Brilliant orange-scarlet. ***Leaves*** Oval, borne along the length of the flowering stem. Dark bronze-green

- NATIVE HABITAT Garden origin
- CULTIVATION Grow in fertile, moist, well-drained soil, in sun or light shade; shelter from wind. Looks good with yellow-flowered and bronze-leaved plants.
- PROPAGATION By division in autumn or spring.
- OTHER NAMES *L.* x *haageana* 'Vesuvius'.

Z 6–8

HEIGHT 18in (45cm)

SPREAD 12in (30cm)

Rosaceae

POTENTILLA 'Gibson's Scarlet'

Habit Clump-forming. ***Flowers*** Saucer-shaped, on slender, borne on branching stems, throughout summer. Brilliant scarlet. ***Leaves*** Palmate, strawberry-like. Dark green.

- NATIVE HABITAT Garden origin.
- CULTIVATION Grow in any moderately fertile, well-drained soil, in sun or light shade. A valuable long-flowering perennial, suitable for the front of an herbaceous border and for cottage gardens.
- PROPAGATION By division in spring or autumn.

Z 5–8

HEIGHT 18in (45cm)

SPREAD 18in (45cm)

Rosaceae

POTENTILLA 'William Rollison'

Habit Clump-forming. ***Flowers*** Saucer-shaped, semi-double, on slender, branching stems, throughout summer. Deep orange, flushed scarlet. ***Leaves*** Palmate, strawberry-like. Dark green.

- NATIVE HABITAT Garden origin.
- CULTIVATION Grow in any moderately fertile, well-drained soil, in sun or light shade. A valuable long-flowering plant, suitable for the front of herbaceous borders and cottage gardens.
- PROPAGATION By division in spring or autumn.

Z 5–8

HEIGHT 18in (45cm)

SPREAD 18in (45cm)

Papaveraceae

PAPAVER 'Fireball'

Habit Spreading, clump-forming. ***Flowers*** Pompon-like, fully double, with narrow, satiny, petals, on wiry stems, in summer. Orange-scarlet. ***Leaves*** Narrowly lance-shaped, doubly toothed, dying back after flowering. Green, bristly-hairy.

- NATIVE HABITAT Garden origin.
- CULTIVATION Grow in well-drained, fertile soil, in full sun. A reliable, long-lived perennial for the front of an herbaceous border and cottage gardens.
- PROPAGATION By root cuttings in winter, or by division in autumn.

Z 4–9

HEIGHT 16in (40cm)

SPREAD 12in (30cm)

Rosaceae

POTENTILLA ATROSANGUINEA

Habit Clump-forming. ***Flowers*** Open cup-shaped, borne on finely hairy, branching stems, throughout summer. Dark red. ***Leaves*** Divided into 3 neatly scalloped leaflets. Mid-green, often silvery beneath.
• NATIVE HABITAT Grassy slopes, Himalayas.
• CULTIVATION Grow in any moderately fertile, cool, moist but well-drained soil, in sun or light shade. Good for the front of an herbaceous border and for cottage gardens.
• PROPAGATION By seed or division in spring or autumn.

Z 5–8

HEIGHT 20in (50cm)

SPREAD 24in (60cm)

Asteraceae/Compositae

GAILLARDIA 'Dazzler'

Habit Lax, open. ***Flowers*** Large, daisy-like, borne singly on lax stems, over a long period in summer. Yellow-tipped, bright orange-red petals, around an orange-red disk. ***Leaves*** Soft, lance-shaped, toothed, and lobed. Mid- to dark green.
• NATIVE HABITAT Garden origin.
• CULTIVATION Grow in light, well-drained, not too fertile soil, in sun. Needs staking, but provides brilliant, long-lasting color in a summer border.
• PROPAGATION By root cuttings in winter.
• OTHER NAMES *Gaillardia* x *grandiflora* 'Dazzler'.

Z 3–8

HEIGHT 24in (60cm)

SPREAD 20in (50cm)

Asphodelaceae/Liliaceae

KNIPHOFIA 'Strawberries and Cream'

Habit Upright, clump-forming. ***Flowers*** Small, narrowly tubular, borne on slender, upright stems in terminal spikes, in late summer. Creamy-white, opening from pinkish-red buds. ***Leaves*** Grass-like, narrowly linear, arching to form basal clumps. Mid-green.
• NATIVE HABITAT Garden origin.
• CULTIVATION Grow in full sun, in moist but well-drained soil. Needs ample moisture when in growth. Mulch crowns in cold winter areas.
• PROPAGATION By division in spring.

Z 6–9

HEIGHT 24in (60cm)

SPREAD 18in (45cm)

Scrophulariaceae

MIMULUS 'Royal Velvet'

Habit Compact. ***Flowers*** Snapdragon-like, tubular with spreading lobes, freely produced throughout summer. Mahogany red with golden-yellow, mahogany-speckled throats. ***Leaves*** Broadly oval, toothed. Mid-green.
• NATIVE HABITAT Garden origin.
• CULTIVATION Grow in moist soil in full sun. In cold areas, overwinter young plants in frost-free conditions as insurance against winter losses.
• PROPAGATION By division in spring or softwood cuttings in late summer.

Z 9–10

HEIGHT 12in (30cm)

SPREAD 9in (23cm)

Polemoniaceae	

POLEMONIUM CARNEUM

Habit Clump-forming, slow-spreading. ***Flowers*** Small, bell- to cup-shaped, in loose clusters, in early summer. Pink or lilac-pink. ***Leaves*** Finely divided into 11–19 elliptic to oval leaflets. Mid-green.

- NATIVE HABITAT Scrub and grassland in the coastal hills of California.
- CULTIVATION Tolerates dry soils. Grows best in humus-rich, sharply drained soil, in a warm, sunny, sheltered site. Suitable for herbaceous borders.
- PROPAGATION By seed or division in spring.

Z 4–9

HEIGHT 18in (45cm)

SPREAD 18in (45cm)

Zingiberaceae	

KAEMPFERIA PULCHRA

Habit Tufted, rhizomatous. ***Flowers*** Small, in short spikes from the center of tufts of foliage during summer. Lilac-pink. ***Leaves*** Aromatic, elliptic. Dark green variegated with pale green, bronze, and silver.

- NATIVE HABITAT Thailand, Malaysia.
- CULTIVATION In cool climates, grow as a house or greenhouse plant in moist, humus-rich soil or potting mix. Maintain high humidity. Water freely when in growth. Withhold water as leaves begin to yellow and keep dry during dormancy.
- PROPAGATION By division in late spring.

Min. 64°F (18°C)

HEIGHT 6in (15cm)

SPREAD 12in (30cm)

Alliaceae/Liliaceae	

TULBAGHIA VIOLACEA

Habit Vigorous, clump-forming. ***Flowers*** Small, star-shaped, borne in terminal clusters, in late summer and autumn. Lilac-purple or lilac-pink. ***Leaves*** Semi-evergreen, linear, in basal clumps. Glaucous green.

- NATIVE HABITAT Eastern Cape, Transvaal, South Africa.
- CULTIVATION Grow in well-drained soil, in a warm, sheltered site, in full sun. Suitable for the front of an herbaceous border or the base of a warm wall.
- PROPAGATION By division or seed in spring.

Z 8–10

HEIGHT 18–24in (45–60cm)

SPREAD 12in (30cm)

Gesneriaceae	FALSE AFRICAN VIOLET

STREPTOCARPUS SAXORUM

Habit Rounded, clump-forming. ***Flowers*** Small, tubular, with long-stalks, in leaf axils, in late summer. Lilac with a white tube. ***Leaves*** Softly hairy, fleshy, elliptic to oval. Dark bluish-green.

- NATIVE HABITAT Tanzania, Kenya.
- CULTIVATION Grow as a house or greenhouse plant in cool climates, in moist, humus-rich soil. Site in bright, indirect light, with high humidity. Avoid wetting the leaves when watering.
- PROPAGATION By seed in spring, by division after flowering, or by tip cuttings in spring or summer.

Min. 50–59°F (10–15°C)

HEIGHT 12in (30cm) or more

SPREAD 12in (30cm) or more

Asteraceae/Compositae

ERIGERON 'Dignity'

Habit Robust, clump-forming. ***Flowers*** Daisy-like, borne in profusion over long periods in summer. Slender, pink-violet ray florets around a greenish-yellow disk. ***Leaves*** Lance- to spoon-shaped. Mid-green.

- NATIVE HABITAT Garden origin.
- CULTIVATION Grow in moderately fertile, well-drained soil in sun. A valuable addition to a summer border, noted for its long flowering period.
- PROPAGATION By division in spring or early autumn, or by softwood cuttings in early summer.

Z 5–8

HEIGHT 18in (45cm)

SPREAD 18in (45cm)

Verbenaceae

VERBENA RIGIDA

Habit Stiffly upright or spreading, tuberous-rooted. ***Flowers*** Small, borne in dense spikes, in late summer. Purple to magenta. ***Leaves*** Coarse, oblong, toothed, mostly along the stems. Mid-green.

- NATIVE HABITAT Argentina, Brazil.
- CULTIVATION Grow in moderately fertile, well-drained soil, in a warm, sunny, sheltered site. Mulch with dry straw in cold winter areas.
- PROPAGATION By division of tubers or seed in autumn, or, in cold areas, in spring.
- OTHER NAMES *V. venosa.*

Z 5–9

HEIGHT 18–24in (45–60cm)

SPREAD 12in (30cm)

Commelinaceae

TRADESCANTIA × *ANDERSONIANA* 'Purple Dome'

Habit Clump-forming. ***Flowers*** 3-petaled, in succession through summer. Rich purple, each surrounded by two leaf-like, green bracts. ***Leaves*** Slightly fleshy, narrowly lance-shaped, borne on jointed stems. Mid-green.

- NATIVE HABITAT Garden origin.
- CULTIVATION Grow in fertile, moist but well-drained soil, in sun or light shade. Protect young growth from slugs. Good for an herbaceous border.
- PROPAGATION By division in spring or autumn.

Z 5–9

HEIGHT to 24in (60cm)

SPREAD 18in (45cm)

Polemoniaceae

POLEMONIUM PULCHERRIMUM

Habit Clump-forming, upright. ***Flowers*** Small, bell- to cup-shaped, borne in dense, terminal clusters, in late spring and summer. Purple-blue with white or yellow throats. ***Leaves*** Finely divided into 11–37 elliptic to oval leaflets. Mid-green.

• NATIVE HABITAT Scrub and grassland, N.W. America.

• CULTIVATION Grow in reasonably fertile, humus-rich, well-drained soil, in full sun. The elegantly divided foliage and profusion of attractive flowers produced over long periods in summer, make this an ideal perennial for the front of an herbaceous or mixed border. It is more compact and lower-growing than the more commonly seen *P. caeruleum* and is also suitable for the larger rock garden. In its native regions it is also used in a wildflower garden.

• PROPAGATION By seed or division in spring.

Z 4–8

HEIGHT
20in (50cm)

SPREAD
12in (30cm)

Asteraceae/Compositae

ERIGERON 'Serenity'

Habit Robust, clump-forming. ***Flowers*** Daisy-like, borne in profusion over long periods in summer. Slender, violet ray florets around a greenish-yellow disk. ***Leaves*** Lance- to spoon-shaped. Mid-green.
• NATIVE HABITAT Garden origin.
• CULTIVATION Grow in moderately fertile, well-drained soil in sun. Suitable for a summer border and valued for its long flowering period. Needs some support.
• PROPAGATION By division in spring or early autumn, or by softwood cuttings in early summer.

Z 5–8

HEIGHT 24in (60cm)

SPREAD 24in (60cm)

Boraginaceae

MOLTKIA DOERFLERI

Habit Upright, rhizomatous. ***Flowers*** Small, tubular to funnel-shaped, in few-flowered, terminal clusters in early summer. Purplish-pink. ***Leaves*** Small, lance-shaped, clothed in tiny bristles pressed closely against the surface. Bright green.
• NATIVE HABITAT Rocky places in Albania.
• CULTIVATION Grow in very well-drained soil in a warm, sheltered site. Suitable for the front of a Mediterranean-type border, or for the crevices of a sunny wall.
• PROPAGATION By seed in autumn.

Z 6–9

HEIGHT to 20in (50cm)

SPREAD 10in (25cm)

Asteraceae/Compositae — PERENNIAL CORNFLOWER

CENTAUREA MONTANA

Habit Clump-forming, rhizomatous. ***Flowers*** Large, cornflower-like, borne on lax stems from early to midsummer. Purple, blue, white, or pink. ***Leaves*** Lance-shaped, soft. Grayish-green, white-hairy beneath at first.
• NATIVE HABITAT Woodland and subalpine meadows, in the mountains of Europe.
• CULTIVATION Grow in moist but well-drained soil, in full sun or light shade. Good for the front of herbaceous borders and for cottage gardens.
• PROPAGATION Seed or division in spring or autumn.

Z 3–8

HEIGHT 20in (50cm)

SPREAD 24in (60cm)

Geraniaceae

GERANIUM HIMALAYENSE 'Gravetye'

Habit Clump-forming. ***Flowers*** Large, cup-shaped, in long-stemmed clusters in summer. Clear violet-blue, with a reddish petal base and white eye. ***Leaves*** Deeply divided into 7 overlapping, lobed and toothed segments. Mid- to bright green.
• NATIVE HABITAT Garden origin.
• CULTIVATION Tolerates dry soils. Grow in any well-drained, fertile soil, in sun or light shade. Good for cottage gardens and herbaceous or mixed borders.
• PROPAGATION By division in autumn or spring.
• OTHER NAMES *G. grandiflorum* var. *alpinum*.

Z 4–8

HEIGHT 12in (30cm)

SPREAD 24in (60cm)

Lamiaceae/Labiatae

STACHYS MACRANTHA 'Superba'

Habit Clump-forming, spreading. ***Flowers*** Tubular, hooded, 2-lipped, borne in dense, whorled, upright spikes, in midsummer. Purple-violet. ***Leaves*** Soft, heart-shaped, wrinkled, and roughly hairy. Mid-green.

• NATIVE HABITAT Garden origin.

• CULTIVATION Grow in any moderately fertile, well-drained soil in sun or light shade. A hardy, easily grown, and undemanding perennial that spreads slowly to form dense clumps of foliage. It makes an attractive display at the front of an herbaceous border where its spreading habit helps soften any straight lines. It is also suitable for cottage gardens and other informal plantings. The flowers are attractive to bees. This is a useful perennial for underplanting or edging borders of old-fashioned shrub roses, since it flowers when many of these are at their peak. Pink- or white-flowered variants are also available (*S. macrantha* 'Rosea', *S. macrantha* 'Nivea'). The cut flowers last well in an indoor display.

• PROPAGATION By division in autumn or spring.

Z 4–9

HEIGHT
12–18in
(30–45cm)

SPREAD
12–24in
(30–60cm)

Commelinaceae	

TRADESCANTIA × *ANDERSONIANA* 'Isis'

Habit Clump-forming. ***Flowers*** Three-petaled, borne in succession throughout summer. Deep blue, surrounded by two leaf-like, green bracts. ***Leaves*** Slightly fleshy, narrowly lance-shaped, borne on jointed stems. Mid-green.

- NATIVE HABITAT Garden origin.
- CULTIVATION Grow in fertile, moist but well-drained soil, in sun or light shade. An excellent, long-flowering plant for herbaceous borders. Protect young growth from slugs.
- PROPAGATION By division in spring or autumn.

Z 6–9

HEIGHT to 24in (60cm)

SPREAD 18in (45cm)

Campanulaceae	BALLOON FLOWER

PLATYCODON GRANDIFLORUS

Habit Clump-forming. ***Flowers*** Large, bell-shaped, opening from balloon-shaped buds, in summer. Gray-blue or blue-violet. ***Leaves*** Elliptic to lance-shaped, neatly toothed. Bluish-green.

- NATIVE HABITAT Grassy slopes, in the hills and mountains of N. China, E. Siberia and Japan.
- CULTIVATION Grow in fertile, moist, well-drained soil, in sun or light shade. Excellent for herbaceous borders. Foliage emerges rather late in spring.
- PROPAGATION By seed in autumn, or by basal cuttings of non-flowering shoots in summer.

Z 4–9

HEIGHT 18–24in (45–60cm)

SPREAD 12–18in (30–45cm)

Geraniaceae	

GERANIUM × *MAGNIFICUM*

Habit Clump-forming, stoloniferous. ***Flowers*** Large, cup-shaped, borne in few-flowered clusters in early summer. Rich violet-blue with darker veins. ***Leaves*** Hairy, divided into 9–11 rounded, overlapping lobes. Grayish-green.

- NATIVE HABITAT Long cultivated, origin unknown.
- CULTIVATION Tolerant of exposed sites. Grow in any well-drained, fertile soil, in light shade, or in full sun for more prolific flowering. Excellent for cottage gardens and herbaceous borders.
- PROPAGATION By division in autumn or spring.

Z 4–8

HEIGHT 18in (45cm)

SPREAD 24in (60cm)

Geraniaceae	

GERANIUM 'Johnson's Blue'

Habit Vigorous, clump-forming. ***Flowers*** Large, cup-shaped, borne in few-flowered clusters, throughout summer. Deep lavender-blue. ***Leaves*** Deeply divided into 7–9 narrow, further lobed and divided segments. Bright green.

- NATIVE HABITAT Garden origin.
- CULTIVATION Grow in any well-drained, fertile soil, in light shade or in full sun. Excellent for cottage gardens and herbaceous or mixed borders, associating well with old-fashioned roses.
- PROPAGATION By division in autumn or spring.

Z 4–8

HEIGHT 12in (30cm)

SPREAD 24in (60cm)

Geraniaceae	

Geranium himalayense

Habit Clump-forming. ***Flowers*** Large, cup-shaped, in long-stemmed clusters, in summer. Deep violet-blue, white-eyed. ***Leaves*** Deeply divided into 7 toothed segments. Mid- to bright green.
• NATIVE HABITAT Forest clearings, scrub, and grassy slopes, in the Himalayas.
• CULTIVATION Tolerates dry soils. Grow in well-drained, fertile soil in sun or light shade. Suited to a cottage garden or herbaceous or mixed border.
• PROPAGATION By division in autumn or spring.
• OTHER NAMES *G. grandiflorum.*

Z 4–8

HEIGHT
12in (30cm)

SPREAD
24in (60cm)

Dipsacaceae	

Scabiosa caucasica 'Clive Greaves'

Habit Clump-forming. ***Flowers*** Borne on strong, wiry stems, throughout summer. Lavender-blue petals arranged around a domed, pincushion-like center. ***Leaves*** Lower leaves lance-shaped, in basal clumps, stem leaves pinnately divided. Gray-green.
• NATIVE HABITAT Garden origin.
• CULTIVATION Grow in moderately fertile, well-drained, preferably alkaline soil, in full sun. Excellent for cutting. Suitable for herbaceous borders and cottage gardens.
• PROPAGATION By division in spring or autumn.

Z 4–9

HEIGHT
18–24in
(45–60cm)

SPREAD
18–24in
(45–60cm)

Asteraceae/Compositae	STOKES' ASTER

Stokesia laevis

Habit Rosette-forming, upright. ***Flowers*** Cornflower-like, produced freely during summer at the ends of hairy, leafy stems. Lavender-blue, purple-blue, or occasionally white. ***Leaves*** Elliptic to narrowly lance-shaped, forming winter-green rosettes. Mid-green.
• NATIVE HABITAT Moist pine woods, S.E. North America.
• CULTIVATION Grow in moist but well-drained, sandy, preferably slightly acid soil, in full sun.
• PROPAGATION Seed or division in spring or autumn.

Z 5–8

HEIGHT
12–18in
(30–45cm)

SPREAD
12–18in
(30–45cm)

Polemoniaceae	JACOB'S LADDER

POLEMONIUM CAERULEUM

Habit Clump-forming, upright. ***Flowers*** Small, cup-shaped, in dense, terminal clusters, in summer. Lavender-blue. ***Leaves*** Finely divided into 17–27 lance-shaped leaflets. Mid- to bright green.
• NATIVE HABITAT Scrub and grassland, from N. and C. Europe to Siberia, the Himalayas, and W. North America.
• CULTIVATION Grow in fertile, humus-rich, moist, well-drained soil, in full sun. Suited to herbaceous borders and cottage gardens. Self-sows freely.
• PROPAGATION By seed or division in spring.

Z 4–8

HEIGHT 18–24in (45–60cm)

SPREAD 18–24in (45–60cm)

Geraniaceae	

GERANIUM ERIANTHUM

Habit Mound-forming. ***Flowers*** Saucer-shaped, 5-petaled, mainly in early summer, but often again later in the season. Pale to deep blue-violet with darker veins. ***Leaves*** Divided into 7–9 deeply lobed and toothed segments. Dark green.
• NATIVE HABITAT Scrub, sub-alpine meadows, and coastal grasslands in E. Siberia, Japan, Alaska, and W. Canada.
• CULTIVATION Grow in well-drained soil in sun or light shade. Good for a border or cottage garden.
• PROPAGATION Seed or division in spring or autumn.

Z 3–7

HEIGHT 20in (50cm)

SPREAD 20in (50cm)

Asteraceae/Compositae	BLUE CUPIDONE, CUPID'S DART

CATANANCHE CAERULEA 'Major'

Habit Clump-forming. ***Flowers*** Small, daisy-like, opening from silvery, papery, oval buds, and borne on wiry stems in summer. Lavender-blue, ***Leaves*** Narrow, linear, in basal clumps. Bluish-green.
• NATIVE HABITAT Species occurs in dry grasslands of S.W. Europe.
• CULTIVATION Grow in well-drained, preferably sandy soil, in full sun. Ideal for an herbaceous border, but propagate regularly to maintain vigorous stock. Flowers and buds dry well.
• PROPAGATION By root cuttings in winter.

Z 3–8

HEIGHT 18–24in (45–60cm)

SPREAD 12in (30cm)

Plumbaginaceae	

LIMONIUM PLATYPHYLLUM 'Blue Cloud'

Habit Clump-forming. ***Flowers*** Tiny, borne in diffuse, airy sprays on branching stems, in late summer. Bluish-mauve. ***Leaves*** Leathery, spoon-shaped, in basal rosettes. Dark green.
• NATIVE HABITAT Species occurs in dry grassland, from S.E. Europe to S. Russia.
• CULTIVATION Grow in well-drained, sandy soil, in full sun. Flowers are good for cutting and drying.
• PROPAGATION By division in spring or root cuttings in winter.
• OTHER NAMES *L. latifolium* 'Blue Cloud'.

Z 4–9

HEIGHT 12in (30cm) often more

SPREAD 18in (45cm)

Lamiaceae/Labiatae | CATMINT

Nepeta × *faassenii*

Habit Mound-forming. ***Flowers*** Small, tubular, 2-lipped, borne in loose spike-like clusters, throughout summer. Soft lavender-blue. ***Leaves*** Aromatic, toothed oblong-oval, finely hairy. Gray-green.

- NATIVE HABITAT Garden origin.
- CULTIVATION Grow in well-drained, preferably alkaline soil, in full sun. Good for softening the edge of a dry, sunny herbaceous border, where it will attract bees, butterflies, and other beneficial insects. Cut back hard after the first flush of flowers to encourage a second flush later in the season. Cats are attracted to the aromatic foliage and may roll on the plant and crush it. They can be deterred by inserting prickly twigs into the base of the clump. The leaves and flowers dry well for potpourri.
- PROPAGATION By division in spring or by stem tip or softwood cuttings in summer.

Z 4–8

HEIGHT
18in (45cm)

SPREAD
18in (45cm)

Ranunculaceae	FALSE ANEMONE

ANEMONOPSIS MACROPHYLLA

Habit Clump-forming, rhizomatous. ***Flowers*** Nodding, waxy, anemone-like, borne in open clusters on wiry stems in late summer. ***Leaves*** Fern-like, finely divided leaflets. Dark, glossy green.

• NATIVE HABITAT Mountain woodland in Japan.

• CULTIVATION Grow in moist, humus-rich, preferably acid soil, in a shady, sheltered site. Excellent for a shaded herbaceous border or woodland garden.

• PROPAGATION By division in spring or fresh seed in late summer.

Z 5–8

HEIGHT 18–24in (45–60cm)

SPREAD 20in (50cm)

Campanulaceae	

CAMPANULA 'Burghaltii'

Habit Mound-forming. ***Flowers*** Nodding, funnel-shaped, borne on erect, wiry stems in summer. Pale lavender-gray, opening from amethyst buds. ***Leaves*** Oval, soft, leathery. Mid-green.

• NATIVE HABITAT Garden origin.

• CULTIVATION Grow in moist but well-drained soil, in sun or partial shade. Provide support. Excellent for herbaceous and mixed borders. Cut flowers last reasonably well in water.

• PROPAGATION By basal cuttings in early summer, or by division in spring or autumn.

Z 4–8

HEIGHT 24in (60cm)

SPREAD 12in (30cm)

Apiaceae/Umbelliferae	

ERYNGIUM BOURGATII

Habit Upright, clump-forming. ***Flowers*** Tiny, in dense, rounded heads amidst long, slender, spiny, metallic-blue-purple bracts, from mid- to late summer. Purplish-blue. ***Leaves*** Rounded, much divided into spiny, leathery leaves. Dark green with silvery venation.

• NATIVE HABITAT Rocky places, in the Pyrenees.

• CULTIVATION Grow in moderately fertile, freely draining soil, in full sun. Flowers dry well.

• PROPAGATION By seed in autumn, by division in spring, or by root cuttings in winter.

Z 5–9

HEIGHT 18–24in (45–60cm)

SPREAD 12in (30cm)

Boraginaceae

MERTENSIA SIMPLICISSIMA

Habit Procumbent, clump-forming. ***Flowers*** Small, tubular, blue, on low stems in early summer. ***Leaves*** Fleshy, rounded to spoon-shaped. Pale blue-gray.
• NATIVE HABITAT Coastal sand and gravel, Japan.
• CULTIVATION Grow in sharply drained soils, with added grit or sand, in full sun. Shelter from dry wind to avoid foliage scorch. Good for coastal gardens.
• PROPAGATION By seed or division in autumn or spring.
• OTHER NAMES *M. asiatica, M. maritima* subsp. *asiatica*.

Z 6–8

HEIGHT
12in (30cm)

SPREAD
12in (30cm)

Scrophulariaceae | DIGGER SPEEDWELL

PARAHEBE PERFOLIATA

Habit Clump-forming, subshrubby, woody-based. ***Flowers*** Small, narrowly funnel-shaped, borne in slender, branching, clusters in early summer. Blue-violet. ***Leaves*** Oval, leathery, clasping, and circling the stems. Glaucous, grayish-green.
• NATIVE HABITAT Mountains of S.E. Australia.
• CULTIVATION Grow in well-drained soil, in a warm, sheltered site. Good for a raised bed, sunny herbaceous border, or sprawling through low shrubs.
• PROPAGATION Semi-ripe cuttings in early summer.
• OTHER NAMES *Veronica perfoliata*.

Z 7–9

HEIGHT
18–24in
(45–60cm)

SPREAD
18in (45cm)

Apocynaceae

AMSONIA ORIENTALIS

Habit Clump-forming subshrubby. ***Flowers*** Small, star-shaped, borne in open, terminal sprays in summer. Pale gray-blue. ***Leaves*** Narrowly oval, borne all along the stems. Grayish-green or green.
• NATIVE HABITAT Grassy places, Greece to Turkey.
• CULTIVATION Grow in any fertile, well-drained soil, in sun or light shade. Leave undisturbed after planting.
• PROPAGATION By division in spring, by softwood cuttings in summer or by seed in autumn.
• OTHER NAMES *Rhazya orientalis*.

Z 6–9

HEIGHT
18–24in
(45–60cm)

SPREAD
12–18in
(30–45cm)

Apiaceae/Umbelliferae

ERYNGIUM VARIIFOLIUM

Habit Upright, rosette-forming. ***Flowers*** Tiny, in dense, conical heads above long, slender, spiny, silvery-white bracts, in late summer. Gray-blue. ***Leaves*** Oval, heart-shaped, scalloped. Dark green, veined and marbled with white.
• NATIVE HABITAT Rocky mountains of N. Africa.
• CULTIVATION Grow in moderately fertile, freely draining soil, in full sun. Flowers are good for drying.
• PROPAGATION By seed in autumn, by division in spring, or by root cuttings in winter.

Z 5–9

HEIGHT
18in (45cm)

SPREAD
10in (25cm)

Linaceae

LINUM NARBONENSE

Habit Clump-forming. ***Flowers*** Small, cup- or bowl-shaped, borne in few-flowered clusters on short, slender stems, from early to midsummer. Pale to azure blue. ***Leaves*** Small, linear-lance-shaped. Grayish-green.

• NATIVE HABITAT Dry hills, around the Mediterranean.

• CULTIVATION Grow in well-drained, moderately fertile soil, in a warm, sunny site. Valued for its long flowering season, the clear blues of its silk-textured blooms and its airy, twiggy habit, it is suitable for an herbaceous border particularly those with a Mediterranean theme. Although usually deciduous, in mild areas it may remain evergreen. Seed-raised plants yield an attractive range of blues that are especially effective if planted in drifts. This perennial tends to be short-lived, so propagate regularly.

• PROPAGATION By seed in autumn.

☼ ◊

Z 5–8

HEIGHT
12–24in
(30–60cm)

SPREAD
12in (30cm)

Scrophulariaceae

VERONICA GENTIANOIDES

Habit Mat-forming. ***Flowers*** Small, 4-lobed, borne in slender, upright spikes, in early summer. Pale blue, occasionally dark blue or white. ***Leaves*** Lance-shaped to oval, in basal clumps. Glossy dark green.

- NATIVE HABITAT Woods and meadows, in mountains from the Caucasus to S.W. Asia.
- CULTIVATION Grow in moist but well drained soil, in full sun or light shade. Excellent for the edge of a border.
- PROPAGATION Seed or division in spring or autumn.

Z 5–8

HEIGHT
18in (45cm)

SPREAD
18in (45cm) or more

Boraginaceae

SYMPHYTUM 'Goldsmith'

Habit Robust, clump-forming, rhizomatous. ***Flowers*** Pendent, tubular, in short, paired clusters, from spring to early summer. Blue, white, and pink. ***Leaves*** Coarse, hairy, oval to lance-shaped. Dark green, edged and splashed with gold and cream.

- NATIVE HABITAT Garden origin.
- CULTIVATION Grow in moist soil in sun or shade. Is less invasive than the species. Cut back after first flowering to produce a second flush of bloom.
- PROPAGATION By division in spring.
- OTHER NAMES *S. ibericum* 'Jubilee'.

Z 5–8

HEIGHT
12in (30cm)

SPREAD
18in (45cm) or more

Apocynaceae

AMSONIA TABERNAEMONTANA

Habit Clump-forming. ***Flowers*** Small, star-shaped, borne in open, terminal clusters, in summer. Pale blue. ***Leaves*** Narrowly oval to oval. Grayish-green or green.

- NATIVE HABITAT Damp grasslands of E. North America.
- CULTIVATION Grow in fertile, moist but well-drained soil, in sun or light shade. Leave undisturbed after planting.
- PROPAGATION By division in spring, by softwood cuttings in summer, or by seed in autumn.

Z 3–9

HEIGHT
18–24in (45–60cm)

SPREAD
12–18in (30–45cm)

Boraginaceae	CHATHAM ISLAND FORGET-ME-NOT

MYOSOTIDIUM HORTENSIA

Habit Clump-forming. ***Flowers*** Small, forget-me-not-like, in dense, rounded clusters, in summer. Blue. ***Leaves*** Evergreen, fleshy, kidney- to heart-shaped, deeply ribbed, glossy. Bright green.
• NATIVE HABITAT Rocky and sandy coastlines of the Chatham Islands (New Zealand).
• CULTIVATION Grow in well-drained, humus-rich soil in partial shade, with shelter from wind. Good for coastal gardens. A seaweed mulch is beneficial.
• PROPAGATION By fresh seed in autumn or division in spring. Not an easy plant.

Z 9

HEIGHT 18–24in (45–60cm)

SPREAD 24in (60cm)

Lamiaceae/Labiatae	

SALVIA CACALIIFOLIA

Habit Upright, rhizomatous. ***Flowers*** Tubular, 2-lipped, in branched, spiky clusters, in late summer. Deep blue. ***Leaves*** Diamond-shaped, glossy. Dark green.
• NATIVE HABITAT Mexico, Guatemala.
• CULTIVATION Grow as a house or greenhouse plant in cool climates, in well-drained potting soil. If grown outdoors, place in fertile, humus-rich soil in full sun.
• PROPAGATION By seed in spring or softwood cuttings in summer.

Z 11

Min. 41°F (5°C)

HEIGHT 18in (45cm)

SPREAD 18in (45cm)

Geraniaceae	

GERANIUM WALLICHIANUM 'Buxton's Variety'

Habit Clump-forming, spreading. ***Flowers*** Large, cup-shaped, from midsummer to autumn. White-centered, blue or blue-purple. ***Leaves*** Divided into 5 toothed, lobes. Mid- to bright green, white-flecked.
• NATIVE HABITAT A selected form of garden origin.
• CULTIVATION Grow in well-drained, soil, in sun or light shade. Good for a cottage garden or border.
• PROPAGATION Division in autumn or spring.
• OTHER NAMES *G.* 'Buxton's Blue'.

Z 4–8

HEIGHT 12in (30cm)

SPREAD 24in (60cm)

Lamiaceae/Labiatae	

SALVIA PATENS

Habit Upright, branching. ***Flowers*** Hooded, tubular, 2-lipped, borne in whorls in long, spike-like clusters, in late summer. Intense bright blue or pale blue. ***Leaves*** Sticky-hairy, oval to diamond-shaped. Mid-green.
• NATIVE HABITAT Scrub and rocks in Mexico.
• CULTIVATION Grow in well-drained soil, in full sun. Excellent for borders, bedding, and for patio tubs. Protect young plants from frost in winter.
• PROPAGATION By seed in spring or by softwood cuttings in midsummer.

Z 7–9

HEIGHT 18–24in (45–60cm)

SPREAD 18in (45cm)

Asteraceae/Compositae	ROMAN WORMWOOD

ARTEMISIA PONTICA

Habit Vigorous, upright. ***Flowers*** Tiny, in slender, nodding plumes, in summer. Gray-white. ***Leaves*** Aromatic, feathery, divided into finely hairy, linear, segments, arranged all along the upright stems. Silvery gray-green.

- NATIVE HABITAT Dry, grassy, and rocky hillsides, in C. and E. Europe.
- CULTIVATION Grow in well-drained soil, in full sun. Invaluable in a river border and excellent for color and texture contrasts in an herbaceous border.
- PROPAGATION Division or seed in spring or autumn.

Z 4–8

HEIGHT
24in (60cm)

SPREAD
8in (20cm) often more

Polygonaceae	

PERSICARIA VIRGINIANA 'Painter's Palette'

Habit Mound-forming. ***Flowers*** Seldom produced in cultivation. ***Leaves*** Oval to elliptic. Green, banded with maroon-brown, splashed and striped ivory-yellow and pink-tinted over all.

- NATIVE HABITAT Garden origin.
- CULTIVATION Grow in moist but well-drained soil, with wind shelter. Good foliage contrast in a border.
- PROPAGATION By division in autumn or spring.
- OTHER NAMES *Tovara virginiana* 'Painter's Palette', *Polygonum virginianum* 'Painter's Palette'.

Z 3–9

HEIGHT
24in (60cm)

SPREAD
24in (60cm)

Rosaceae	

ALCHEMILLA CONJUNCTA

Habit Clump-forming. ***Flowers*** Tiny, star-shaped, in many-branched clusters, in mid-summer. Greenish-yellow. ***Leaves*** Circular, with 7–9 segments joined at the base, with teeth almost hidden by silky hair. Blue-green above, silver below.

- NATIVE HABITAT Sub-alpine meadows and rocky streamsides, in the Jura and S.W. Alps.
- CULTIVATION Grow in moist, well-drained soil, in an open sunny site. Often confused with *A. alpina*.
- PROPAGATION By seed or division in spring or autumn.

Z 3–7

HEIGHT
12in (30cm)

SPREAD
12in (30cm)

Rosaceae	LADY'S MANTLE

ALCHEMILLA MOLLIS

Habit Clump-forming, vigorous. ***Flowers*** Tiny, star-shaped, in rounded, open sprays throughout summer. Bright greenish-yellow. ***Leaves*** Circular, with 9–11 rounded, neatly toothed lobes. Soft green.

- NATIVE HABITAT Streambanks, meadows, and forests, in the eastern Carpathians and Caucasus.
- CULTIVATION Grow in moist, well-drained soil, in an open sunny site. Suitable for herbaceous borders, screes, and paving crevice plantings. Flowers dry well for winter arrangements. Self-sows freely.
- PROPAGATION Seed or division in spring or autumn.

Z 4–7

HEIGHT
12in (30cm)

SPREAD
12in (30cm)

HOSTAS

Hostas, also known as plantain lilies, are grown primarily for their luxuriant and decorative foliage, which provides a wide range of colors and textural contrasts in an herbaceous border. Many hostas also produce attractive spike-like heads of bell-, trumpet-shaped, or tubular flowers, which rise gracefully above the foliage in mid-summer. Some flowers are strongly fragrant.

Hostas are suitable for many situations from damp, shady borders and poolsides to containers. The large clump-forming species provide excellent ground cover.

Grow in moist but well-drained, humus-rich, neutral soil, in partial shade, but take care to protect the leaves against slug and snail damage.

Propagate by division in early spring.

H. UNDULATA var. *UNIVITTATA*

Habit Vigorous, clump-forming.
Flowers Trumpet-shaped, in long spikes above the foliage in midsummer. Pale mauve.
Leaves Narrowly oval, twisted at the tip, to 6in (15cm) long. Mid-green, with a narrow creamy-white, central blotch.
• HEIGHT 1½ft (45cm).
• SPREAD 2ft (60cm).

H. undulata* var. *univittata

Z 3–9

H. DECORATA

Habit Slow-growing, stoloniferous.
Flowers Trumpet-shaped, in dense heads in midsummer. Violet.
Fruits Large, oval, glossy brown seed heads.
Leaves Oval, tapering, 6in (15cm) long. Dark green with neat, narrow, white margins.
• HEIGHT 1½ft (45cm).
• SPREAD 3ft (1m).

H. decorata

Z 3–9

H. CRISPULA

Habit Slow-growing, clump-forming.
Flowers Trumpet-shaped, borne above the foliage in early summer. Pale mauve.
Leaves Large, oval to heart-shaped, with wavy margins, tips twisted. Dark green, white edged.
• TIPS May be damaged by late frosts.
• HEIGHT 2½ft (75cm).
• SPREAD 3ft (1m).

H. crispula

Z 3–9

H. UNDULATA var. *ALBOMARGINATA*

Habit Clump-forming.
Flowers Trumpet-shaped, in spikes well above foliage in midsummer. Pale violet.
Leaves Lance-shaped to oval, round-tipped. Mid-green, with a cream edge extending down the stalk.
• OTHER NAMES *H. undulata* 'Albomarginata'.
• HEIGHT 2½ft (75cm).
• SPREAD 3ft (1m).

H. undulata* var. *albomarginata

Z 3–9

H. 'Ginko Craig'

Habit Low-growing, clump-forming.
Flowers Bell-shaped, borne in tall spires above the foliage in late summer. Deep violet.
Leaves Small, lance-shaped. Dark green with a fine white edge.
• TIPS Good for a border edge.
• HEIGHT to 1ft (30cm).
• SPREAD 1–1½ft (30–45cm).

***H.* 'Ginko Craig'**

Z 3–9

H. 'Shade Fanfare'

Habit Vigorous, clump-forming, free-flowering.
Flowers Trumpet-shaped, in many spikes in summer. Lavender.
Leaves Medium, to 5in (12cm) long, heart-shaped. Pale green, with cream margins; pale green becomes yellow in sun.
• TIPS For sun or partial shade.
• HEIGHT 1½ft (45cm).
• SPREAD 2½ft (75cm).

***H.* 'Shade Fanfare'**

Z 3–9

H. 'Ground Master'

Habit Low-growing, clump-forming.
Flowers Trumpet-shaped, borne above the foliage in late summer. Violet-purple.
Leaves Narrow, lance-shaped. Mid-green, edged with a broad creamy-white band.
• TIPS Good for the border front.
• HEIGHT 12in (30cm).
• SPREAD 18in (45cm).

H. 'Ground Master'

Z 3–9

H. 'Regal Splendor'

Habit Clump-forming.
Flowers Trumpet-shaped, borne in tall spikes in summer. Lilac.
Leaves Large, to 12in (30cm) long, arching. Dark grayish-blue with an irregular cream or creamy-white edge.
• HEIGHT 3ft (1m).
• SPREAD 3ft (1m).

H. 'Regal Splendor'

Z 3–9

H. SIEBOLDIANA var. ELEGANS

Habit Robust, clump-forming, slow-growing.
Flowers Bell-shaped, borne just above the foliage in early summer. Very pale lilac.
Leaves Large, heart-shaped, deeply ribbed, puckered. Bluish-green.
• TIPS Leaves become dull green in sun.
• HEIGHT 3ft (1m).
• SPREAD 5ft (1.5m).

H. sieboldiana var. *elegans*

Z 3–9

H. ROHDEIFOLIA

Habit Upright, clump-forming.
Flowers Trumpet-shaped, in erect heads, in summer. Pale mauve with a purple stripe.
Leaves Erect, lance-shaped, pointed, to 7in (18cm) long, veined. Glossy bluish-green, usually with a fine yellow edge.
• HEIGHT to 3ft (1m).
• SPREAD to 3ft (1m).

H. rohdeifolia

Z 3–9

H. 'Halcyon'

Habit Robust, clump-forming.
Flowers Trumpet-shaped, in dense spikes just above foliage in mid-summer. Violet-mauve.
Leaves Heart-shaped, pointed, to 6in (15cm) long. Gray-blue, turning muddy green in sun.
• TIPS Heavy rain may spoil leaves.
• HEIGHT 1ft (30cm).
• SPREAD 3ft (1m).

H. 'Halcyon'

Z 3–9

H. 'Snowden'

Habit Clump-forming.
Flowers Trumpet-shaped, in tall spikes in summer. White, tinged green.
Leaves Large, to 12in (30cm) long, narrowly heart-shaped, pointed, slightly corrugated. Gray-blue, maturing to grayish-green.
• HEIGHT 3ft (1m).
• SPREAD 3ft (1m).

H. 'Snowden'

Z 3–9

H. 'Krossa Regal'

Habit Forms a vase-shaped clump.
Flowers Trumpet-shaped, in tall, wavy spikes in summer. Pale lilac.
Leaves Very large, to 18in (45cm) long, gracefully arching, ribbed. Gray-blue.
• TIPS Makes an excellent specimen plant.
• HEIGHT 3ft (1m).
• SPREAD 3ft (1m).

H. 'Krossa Regal'

Z 3–9

H. 'Blue Wedgwood'

Habit Slow-growing, clump-forming.
Flowers Bell-shaped, borne above the foliage in midsummer. Pale lavender.
Leaves Medium, to 7in (18cm) long, broadly triangular, lightly puckered, with rippled margins. Blue-gray.
• HEIGHT 9in (23cm).
• SPREAD 1½ft (45cm).

H. 'Blue Wedgwood'

Z 3–9

H. SIEBOLDIANA
Habit Robust, clump-forming, slow-growing.
Flowers Bell-shaped, borne just above the foliage in early summer. Very pale lilac.
Leaves Large, to 15in (38cm) long, heart-shaped, deeply ribbed and puckered. Bluish gray-green.
• TIPS Best in semi-shade or shade. Leaves become dull green in sun.
• HEIGHT 3ft (1m).
• SPREAD 5ft (1.5m).

H. sieboldiana

Z 3–9

H. TOKUDAMA f. AUREONEBULOSA
Habit Slow-growing, clump-forming.
Flowers Trumpet-shaped, just above foliage in midsummer. Pale lilac-gray.
Leaves Cup-shaped, puckered. Cloudy yellow at the center, glaucous blue at the edge.
• OTHER NAMES *H. tokudama* 'Variegata'.
• HEIGHT 1½ft (45cm).
• SPREAD 2½ft (75cm).

H. tokudama* f. *aureonebulosa

Z 3–9

H. 'Love Pat'
Habit Vigorous, clump-forming.
Flowers Trumpet-shaped, borne in spikes in summer. Pale lilac.
Leaves To 6in (15cm) long, rounded, cupped, deeply puckered. Deep glaucous blue.
• HEIGHT 2ft (60cm).
• SPREAD 2ft (60cm).

***H.* 'Love Pat'**

Z 3–9

H. 'Hadspen Blue'
Habit Slow-growing, mound-forming.
Flowers Trumpet-shaped, in short spikes in midsummer. Lavender.
Leaves Heart-shaped, to 6in (15cm) long, smooth and closely veined. Deep glaucous blue.
• TIPS Good for a smaller border, or where space is limited.
• HEIGHT 12in (30cm).
• SPREAD 12in (30cm).

***H.* 'Hadspen Blue'**

Z 3–9

H. TARDIFLORA
Habit Clump-forming.
Flowers Trumpet-shaped, in dense heads just above foliage in late summer and early autumn. Lilac-purple.
Leaves Erect, lance-shaped to narrowly elliptic, to 6in (15cm) long, thick textured. Glossy dark green.
• HEIGHT 1ft (30cm).
• SPREAD 2½ft (75cm).

H. tardiflora

Z 3–9

H. PLANTAGINEA
Habit Clump-forming.
Flowers Fragrant, trumpet-shaped, long-tubed, in late summer and early autumn. White.
Leaves Heart-shaped, to 11in (28cm) long, conspicuously veined. Glossy yellow-green.
• TIPS Grows well in sun.
• HEIGHT 2ft (60cm).
• SPREAD 4ft (1.2m).

H. plantaginea
August lily

Z 3–9

H. VENTRICOSA
Habit Clump-forming.
Flowers Bell-shaped, borne in racemes above the foliage in late summer. Deep purple.
Leaves Heart-shaped, to 10in (24cm) long, slightly wavy-edged. Glossy dark green.
• TIPS Usually comes true from seed.
• HEIGHT 28in (70cm).
• SPREAD 3ft (1m) or more.

H. ventricosa

Z 3–9

H. 'Tall Boy'

Habit Upright, clump-forming.
Flowers Trumpet-shaped, borne on tall stems 4ft (1.2m) or more in height, in late summer. Rich lilac.
Leaves Oval to broadly lance-shaped, long-pointed. Dull green.
• TIPS Good by the edge of water.
• HEIGHT 2ft (60cm).
• SPREAD 2ft (60cm).

H. 'Tall Boy'

Z 3–9

H. 'Royal Standard'

Habit Upright, clump-forming.
Flowers Trumpet-shaped, fragrant, in tall spikes, opening on summer evenings. Pure white.
Leaves Large, to 10in (25cm) long, rather stiff, broadly oval, ribbed. Glossy bright green.
• TIPS Grows well in full sun.
• HEIGHT 2ft (60cm).
• SPREAD 4ft (1.2m).

H. 'Royal Standard'

Z 3–9

H. 'Honeybells'

Habit Rapidly growing, lax, clump-forming.
Flowers Bell-shaped, fragrant, in late summer. White, streaked violet.
Leaves Large, to 10in (25cm) long, oval, blunt-tipped, veined, smooth, slightly wavy-edged. Light green.
• TIPS Very tolerant of sun.
• HEIGHT 3ft (1m).
• SPREAD 2ft (60cm).

H. 'Honeybells'

Z 3–9

H. VENUSTA

Habit Vigorous, mat-forming.
Flowers Trumpet-shaped, borne well above the foliage in midsummer. Purple.
Leaves Small, oval to lance-shaped. Matt, mid- to dark olive green.
• TIPS Good ground cover.
• HEIGHT 2in (5cm).
• SPREAD to 12in (30cm).

H. venusta

Z 3–9

H. LANCIFOLIA

Habit Arching, clump-forming.
Flowers Trumpet-shaped, borne above foliage in late summer and autumn. Deep violet.
Leaves Narrowly lance-shaped, to 7in (17cm) long, thin-textured. Glossy dark green.
• TIPS Needs shade or semi-shade.
• HEIGHT 1½ft (45cm).
• SPREAD 2½ft (75cm).

H. lancifolia

Z 3–9

H. 'August Moon'

Habit Clump-forming.
Flowers Trumpet-shaped, borne above foliage in midsummer. Pale gray-mauve.
Leaves Large, to 10in (25cm) long, broadly oval, slightly corrugated. Pale golden-yellow with a faint glaucous bloom.
• TIPS Tolerates full sun.
• HEIGHT 2ft (60cm).
• SPREAD 3ft (1m).

H. 'August Moon'

Z 3–9

H. 'Blue Skies'

Habit Slow-growing, clump-forming.
Flowers Bell-shaped, in dense spikes. Palest lavender to nearly white.
Leaves Small, heart-shaped, abruptly tipped, smooth. Dark bluish-green.
• TIPS Grow in dappled shade.
• HEIGHT to 9in (23cm).
• SPREAD 12in (30cm).

H. 'Blue Skies'

Z 3–9

H. 'Frances Williams'

Habit Slow-growing, but robust, clump-forming. ***Flowers*** Trumpet-shaped, borne just above foliage in early summer. Very pale lavender. ***Leaves*** Large, to 15in (38cm) long, heart-shaped, deeply ribbed, puckered. Bluish gray, with a broad, irregular yellow edge.
• HEIGHT 3ft (1m).
• SPREAD 3ft (1m).

***H.* 'Frances Williams'**

Z 3–9

H. FORTUNEI var. *AUREOMARGINATA*

Habit Clump-forming. ***Flowers*** Trumpet-shaped, violet, in midsummer. ***Leaves*** Oval to heart-shaped. Mid-green with irregular creamy-yellow edges.
• TIPS Tolerates sun.
• HEIGHT 2½–3ft (75cm–1m).
• SPREAD 3ft (1m).

H. fortunei* var. *aureomarginata

Z 3–9

H. MONTANA 'Aureomarginata'

Habit Clump-forming. ***Flowers*** Trumpet-shaped, in tall heads in midsummer. Pale violet. ***Leaves*** Large, with prominent veins. Dark glossy green, gold-edged.
• TIPS Comes up early can be damaged by frost.
• OTHER NAMES *H.* 'Aureomarginata'.
• HEIGHT 3½ft (1.1m).
• SPREAD 3ft (1m).

***H. montana* 'Aureomarginata'**

Z 3–9

H. 'Golden Tiara'

Habit Neat, rapidly growing, clump-forming. ***Flowers*** Trumpet-shaped, borne in tall heads, in midsummer, and sometimes repeating. Lavender-purple. ***Leaves*** Broadly heart-shaped, to 6in (15cm) long. Dark green with irregular, chartreuse-yellow edges.
• HEIGHT 6in (15cm).
• SPREAD 12in (30cm).

***H.* 'Golden Tiara'**

Z 3–9

H. FORTUNEI var. *ALBOPICTA*

Habit Vigorous, clump-forming. ***Flowers*** Trumpet-shaped, in early summer. Pale violet. ***Leaves*** Oval to heart-shaped. Creamy-yellow, with irregular mid-green margins; the centers fade to pale green.
• OTHER NAMES *H. fortunei* 'Albopicta', *H.* 'Aureomaculata'.
• HEIGHT 2½–3ft (75cm–1m).
• SPREAD 3ft (1m).

H. fortunei* var. *albopicta

Z 3–9

H. VENTRICOSA 'Aureomarginata'

Habit Clump-forming. ***Flowers*** Bell-shaped, borne above foliage in late summer. Deep purple. ***Leaves*** Heart-shaped, to 10in (24cm) long. Glossy dark green, with irregular, creamy-white, wavy edge.
• OTHER NAMES *H. ventricosa* 'Variegata'.
• HEIGHT 28in (70cm).
• SPREAD 3ft (1m) or more.

***H. ventricosa* 'Aureomarginata'**

Z 3–9

H. 'Piedmont Gold'

Habit Slow-growing, clump-forming. ***Flowers*** Trumpet-shaped, in summer. Pale lavender. ***Leaves*** Large, heart-shaped, to 10in (25cm) long, smooth, with slightly fluted margins. Bright golden-yellow.
• TIPS Best in light shade.
• HEIGHT 2ft (60cm).
• SPREAD 2½ft (75cm).

***H.* 'Piedmont Gold'**

Z 3–9

H. 'Wide Brim'

Habit Vigorous, clump-forming.
Flowers Trumpet-shaped, borne in abundant spikes in summer. Pale lavender.
Leaves Medium, to 7in (18cm) long, ribbed and puckered. Dark green with a broad, irregular, creamy-white margin.
- HEIGHT 2½ft (75cm).
- SPREAD 2½ft (75cm).

H. 'Wide Brim'

Z 3–9

H. 'Birchwood Parky's Gold'

Habit Vigorous, clump-forming.
Flowers Bell-shaped in profusion. Lavender.
Leaves Small, wavy, heart-shaped. Chartreuse on unfurling, becoming bright yellow.
- TIPS Dense ground cover. Ideal for woodland gardens.
- HEIGHT 18in (45cm).
- SPREAD 30in (75cm).

H. 'Birchwood Parky's Gold'

Z 3–9

H. VENTRICOSA var. *AUREOMACULATA*

Habit Clump-forming.
Flowers Bell-shaped, in racemes above foliage in late summer. Deep purple.
Leaves Heart-shaped, to 10in (24cm) long, slightly wavy-edged. Glossy dark green with irregular central creamy-yellow markings.
- HEIGHT 28in (70cm).
- SPREAD 3ft (1m) or more.

H. ventricosa var. *aureomaculata*

Z 3–9

H. SIEBOLDIANA f. *KABITAN*

Habit Clump-forming, stoloniferous.
Flowers Small, trumpet-shaped, in tall spikes in early summer. Mid-violet.
Leaves Lance-shaped, thin-textured, ruffled. Greenish-yellow, with a narrow, dark green edge.
- OTHER NAMES *H.* 'Kabitan'.
- HEIGHT to 1ft (30cm).
- SPREAD 2ft (60cm).

H. sieboldiana* f. *kabitan

Z 3–9

H. 'Gold Standard'

Habit Vigorous, clump-forming.
Flowers Trumpet-shaped, borne above leaves in midsummer. Violet.
Leaves Large, oval to heart-shaped, 10in (25cm) long, pale green, then pale yellow, turning golden with age, with a narrow, irregular, darker green margin.
- HEIGHT 2½ft (75cm).
- SPREAD 3ft (1m).

H. 'Gold Standard'

Z 3–9

H. 'Golden Prayers'

Habit Upright, clump-forming.
Flowers Funnel-shaped, borne in dense heads in midsummer. White, suffused with lavender.
Leaves To 6in (15cm) long, heart-shaped, cupped and puckered. Bright golden-yellow.
- TIPS Suited to a rock garden.
- HEIGHT 6in (15cm).
- SPREAD 12in (30cm).

H. 'Golden Prayers'

Z 3–9

H. 'Sum and Substance'

Habit Vigorous, clump-forming.
Flowers Trumpet-shaped, in tall spikes in late summer. Pale lavender.
Leaves Very large, to 18in (45cm) long, heart-shaped, thick-textured, smooth, ribbed. Glossy golden green.
- HEIGHT 3ft (1m).
- SPREAD 3ft (1m).

H. 'Sum and Substance'

Z 3–9

Lamiaceae/Labiatae	

STACHYS BYZANTINA 'Primrose Heron'

Habit Mat-forming. ***Flowers*** Small, tubular, 2-lipped, in white-woolly, upright spikes, in summer. Pink. ***Leaves*** Evergreen, thick, oblong to spoon-shaped or elliptic, densely white-woolly, mainly in basal rosettes. Yellow-green beneath the hairs.

- NATIVE HABITAT Garden origin.
- CULTIVATION Grow in well-drained soil, ideally in a hot, sunny site. Good for ground cover and border edging, especially in a silver border.
- PROPAGATION By division in spring.

Z 4–9

HEIGHT 12–15in (30–38cm)

SPREAD 2ft (60cm)

Sarraceniaceae	TRUMPETS, YELLOW PITCHER PLANT

SARRACENIA FLAVA

Habit Upright, rhizomatous, insectivorous. ***Flowers*** Musk-scented, nodding, to 4in (10cm) across, from late spring to early summer. Yellow or greenish-yellow. ***Leaves*** Modified to form erect, hooded, trumpet-shaped pitchers, 1–3ft (30–100cm) tall. Yellow green, veined maroon.

- NATIVE HABITAT Pinelands, E. North America.
- CULTIVATION Grow as a house or greenhouse plant in cool climates, on damp peat or moss, in sun or partial shade. Keep slightly drier in winter.
- PROPAGATION By seed in spring.

Z 11

Min. 41°F (5°C)

HEIGHT 18in (45cm)

SPREAD 18in (45cm)

Iridaceae	

SISYRINCHIUM STRIATUM

Habit Upright, tuft-forming. ***Flowers*** Small, slightly cupped, borne in sturdy, upright spikes in summer. Creamy-yellow, striped purple. ***Leaves*** Evergreen or semi-evergreen, long, lance-shaped, in basal, fan-shaped clumps. Blue-green.

- NATIVE HABITAT Scrub, woods, Chile, Argentina.
- CULTIVATION Grow in moist, well-drained soil, in sun, at the border front, or in scree plantings.
- PROPAGATION By division in early spring, or by seed in autumn. Self-sows freely.
- OTHER NAMES *Phaiophleps nigricans*.

Z 7–8

HEIGHT 18–24in (45–60cm)

SPREAD 12in (30cm)

Lamiaceae/Labiatae	GOLDEN MARJORAM

ORIGANUM VULGARE 'Aureum'

Habit Mat-forming, woody-based. ***Flowers*** Tiny, 2-lipped, in short spikes in summer, but only occasionally produced. Lavender-mauve. ***Leaves*** Very aromatic, rounded-oval. Golden-yellow on emergence, pale greenish-yellow at maturity.
• NATIVE HABITAT Garden origin. Species occurs in open woodland and dry grassland, in Europe.
• CULTIVATION Grow in well-drained, alkaline soil, in full sun. Good for border fronts and sunny banks.
• PROPAGATION By division in spring, or cuttings of non-flowering shoots in early summer.

Z 4–8

HEIGHT
3in (8cm)

SPREAD
indefinite

Rosaceae	

FILIPENDULA ULMARIA 'Aurea'

Habit Clump-forming, upright. ***Flowers*** Tiny, in feathery plumes, on branching stems, in midsummer. Creamy-white. ***Leaves*** Aromatic, divided into 3–5 pairs of oval-oblong leaflets. Golden, turning pale creamy-green.
• NATIVE HABITAT Species occurs by streambanks and in damp meadows from Europe to N.W. China.
• CULTIVATION Grow in moist soils, in partial shade; leaves scorch in full sun. Excellent for a foliage border.
• PROPAGATION By division in autumn or winter.

Z 3–9

HEIGHT
1ft (30cm)

SPREAD
1ft (30cm)

Asphodelaceae/Liliaceae	

KNIPHOFIA 'Little Maid'

Habit Upright, clump-forming. ***Flowers*** Small, narrowly tubular, borne on upright stems in dense, terminal spikes, over long periods in late summer. Creamy-yellow, opening from pale green buds. ***Leaves*** Grass-like, narrowly linear, arching to form basal clumps. Mid-green.
• NATIVE HABITAT Garden origin.
• CULTIVATION Grow in full sun, in moist, well-drained soil. Needs ample moisture when in growth. Mulch crowns in cold winter areas.
• PROPAGATION By division in spring.

Z 5–9

HEIGHT
24in (60cm)

SPREAD
18in (45cm)

Asteraceae/Compositae

OSTEOSPERMUM 'Buttermilk'

Habit Clump-forming, woody-based. ***Flowers*** Large, single, daisy-like, borne on slender, sturdy stems throughout summer. Pale yellow petals surround a dark reddish-brown central disk. ***Leaves*** Evergreen, aromatic, long, narrow, and serrated. Gray-green.

- NATIVE HABITAT Garden origin.
- CULTIVATION Grow in fertile, well-drained soil, in full sun. Protect young plants from frost in winter.
- PROPAGATION By cuttings of non-flowering shoots in midsummer.

Z 9–10

HEIGHT 24in (60cm)

SPREAD 12in (30cm)

Asteraceae/Compositae

ACHILLEA 'Taygetea'

Habit Upright. ***Flowers*** Tiny, in large, flat heads, borne on rigid, leafy stems during summer. Pale lemon-yellow. ***Leaves*** Feathery, finely divided into oblong to lance-shaped finely hairy segments. Silver-gray.

- NATIVE HABITAT Garden origin.
- CULTIVATION Grow in well-drained soil, in full sun. Excellent for a silver border. Divide and replant every third year to maintain vigor. The flower heads dry well and retain their color and fragrance.
- PROPAGATION Division in early spring or autumn.

Z 7–9

HEIGHT 24in (60cm)

SPREAD 20in (50cm)

Polemoniaceae

POLEMONIUM PAUCIFLORUM

Habit Clump-forming, slow-spreading. ***Flowers*** Nodding, long-tubed, with spreading petal lobes, in loose clusters, in late summer. Pale yellow, flushed red. ***Leaves*** Finely divided into 11–25 elliptic to lance-shaped leaflets. Mid-green.

- NATIVE HABITAT Mountain streamsides, Arizona and N. Mexico.
- CULTIVATION Grow in humus-rich, moist, well-drained soil, in a sheltered spot. Suitable for an herbaceous border. Self-sows freely.
- PROPAGATION By seed or division in spring.

Z 7–9

HEIGHT 12–18in (30–45cm)

SPREAD 18in (45cm)

Asteraceae/Compositae

x *SOLIDASTER LUTEUS*

Habit Clump-forming. ***Flowers*** Small, daisy-like, borne in slender-stemmed, branched heads, from midsummer to autumn. Bright creamy-yellow. ***Leaves*** Lance-shaped to elliptic. Mid-green.

- NATIVE HABITAT A natural hybrid of garden origin.
- CULTIVATION Grow in any fertile, well-drained soil, in full sun. A valuable, long-flowering perennial for a late summer border.
- PROPAGATION By division in spring or autumn.
- OTHER NAMES x *S. hybridus*.

Z 4–9

HEIGHT 24in (60cm)

SPREAD 30in (75cm)

Asteraceae/Compositae

ACHILLEA 'Moonshine'

Habit Upright. ***Flowers*** Tiny, in large, flat heads, borne on rigid, leafy, gray stems during summer. Bright yellow. ***Leaves*** Feathery, finely divided into linear to lance-shaped segments, densely hairy. Silvery gray-green.
• NATIVE HABITAT Garden origin.
• CULTIVATION Grow in fertile, well-drained soil, in full sun. Excellent for a silver border. Divide and replant every second or third year to maintain vigor. The flower heads dry well for arrangements.
• PROPAGATION Division in early spring or autumn.

Z 3–7

HEIGHT 18–24in (45–60cm)

SPREAD 20in (50cm)

Asteraceae/Compositae

ACHILLEA 'Schwellenburg'

Habit Low-growing, spreading. ***Flowers*** Tiny, in large, flat heads, borne on rigid, leafy stems during summer. Lemon-yellow. ***Leaves*** Feathery, finely divided into oblong to lance-shaped segments, hairy. Grayish-green.
• NATIVE HABITAT Garden origin.
• CULTIVATION Grow in fertile, moisture-retentive, well-drained soil, in full sun. Divide and replant every third year to maintain vigor. The flower heads dry well for winter decoration.
• PROPAGATION Division in early spring or autumn.

Z 4–8

HEIGHT 18in (45cm)

SPREAD 24in (60cm)

Brassicaceae/Cruciferae | VARIEGATED WINTER CRESS

BARBAREA VULGARIS 'Variegata'

Habit Lax, rosette-forming. ***Flowers*** Small, 4-petaled, in branching heads, in early summer. Silvery-yellow. ***Leaves*** Basal leaves have 2–5 pairs of lateral lobes; stem leaves simple. Glossy green, blotched cream.
• NATIVE HABITAT Species occurs in damp hedges and ditches, throughout Europe. Garden origin.
• CULTIVATION Grow in moist but well-drained soil, in full sun or partial shade. Suitable for a cottage garden or wild garden. Self-sows freely.
• PROPAGATION By division in spring or autumn.

Z 4–9

HEIGHT 10–18in (25–45cm)

SPREAD to 9in (23cm)

Asteraceae/Compositae

HELICHRYSUM 'Schweffellicht'

Habit Clump-forming, tufted. ***Flowers*** Tiny, papery, borne in dense heads on upright stems, from mid- to late summer. Orange-tinted, pale sulfur-yellow. ***Leaves*** Narrowly lance-shaped, softly and densely woolly-hairy. Silver-green.
• NATIVE HABITAT Garden origin.
• CULTIVATION Grow in light, well-drained, fertile soil, in full sun. Excellent for the front of a silver border. Cut flowers dry well for winter arrangements.
• PROPAGATION By division in spring.
• OTHER NAMES *H.* 'Sulfur Light'.

Z 5–9

HEIGHT 16–24in (40–60cm)

SPREAD 12in (30cm)

Rosaceae

POTENTILLA RECTA 'Warrenii'

Habit Clump-forming. ***Flowers*** Open cup-shaped, borne in open, branching clusters, through summer. Rich golden-yellow. ***Leaves*** Divided into 5–7 lance-shaped, serrated, finely hairy leaflets. Green.

- NATIVE HABITAT Garden origin.
- CULTIVATION Grow in any moderately fertile, moist but well-drained soil, in sun or light shade. Good for a cottage garden, or the front of an herbaceous border.
- PROPAGATION By division in spring or autumn.
- OTHER NAMES *P. recta* 'Macrantha'.

Z 4–8

HEIGHT 20in (50cm)

SPREAD 24in (60cm)

Scrophulariaceae

CALCEOLARIA BIFLORA

Habit Mat-forming, rhizomatous. ***Flowers*** Small, pouched, borne in loose clusters of 2–8, on slender stems in summer. Yellow. ***Leaves*** Variable, softly hairy, oval-lance-shaped to diamond-shaped, in basal rosettes. Dark green.

- NATIVE HABITAT Chile and Argentina.
- CULTIVATION Grow in moist but well-drained, humus-rich soil, in partial shade. Suitable for a peat bed, shady border front, or rock garden.
- PROPAGATION By seed in autumn or spring, or by division in spring.

Z 9–10

HEIGHT 12in (30cm)

SPREAD 6in (15cm) or more

Asteraceae/Compositae

GAILLARDIA ARISTATA

Habit Upright, open clump-forming. ***Flowers*** Large, daisy-like, borne singly on slender, sturdy stems, over long periods in summer. Rich yellow, with an orange-red center. ***Leaves*** Aromatic, soft, lance-shaped, entire, toothed, or lobed. Mid-green.

- NATIVE HABITAT Dry meadows and prairies, W. North America.
- CULTIVATION Grow in light, well-drained soil, in sun. Needs staking and may be short-lived.
- PROPAGATION By seed in spring or autumn, or by root cuttings in winter.

Z 3–9

HEIGHT 24in (60cm)

SPREAD 20in (50cm)

Ranunculaceae

RANUNCULUS CONSTANTINOPOLITANUS 'Plenus'

Habit Clump-forming. ***Flowers*** Double, pompon-like, borne on short stems above the foliage, in early summer. Yellow, with a green center. ***Leaves*** Divided into 3 deeply toothed lobes. Dark green.

- NATIVE HABITAT Species occurs in damp meadows, from Europe to N. Africa and W. Asia.
- CULTIVATION Grow in moist, fertile soil, in sun or partial shade. Good for a border or cottage garden.
- PROPAGATION By division in spring or autumn.
- OTHER NAMES *R. bulbosus* 'Speciosus'.

Z 4–8

HEIGHT 20in (50cm)

SPREAD 12in (30cm)

Onagraceae

OENOTHERA FRUTICOSA 'Fyrverkeri'

Habit Clump-forming. ***Flowers*** Fragrant, cup-shaped, in upright or ascending spikes, from mid- to late summer. Bright yellow. ***Leaves*** Broadly lance-shaped to broadly oval. Glossy mid-green, flushed purple, on red-tinted stems.

• NATIVE HABITAT Garden origin.

• CULTIVATION Grow in light, preferably sandy, well-drained soil, in full sun. It is good for the front of a warm, sunny herbaceous border and is suitable for rock and cottage gardens. Although the individual flowers are not long-lived, there are sufficient numbers to give a continuous display of color toward the end of the season. Valued also for its handsome glossy foliage and purple-tinted young leaves that contrast beautifully with the red stems. It associates particularly well with bronze- or copper-leaved plants.

• PROPAGATION By division in autumn or spring, or by softwood cuttings in late spring.

• OTHER NAMES *O. fruticosa* 'Fireworks', *O. tetragona* 'Fireworks', *O. tetragona* 'Illumination'.

Z 5–9

HEIGHT
12–15in
(30–38cm)

SPREAD
12–15in
(30–38cm)

Scrophulariaceae	YELLOW MUSK

MIMULUS LUTEUS

Habit Creeping, upright. ***Flowers*** Snapdragon-like, tubular with spreading lobes, borne in the leaf axils throughout summer. Bright yellow, with occasional dark red or purple-red spots. ***Leaves*** Broadly oval, toothed, finely hairy. Mid-green.

• NATIVE HABITAT By streamsides and in wet places; Chile, but naturalized elsewhere.

• CULTIVATION Grow in moist or wet soil, in full sun. Good for a bog garden, streambank, or pondside.

• PROPAGATION By seed or division in spring or softwood cuttings in late summer.

Z 9–10

HEIGHT
12in (30cm)

SPREAD
12in (30cm)

Papaveraceae	LAMPSHADE POPPY

MECONOPSIS INTEGRIFOLIA

Habit Rosette-forming, short-lived perennial or biennial. ***Flowers*** Large, poppy-like, with satiny petals, borne in branched clusters on long, bristly stems, in late spring and early summer. Pale yellow. ***Leaves*** Large, lance-shaped to oval. Pale green, clothed in downy, orange-red hairs.

• NATIVE HABITAT Tibet, Upper Burma, W. China.

• CULTIVATION Grow in moist, humus-rich soils, in partial shade or shade, in a cool, sheltered site. Excellent for a peat bed or woodland garden.

• PROPAGATION By fresh seed in late summer.

pH

Z 7–9

HEIGHT
18–24in
(45–60cm)

SPREAD
24in (60cm)

Rosaceae	

GEUM 'Lady Stratheden'

Habit Clump-forming. ***Flowers*** Double, cup-shaped, borne on arching, branching stems, over long periods in summer. Clear, bright yellow. ***Leaves*** Large, lobed, heart-shaped at the base. Mid-green.

• NATIVE HABITAT Garden origin.

• CULTIVATION Grow in moist but well-drained soil, in sun. An easily grown herbaceous border plant, valued for its long flowering period.

• PROPAGATION By division in spring or autumn. Seed sown in spring comes reasonably true.

Z 5–9

HEIGHT
18–24in
(45–60cm)

SPREAD
18in (45cm)

Rosaceae	

POTENTILLA MEGALANTHA

Habit Clump-forming. ***Flowers*** Open cup-shaped, borne singly on slender stems, in profusion in summer. Rich yellow. ***Leaves*** Large, palmate, with 3 softly hairy leaflets. Soft green.

• NATIVE HABITAT Meadows and woodland, Japan.

• CULTIVATION Grow in any moderately fertile, moist but well-drained soil, in sun or light shade. Good for the front of herbaceous borders and cottage gardens.

• PROPAGATION By seed or division in spring or autumn.

Z 5–9

HEIGHT
8in (20cm)

SPREAD
6in (15cm)

Asteraceae/Compositae	YELLOW OX-EYE

BUPHTHALMUM SALICIFOLIUM

Habit Upright, spreading. ***Flowers*** Daisy-like, borne singly on sturdy, leafy stems throughout summer. Clear yellow, with narrow, widely spaced ray florets around a darker yellow disk. ***Leaves*** Lance-shaped to linear-lance-shaped, toothed or entire. Mid-green.

• NATIVE HABITAT Damp, rocky places, C. Europe.

• CULTIVATION Grow in moist, well-drained soil, in sun or light shade. May need staking. Spreads on fertile soils. Good for wild or cottage gardens.

• PROPAGATION Seed or division in spring or autumn.

Z 3–7

HEIGHT 2ft (60cm)

SPREAD 3ft (1m)

Asteraceae/Compositae	

BIDENS FERULIFOLIA

Habit Clump-forming, spreading, short-lived. ***Flowers*** Starry, 1½in (4cm) across, in profusion, from mid spring to first frost. Golden-yellow. ***Leaves*** Divided, fern-like. Fresh green.

• NATIVE HABITAT Grassland and waste ground in southern US, Mexico, Guatemala.

• CULTIVATION Grow in sun, in well-drained soil. Good for a border, scree plantings, hanging basket, and other containers. May be grown as an annual.

• PROPAGATION Seed, division, or stem cuttings in spring.

Z 8–10

HEIGHT 12in (30cm) or more

SPREAD 12in (30cm)

Asteraceae/Compositae	

GAZANIA RIGENS var. *UNIFLORA*

Habit Mat-forming. ***Flowers*** Daisy-like, with pointed, borne singly on short stems, in early summer. Yellow-orange or yellow ray florets around a yellow disk. ***Leaves*** Spoon-shaped or divided, smooth. Dark green above, silvery-white beneath.

• NATIVE HABITAT South Africa.

• CULTIVATION Tolerant of dry soils and salt-laden winds. Suitable for containers. Treat as an annual in cool areas. Grow in well-drained soil in a warm, sunny, sheltered site.

• PROPAGATION By seed or division in spring.

Z 8–10

HEIGHT 9in (23cm)

SPREAD 8–12in (20–30cm)

Crassulaceae	

SEDUM AIZOON 'Euphorbioides'

Habit Clump-forming, rhizomatous. ***Flowers*** Small, star-shaped, borne in dense, slightly rounded heads, over long periods in summer. Dark yellow, opening from red buds. ***Leaves*** Fleshy, oblong-lance-shaped. Bluish-green.

• NATIVE HABITAT Species occurs on dry hills, in scrub, and on rocky streambanks, in N. Asia.

• CULTIVATION Grow in fertile, moist but well-drained soil, in sun or light shade.

• PROPAGATION By division in spring or autumn.

• OTHER NAMES *S. aizoon* 'Aurantiacum'.

Z 4–9

HEIGHT 18in (45cm)

SPREAD 18in (45cm)

Ranunculaceae	DOUBLE MEADOW BUTTERCUP

RANUNCULUS ACRIS 'Flore Pleno'

Habit Clump-forming. ***Flowers*** Double, pompon-like, borne on sturdy, slender, branching stems, in late spring and early summer. Golden-yellow, with a less pronounced green center than *R. constantinopolitanus* 'Plenus'. ***Leaves*** Deeply cut and lobed. Mid- to dark green.

• NATIVE HABITAT Said to have occurred naturally in damp pastures, in northern England. Grown in gardens since the 16th century.

• CULTIVATION Grow in moist, fertile soil, in sun or partial shade. Valued for its dark foliage and wiry stems topped by neat, shining, golden-yellow, pompon-like blooms, it is a charming plant that is happy in the wilder parts of the garden in damp borders, cottage gardens, and bog gardens. It often benefits from gentle support by way of branches placed discreetly around the clump. Unlike its parent species, the meadow buttercup, *R. acris*, this variant does not self-sow or produce runners and it is unlikely to spread invasively.

• PROPAGATION By division in spring or autumn.

Z 4–8

HEIGHT
18–24in
(45–60cm)

SPREAD
18–24in
(45–60cm)

Tropaeoleaceae

TROPAEOLUM POLYPHYLLUM

Habit Prostrate, trailing. ***Flowers*** Spurred, short trumpet-shaped, singly on long stalks in the leaf axils; in summer. Bright yellow. ***Leaves*** Divided into 5- to 7 or more, rounded lobes. Gray-green.
• NATIVE HABITAT Chile, Argentina.
• CULTIVATION Grow in very well-drained soil, in sun. Suitable for sunny banks, or raised beds and very effective when allowed to cascade over a sunny wall. Dies back completely after flowering. Needs to be planted deeply to be successful.
• PROPAGATION By seed in spring.

Z 7–9

HEIGHT
2–3in
(5–8cm)
or more

SPREAD
3ft (1m)

Asteraceae/Compositae

COREOPSIS LANCEOLATA

Habit Bushy, clump-forming. ***Flowers*** Daisy-like, with toothed, ray florets, borne on branching stems, in profusion throughout summer. Bright yellow with a golden-yellow center. ***Leaves*** Narrowly lance-shaped, spoon-shaped to linear, all along the flowering stems. Mid-green.
• NATIVE HABITAT C. and S.E. US
• CULTIVATION Easily grown in any fertile, well-drained soil, in full sun. Good for the summer border; the cut flowers last very well in water.
• PROPAGATION Seed or division in spring or autumn.

Z 3–8

HEIGHT
18in (45cm)

SPREAD
12in (30cm)

Rosaceae

POTENTILLA 'Yellow Queen'

Habit Clump-forming. ***Flowers*** Open cup-shaped, semi-double, borne on slender stems, in profusion in midsummer. Bright yellow. ***Leaves*** Divided into 3 finely hairy, neatly toothed leaflets. Dark green, usually silvery beneath.
• NATIVE HABITAT Garden origin.
• CULTIVATION Grow in any moderately fertile, moist but well-drained soil, in sun or light shade. Good for the front of herbaceous or mixed borders and cottage gardens.
• PROPAGATION By division in spring or autumn.

Z 5–8

HEIGHT
to 24in
(60cm)
or more

SPREAD
18in (45cm)

Asteraceae/Compositae

HIERACIUM LANATUM

Habit Clump- or rosette-forming. ***Flowers*** Small, dandelion-like, borne on wiry, branching, gray-hairy stems, in summer. Bright yellow. ***Leaves*** Broad, lance-shaped, densely white-felted, in large basal rosettes. Gray.
• NATIVE HABITAT Limestone rocks and cliffs in the Alps and Jura mountains.
• CULTIVATION Grow in sharply drained, preferably alkaline, and not too fertile soil, in full sun. Excellent for planting on a sunny wall or raised bed.
• PROPAGATION Seed or division in spring or autumn.

Z 5–8

HEIGHT
12–18in
(30–45cm)

SPREAD
12in (30cm)

Asteraceae/Compositae

COREOPSIS VERTICILLATA

Habit Bushy, rhizomatous. ***Flowers*** Star-shaped, daisy-like, borne on branching stems, in profusion throughout summer. Bright golden-yellow. ***Leaves*** Finely divided into hair-like segments. Bright green.
• NATIVE HABITAT Dry woodland clearings, E. North America.
• CULTIVATION Tolerant of dry soils. Easily grown in any fertile, well-drained soil, in full sun. Good for a summer border; the cut flowers last very well in water. Divide regularly to maintain vigor.
• PROPAGATION By seed or division in spring.

Z 3–9

HEIGHT 16–24in (40–60cm)

SPREAD 12in (30cm)

Balsaminaceae

IMPATIENS REPENS

Habit Creeping, stem-rooting. ***Flowers*** 5-petaled, with a large, finely hairy spur, in summer. Rich yellow. ***Leaves*** Evergreen, small, scalloped, kidney-shaped. Mid-green.
• NATIVE HABITAT Sri Lanka, India.
• CULTIVATION Grow as a house or greenhouse plant in cool climates in moist, well-drained potting soil. If grown outdoors site in full sun. Provides very effective ground cover in a border.
• PROPAGATION By seed or stem cuttings in spring or summer.

Min. 50°F (10°C)

HEIGHT to 2in (5cm)

SPREAD indefinite

Brassicaceae/Cruciferae

ERYSIMUM 'Moonlight'

Habit Mat-forming. ***Flowers*** Small, 4-petaled, borne in dense, terminal clusters, in succession throughout summer. Pale yellow. ***Leaves*** Evergreen, narrowly lance-shaped. Gray-green.
• NATIVE HABITAT Garden origin.
• CULTIVATION Grow in poor, gritty, well-drained soil, in a sheltered site, in full sun. Is often short-lived, so propagate regularly. Good for the front of a border, sunny bank, or rock garden.
• PROPAGATION By softwood cuttings in summer.
• OTHER NAMES *Cheiranthus* 'Moonlight'.

Z 6–9

HEIGHT 6in (15cm)

SPREAD 8in (20cm)

Asteraceae/Compositae

ERIOPHYLLUM LANATUM

Habit Clump- or cushion-forming. ***Flowers*** Star-shaped, daisy-like, usually borne singly on slender, sturdy stems, in profusion over long periods in summer. Bright yellow. ***Leaves*** Dense, finely divided. Silvery-gray, white-woolly beneath.
• NATIVE HABITAT Dry scrub, in the foothills and mountains of W. North America.
• CULTIVATION Grow in sharply drained, not too fertile soil, in full sun.
• PROPAGATION By seed or division in spring.

Z 5–8

HEIGHT 12in (30cm)

SPREAD 12in (30cm)

Asteraceae/Compositae

INULA ENSIFOLIA

Habit Clump-forming. ***Flowers*** Daisy-like, with slender, ray florets, borne on slender, wiry stems, in late summer. Bright yellow with a golden disk. ***Leaves*** Small, lance-shaped to elliptic. Mid-green.
• NATIVE HABITAT Scrub and grasslands. E. Europe and eastern C. Europe.
• CULTIVATION Grow in any moist but well-drained soil, in sun or light shade. May spread rapidly. Suitable for borders and wild or woodland gardens.
• PROPAGATION By seed or division in spring or autumn.

Z 4–9

HEIGHT
12in (30cm)

SPREAD
12in (30cm)

Rosaceae

GEUM 'Borisii'

Habit Clump-forming. ***Flowers*** Single, cup-shaped, borne on hairy, slender, branching stems, over long periods in summer. Bright orange. ***Leaves*** Large, irregularly lobed. Pale to mid-green.
• NATIVE HABITAT Damp meadows, Balkans, N. Turkey.
• CULTIVATION Grow in moist but well-drained soil, in sun. An easily grown herbaceous border plant, associating well with blue- or yellow-flowered perennials.
• PROPAGATION By division in spring or autumn.

Z 5–8

HEIGHT
12in (30cm)

SPREAD
12in (30cm)

Scrophulariaceae

CALCEOLARIA 'John Innes'

Habit Clump-forming, stoloniferous. ***Flowers*** Small, pouched, borne in loose, slender-stemmed clusters, in late spring and summer. Yellow, freckled red-brown. ***Leaves*** Evergreen, broadly oval, in basal clumps. Mid-green.
• NATIVE HABITAT Garden origin.
• CULTIVATION Grow in moist but well-drained, humus-rich soil, in sun or light shade. Suitable for a peat bed, border front, or rock garden.
• PROPAGATION By division in spring.

Z 7–8

HEIGHT
6–8in
(15–20cm)

SPREAD
10–12in
(25–30cm)

Crassulaceae

RHODIOLA HETERODONTA

Habit Clump-forming. ***Flowers*** Small, borne in dense, slightly rounded heads on leafy stems, in late spring and early summer. Orange-red to purple, sometimes greenish beneath. ***Leaves*** Fleshy, oval, toothed. Bluish-green.
• NATIVE HABITAT Dry, rocky places, Afghanistan to Nepal.
• CULTIVATION Grow in well-drained soil in sun.
• PROPAGATION By division from spring to midsummer, or by seed in autumn or spring.
• OTHER NAMES *Sedum heterodontum*.

Z 2–8

HEIGHT
18in (45cm)

SPREAD
10in (25cm)

Liliaceae Convallariaceae	TOAD LILY

TRICYRTIS HIRTA ALBA

Habit Upright, rhizomatous. ***Flowers*** Large, spurred, bell-shaped, borne in the upper leaf axils, in late summer and early autumn. White, usually spotted deep purple. ***Leaves*** Lance-shaped, hairy, and stem-clasping. Mid-green.
• NATIVE HABITAT Damp, shady rocks, Japan.
• CULTIVATION Grow in moist, humus-rich, fertile soil, in a sheltered site, in sun, or in warm areas, in partial shade. Good for woodland gardens.
• PROPAGATION By division in spring or seed in autumn.

Z 4–9

HEIGHT 18–24in (45–60cm)

SPREAD 18in (45cm)

Crassulaceae	ICE-PLANT

SEDUM SPECTABILE 'Brilliant'

Habit Clump-forming. ***Flowers*** Small, bright borne in dense, flattened heads on leafy stems, in profusion from late summer to autumn. Rose-pink. ***Leaves*** Fleshy, oval-elliptic. Gray-green.
• NATIVE HABITAT Garden origin.
• CULTIVATION Grow in fertile, well-drained soil, with adequate moisture during summer, in full sun. Excellent for the border front and very attractive to bees and butterflies.
• PROPAGATION By division in spring.
• OTHER NAMES *Hylotelephium spectabile* 'Brilliant'.

Z 4–9

HEIGHT 12–18in (30–45cm)

SPREAD 12–18in (30–45cm)

Iridaceae	

SCHIZOSTYLIS COCCINEA 'Sunrise'

Habit Clump-forming, rhizomatous. ***Flowers*** Large, shallowly cup-shaped, in upright spikes, in early autumn. Clear pink. ***Leaves*** Long, narrowly sword-shaped, ribbed, in basal clumps. Mid-green.
• NATIVE HABITAT Garden origin.
• CULTIVATION Grow in fertile, moist but well-drained soil, in full sun. Divide and replant regularly to maintain vigor. Excellent for front border placement and for pondside plantings above water level. Cut flowers last well in water.
• PROPAGATION By division in spring.

Z 6–9

HEIGHT 24in (60cm)

SPREAD 9–12in (23–30cm)

Polygonaceae	

PERSICARIA MILLETII

Habit Clump-forming, spreading, rhizomatous. ***Flowers*** Tiny, borne in dense, broadly cylindrical spikes, on strong, slender stems, in summer and autumn. Deep rose-crimson. ***Leaves*** Linear-lance-shaped to oblong. Dark green.
• NATIVE HABITAT Alpine scrub, rocks, Himalayas.
• CULTIVATION Grow in any moist, fertile soil, in sun or partial shade. A vigorous and long-flowering specimen for a damp border.
• PROPAGATION Seed or division in spring or autumn.
• OTHER NAMES *Polygonum milletii*.

Z 5–9

HEIGHT 24in (60cm)

SPREAD 24in (60cm) often more

Lamiaceae/Labiatae

SALVIA BLEPHAROPHYLLA

Habit Spreading, subshrubby. ***Flowers*** Tubular, 2-lipped, in slender clusters, in summer and autumn. Bright red with maroon calyces. ***Leaves*** Oval to diamond-shaped, glossy. Dark green.

• NATIVE HABITAT Mexico.

• CULTIVATION Grow in fertile, well-drained soil, in a warm, sheltered site, in full sun. A useful plant for late in the season, this colorful sage should be propagated annually and young plants overwintered in a warm greenhouse. In frost-prone areas, it is suitable for large pots or tubs in a cool sunroom and may be moved outdoors to a patio or sheltered courtyard during the frost-free summer months. Container-grown plants will need support to control the plant's spreading habit. Water pot-grown specimens freely and apply a balanced liquid fertilizer every 7–10 days when in growth; water very sparingly in winter. Cut back and repot in spring.

• PROPAGATION By seed in spring or softwood cuttings in summer.

Z 9–10

HEIGHT
18in (45cm)

SPREAD
18in (45cm)

Iridaceae

SCHIZOSTYLIS COCCINEA 'Major'

Habit Clump-forming, rhizomatous. ***Flowers*** Large, shallowly cup-shaped, in upright spikes, in early autumn. Bright crimson-scarlet. ***Leaves*** Long, sword-shaped, in basal clumps. Mid-green.

• NATIVE HABITAT Garden origin.

• CULTIVATION Grow in fertile, moist, well-drained soil, in full sun. Divide and replant regularly to maintain vigor. Cut flowers last well in water. Good for border fronts or pondsides, above water level.

• PROPAGATION By division in spring.

• OTHER NAMES *S. coccinea* 'Grandiflora'.

Z 6–9

HEIGHT
24in (60cm)
or more

SPREAD
12in (30cm)
or more

Zingiberaceae

CAUTLEYA SPICATA

Habit Upright, rhizomatous. ***Flowers*** Funnel-shaped, borne in upright spikes above the foliage, in late summer and early autumn. Pale orange or soft yellow, with maroon-purple bracts. ***Leaves*** Large, lance-shaped, glossy, on reed-like stems. Rich-green.

• NATIVE HABITAT Himalayas.

• CULTIVATION Grow in deep, fertile, moist but well-drained soil, in sun, and with shelter from cold, dry winds.

• PROPAGATION By seed or division in spring.

Z 7–9

HEIGHT
24in (60cm)

SPREAD
20in (50cm)

Asteraceae/Compositae	

SENECIO PULCHER

Habit Upright. ***Flowers*** Large, daisy-like, borne in loose, few-flowered, terminal clusters, in late summer and autumn. Bright purplish-pink ray florets around a golden-yellow disk. ***Leaves*** Leathery, elliptic, scalloped or lobed, hairy. Dark green.

- NATIVE HABITAT S. Brazil, Uruguay, Argentina.
- CULTIVATION Grow in light, well-drained soil, in full sun, in a warm, sheltered site. The strongly colored flowers associate well with silver-leaved plants.
- PROPAGATION By seed or division in spring.

Z 8–10

HEIGHT 18–24in (45–60cm)

SPREAD 20in (50cm)

Gesneriaceae	

CHIRITA LAVANDULACEA

Habit Upright. ***Flowers*** Funnel-shaped, in the leaf axils, from spring to autumn, if sown in succession. White tube, with lavender-blue petal lobes. ***Leaves*** Evergreen, downy, to 8in (20cm) long. Pale green.

- NATIVE HABITAT Tropical Asia.
- CULTIVATION Grow as a house or greenhouse plant in cool climates. Site in moist soil, in bright, indirect light, with high humidity. Avoid wetting the leaves when watering.
- PROPAGATION By tip cuttings in summer, or by seed, if available, in late winter or spring.

Min. 59°F (15°C)

HEIGHT 24in (60cm)

SPREAD 24in (60cm)

Convallariaceae/ Liliaceae	LILY TURF

LIRIOPE MUSCARI

Habit Spreading, tufted, tuberous-rooted. ***Flowers*** Small, rounded bell-shaped, in dense, upright, spikes in autumn. Lavender or purple-blue. ***Leaves*** Evergreen, strap-shaped. Glossy dark green.

- NATIVE HABITAT Woodlands of China and Japan.
- CULTIVATION Tolerates dry soils and shade, but flowers best in sun. Grow in fertile, humus-rich, moist but well-drained soil. Provide shelter from strong winds to avoid foliage scorch.
- PROPAGATION By division in spring or seed in autumn.

Z 6–10

HEIGHT 12in (30cm)

SPREAD 18in (45cm)

Asteraceae/Compositae	CAPE DANDELION

ARCTOTHECA CALENDULA

Habit Mound-forming, carpeting. ***Flowers*** Daisy-like, borne from late spring to autumn. Yellow ray florets around a darker yellow disk. ***Leaves*** Divided or entire. Mid- to dark green, roughly hairy above, white-downy beneath.

- NATIVE HABITAT South Africa, naturalized in C. Portugal, S.W. Spain.
- CULTIVATION Grow as a house or greenhouse plant in cool climates. Site in full light. Grow outdoors only where there is no danger of frost.
- PROPAGATION By seed or division in spring.

Z 11

Min. 41°F (5°C)

HEIGHT 12in (30cm)

SPREAD 12in (30cm)

Begonias

Begonias form a varied genus of plants that provide flowers, foliage, and attractive habit all year round. Because they are mostly tropical or subtropical, in cool climates they are grown as houseplants or in the greenhouse, where the trailing types are well-suited to hanging baskets.

All begonias need light, well-drained and neutral to slightly acid soil or potting mix, with bright but indirect light. Water more when in full growth, and less in winter, and fertilize in late spring and summer at every other watering. Repot every spring.

The more commonly cultivated begonias are grouped as follows.

Cane-stemmed – frost tender, grown mainly for their attractive assymetrical heart-shaped leaves. Take leaf, tip, or stem cuttings in spring or summer.

Rex-cultorum – grown for their foliage. Keep at 70–75°F (21–24°C). Take leaf or rhizome cuttings in summer.

Rhizomatous – grown for their foliage and/or flowers, keep at around 66°F (19°C) and water from below. Take leaf cuttings in spring or rhizome cuttings in summer.

Semperflorens – grown for clusters of rounded flowers. Plant out when danger of frost has passed. Sow seed or take basal cuttings in spring.

Shrub-like – grown for their foliage and habit. Keep humid and provide bright light in winter to enhance leaf color. Pinching growing tips makes them bushier. Sow ripe seed or take leaf, stem or tip cuttings.

Tuberous (the Tuberhybrida Group in particular) – grown for exhibition, as pot plants, or for summer beds. Start tubers in spring, and remove all flower buds until at least 3 pairs of leaves show. Sow seed in spring, or take stem cuttings in summer

Winter-flowering – grown for their bronze-green leaves and profusion of winter flowers. Keep humid. Take basal cuttings.

B. 'Billie Langdon'
Habit Upright, tuberous.
Flowers Double, to 7in (18cm) across, produced in profusion throughout summer. Pure white, with broad, veined petals, and a rose-bud center.
Leaves Oval, to 8in (20cm) long. Rich green.
• HEIGHT 24in (60cm).
• SPREAD 18in (45cm).

***B.* 'Billie Langdon'**
(Tuberhybrida Group)
◐ ◇
Min. 50°F (10°C)

B. *FOLIOSA*
Habit Shrubby, with pendent stems.
Flowers Small, to ½in (1.5cm) across, single, produced from autumn to spring. White.
Leaves Evergreen, oval, notched, to ⅜in (8mm) long, in two ranks along the stems. Dark green.
• TIPS Prone to whitefly. Needs light and humidity.
• HEIGHT 18in (45cm).
• SPREAD 12in (30cm).

B. foliosa
(Shrub-like)
Fern begonia
◐ ◇
Min. 50°F (10°C)

B. *ALBOPICTA*
Habit Fast-growing.
Flowers Pendent, small, single, in clusters in late summer. Green-white.
Leaves Evergreen, oval-lance-shaped, 3in (8cm) long, with wavy margins. Green, silver-spotted above, pale green beneath.
• TIPS Pinch out tips to encourage bushy growth.
• HEIGHT 2–3ft (60–100cm).
• SPREAD 12in (30cm).

B. albopicta
(Cane-stemmed)
Guinea-wing begonia
◐ ◇
Min. 50°F (10°C)

B. *OLSONIAE*
Habit Compact, upright.
Flowers Single, to 1¼in (3cm) across, on arching stems above the foliage, year-round. Pale pink or white.
Leaves Evergreen, obliquely oval to rounded, 5–8in (12–20cm) long. Satiny, bronze-green with prominent creamy-white veins, brown-red beneath.
• HEIGHT 9in (22cm).
• SPREAD 12in (30cm).

B. olsoniae
(Shrub-like)
◐ ◇
Min. 50°F (10°C)

B. manicata

Habit Upright, then arching.
Flowers Single, ½in (1.5cm) across, in small clusters above the foliage in late winter. Pink.
Leaves Evergreen, obliquely heart-shaped, 6in (15cm) long. Glossy light green, with a fringe of red bristles below the leaf base.

- TIPS Grow under glass in cool climates in partial shade and in well-drained soil. Pot up small plantlets during the growing season.
- HEIGHT 24in (60cm).
- SPREAD 14in (35cm).

B. manicata
(Rhizomatous)

Min. 50°F (10°C)

B. scharffii

Habit Upright, shrubby.
Flowers Single, prolific, in clusters, to 2in (5cm) across, from autumn to summer. Pink-white.
Leaves Obliquely oval, to 10in (25cm) long. Dark metallic gray-green, red-tinted beneath.

- OTHER NAMES *B. haageana*.
- HEIGHT 2–4ft (60cm–1.2m).
- SPREAD 2ft (60cm).

B. scharffii
(Shrub-like)

Min. 50°F (10°C)

B. 'Weltoniensis'

Habit Shrub-like.
Flowers Single, to 1¼in (3cm) across, in profuse sprays from early summer to mid autumn. Pink.
Leaves Oval, shallowly lobed, with toothed margins. Apple-green with purple-red veins.

- HEIGHT 12–18in (30–45cm).
- SPREAD 12in (30cm).

***B.* 'Weltoniensis'**
(Shrub-like)
Grapevine begonia

Min. 50°F (10°C)

B. 'Ingramii'

Habit Shrubby, upright, slender-stemmed.
Flowers Single, to 1¼in (3cm) across, more or less continuously throughout the year. Deep pink.
Leaves Evergreen, oval-lance-shaped, toothed, 3in (7–8cm) long. Bright green.

- HEIGHT 30in (75cm).
- SPREAD 18in (45cm).

***B.* 'Ingramii'**
(Shrub-like)

Min. 50°F (10°C)

B. metallica

Habit Upright.
Flowers Single, to 1½in (3.5cm) across, in autumn. Pink, red-hairy.
Leaves Evergreen, obliquely oval-heart-shaped, 7in (18cm) long. Dark green, red-hairy, with a bright metallic sheen and sunken, dark red veins.

- HEIGHT 3ft (90cm).
- SPREAD 2ft (60cm).

B. metallica
(Shrub-like)
Metallic-leaf begonia

Min. 50°F (10°C)

B. 'Merry Christmas'

Habit Upright, rhizomatous.
Flowers Single, to ½in (1cm) across, sparse, from autumn to early winter. Pale rose-pink.
Leaves Obliquely heart-shaped, 6–8in (15–20cm) long. Satiny bright red with a broad emerald-green outer band and a velvety, deep red-pink center, sometimes edged with gray.

- OTHER NAMES *B.* 'Ruhrtal'.
- HEIGHT 10–12in (25–30cm).
- SPREAD 10–12in (25–30cm).

***B.* 'Merry Christmas'**
(Rex-cultorum)

Min. 50°F (10°C)

B. 'Roy Hartley'
Habit Upright, tuberous.
Flowers Double, to 6in (15cm) across, with slightly serrated petals, profusely throughout summer. Soft pink tinted salmon-pink.
Leaves Oval, to 6in (15cm) long. Rich green.
• TIPS Depth of flower color depends on light intensity.
• HEIGHT 24in (60cm).
• SPREAD 18in (45cm).

B. 'Roy Hartley'
(Tuberhybrida Group)

☼ 💧
Min. 50°F (10°C)

B. × *CORALLINA* 'Lucerna'
Habit Vigorous, upright.
Flowers Single, to 1½in (4cm) across, in clusters, in summer. Rose-pink.
Leaves Evergreen, oval, 8–14in (20–35cm) long. Olive-green, heavily spotted silver above, dark red beneath.
• OTHER NAMES *B.* 'Lucerna'.
• HEIGHT 6–7ft (2–2.2m).
• SPREAD 14in (35cm).

B. × *corallina* 'Lucerna'
(Cane-stemmed)

☼ 💧
Min. 50°F (10°C)

B. 'Red Ascot'
Habit Dense, branching.
Flowers Single, to ¾in (2cm) across, produced from the leaf axils in profusion in summer. Crimson-red.
Leaves Evergreen, rounded, to 3in (8cm) across, waxy and fleshy. Emerald-green, paler beneath.
• HEIGHT 6in (15cm).
• SPREAD 6in (15cm).

B. 'Red Ascot'
(Semperflorens Cultorum)

☼ 💧
Min. 45°F (7°C)

B. 'Organdy'
Habit Dense, branching.
Flowers Single, to ¾in (2cm) across, produced from leaf axils profusely in summer. Shades of red, pink and white.
Leaves Evergreen, rounded, to 3in (8cm) long, waxy and fleshy. Green-bronze, paler beneath.
• HEIGHT 6in (15cm).
• SPREAD 6in (15cm).

B. 'Organdy'
(Semperflorens Cultorum)

☼ 💧
Min. 45°F (7°C)

B. 'Flamboyant'
Habit Low, bushy, compact, and tuberous.
Flowers Single, 2in (5cm) across, produced in profuse clusters in summer. Deep cerise to red.
Leaves Heart-shaped, to 6in (15cm) long. Rich green.
• TIPS Tolerates full sun.
• HEIGHT 7in (17cm).
• SPREAD 6in (15cm).

B. 'Flamboyant'
(Tuberhybrida Group: Multiflora)

☼ 💧
Min. 50°F (10°C)

B. 'Helen Lewis'
Habit Upright.
Flowers Single, to ½in (1cm) across, sparsely hairy, in early summer. Creamy-white.
Leaves Obliquely oval, 6–8in (15–20cm) long, silky. Dark wine-red with a broad, irregular silver band toward the margins.
• HEIGHT 18–24in (45–60cm).
• SPREAD 18–24in (45–60cm).

B. 'Helen Lewis'
(Rex-cultorum)

☼ 💧
Min. 50°F (10°C)

B. 'Duartei'
Habit Upright.
Flowers Single, to ½in (1cm) across, sparse, in late winter/early spring. Pink.
Leaves Obliquely heart-shaped, to 7in (17cm) long, spirally twisted. Red-hairy, dark green, with silver-gray streaks and almost black edges.
• HEIGHT 18–24in (45–60cm).
• SPREAD 18–24in (45–60cm).

B. 'Duartei'
(Rex-cultorum)

☼ 💧
Min. 50°F (10°C)

B. 'Thurstonii'
Habit Upright.
Flowers Single, to ½–¾in (1.5–2cm) across, relatively insignificant, and sparsely produced in summer. Pink.
Leaves Evergreen, oval, taper-pointed, 6in (15cm) long, glossy. Green, deeply veined, rich red-brown beneath.
• HEIGHT 6ft (2m).
• SPREAD 18in (45cm).

B. 'Thurstonii'
(Shrub-like)

☼ 💧
Min. 50°F (10°C)

B. SERRATIPETALA
Habit Trailing.
Flowers Single, ¾–1¼in (2–3cm) across produced sparsely year-round. Deep pink.
Leaves Evergreen, obliquely oval, 3in (8cm) long, deeply serrated, with waved margins. Dark bronze-green, with raised, deep pink spots.
• TIPS Prefers moderate humidity, with fairly dry roots.
• HEIGHT 18in (45cm).
• SPREAD 18in (45cm).

B. serratipetala
(Shrub-like)

Min. 55°F (13°C)

B. 'Orpha C. Fox'
Habit Upright.
Flowers Single, to 1¼in (3cm) across, in clusters, mainly in summer. Rose-pink.
Leaves Evergreen, oval, 6in (15cm) long. Gray-green, splashed silver and maroon beneath.
• HEIGHT 36in (90cm).
• SPREAD 12in (30cm).

B. 'Orpha C. Fox'
(Cane-stemmed)

Min. 50°F (10°C)

B. 'Silver Queen'
Habit Upright.
Flowers Small, single, to ½–¾in (1.5–2cm) across, relatively insignificant, in autumn. Pink.
Leaves Evergreen, oval, 8in (20cm) long. Silver, with metallic purple centers that become dull purple in bright light.
• HEIGHT 12in (30cm).
• SPREAD 18in (45cm)

B. 'Silver Queen'
(Rex-cultorum)

Min. 50°F (10°C)

B. PUSTULATA 'Argentea'
Habit Creeping.
Flowers Single, small, in clusters in summer. White.
Leaves Oval, 6in (15cm) long. Dark green, finely hairy, with blisters, and silvery markings.
• OTHER NAMES *B.* 'Silver'.
• HEIGHT 6–8in (15–20cm).
• SPREAD 8–10in (20–25cm).

***B. pustulata* 'Argentea'**
(Rhizomatous)

Min. 55°F (13°C)

B. MASONIANA
Habit Upright to arching.
Flowers Single, to ¾in (2cm) across, freely in summer. Green-white.
Leaves Evergreen, obliquely oval-heart-shaped, to 8in (20cm) long, warty. Dark green, red-hairy, with a brown cross-shaped central mark.
• OTHER NAMES *B.* 'Iron Cross'.
• HEIGHT 20in (50cm).
• SPREAD 18in (45cm).

B. masoniana
(Rhizomatous)
Iron-cross begonia
Min. 55°F (13°C)

B. BOWERAE
Habit Creeping.
Flowers Single, about ½–¾in (1.5–2cm) across, produced freely in winter. White, tinted pink.
Leaves Evergreen, oval, 1in (2.5cm) long. Bright green, marked chocolate-brown, and fringed with fine hairs.
• HEIGHT 10in (25cm).
• SPREAD 7in (18cm).

B. bowerae
(Rhizomatous)
Eyelash begonia
Min. 50°F (10°C)

B. MANICATA 'Crispa'
Habit Upright, then arching. ***Flowers*** Single, small, ½in (1.5cm) across, in clusters in late winter. Deep pink
Leaves Evergreen, obliquely heart-shaped, 6in (15cm) long. Glossy light green, with crested margins, and a fringe of red bristles at the base.
• HEIGHT 24in (60cm).
• SPREAD 14in (35cm).

***B. manicata* 'Crispa'**
(Rhizomatous)

Min. 50°F (10°C)

B. 'Norah Bedson'
Habit Bushy, upright.
Flowers Single, about ½–¾in (1.5–2cm) across, in early spring. Pink.
Leaves Evergreen, oval, taper-pointed, to 2in (5cm) long. Bright green, mottled chocolate-brown, splashed red beneath.
• HEIGHT 9in (23cm).
• SPREAD 10in (25cm).

B. 'Norah Bedson'
(Rhizomatous)

Min. 50°F (10°C)

B. 'Oliver Twist'
Habit Bushy, upright.
Flowers Single, about ½–¾in (1.5–2cm) across, in winter or early spring. Pink.
Leaves Evergreen, oval, 6–12in (15–30cm) long, ruffled and crested. Pale to mid-green, with brown markings along the veins.
• HEIGHT 18in (45cm).
• SPREAD 10in (25cm).

B. 'Oliver Twist'
(Rhizomatous)

Min. 50°F (10°C)

B. PRISMATOCARPA
Habit Creeping.
Flowers Single, to ½in (1.5cm) across, year-round. Yellow.
Leaves Evergreen, obliquely oval, 2–3 lobed, 1¼in (3cm) long. Shining bright green.
• TIPS Suited to a terrarium.
• HEIGHT 6–8in (15–20cm).
• SPREAD 8–10in (20–25cm).

B. prismatocarpa
(Rhizomatous)

Min. 62°F (16°C)

B. NELUMBIIFOLIA
Habit Upright. ***Flowers*** Single, ½in (1.5cm) across, sparsely produced in branching clusters in late winter. Greyish white.
Leaves Evergreen, peltate, rounded, to 12in (30cm) across. Green, fringed at the margins, hairy beneath.
• HEIGHT 18in (45cm).
• SPREAD 24in (60cm).

B. nelumbiifolia
(Rhizomatous)
Lily-pad begonia

Min. 50°F (10°C)

B. 'Apricot Cascade'
Habit Pendent, tuberous.
Flowers Double, to 3in (7cm) across, with serrated petals, profusely from summer to autumn. Pale apricot-orange.
Leaves Oval, to 8in (20cm) long. Emerald-green.
• TIPS Grow indoors in cool climates. Good for hanging baskets.
• HEIGHT 24in (60cm).
• SPREAD 24in (60cm).

B. 'Apricot Cascade'
(Tuberhybrida Group: Pendula)

Min. 50°F (10°C)

B. 'Can-Can'
Habit Upright, tuberous.
Flowers Double, to 7in (18cm) across, in profusion through summer. Rich yellow, the serrated petals having a heavy red-picotee margin.
Leaves Oval, to 8in (20cm) long. Rich green.
• HEIGHT 36in (90cm).
• SPREAD 18in (45cm).

B. 'Can-Can'
(Tuberhybrida Group)

Min. 50°F (10°C)

B. 'Orange Rubra'
Habit Slow-growing.
Flowers Single, ¾–1¼in (2–3cm) across, in panicles year-round. Vivid orange.
Leaves Evergreen, lance-shaped, 5in (12cm) long. Emerald-green, sometimes silver-spotted.
• TIPS Stake and pinch for a bushy plant.
• HEIGHT 24in (60cm).
• SPREAD 18in (45cm).

B. 'Orange Rubra'
(Cane-stemmed)

Min. 50°F (10°C)

B. SUTHERLANDII
Habit Trailing, tuberous.
Flowers Single, to 1in (2.5cm) across, in sprays through summer. Orange.
Leaves Oval-lance-shaped, to 6in (15cm) long, serrated. Bright green with red veins and margins.
• TIPS Good for hanging baskets. Susceptible to mildew.
• HEIGHT 18in (45cm–1m).
• SPREAD indefinite.

B. sutherlandii
(Tuberous)

Min. 50°F (10°C)

Araceae

SPATHIPHYLLUM FLORIBUNDUM 'Mauna Loa'

Habit Compact, tufted, rhizomatous. ***Flowers*** Fragrant, produced intermittently and irregularly. Each flower is formed by a fleshy, white spadix surrounded by a large, white spathe. ***Leaves*** Large, lance-shaped to elliptic, glossy. Dark green.

• NATIVE HABITAT Garden origin. Species occurs in damp tropical forests in Central America, the Philippines, and Indonesia.

• CULTIVATION Grow as a house or greenhouse plant in cool climates. Site in bright, indirect light, providing shade from the summer sun. It is essential for maximum flower production to maintain humidity: water freely when in growth and keep drier in winter. The growing medium should be equal parts of leaf mold and bark with soil added. The addition of pieces of charcoal will ensure this mixture is kept "sweet." The requirements for high humidity are more easily met in a greenhouse or sunroom. In the home, keep humid by standing the plant's pot on a saucer of pebbles kept permanently wet.

• PROPAGATION By division in spring or summer.

Min. 59°F (15°C)

HEIGHT 18–24in (45–60cm)

SPREAD 18–24in (45–60cm)

Gesneriaceae | LACE FLOWER

EPISCIA DIANTHIFLORA

Habit Prostrate, creeping, stoloniferous. ***Flowers*** Small, broadly tubular with fringed petals. White. ***Leaves*** Evergreen, thick, elliptic to oval, toothed, velvety. Dark green.

- NATIVE HABITAT Tropical Costa Rica and Mexico.
- CULTIVATION Grow as a house or greenhouse plant in cool climates in well-drained potting mix or soil, in bright indirect light. Water freely during growth.
- PROPAGATION By division, by removal of rooted stems, or by stem cuttings in summer.
- OTHER NAMES *Alsobia dianthiflora*.

Min. 59°F (15°C)

HEIGHT 4in (10cm)

SPREAD indefinite

Commelinaceae

TRADESCANTIA FLUMINENSIS 'Albovittata'

Habit Vigorous, trailing, with rooting stems. ***Flowers*** Tiny, 3-petaled, produced intermittently. White. ***Leaves*** Evergreen, broadly oval to lance-shaped. Bluish-green with broad, white stripes.

- NATIVE HABITAT Garden origin.
- CULTIVATION Grow as a house or greenhouse plant in cool climates. Fertilize and water freely when in growth. Cut straggly stems back in spring.
- PROPAGATION By tip cuttings in spring, summer, or autumn.

Min. 59°F (15°C)

HEIGHT 12in (30cm)

SPREAD indefinite

Acanthaceae

HEMIGRAPHIS REPANDA

Habit Prostrate, with spreading, rooting stems. ***Flowers*** Tiny, tubular, borne intermittently. White. ***Leaves*** Narrowly lance-shaped, toothed, scalloped, or lobed, satiny. Grayish-green, flushed red-purple above and darker purple beneath.

- NATIVE HABITAT Tropical Malaysia.
- CULTIVATION In cool climates grow as a house or greenhouse plant in well-drained soil or potting mix. Protect from hot sun. Water freely during growth; less in winter. Cut back straggly growth in spring.
- PROPAGATION By stem cuttings in summer.

Min. 59°F (15°C)

HEIGHT to 6in (15cm)

SPREAD indefinite

Lamiaceae/Labiatae | VARIEGATED GROUND IVY

GLECHOMA HEDERACEA 'Variegata'

Habit Mat-forming, rhizomatous. ***Flowers*** Insignificant, produced in summer. Mauve or white. ***Leaves*** Evergreen, toothed, oval, heart-shaped at the base. Green, marbled with white and silver-gray.

- NATIVE HABITAT Garden origin.
- CULTIVATION Grow in moist but well-drained soil, in sun or shade. Excellent ground cover, but may be invasive. Also suitable for hanging baskets and other containers.
- PROPAGATION By division in spring or autumn, or by softwood cuttings in spring.

Z 5–9

HEIGHT 6in (15cm)

SPREAD indefinite

Ranunculaceae	LENTEN ROSE

HELLEBORUS ORIENTALIS white

Habit Clump-forming. ***Flowers*** Nodding, cup-shaped, borne in clusters of 1–4 in late winter and early spring. White, sometimes with darker spots. ***Leaves*** Evergreen (deciduous in cold winters) divided into 7–10 segments. Light to dark green.

• NATIVE HABITAT Scrub, woodland edge, in grass, from N.E. Greece, N. and N.E. Turkey to the Caucasus.

• CULTIVATION Grow in fertile, heavy, moist but well-drained soil, in a sunny or partially shaded site, with shelter from cold winds. Particularly suited to woodland gardens, but also excellent in a shady herbaceous border or beneath deciduous shrubs. It associates particularly well with snowdrops (*Galanthus* species) and makes an attractive feature when planted with the pink and purple color forms of the species (see pages 280 and 284).

• PROPAGATION By fresh seed, or division in autumn.

Z 4–9

HEIGHT
18in (45cm)

SPREAD
18in (45cm)

Commelinaceae	

TRADESCANTIA FLUMINENSIS 'Aurea'

Habit Vigorous, trailing, with rooting stems. ***Flowers*** Tiny, 3-petalled, produced intermittently. ***Leaves*** Evergreen, broadly oval to lance-shaped. Green with irregular, creamy-white stripes.

• NATIVE HABITAT Garden origin.

• CULTIVATION Grow as a house or greenhouse plant in cool climates. Cut straggly stems in spring.

• PROPAGATION By tip cuttings in spring, summer or autumn.

• OTHER NAMES *T. fluminensis* 'Variegata'. *T. albiflora* 'Variegata'.

Min. 59°F (15°C)

HEIGHT 12in (30cm)

SPREAD indefinite

Piperaceae	EMERALD-RIPPLE PEPPER

PEPEROMIA CAPERATA

Habit Bushy, upright. ***Flowers*** Minute, densely clustered in upright spikes, produced irregularly. Creamy-white. ***Leaves*** Evergreen, heart-shaped, with pink leaf stalks, sunken veins, and a wrinkled surface. Dark green.

• NATIVE HABITAT Origin uncertain, probably Brazil.

• CULTIVATION Grow as a house or greenhouse plant in cool climates. Best in peaty soil or potting mix. Water moderately, less in winter.

• PROPAGATION By division, seed, or leaf or stem cuttings in spring or summer.

Min. 50°F (10°C)

HEIGHT to 6in (15cm)

SPREAD 6in (15cm)

Acanthaceae	SILVER-NET LEAF

FITTONIA VERSCHAFFELTII var. *ARGYRONEURA*

Habit Creeping, stem-rooting. ***Flowers*** Small, in spikes, produced occasionally, but best removed as they appear. White. ***Leaves*** Evergreen, oval to elliptic. Emerald green, net-veined with white.

• NATIVE HABITAT Tropical Peru.

• CULTIVATION Grow as a house or greenhouse plant in cool climates. Needs high humidity. Water freely during growth; less in winter.

• PROPAGATION Division or stem cuttings in summer.

• OTHER NAMES *F. argyroneura.*

Min. 59°F (15°C)

HEIGHT 6in (15cm)

SPREAD indefinite

Anthericaceae/Liliaceae	SPIDER PLANT

CHLOROPHYTUM COMOSUM 'Vittatum'

Habit Tufted, rosette-forming, forming plantlets at the nodes of stems. ***Flowers*** Tiny, star-shaped, borne intermittently on slender, white stems. White. ***Leaves*** Evergreen, long, narrow, lance-shaped. Green with a central white stripe.

• NATIVE HABITAT Garden origin.

• CULTIVATION Grow as a house or greenhouse plant in cool climates. Site in bright, indirect light. Water freely when in growth, otherwise sparingly.

• PROPAGATION Divide, or pot up young plantlets at any time except during winter.

Z 11

Min. 41°F (5°C)

HEIGHT 12in (30cm)

SPREAD 12in (30cm)

Convallariaceae/ Liliaceae

ASPIDISTRA ELATIOR 'Variegata'

Habit Clump-forming, rhizomatous. ***Flowers*** Small, inconspicuous, usually borne in late winter at soil level. Green or purplish. ***Leaves*** Evergreen, oval to lance-shaped, on long stalks, glossy. Dark green, with irregular, longitudinal, creamy stripes.

- NATIVE HABITAT Garden origin.
- CULTIVATION Grow as a house or greenhouse plant in cool climates. Tolerant of a wide range of growing conditions but best in fertile, well-drained soil in full shade. Full sun will scorch the foliage.
- PROPAGATION By division in spring.

Min. 41–50°F (5–10°C)

HEIGHT 24in (60cm)

SPREAD 18in (45cm)

Ranunculaceae

HELLEBORUS NIGER 'Potter's Wheel'

Habit Clump-forming. ***Flowers*** Nodding, cup-shaped, rounded, borne singly or in clusters of 2–3, in winter and early spring. White, larger than the species, and with a distinct green eye. ***Leaves*** Evergreen (deciduous in cold winters) divided into 7–9 segments. Dark green.

- NATIVE HABITAT Garden origin.
- CULTIVATION Grow in deep, fertile, moist but well-drained soil, preferably alkaline, with shelter from cold wind.
- PROPAGATION By division in autumn.

Z 4–8

HEIGHT 12in (30cm)

SPREAD 12in (30cm)

Ranunculaceae | CHRISTMAS ROSE

HELLEBORUS NIGER

Habit Clump-forming. ***Flowers*** Nodding, cup-shaped, borne singly or in clusters of 2–3, in winter and early spring. White. ***Leaves*** Evergreen (deciduous in cold winters) divided into 7–9 segments, toothed at the tip. Dark green.

- NATIVE HABITAT Mountain woodland, open grassland, C. Europe (Alps).
- CULTIVATION Grow in deep, fertile, moist but well-drained, preferably alkaline soil, in sun or partial shade, with shelter from cold wind.
- PROPAGATION Fresh seed, or division in autumn.

Z 4–8

HEIGHT 12in (30cm)

SPREAD 12in (30cm)

Ranunculaceae

HELLEBORUS x *STERNII* 'Boughton Beauty'

Habit Clump-forming, compact. ***Flowers*** Nodding, cup-shaped, borne in terminal clusters, in winter and early spring. Pale lime-green, tinged rose-pink. ***Leaves*** Evergreen (deciduous in cold winters) divided into segments. Dark grayish-green often veined gray or silver and pink-tinted.

- NATIVE HABITAT Garden origin.
- CULTIVATION Grow in deep, moist, well-drained soil, preferably alkaline, with shelter from cold wind.
- PROPAGATION By division in autumn.

Z 6–9

HEIGHT 18in (45cm)

SPREAD 18in (45cm)

Poaceae/Gramineae

OPLISMENUS AFRICANUS 'Variegatus'

Habit Creeping, stem-rooting grass. ***Flowers*** Inconspicuous, borne intermittently. ***Leaves*** Evergreen, narrowly lance-shaped to oval, wavy-margined. Green, striped white, and often tinted pink.

• NATIVE HABITAT Garden origin. The species originates in shady tropical forests.

• CULTIVATION Grow as a house or greenhouse plant in cool climates. Does best in fertile, moist but well-drained soil, in bright, indirect light or partial shade. Water pot-grown plants freely when in full growth and apply a balanced liquid fertilizer once a month; keep drier in winter. In frost-prone areas, its trailing habit makes it especially suitable for hanging baskets. It is also useful for underplanting in a greenhouse border. In warmer regions, use in a mixed or herbaceous border, or site where it can trail over terrace walls or similar.

• PROPAGATION By division of rooted stems in spring.

• OTHER NAMES *O. hirtellus* 'Variegatus'.

☼ ◊

Min. 60°F (15°C)

HEIGHT
8in (20cm) or more

SPREAD
indefinite

Ranunculaceae	

HELLEBORUS × *STERNII*

Habit Clump-forming. ***Flowers*** Nodding, cup-shaped, borne in terminal clusters, in winter and early spring. Pale green, tinged pink or purple-brown. ***Leaves*** Evergreen (deciduous in cold winters) divided into segments. Dark grayish-green often veined gray or silver.
• NATIVE HABITAT Garden origin.
• CULTIVATION Grow in deep, fertile, moist but well-drained, preferably alkaline soil, in sun or partial shade. Provide shelter from cold wind.
• PROPAGATION By division in autumn.

Z 6–9

HEIGHT
18in (45cm)

SPREAD
18in (45cm)

Ranunculaceae	LENTEN ROSE

HELLEBORUS ORIENTALIS pink

Habit Clump-forming. ***Flowers*** Nodding, cup-shaped, borne in clusters of 1–4 in late winter and early spring. Pink, sometimes with darker spots. ***Leaves*** Evergreen (deciduous in cold winters) divided into 7–10 segments. Green.
• NATIVE HABITAT Scrub, woodland edge, from N.E. Greece, N. and N.E. Turkey to the Caucasus.
• CULTIVATION Grow in fertile, heavy, moist but well-drained soil, in sun or partial shade, with shelter from cold wind. Good for woodland gardens.
• PROPAGATION Fresh seed, or division in autumn.

Z 4–9

HEIGHT
18in (45cm)

SPREAD
18in (45cm)

Ranunculaceae	LENTEN ROSE

HELLEBORUS ORIENTALIS subsp. *GUTTATUS*

Habit Clump-forming. ***Flowers*** Nodding, cup-shaped, borne in clusters of 1–4 in late winter and early spring. White or cream, spotted red-purple. ***Leaves*** Evergreen (deciduous in cold winters) divided into 7–10 segments. Light to dark green.
• NATIVE HABITAT Garden origin.
• CULTIVATION Grow in fertile, heavy, moist but well-drained soil, in sun or partial shade. Provide shelter from cold wind. Good for woodland gardens.
• PROPAGATION By division in autumn.

Z 4–9

HEIGHT
18in (45cm)

SPREAD
18in (45cm)

Gesneriaceae	

STREPTOCARPUS 'Nicola'

Habit Upright, rosette-forming. ***Flowers*** Small, semi-double, funnel-shaped, borne intermittently in small, long-stalked clusters. Deep rose-pink. ***Leaves*** Evergreen, fleshy, strap-shaped, wrinkled. Dark green.
• NATIVE HABITAT Garden origin.
• CULTIVATION Grow as a house or greenhouse plant in cool climates. Needs high humidity. Water freely when in growth; avoid wetting leaves.
• PROPAGATION By division after flowering, or by leaf cuttings in spring or summer.

Min.
50–59°F
(10–15°C)

HEIGHT
10in (25cm)

SPREAD
20in (50cm)

Commelinaceae	SILVER INCH PLANT

TRADESCANTIA ZEBRINA

Habit Trailing, with rooting stems. ***Flowers*** Tiny, 3-petaled, borne intermittently. Pink or violet-blue. ***Leaves*** Evergreen, oval-oblong, fleshy. Purple-tinted, bluish-green, with 2 broad silvery bands.

- NATIVE HABITAT Tropical Mexico.
- CULTIVATION Grow as a house or greenhouse plant in cool climates. Fertilize and water freely when in growth; avoid wetting the foliage.
- PROPAGATION By tip cuttings in spring, summer, or autumn.
- OTHER NAMES *T. pendula*, *T. zebrina pendula*.

Min. 59°F (15°C)

HEIGHT 6in (15cm)

SPREAD indefinite

Asteraceae/Compositae	BARBERTON DAISY

GERBERA JAMESONII

Habit Upright. ***Flowers*** Large, long-stemmed, daisy-like, borne from summer to winter. Variably colored from white, yellow, and orange, to dark red. ***Leaves*** Evergreen, oblong-spoon-shaped, jaggedly divided. Dark green.

- NATIVE HABITAT South Africa, Swaziland.
- CULTIVATION Grow in sandy soil or potting mix in sun. Protect from frost in well-ventilated conditions. Good for cool sunrooms. Cut flowers last well.
- PROPAGATION By seed in autumn or spring, or by heel cuttings from side shoots in summer.

Z 8–10

HEIGHT 24in (60cm)

SPREAD 18in (45cm)

Gesneriaceae	FLAME VIOLET

EPISCIA CUPREATA

Habit Prostrate, creeping, stoloniferous. ***Flowers*** Small, tubular, borne intermittently. Scarlet with a yellow throat. ***Leaves*** Evergreen, small, thick, downy, and wrinkled. Purple-tinted with silver veins.

- NATIVE HABITAT Colombia, Venezuela, Brazil.
- CULTIVATION In cool climates, grow as a house or greenhouse plant in moist, well-drained soil or potting mix. Site in bright, indirect light, with shade from summer sun. Water freely when in full growth.
- PROPAGATION By division, by removal of rooted stems, or by stem cuttings in summer.

Min. 59°F (15°C)

HEIGHT 4in (10cm)

SPREAD indefinite

Saxifragaceae	

TELLIMA GRANDIFLORA 'Rubra'

Habit Spreading, clump-forming. ***Flowers*** Small, bell-shaped, in erect clusters, in late spring. Greenish-white, with pink-fringed petals. ***Leaves*** Semi-evergreen, hairy, 3- to 7-lobed, heart-shaped. Dark green, flushed red-purple.

- NATIVE HABITAT Species occurs in coniferous woods of W. North America.
- CULTIVATION Grow in moist but well-drained soil in shade or partial shade.
- PROPAGATION By division at any time.
- OTHER NAMES *T. grandiflora* 'Purpurea'.

Z 4–9

HEIGHT 24in (60cm)

SPREAD 24in (60cm)

AFRICAN VIOLETS

African violet is the common name for the genus *Saintpaulia*. These small, evergreen, rosette-forming perennials may be grown as summer bedding in warm, humid climates, or as attractive, indoor pot plants.

Grow in soilless potting mix in bright, indirect light at a temperature of 55–59°F (13-15°C). Keep the mix moist but not waterlogged and avoid splashing the foliage when watering. In summer, feed with dilute liquid fertilizer every 10 days. Provide high humidity by standing plant on a saucer or tray of pebbles, topped up with soft water. Repot every year in spring.

Propagate by leaf cuttings in summer: root in a mix of equal parts peat and sand at 64–70°F (18–21°C). Sow seed in early spring at 64–70°F (18–21°C).

S 'Garden News'

Habit Stemless, rosette-forming.
Flowers Fully double, with frilled petals, borne in clusters of 2–8, throughout the year. Pure white.
Leaves Evergreen, almost round, to 3in (8cm) long, slightly scalloped and finely hairy. Bright green.
- HEIGHT to 4in (10cm).
- SPREAD to 10in (25cm).

S. 'Garden News'

Min. 59°F (15°C)

S. 'Fancy Pants'

Habit Stemless, rosette-forming.
Flowers Single, produced year-round, in clusters of 2–8. Pure white petals with red-frilled edges, surrounding a yellow eye.
Leaves Evergreen, almost round, to 3in (8cm). long, slightly scalloped and finely hairy. Mid-green.
- HEIGHT to 4in (10cm).
- SPREAD to 10in (25cm).

S. 'Fancy Pants'

Min. 59°F (15°C)

S. 'Miss Pretty'

Habit Stemless, rosette-forming.
Flowers Large, single, in clusters of 2–8, all year. White, pink-frilled petals.
Leaves Evergreen, almost round, to 3in (8cm). long, slightly scalloped and finely hairy. Pale green.
- HEIGHT to 4in (10cm).
- SPREAD to 10in (25cm).

S. 'Miss Pretty'

Min. 59°F (15°C)

S. 'Pip Squeak'

Habit Stemless, rosette-forming.
Flowers Small, to ½in (1cm) across, single, bell-shaped, 5-lobed, produced singly or in pairs, well above the foliage, throughout the year. Pale pink.
Leaves Evergreen, oval, ½–¾in (1–2cm) long, unscalloped, deep green.
- HEIGHT 3in (8cm).
- SPREAD 4in (10cm).

S. 'Pip Squeak'

Min. 59°F (15°C)

S. 'Rococo Pink'

Habit Stemless, rosette-forming.
Flowers Fully double, in clusters of 2–8, throughout the year. Iridescent pink.
Leaves Evergreen, almost round, to 3in (8cm) long, slightly scalloped and finely hairy. Dark green, edged with emerald green with a small, pale area at base of leaf blade.
- HEIGHT to 4in (10cm).
- SPREAD to 10in (25cm).

S. 'Rococo Pink'

Min. 59°F (15°C)

S. 'Colorado'

Habit Stemless, rosette-forming.
Flowers Single, borne in clusters of 2–8, throughout the year. Frilled, magenta petals with a yellow eye.
Leaves Evergreen almost round, to 3in (8cm) long, slightly scalloped and finely hairy. Dark green.

- HEIGHT to 4in (10cm).
- SPREAD to 10in (25cm).

S. 'Colorado'

Min. 59°F (15°C)

S. 'Kristi Marie'

Habit Stemless, rosette-forming.
Flowers Semi-double, borne in clusters of 2–8, throughout the year. Dusky red petals, finely edged with white.
Leaves Evergreen, almost round, to 3in (8cm) long, slightly scalloped and finely hairy. Dark green.

- HEIGHT to 4in (10cm).
- SPREAD to 10in (25cm).

S. 'Kristi Marie'

Min. 59°F (15°C)

S. 'Bright Eyes'

Habit Stemless, rosette-forming.
Flowers Single, borne in clusters of 2–8, throughout the year. Deep violet-blue with a yellow eye.
Leaves Evergreen, almost round, to 3in (8cm) long, slightly scalloped and finely hairy. Dark green.

- HEIGHT to 4in (10cm).
- SPREAD to 10in (25cm).

S. 'Bright Eyes'

Min. 59°F (15°C)

S. 'Porcelain'

Habit Stemless, rosette-forming.
Flowers Semi-double borne in clusters of 2–8, throughout the year. White petals, edged with rich purple-blue.
Leaves Evergreen, almost round, to 3in (8cm). long, slightly scalloped and finely hairy. Dark green.

- HEIGHT to 4in (10cm).
- SPREAD to 10in (25cm).

S. 'Porcelain'

Min. 15°C (59°F).

S. 'Delft'

Habit Stemless, rosette-forming.
Flowers Semi-double, borne in clusters of 2–8, throughout the year. Slightly frilled, violet-blue petals, with a yellow eye.
Leaves Evergreen, almost round, to 3in (8cm). long, slightly scalloped and finely hairy. Dark green.

- HEIGHT to 4in (10cm).
- SPREAD to 10in (25cm).

S. 'Delft'

Min. 59°F (15°C)

Ranunculaceae	LENTEN ROSE

HELLEBORUS ORIENTALIS purple

Habit Clump-forming. ***Flowers*** Nodding, cup-shaped, borne in clusters of 1–4 in late winter and early spring. Purple, sometimes with darker spots. ***Leaves*** Evergreen (deciduous in cold winters) divided into 7–10 segments. Green.

• NATIVE HABITAT Scrub, or woodland edge, from N.E. Greece, N. and N.E. Turkey to the Caucasus.

• CULTIVATION Grow in fertile, heavy, moist but well-drained soil, in sun or partial shade. Provide shelter from cold wind. Good for woodland gardens.

• PROPAGATION Fresh seed, or division in autumn.

Z 4–9

HEIGHT 18in (45cm)

SPREAD 18in (45cm)

Acanthaceae	MOSAIC PLANT, PAINTED NET-LEAF

FITTONIA VERSCHAFFELTII

Habit Creeping, stem-rooting. ***Flowers*** Small, in 4-angled spikes produced occasionally. White, with overlapping green bracts. Remove flowers as they appear. ***Leaves*** Evergreen, oval to elliptic, olive-green, net-veined with ruby red or scarlet.

• NATIVE HABITAT Tropical Peru.

• CULTIVATION Grow as a house or greenhouse plant in cool climates. Needs high humidity. Water freely when in full growth; less in winter. Cut back straggly growth in spring.

• PROPAGATION Division or stem cuttings in summer

Min. 59°F (15°C)

HEIGHT 6in (15cm)

SPREAD indefinite

Agavaceae/Phormiaceae	

PHORMIUM TENAX 'Bronze Baby'

Habit Upright, clump-forming, dwarf. ***Flowers*** Tubular, in branched heads, borne on red-purple stems, occasionally in summer. Dull dark red. ***Leaves*** Evergreen, stiff, sword-shaped, in basal clumps. Bronze-tinted, red-purple,

• NATIVE HABITAT Garden origin.

• CULTIVATION Grow in deep, fertile, humus-rich soil, in a warm, sunny, sheltered site. Excellent for coastal gardens. Suitable for raised beds, scree plantings, and the front of a border.

• PROPAGATION By division in spring.

Z 9–10

HEIGHT 18–24in (45–60cm)

SPREAD 18–24in (45–60cm)

Convallariaceae/ Liliaceae	

OPHIOPOGON PLANISCAPUS 'Nigrescens'

Habit Spreading, clump-forming. ***Flowers*** Small, tubular, in upright clusters, in summer. White or lilac. ***Fruits*** Berry-like, small. Dull blue. ***Leaves*** Evergreen, linear, grass-like. Purple-black.

• NATIVE HABITAT Garden origin; species originates in Japanese woodlands.

• CULTIVATION Grow in humus-rich, well-drained soil, in sun or partial shade. Good ground cover; can be used as a low-maintenance grass substitute.

• PROPAGATION By division in spring.

Z6–10

HEIGHT 9in (23cm)

SPREAD 12in (30cm) or more

Commelinaceae

TRADESCANTIA PALLIDA 'Purple Heart'

Habit Trailing, with rooting stems. ***Flowers*** Tiny, 3-petaled, borne singly at the stem tips in summer. Pink or pink-and-white. ***Leaves*** Evergreen, elliptic to lance-shaped, slightly fleshy. Dark purple.

• NATIVE HABITAT Tropical E. Mexico.
• CULTIVATION In cool climates, grow as a house or greenhouse plant. Grow in well-drained potting mix or soil in bright, indirect light. Water well in growth.
• PROPAGATION By tip cuttings in spring, summer, or autumn.
• OTHER NAMES *Setcreasea purpurea*.

Min. 59°F (15°C)

HEIGHT 6in (15cm)

SPREAD Indefinite

Lamiaceae/Labiatae

AJUGA REPTANS 'Atropurpurea'

Habit Carpet-forming, stoloniferous. ***Flowers*** Small, 2-lipped, tubular, in short, whorled spikes in spring. Blue. ***Leaves*** Evergreen, oblong to spoon-shaped, in rosettes. Glossy. Dark bronze-purple.

• NATIVE HABITAT Garden origin.
• CULTIVATION Tolerates sun or shade and most soils, but grows best in fertile, moist but well-drained soil. Invaluable for border edging and as ground cover beneath shrubs and robust perennials. Spreads freely in good, moist soils.
• PROPAGATION By division in spring.

Z 3–9

HEIGHT 6in (15cm)

SPREAD 3ft (1m)

Commelinaceae

TRADESCANTIA SILLAMONTANA

Habit Upright. ***Flowers*** Tiny, 3-petaled, borne at the stem tips in summer. Bright purplish-pink. ***Leaves*** Evergreen, elliptic-oval, stem-clasping. Green, flushed purple-red, white-hairy.

• NATIVE HABITAT Tropical N.E. Mexico.
• CULTIVATION Grow as a house or greenhouse plant in cool climates. Fertilize and water freely when in growth; avoid wetting leaves.
• PROPAGATION By tip cuttings in spring, summer, or autumn.

Min. 50–59°F (10–15°C)

HEIGHT 12in (30cm)

SPREAD 12in (30cm)

Urticaceae | WATERMELON BEGONIA

PELLIONIA REPENS

Habit Creeping, with rooting stems. ***Flowers*** Insignificant. ***Leaves*** Evergreen, broadly oval, scalloped. Soft gray green at the center, edged with purplish-brown.

- NATIVE HABITAT Vietnam to Malaysia and Burma.
- CULTIVATION Grow as a house or greenhouse plant in cool climates. Needs a humid atmosphere.
- PROPAGATION Separate rooted stems or take stem cuttings in spring or summer.
- OTHER NAMES *P. daveauana, Elatostema daveauana, E. repens.*

Min. 59°F (15°C)

HEIGHT 4in (10cm)

SPREAD indefinite

Scrophulariaceae | MEXICAN FOXGLOVE, MEXICAN VIOLET

TETRANEMA ROSEUM

Habit Rosette-forming. ***Flowers*** Nodding, trumpet-shaped, shallowly lobed, mostly in summer, but intermittently throughout the year. Lilac to mauve with darker markings. ***Leaves*** Evergreen, stalkless, broadly oval, slightly leathery. Dark green.

- NATIVE HABITAT Damp, shady habitats in Mexico.
- CULTIVATION Grow as a house or greenhouse plant in cool climates. Needs a humid, draught-free atmosphere. Take care not to overwater.
- PROPAGATION By division or seed in spring.
- OTHER NAMES *T. mexicanum.*

Min. 55°F (13°C)

HEIGHT to 8in (20cm)

SPREAD 12in (30cm)

Ranunculaceae

HELLEBORUS TORQUATUS 'Dido'

Habit Clump-forming. ***Flowers*** Nodding or held horizontally, double, cup-shaped, borne in clusters in late winter and early spring. Purple outside, lime-green within. ***Leaves*** Deciduous, emerging with or after the flowers, divided into 10–30 narrow, segments. Dark green.

- NATIVE HABITAT Garden origin.
- CULTIVATION Grow in fertile, heavy, moist but well-drained soil, in sun or partial shade. Provide shelter from cold wind. Good for woodland gardens.
- PROPAGATION By division in autumn.

Z 6–9

HEIGHT 16–18in (40–45cm)

SPREAD 18in (45cm)

Lamiaceae/Labiatae

AJUGA REPTANS 'Multicolor'

Habit Carpet-forming, stoloniferous. ***Flowers*** Small, 2-lipped, tubular, in short, whorled spikes in spring. Blue. ***Leaves*** Evergreen, spoon-shaped, in basal rosettes. Dark green, marked cream and pink,

- NATIVE HABITAT Garden origin.
- CULTIVATION Tolerates sun or shade and most soil types. Good for border edging and as ground cover beneath shrubs and robust perennials.
- PROPAGATION By division in spring.
- OTHER NAMES *A. reptans* 'Rainbow', *A. reptans* 'Tricolor'.

Z 3–9

HEIGHT 5in (12cm)

SPREAD 18in (45cm)

Gesneriaceae

STREPTOCARPUS 'Constant Nymph'

Habit Upright, rosette-forming. ***Flowers*** Small, funnel-shaped, borne intermittently in small clusters. Purple-blue, with dark veins and yellow throats. ***Leaves*** Evergreen, fleshy, strap-shaped, wrinkled. Dark green.

- NATIVE HABITAT Garden origin.
- CULTIVATION Grow as a house or greenhouse plant in cool climates. Needs high humidity. Water freely during growth; avoid wetting leaves.
- PROPAGATION By division after flowering, or by leaf cuttings in spring or summer.

Min. 50–59°F (10–15°C)

HEIGHT 10in (25cm)

SPREAD 20in (50cm)

Marantaceae — HERRINGBONE PLANT

MARANTA LEUCONEURA var. *ERYTHRONEURA*

Habit Low-growing, rhizomatous. ***Flowers*** Small, 3-petaled, in an upright spike, year-round. White or violet. ***Leaves*** Evergreen, oblong, velvety. Black-green, with red veins and lime-green midrib zone.

- NATIVE HABITAT Garden origin.
- CULTIVATION Grow as a house or greenhouse plant in cool climates. Needs constant humidity and a draft-free position. Good for a terrarium.
- PROPAGATION By division in spring or summer, or stem cuttings in summer.

Min. 59°F (15°C)

HEIGHT to 12in (30cm)

SPREAD to 12in (30cm)

Commelinaceae — PUSSY EARS

CYANOTIS SOMALIENSIS

Habit Creeping, with rooting shoots. ***Flowers*** Small, stemless, 3-petaled, in the leaf axils, in winter and spring. Purplish-blue. ***Leaves*** Evergreen, fleshy, narrowly oblong, with round-pointed tips, glossy, densely hairy, and fringed with long hairs beneath. Dark green.

- NATIVE HABITAT Uncertain, probably Somalia.
- CULTIVATION Grow as a house or greenhouse plant in cool climates, in humus-rich, well-drained potting soil. Water moderately, less in winter.
- PROPAGATION Tip cuttings from spring to autumn.

Min. 50–59°F (10–15°C)

HEIGHT 2in (5cm)

SPREAD indefinite

Dracaenaceae

SANSEVIERIA TRIFASCIATA 'Hahnii'

Habit Upright, stemless, rosette-forming, and rhizomatous. ***Flowers*** Small, but seldom produced. Pale green. ***Leaves*** Evergreen, stiff, erect, broadly lance-shaped, with a pointed tip. Banded horizontally with dark green, pale green, and white.

- NATIVE HABITAT Garden origin.
- CULTIVATION Grow as a house or greenhouse plant in cool climates, in any moderately fertile potting soil. Water moderately when in growth. A tough and adaptable plant.
- PROPAGATION By division in summer.

Min. 50–59°F (10–15°C)

HEIGHT 6–12in (15–30cm)

SPREAD 4in (10cm)

Marantaceae	CATHEDRAL WINDOWS, PEACOCK PLANT

CALATHEA MAKOYANA

Habit Clump-forming. ***Flowers*** Tubular, in short, dense spikes, produced intermittently. White with purple lobes. ***Leaves*** Evergreen, oval. Pale green, with oblong, dark green blotches, and creamy-white feathering above, patterned red-purple beneath.

- NATIVE HABITAT Damp forests, E. Brazil.
- CULTIVATION Grow as a house or greenhouse plant in cool climates. Keep just moist with soft water in winter. Needs high humidity, a constant temperature, and draft-free conditions.
- PROPAGATION By division in spring.

Min. 59°F (15°C)

HEIGHT to 2ft (60cm)

SPREAD to 4ft (1.2m)

Araceae	

AGLAONEMA COMMUTATUM 'Silver King'

Habit Upright, tufted. ***Flowers*** Greenish-white spathes, in summer. ***Leaves*** Evergreen, lance-shaped, to 12in (30cm) long. Mid-green, irregularly marked with dark green and pale silvery-green.

- NATIVE HABITAT Garden origin.
- CULTIVATION Grow as a house or greenhouse plant in cool climates. Site in moist but well-drained soil. Needs moderate humidity. Keep moist in winter, but allow to become drier in winter.
- PROPAGATION By division or stem cuttings in summer.

Min. 59°F (15°C)

HEIGHT 18in (45cm)

SPREAD 18in (45cm)

Araceae	

AGLAONEMA PICTUM

Habit Upright, tufted. ***Flowers*** Creamy-white spathes, in summer. ***Leaves*** Evergreen, narrowly elliptic, to 6in (15cm) long. Lustrous, dark bluish-green, irregularly marked gray-green or gray-white.

- NATIVE HABITAT Sumatra.
- CULTIVATION Grow as a house or greenhouse plant in cool climates. Grow in moist but well-drained soil, in bright, indirect light or partial shade. Water moderately and maintain humidity when in growth; keep drier in winter.
- PROPAGATION Division or stem cuttings in summer.

Min. 59°F (15°C)

HEIGHT to 24in (60cm)

SPREAD to 24in (60cm)

Marantaceae	RABBIT TRACKS

MARANTA LEUCONEURA var. *KERCHOVEANA*

Habit Low-growing, rhizomatous. ***Flowers*** Small, 3-petaled, borne intermittently, in an upright spike. White or mauve. ***Leaves*** Evergreen, oblong. Gray-green, with dark brown blotches fading with age.

- NATIVE HABITAT Damp, tropical forests, Brazil.
- CULTIVATION Grow as a house or greenhouse plant in cool climates. Needs constant high humidity. Good for a terrarium.
- PROPAGATION By division in spring or summer, or stem cuttings in summer.

Min. 59°F (15°C)

HEIGHT to 12in (30cm)

SPREAD to 12in (30cm)

Welwitschiaceae

WELWITSCHIA MIRABILIS

Habit Long-lived, deep-rooting. ***Flowers*** Small, cone-like, seldom produced. Reddish-brown. ***Leaves*** Evergreen; the 2 strap-shaped leaves continuously grow to 8ft (2.5m) or more, splitting and twisting at the tips with age. Pale gray-green.

- NATIVE HABITAT Coastal desert, S.W. Africa.
- CULTIVATION Grow as a house or greenhouse plant in cool climates in tall, narrow pots. Difficult to grow.
- PROPAGATION By seed when ripe.
- OTHER NAMES *W. bainesii*.

Min. 50°F (10°C)

HEIGHT 12in (30cm) or more

SPREAD indefinite

Lamiaceae/Labiatae | LAMB'S TONGUE, BUNNIES' EARS

STACHYS BYZANTINA

Habit Mat-forming. ***Flowers*** Small, tubular, 2-lipped, in white-woolly, upright spikes, in summer. Pink. ***Leaves*** Evergreen, thick, oblong to spoon-shaped or elliptic, mainly in basal rosettes. Densely white-woolly.

- NATIVE HABITAT Rocky hills, Caucasus to Iran.
- CULTIVATION Grow in well-drained soil, ideally in a hot, sunny site. Good for ground cover and border edging, especially in a silver border.
- PROPAGATION By seed or division in spring.
- OTHER NAMES *S. lanata, S. olympica.*

Z 4–9

HEIGHT 12–15in (30–38cm)

SPREAD 2ft (60cm)

Lamiaceae/Labiatae

STACHYS BYZANTINA 'Silver Carpet'

Habit Mat-forming. ***Flowers*** Seldom produced. ***Leaves*** Evergreen, thick, oblong to spoon-shaped or elliptic, mainly in basal rosettes. Densely white-woolly.

- NATIVE HABITAT Garden origin.
- CULTIVATION Grow in well-drained soil, preferably in a hot, sunny site. Tolerates poor soil. Good for ground cover and border edging, and is especially useful in a silver border or for edging in an herb garden.
- PROPAGATION By division in spring.

Z 4–9

HEIGHT 6in (15cm)

SPREAD 2ft (60cm)

Convallariaceae/Liliaceae

OPHIOPOGON JAPONICUS

Habit Spreading, clump-forming, stoloniferous. ***Flowers*** Small, tubular, in spike-like heads, in summer. Lilac. ***Fruits*** Berry-like, small. Blue. ***Leaves*** Evergreen, narrow-linear, grass-like, glossy. Dark green.

- NATIVE HABITAT Damp habitats, Japan.
- CULTIVATION Grow in fertile, humus-rich, moist but well-drained soil, in sun or light shade. Good for ground cover: may also be grown in the edge of a pond, but it will not flower.
- PROPAGATION By division in spring.

Z 6–10

HEIGHT 12in (30cm)

SPREAD indefinite

Ranunculaceae

HELLEBORUS MULTIFIDUS subsp. *HERCEGOVINUS*

Habit Clump-forming. ***Flowers*** Small, scented, nodding, cup-shaped, borne in clusters in winter and early spring. Green. ***Leaves*** Deciduous, very finely divided into 45–70 linear, leathery leaflets, hairy beneath. Green, tinted dull brown.

- NATIVE HABITAT Woods and scrub on the hillsides of the S. Balkans.
- CULTIVATION Grow in fertile, moist, well-drained soil, in a warm site, sheltered from wind.
- PROPAGATION Fresh seed, or division in autumn.

Z 6–9

HEIGHT to 20in (50cm)

SPREAD 12in (30cm)

Ranunculaceae

HELLEBORUS ARGUTIFOLIUS

Habit Clump-forming. ***Flowers*** Nodding, cup-shaped, borne in large clusters, in winter and early spring. Pale green. ***Leaves*** Evergreen, divided into 3 elliptic, sharply toothed leaflets. Dark green.

- NATIVE HABITAT Maquis scrub in Corsica and Sardinia.
- CULTIVATION Grow in fertile, well-drained soil, in sun, with shelter from cold wind. May be short-lived but usually self-sows.
- PROPAGATION Fresh seed, or division in autumn.
- OTHER NAMES *H. corsicus, H. lividus* subsp. *corsicus.*

Z 7–9

HEIGHT 24in (60cm) or more

SPREAD 18in (45cm)

Urticaceae | BABY'S TEARS

SOLEIROLIA SOLEIROLII

Habit Mat-forming, often vigorously invasive. ***Flowers*** Tiny, seldom produced. Yellow-white. ***Leaves*** Evergreen, small, thin, rounded, brilliant green, on delicate, translucent, rooting stems.

- NATIVE HABITAT Asia to Malaysia.
- CULTIVATION Grow in moist, well-drained soil in sun or partial shade. Good for ground cover beneath other, more robust plants, in paving crevices, and very attractive grown indoors in pots.
- PROPAGATION Division from spring to summer.
- OTHER NAMES *Helxine soleirolii.*

Z 10–11

HEIGHT 2in (5cm)

SPREAD indefinite

Lamiaceae/Labiatae

BALLOTA PSEUDODICTAMNUS

Habit Mound-forming, sub-shrubby. ***Flowers*** Small, tubular, 2-lipped, in summer. White or pale pink, borne within curious, pale green calyces. ***Leaves*** Evergreen, oval, woolly. Gray-green.
• NATIVE HABITAT Dry hills in the Greek Islands.
• CULTIVATION Grow in well-drained soil in a warm, sunny, sheltered site. Good for the front of a silver-leaved border. Cut back in spring before new growth begins.
• PROPAGATION By seed in spring or semi-ripe cuttings in summer.

Z 7–9

HEIGHT
24in (60cm)

SPREAD
36in (90cm)

Droseraceae — SPOON-LEAF SUNDEW

DROSERA SPATHULATA

Habit Rosette-forming, insectivorous. ***Flowers*** Tiny, 5-petaled, borne in clusters of up to 15, on leafless stems, to 8in (20cm) high, in summer. White to pink. ***Leaves*** Evergreen, spoon-shaped, clothed in sensitive, glandular, red hairs. Mid-green.
• NATIVE HABITAT Bogs, S. Japan to E. China, south to New Zealand.
• CULTIVATION Grow as a house or greenhouse plant in cool climates. Plant in a mix of peat and sphagnum moss, in sun. Keep moist with soft water.
• PROPAGATION By seed or division in spring.

Min.
41–50°F
(5–10°C)

HEIGHT
3in (8cm)

SPREAD
3in (8cm)

Commelinaceae

CALLISIA REPENS

Habit Creeping, dense, stem-rooting. ***Flowers*** Inconspicuous, 3-petaled, in winter, but seldom produced. White. ***Leaves*** Evergreen, small, rounded, slightly fleshy, heart-shaped at the base. Green above, purplish-green and sometimes banded white beneath.
• NATIVE HABITAT Texas and West Indies to Argentina.
• CULTIVATION Grow as a house or greenhouse plant in cool climates. Shade from hot sun.
• PROPAGATION By tip cuttings in spring.

Min. 59°F
(15°C)

HEIGHT
4in (10cm)

SPREAD
Indefinite

Piperaceae — WAX PRIVET

PEPEROMIA GLABELLA

Habit Upright or sprawling. ***Flowers*** Minute, insignificant, produced irregularly. ***Leaves*** Evergreen, softly fleshy, broadly oval, glossy. Bright green, on long red leaf stalks, on red stems.
• NATIVE HABITAT C. and S. America, West Indies.
• CULTIVATION Grow as a house or greenhouse plant in cool climates. Plant in peaty soil or potting mix. Water moderately when in growth, less in winter.
• PROPAGATION By division, seed, or leaf or stem cuttings in spring or summer.

Min. 50°F
(10°C)

HEIGHT
to 6in
(15cm)

SPREAD
12in (30cm)

Ranunculaceae	GREEN HELLEBORE

HELLEBORUS VIRIDIS

Habit Clump-forming. ***Flowers*** Small, nodding, cup-shaped, borne in clusters of 2–4, in winter and early spring. Green, often blotched purple at the petal base. ***Leaves*** Deciduous, divided into 7–11 narrowly elliptic, toothed leaflets. Dark green.
• NATIVE HABITAT Woods, sunny banks, on alkaline soils, from C. France to Austria and N. Italy.
• CULTIVATION Grow in fertile, moist, well-drained, preferably alkaline soil, in partial shade, with shelter from wind. A graceful specimen for a winter border.
• PROPAGATION Fresh seed, or division in autumn.

Z 6–8

HEIGHT
12in (30cm)

SPREAD
12in (30cm)

Saxifragaceae	

TOLMIEA MENZIESII 'Taff's Gold'

Habit Spreading, mat-forming. ***Flowers*** Tiny, nodding, tubular to bell-shaped, borne in slender, upright spikes in spring. Green and chocolate brown. ***Leaves*** Semi-evergreen, 3-lobed, ivy-like. Pale lime-green, spotted and mottled with cream and gold.
• NATIVE HABITAT Garden origin.
• CULTIVATION Grow in moist but well-drained soil in shade or partial shade. Good ground cover for woodland gardens. Also grown as a houseplant.
• PROPAGATION By division in spring or autumn.

Z 6–9

HEIGHT
18–24in
(45–60cm)

SPREAD
12in (30cm)

Piperaceae	VARIEGATED BABY RUBBER PLANT

PEPEROMIA OBTUSIFOLIA 'Variegata'

Habit Bushy, upright, stoloniferous. ***Flowers*** Minute, insignificant, produced irregularly. ***Leaves*** Evergreen, firm, fleshy, broadly oval. Mid-green and pale green, with irregular cream margins.
• NATIVE HABITAT Garden origin.
• CULTIVATION Grow as a house or greenhouse plant in cool climates. Prefers peaty soil or potting mix and a bright position out of direct sunlight. Water moderately when in growth, less in winter.
• PROPAGATION By division, leaf or stem cuttings in spring or summer.

Min. 50°F
(10°C)

HEIGHT
to 6in
(15cm)

SPREAD
to 6in
(15cm)

Amaranthaceae	

IRESINE HERBSTII 'Aureoreticulata'

Habit Bushy. ***Flowers*** Insignificant. White or greenish-white. ***Leaves*** Evergreen, oval, to 4in (10cm) long, waxy, borne on succulent red stems. Mid-green, with bright to pale yellow or red veins.
• NATIVE HABITAT Garden origin.
• CULTIVATION Grow as a house or greenhouse plant in cool climates. Grow in well-drained, soil-based potting mix in bright light. Water freely when in growth, otherwise moderately. Pinch young growing tips to encourage bushiness.
• PROPAGATION By stem cuttings in spring.

Min.
50–59°F
(10–15°C)

HEIGHT
to 24in
(60cm)

SPREAD
18in (45cm)

Droseraceae	VENUS FLYTRAP

DIONAEA MUSCIPULA

Habit Rosette-forming, insectivorous. ***Flowers*** Small, 5-petaled, in clusters of 3–10, in summer. White. ***Leaves*** Evergreen, 2-lobed, hinged at the midrib, pink-flushed inside, fringed with stiff bristles, and with touch-sensitive hairs within.

- NATIVE HABITAT Bogs, N. and S. Carolina.
- CULTIVATION Grow as a house or greenhouse plant in cool climates in a mix of vermiculite, peat, and sphagnum moss in sun. Stand in a saucer filled with soft water to a depth of about ½in (1cm).
- PROPAGATION By seed or division in spring.

Z 8–9

HEIGHT 4in (10cm)

SPREAD to 12in (30cm)

Dracaenaceae	

SANSEVIERIA TRIFASCIATA 'Golden Hahnii'

Habit Upright, stemless, rosette-forming, and rhizomatous. ***Flowers*** Small, seldom produced. Pale green, ***Leaves*** Evergreen, stiff, erect, broadly lance-shaped. Green, with broad yellow margins.

- NATIVE HABITAT Garden origin.
- CULTIVATION In cool climates, grow as a house or greenhouse plant in moderately fertile potting mix or soil. Tolerates sun or shade. Increase water during growth. A tough and adaptable plant.
- PROPAGATION By division in summer.

Min. 50–59°F (10–15°C)

HEIGHT 6–12in (15–30cm)

SPREAD 4in (10cm)

Ranunculaceae	STINKING HELLEBORE

HELLEBORUS FOETIDUS

Habit Clump-forming. ***Flowers*** Small, nodding, cup-shaped, borne in clusters of 2–4, in winter and early spring. Green, with red petal margins. ***Leaves*** Evergreen, divided into 7–10 narrow, elliptic toothed glossy leaflets. Very dark green.

- NATIVE HABITAT Woods, rocky slopes usually on limy soils, in S.W. and C. Europe.
- CULTIVATION Grow in a sheltered site, preferably in alkaline soil. Tolerant of dry shade.
- PROPAGATION Fresh seed, or division in autumn.

Z 6–9

HEIGHT 18in (45cm)

SPREAD 18in (45cm)

Gesneriaceae	

NAUTILOCALYX LYNCHII

Habit Robust upright, bushy. ***Flowers*** Small, tubular, borne in axillary clusters in summer. Pale yellow, red-haired, purple-flecked within. ***Leaves*** Evergreen, elliptic lance-shaped, glossy, wrinkled. Dark greenish-red above, red-tinted beneath.

- NATIVE HABITAT Tropical Colombia.
- CULTIVATION Grow as a house or greenhouse plant in cool climates. Needs high humidity. Water moderately when in growth, less in winter.
- PROPAGATION By stem cuttings in summer or by seed in spring.

Min. 59°F (15°C)

HEIGHT to 24in (60cm)

SPREAD to 24in (60cm)

GRASSES, SEDGES, AND RUSHES

Grasses (Gramineae), sedges (Cyperaceae), and rushes (Juncaceae) together form part of a group of generally trouble-free plants grown mainly for their foliage, which offers contrasts of form, color and texture in borders and rock gardens. A number of grasses also have attractive flower heads some of which are useful for drying. Most grasses thrive in any well-drained soil and flourish in a range of light conditions. Rushes prefer moist or wet soil in sun or partial shade, although *Luzula* species often prefer drier conditions. Sedges grow in sun or partial shade, and although many occur naturally in water, most will grow well in moist, well-drained, moderately fertile soils.

Propagate species by seed in autumn, or division in autumn or spring.

***PHALARIS ARUNDINACEA* var. *PICTA*'**
Habit Clump-forming.
Flowers Tiny, in narrow panicles in summer. Pale greenish-brown.
Leaves Evergreen, broadly linear. Green, striped white.
• TIPS Grow in damp, shady borders and by water. Invasive.
• HEIGHT 3ft (1m).
• SPREAD indefinite.

Phalaris arundinacea* var. *picta
Gardener's garters, Ribbon grass
Z 4–9

***CORTADERIA SELLOANA* 'Silver Comet'**
Habit Clump-forming.
Flowers Tiny, borne in dense, silky, plume-like panicles in late summer. Silver.
Leaves Evergreen, narrow, sharp-edged, arching. Pale, silvery green.
• TIPS Protect young plants with a winter mulch. Avoid heavy soils. An excellent specimen plant. Propagate by division in spring.
• HEIGHT 4–5ft (1.2–1.5m).
• SPREAD 3ft (1m).

***Cortaderia selloana* 'Silver Comet'**
Z 7–10

***HOLCUS MOLLIS* 'Albovariegatus'**
Habit Clump-forming, spreading.
Flowers Tiny, in purplish-white flower spikes, in summer.
Leaves Evergreen, linear, with hairy nodes. Green, striped white.
• OTHER NAMES *H. mollis* 'Variegatus'.
• HEIGHT 3ft (1m).
• SPREAD indefinite.

***Holcus mollis* 'Albovariegatus'**
Variegated creeping soft grass
Z 5–9

ARUNDO DONAX* var. *VERSICOLOR
Habit Clump-forming, rhizomatous.
Flowers Feathery, in dense, erect heads in late summer, but produced reliably only in hot summers. Creamy-white.
Leaves Broadly linear. Bluish-green, striped and edged creamy-white.
• TIPS Needs moist soil. Propagate by division in spring.
• OTHER NAMES *A. donax* 'Variegata'.
• HEIGHT 8–10ft (2.5–3m).
• SPREAD 2ft (60cm).

Arundo donax* var. *versicolor
Variegated giant reed
Z 8–10

GLYCERIA MAXIMA var. *VARIEGATA*

Habit Clump-forming.
Flowers Tiny, in open heads in summer. Green, purple-tinted.
Leaves Broadly linear. Green, with cream stripes, pink-flushed when young.
• TIPS Ideally suited to waterside plantings. Propagate by division in spring.
• OTHER NAMES *G. aquatica variegata*.
• HEIGHT 32in (80cm).
• SPREAD indefinite.

Glyceria maxima* var. *variegata

Z 5–9

CORTADERIA SELLOANA 'Sunningdale Silver'

Habit Sturdy, clump-forming.
Flowers Tiny, borne in long, dense, silky plumes in late summer. Silvery-cream.
Leaves Evergreen, narrow, very sharp-edged, arching. Pale olive-green.
• TIPS Protect young plants with a winter mulch. Avoid heavy soil. A robust and excellent specimen plant. Propagate by division in spring.
• HEIGHT 7ft (2.1m).
• SPREAD 4ft (1.2m).

***Cortaderia selloana* 'Sunningdale Silver'**

Z 7–10

LUZULA NIVEA

Habit Clump-forming.
Flowers Tiny, in early summer. Shining white.
Leaves Evergreen, linear, mostly basal. Dark green, fringed with white hairs.
• TIPS Grow in moist but well-drained soil. Suited to a woodland garden. Propagate by seed in autumn; division in spring.
• HEIGHT 24in (60cm).
• SPREAD 18–24in (45–60cm).

Luzula nivea
Snowy woodrush

Z 4–9

SCHOENOPLECTUS LACUSTRIS subsp. *TABERNAEMONTANI* 'Zebrinus'

Habit Clump-forming.
Flowers Tiny, in spikelets in summer. Red-brown.
Leaves Almost leafless, stems banded with white.
• TIPS Grows well by water. Divide in spring.
• OTHER NAMES *Scirpus tabernaemontani* 'Zebrinus'.
• HEIGHT 5ft (1.5m).
• SPREAD indefinite.

***Schoenoplectus lacustris* subsp. *tabernaemontani* 'Zebrinus'**

Z 6–9

MISCANTHUS SINENSIS 'Zebrinus'

Habit Clump-forming.
Flowers Tiny, in silky-haired spikelets borne in fan-shaped heads in early autumn. White.
Leaves Long, arching, linear. Bluish-green, with transverse, creamy-white or yellow-gold banding.
• TIPS Well-suited for placing at the back of a border, but flowers reliably only in warm summers. Propagate by division in spring.
• HEIGHT 4ft (1.2m).
• SPREAD 18in (45cm).

***Miscanthus sinensis* 'Zebrinus'**
Zebra grass

Z 5–10

HORDEUM JUBATUM

Habit Tufted.
Flowers Tiny, silky-bristled spikelets, borne in arching spikes from early to midsummer. Pale green, flushed red, turning beige when mature.
Leaves Linear. Green.
• TIPS An annual or short-lived perennial grown for its flowers that dry well for winter arrangements. Propagate by seed in spring.
• HEIGHT 1–2ft (30–60cm).
• SPREAD 1ft (30cm).

Hordeum jubatum
Foxtail barley,
Squirreltail grass

Z 4–8

PENNISETUM VILLOSUM

Habit Tuft-forming.
Flowers Tiny, bearded spikelets, in plumes in late summer. Creamy-pink.
Leaves Flat, linear, on hairy stems. Mid-green.
• TIPS Flower heads cut and dry well. Propagate by seed in spring.
• OTHER NAMES *P. longistylum*
• HEIGHT to 3ft (1m).
• SPREAD 20in (50cm).

Pennisetum villosum
Feather-top

Z 8–10

STIPA GIGANTEA

Habit Tufted.
Flowers Tiny, in open, airy panicles in summer. Silvery, with golden anthers.
Leaves Evergreen, narrow, smooth, or slightly rough. Dark green.
• TIPS An imposing specimen at the back of a border. Sow seed in spring or divide in autumn.
• HEIGHT 8ft (2.5cm).
• SPREAD 3ft (1m).

Stipa gigantea
Golden oats

Z 6–9

CYPERUS PAPYRUS

Habit Clump-forming.
Flowers Tiny, in large terminal umbels, in summer. Brownish-yellow.
Leaves Evergreen, insignificant, but with a whorl of short, linear, dark green, leaf-like bracts beneath the flowers.
• TIPS Grow as a house or conservatory plant in cooler climates. Suitable for planting in a large pot. Needs permanently wet soil and protection from direct sun. Propagate by division in spring.
• HEIGHT to 10–15ft (3–5m).
• SPREAD 3ft (1m).

Cyperus papyrus
Egyptian paper reed,
Papyrus

Min. 45–50°F (7–10°C)

HELICTOTRICHON SEMPERVIRENS

Habit Tuft-forming.
Flowers Tiny, borne in spikes, in erect heads, in summer. Straw-color.
Leaves Evergreen, narrowly linear, stiff. Silvery-blue, up to 12in (30cm) or more.
• OTHER NAMES *Avena candida* of gardens.
• HEIGHT 20in (50cm).
• SPREAD 8in (20cm).

Helictotrichon sempervirens

Z 4–9

CHONDROSUM GRACILE

Habit Tuft-forming.
Flowers Tiny, in spikelets, in summer. Purple-brown.
Leaves Semi-evergreen, narrowly linear. Dark grayish-green.
• TIPS Must have good drainage. Divide or sow seed in spring.
• OTHER NAMES *Bouteloua gracilis.*
• HEIGHT 20in (50cm).
• SPREAD 8in (20cm).

Chondrosum gracile
Blue grama
Mosquito grass

Z 5–9

MELICA ALTISSIMA 'Atropurpurea'

Habit Tuft-forming.
Flowers Tiny spikelets, borne in narrow, terminal, arching heads in summer. Deep mauve.
Leaves Broadly linear, arching, roughly hairy beneath. Mid-green.

- TIPS Needs well-drained soil and sun. Propagate by division in spring.
- HEIGHT 2ft (60cm).
- SPREAD 2ft (60cm).

Melica altissima 'Atropurpurea'

Z 6–9

JUNCUS EFFUSUS 'Spiralis'

Habit Tuft-forming.
Flowers Tiny, in short, dense heads in summer. Greenish-brown.
Leaves Leafless, but with spiraling, evergreen stems that are often prostrate.

- TIPS Plant by water or in a moist border. Divide in spring.
- HEIGHT 3ft (1m).
- SPREAD 2ft (60cm).

Juncus effusus 'Spiralis'
Corkscrew rush

Z 5–9

MISCANTHUS SINENSIS 'Gracillimus'

Habit Clump-forming.
Flowers Tiny spikelets in fan-shaped heads in early autumn. Hairy, white.
Leaves Long, arching, narrow. Bluish-green, with a white midrib, often bronze-flushed.

- TIPS Ideal for the back of a border. Divide in spring.
- HEIGHT 4ft (1.2m).
- SPREAD 18in (45cm).

Miscanthus sinensis 'Gracillimus'

Z 5–10

CYPERUS INVOLUCRATUS

Habit Tuft-forming.
Flowers Tiny, surrounded by green bracts, in summer. Creamy-yellow.
Leaves Evergreen, insignificant.

- TIPS Grow indoors in a big pot in cooler climates. Keep wet. Divide in spring.
- OTHER NAMES *C. alternifolius* (of gardens).
- HEIGHT to 3ft (1m).
- SPREAD 1ft (30cm).

Cyperus involucratus
Umbrella plant
Nile grass

Min. 39–45°F (4–7°C) Z 1

CAREX PENDULA

Habit Densely tufted.
Flowers Tiny, in catkin-like spikes on long stems in summer. Brown.
Leaves Evergreen, narrow, rigid, keeled. Shining yellow-green, blue-green beneath.
• TIPS Suited to a woodland garden. Divide in spring or sow seed in autumn.
• HEIGHT 3ft (1m).
• SPREAD 1ft (30cm).

Carex pendula
Nodding sedge

Z 5–9

SPARTINA PECTINATA 'Aureomarginata'

Habit Clump-forming, rhizomatous.
Flowers Tiny, in narrow spikes in late summer. Straw-colored.
Leaves Tough, narrow, arching. Olive-green with yellow stripes and margin; orange-brown in autumn.
• TIPS Ideally suited to waterside plantings but will also thrive in a dry garden. Propagate by division in spring.
• OTHER NAMES *S. pectinata* 'Aureovariegata'.
• HEIGHT to 6ft (2m).
• SPREAD indefinite.

***Spartina pectinata* 'Aureomarginata'**

Z 5–9

CAREX HACHIJOENSIS 'Evergold'

Habit Densely tufted.
Flowers Tiny, in small clusters at the tips of solid triangular stems in mid- to late spring. Dark brown.
Leaves Evergreen, linear, Dark green, yellow striped.
• TIPS Needs good drainage. Divide in spring.
• OTHER NAMES *C. oshimensis* 'Evergold'.
• HEIGHT 12in (30cm).
• SPREAD 14in (35cm).

***Carex hachijoensis* 'Evergold'**

Z 7–9

CAREX ELATA 'Aurea'

Habit Tussock-forming.
Flowers Tiny, in small clusters, on triangular stems in spring and early summer. Dark brown.
Leaves Evergreen, linear. Golden-yellow.
• TIPS Suited to poolside plantings. Divide in spring.
• OTHER NAMES *C. stricta* 'Aurea'.
• HEIGHT to 16in (40cm).
• SPREAD 6–8in (15–20cm).

***Carex elata* 'Aurea'**
Bowles' golden sedge

Z 5–9

HAKENOCHLOA MACRA 'Aureola'

Habit Mound-forming, rhizomatous.
Flowers Tiny spikelets, in open heads in late summer. Red-tinted.
Leaves Linear, arching. Bright yellow with narrow cream and green stripes, flushing red in autumn.
• TIPS Grow in moist but well-drained soil in partial shade or sun. Propagate by division in spring.
• HEIGHT 16in (40cm).
• SPREAD 18–24in (45–60cm).

***Hakenochloa macra* 'Aureola'**

Z 4–9

ALOPECURUS PRATENSIS 'Aureovariegatus'

Habit Tuft-forming.
Flowers Dense spikes, in summer. Pale green.
Leaves Flat, linear. Yellowish-green, striped and edged with gold.
• OTHER NAMES *A. pratensis* 'Aureomarginatus'.
• HEIGHT to 12in (30cm).
• SPREAD to 12in (30cm).

***Alopecurus pratensis* 'Aureovariegatus'**
Golden foxtail

Z 5–8

FERNS

Among the most popular of all foliage plants, ferns add texture and atmosphere to the house or garden, where they are particularly effective in settings by streams or in damp, shady corners.

Hardy ferns are suitable for growing in woodland gardens, or in the open garden where they benefit from moist, neutral to acid conditions. Many of the smaller types are excellent for a shady rock garden.

Tender tropical ferns are best cultivated indoors in a greenhouse or sunroom, or as house plants where they should be kept moist, but not waterlogged. Protection should be given from direct sunlight.

Ferns are raised mainly by spores but may be propagated by division, or, in some species, by bulbils.

PTERIS CRETICA ALBOLINEATA
Habit Clump-forming.
Leaves Evergreen or semi-evergreen, to 8in (20cm) long, forked in linear segments. Pale green with a creamy-white central stripe.
• TIPS Grow indoors in cooler climates. Propagate by division in spring or spores in summer.
• HEIGHT 18in (45cm).
• SPREAD 12in (30cm).

Pteris cretica albolineata

Min. 41°F (5°C) Z 11

POLYPODIUM AUREUM
'Mandaianum'
Habit Creeping.
Leaves Evergreen, to 3ft (1m) long, deeply lobed, with orange sporangia beneath. Blue-green.
• TIPS Grow indoors in cooler climates. Divide in spring.
• OTHER NAMES *Phlebodium aureum* 'Mandaianum'.
• HEIGHT 3–5ft (1–1.5m).
• SPREAD 2ft (60cm).

Polypodium aureum 'Mandaianum'

Min. 41°F (5°C) Z 11

DRYOPTERIS FILIX-MAS
Habit Arching.
Leaves Deciduous or semi-evergreen, lance-shaped, arising like a shuttlecock from a crown of thick, brown-scaly rhizomes. Mid-green.
• TIPS Grow in humus-rich soil in a shady border. Sow spores in summer or divide in spring or autumn.
• HEIGHT 4ft (1.2m).
• SPREAD 3ft (1m).

Dryopteris filix-mas
Male fern

Z 4–8

DICKSONIA ANTARCTICA
Habit Slow-growing, trunk-forming.
Leaves Evergreen or semi-evergreen, to 10ft (3m) long, arching, divided into linear segments. Dark green, pale green when young.
• TIPS Needs fibrous, peaty soil and moderate humidity. Excellent for a cool sunroom. Propagate by spores in summer.
• HEIGHT 30ft (10m) or more.
• SPREAD 12ft (4m).

Dicksonia antarctica
Man fern, Soft tree fern

Z 9–10

PLATYCERIUM BIFURCATUM
Habit Epiphytic.
Leaves Evergreen, with round, papery sterile fronds, and arching, forked, fertile fronds with velvety-brown spores beneath. Gray-green.
TIPS Grow indoors in cooler climates, on bark attached to a wad of moss. Needs high humidity.
• HEIGHT 3ft (1m).
• SPREAD 3ft (1m).

Platycerium bifurcatum
Common stag's horn fern

Min. 41°F (5°C) Z 11

POLYSTICHUM ACULEATUM 'Pulcherrimum'

Habit Arching, with woody, scaly rhizomes.
Leaves Evergreen or semi-evergreen, rigid, lance-shaped, to 36in (90cm) long, daintily cut into toothed segments, Bright green, maturing to dark green.
• TIPS Needs fibrous, moist but well-drained soil. Propagate by division in spring.
• HEIGHT 24in (60cm).
• SPREAD 30in (75cm).

***Polystichum aculeatum* 'Pulcherrimum'**

Z 4–8

MICROLEPIA STRIGOSA

Habit Creeping, rhizomatous.
Leaves Evergreen, irregularly lance-shaped, to 32in (80cm) long, finely divided into segments. Pale green.
• TIPS Grow indoors in cooler climates. Excellent for shallow pots or hanging baskets in the home or sunroom. Propagate by division in spring or spores in summer.
• HEIGHT 3ft (90cm).
• SPREAD 2ft (60cm).

Microlepia strigosa

Min. 41°F (5°C) Z 11

POLYSTICHUM MUNITUM

Habit Upright.
Leaves Evergreen, rigid, lance-shaped fronds, divided into leathery, spiny-margined segments. Dark green.
• TIPS Needs moist, fibrous soil. Propagate by division in spring or spores in summer.
• HEIGHT 4ft (1.2m).
• SPREAD 1ft (30cm).

Polystichum munitum
Giant holly fern

Z 5–8

BLECHNUM TABULARE

Habit Upright.
Leaves Evergreen or semi-evergreen, with oval, sterile outer fronds, divided into paired, lance-shaped segments. Dark green. Inner fronds are upright, with linear segments.
• TIPS Needs neutral to acid soil. Sow spores in late summer.
• HEIGHT 1–3ft (30cm–1m).
• SPREAD 1–2ft (30–60cm).

Blechnum tabulare

Z 8–10

POLYPODIUM GLYCYRRHIZA

Habit Upright, with a licorice-scented rhizome.
Leaves Deciduous, narrowly oval, to 14in (35cm) long, cut into bright green segments.
• TIPS Needs fibrous, moist, well-drained soil. Divide in spring or sow spores in late summer.
• HEIGHT 18in (45cm).
• SPREAD 18in (45cm).

Polypodium glycyrrhiza
Licorice fern

Z 3–8

POLYPODIUM SCOULERI

Habit Creeping.
Leaves Evergreen, oval rigid, leathery, and divided into paired oblong segments. Dark green.
• TIPS Good for coastal gardens. Needs good drainage. Divide in spring or sow spores in summer.
• HEIGHT 12–16in (30–40cm).
• SPREAD 12–16in (30–40cm).

Polypodium scouleri
Coast polypody, Leathery polypody

Z 6–8

RUMOHRA ADIANTIFORMIS

Habit Creeping, stoutly rhizomatous, epiphytic. ***Leaves*** Evergreen, to 24in (60cm) long, oval, diamond- or lance-shaped, leathery, with pairs of stalked segments. Dark green.
• TIPS Grow as a house or conservatory plant in cooler climates. Grow epiphytically on bark attached to a wad of moss. Needs high humidity. Propagate by division in spring.
• HEIGHT 30–36in (75–90cm).
• SPREAD 30–36in (75–90cm).

Rumohra adiantiformis
Leather fern,
Leatherleaf fern
Min. 50°F (10°C)

CYRTOMIUM FALCATUM

Habit Clump-forming, with an erect rhizome. ***Leaves*** Evergreen (deciduous in cool climates), to 2ft (60cm) long, with holly-like segments. Glossy, bright green.
• TIPS An excellent house plant. If grown outdoors, protect with a straw mulch in winter. Needs a sheltered site. Propagate by spores in summer.
• HEIGHT 1–2ft (30–60cm).
• SPREAD 12–18in (30–45cm).

Cyrtomium falcatum
Fishtail fern,
Japanese holly fern
Z 7–9

SELAGINELLA MARTENSII

Habit Upright, rhizomatous. ***Leaves*** Evergreen, tiny, scale-like, glossy, in dense, multi-branched, frond-like sprays. Rich green.
• TIPS Grow indoors in cool climates. Needs moist peaty soil. Separate rooted stems at any time.
• HEIGHT 9in (23cm).
• SPREAD 9in (23cm).

Selaginella martensii
Min. 41°F (5°C) Z 11

ASPLENIUM CETERACH

Habit Rosette-forming. ***Leaves*** Evergreen, with lance-shaped fronds divided into alternate, bluntly rounded lobes. Dark green with silver scales beneath that age to red-brown.
TIPS Grow in moist, well-drained, alkaline soil. Sow spores in summer; divide in spring.
• HEIGHT 6in (15cm).
• SPREAD 6in (15cm).

Asplenium ceterach
Rusty-back fern
Z 7–9

PTERIS CRETICA

Habit Clump-forming. ***Leaves*** Evergreen or semi-evergreen, broadly oval to triangular, divided into finger-like segments. Pale green.
• TIPS Needs high humidity. Grow indoors in cool climates. By division in spring or spores in summer.
• HEIGHT 18in (45cm).
• SPREAD 12in (30cm).

Pteris cretica
Cretan brake
Min. 5°C (41°F) Z 11

ASPLENIUM TRICHOMANES

Habit Rosette-forming. ***Leaves*** Evergreen, narrowly lance-shaped, divided into leathery, oblong to rounded segments. Bright green.
• TIPS Needs moist, well-drained, alkaline soil. Good for rock crevices. Sow spores in summer.
• HEIGHT 6in (15cm).
• SPREAD 6–12in (15–30cm).

Asplenium trichomanes
Maidenhair spleenwort
Z 3–8

POLYPODIUM AUREUM

Habit Creeping.
Leaves Evergreen, arching, deeply lobed. Mid-green with orange-yellow sporangia beneath.
• TIPS Grow indoors in cool climates. Tolerates part-day sun. Propagate by division in spring; spores in summer.
OTHER NAMES *Phlebodium aureum*.
• HEIGHT 3–5ft (1–1.5m).
• SPREAD 2ft (60cm).

Polypodium aureum
Golden polypody

Min. 41°F (5°C)

POLYSTICHUM SETIFERUM 'Divisilobum'

Habit Arching.
Leaves Evergreen or semi-evergreen, narrowly oval, finely divided into soft-textured segments. Fresh green, covered with white scales as they unfurl.
• TIPS Needs fibrous, moist, well-drained soil. Divide in spring.
• HEIGHT 2ft (60cm).
• SPREAD 1ft (30cm).

***Polystichum setiferum* 'Divisilobum'**

Z 5–8

ADIANTUM PEDATUM

Habit Clump-forming with a thick, creeping rootstock.
Leaves Deciduous, with linear-lance-shaped fronds, to 12in (30cm) long, divided into triangular to oblong segments, on a slender dark brown stem. Fresh green.
• TIPS Needs moist, humus-rich, acid soil. Propagate by dividing very carefully in early spring or by sowing spores in summer.
• HEIGHT 18in (45cm).
• SPREAD 18in (45cm).

Adiantum pedatum
Northern maidenhair fern

Z 3–8

THELYPTERIS PALUSTRIS

Habit Erect or gently arching, creeping.
Leaves Deciduous, lance-shaped, to 15–39in (30–100cm) long, with widely spaced, deeply cut pinnae. Pale green.
• TIPS Tolerates sun. Suited to waterside plantings. Propagate by division in spring.
• HEIGHT 30in (75cm).
• SPREAD 12in (30cm).

Thelypteris palustris
Marsh buckler fern, Marsh fern

Z 5–8

CRYPTOGRAMMA CRISPA

Habit Tuft-forming.
Leaves Deciduous, with oval outer, sterile fronds, divided into toothed segments. Bright green.
• TIPS Grow in a sheltered, damp site in well- drained, gritty, humus-rich soil. Sow spores in late summer.
• HEIGHT 6–9in (15–23cm).
• SPREAD 6–12in (15–30cm).

Cryptogramma crispa
European parsley fern

Z 5–8

DAVALLIA FEJEENSIS

Habit Arching, with scaly rhizomes clothed in curly brown hair.
Leaves Evergreen, to 18in (45cm) long, finely divided into lance-shaped segments. Mid-green.
• TIPS Needs fibrous, peaty soil and high humidity. Grow indoors in cool climates. Excellent for hanging baskets. Propagate by division or spores in summer.
• HEIGHT 8in–3ft2 (0–100cm).
• SPREAD 8in–3ft (20–100cm).

Davallia fejeensis

Min. 50°F (10°C)

POLYPODIUM VULGARE
'Cornubiense'
Habit Upright, creeping.
Leaves Evergreen, lance-shaped, finely divided into lacy segments. Fresh green.
• TIPS Needs fibrous, moist but well-drained soil. Divide in spring or sow spores in summer.
• HEIGHT 10–12in (25–30cm).
• SPREAD 10–12in (25–30cm).

Polypodium vulgare
'Cornubiense'

Z 5–8

SELAGINELLA KRAUSSIANA
Habit Prostrate, trailing.
Leaves Evergreen, tiny, scale-like, and overlapping along jointed stems, with a moss-like appearance. Bright green.
• TIPS Needs moist, peaty soil. An excellent foliage plant for the home or sunroom. Separate rooted stems at any time.
• HEIGHT ½in (1cm).
• SPREAD indefinite.

Selaginella kraussiana
Spreading club moss, Trailing spike moss

Min. 41°F (5°C) Z 11

ONOCLEA SENSIBILIS
Habit Arching, creeping, rhizomatous.
Leaves Deciduous, broadly triangular, finely divided into segments. Pale green, flushed pink when young.
• TIPS Good for waterside planting in humus-rich soil. Divide in autumn or winter.
• HEIGHT 18in (45cm).
• SPREAD 18in (45cm) or more.

Onoclea sensibilis
Sensitive fern, Bead fern

Z 4–8

ADIANTUM PEDATUM var. *ALEUTICUM*
Habit Clump-forming.
Leaves Deciduous, with finger-like fronds, divided into triangular segments, densely arranged on dark brown stems. Bluish-green.
• TIPS Needs moist, humus-rich, alkaline soil. Divide carefully in early spring or sow spores in summer.
• HEIGHT 18in (45cm).
• SPREAD 18in (45cm).

Adiantum pedatum* var. *aleuticum
Aleutian maidenhair

Z 3–8

TODEA BARBARA
Habit Slow-growing, trunk-forming with a massive rhizome.
Leaves Evergreen, semi-erect, fronds to 4ft (1.2m) long, with lance-shaped segments. Bright grass-green.
• TIPS Grow indoors in cool climates. Needs fibrous, peaty soil and moderate humidity. Suitable for a warm greenhouse. Propagate by sowing ripe spores.
• HEIGHT to 6ft (2m) or more.
• SPREAD 6ft (2m).

Todea barbara
Crepe fern, King fern

Min. 50–55°F (10–13°C)

OSMUNDA REGALIS

Habit Clump-forming, with fibrous rootstock. ***Leaves*** Deciduous, broadly oval to oblong, to 6ft (1.8m) long. Bright green, bearing tassel-like, rusty-brown, fertile segments, at tips of mature fronds.
- TIPS Excellent for waterside plantings. Propagate by spores sown immediately as they ripen or by division in autumn or winter.
- HEIGHT 6ft (2m).
- SPREAD 3ft (1m).

Osmunda regalis
Royal fern

Z 3–9

MATTEUCCIA STRUTHIOPTERIS

Habit Upright or gently arching, rhizomatous. ***Leaves*** Deciduous, lance-shaped. Fresh green. Dark brown inner, fertile fronds are winter-persistent.
- TIPS Excellent for waterside plantings. Tolerates part-day sun. Divide in autumn or winter.
- HEIGHT 3ft (1m)
- SPREAD 18in (45cm).

Matteuccia struthiopteris
Ostrich fern
Ostrich-feather fern,

Z 2–8

POLYSTICHUM SETIFERUM PROLIFERUM

Habit Slightly arching. ***Leaves*** Evergreen or semi-evergreen, oval, finely divided into soft, moss-like segments. Fresh green, covered with white scales as they unfurl.
- TIPS Needs well-drained soil. Divide or plant bulbils in spring.
- HEIGHT 24in (60cm).
- SPREAD 18in (45cm).

Polystichum setiferum proliferum

Z 5–8

ASPLENIUM SCOLOPENDRIUM Crispum Group

Habit Upright. ***Leaves*** Evergreen, strap-shaped, in an irregular rosette, with waved and ruffled margins. Glossy bright green.
- TIPS Needs moist, humus-rich, alkaline soil. Propagate by root leaf bases in summer.
- HEIGHT 18in (45cm).
- SPREAD 30in (75cm).

Asplenium scolopendrium
Crispum Group

Z 4–8

ASPLENIUM SCOLOPENDRIUM

Habit Upright. ***Leaves*** Evergreen, strap-shaped, to 16in (40cm) long, in an irregular rosette. Bright green.
- TIPS Needs moist, humus-rich, alkaline soil. Sow spores in summer.
- OTHER NAMES *Phyllitis scolopendrium.*
- HEIGHT 18–30in (45–75cm).
- SPREAD to 18in (45cm).

Asplenium scolopendrium
Hart's tongue fern

Z 4–8

POLYPODIUM VULGARE

Habit Upright, creeping. ***Leaves*** Evergreen, narrowly lance-shaped, with thin-textured segments. Mid-green.
- TIPS Needs fibrous, moist but well-drained soil. Divide in spring or sow spores in late summer.
- HEIGHT 10–12in (25–30cm).
- SPREAD 10–12in (25–30cm).

Polypodium vulgare
Common polypody,
Polypody

Z 5–8

ASPLENIUM SCOLOPENDRIUM Marginatum Group

Habit Upright, thickly rhizomatous.
Leaves Evergreen, sword-shaped, leathery, with frilled margins, often "winged" beneath, arranged in an irregular rosette. Bright green.
• TIPS Needs moist, humus-rich, alkaline soil. Propagate by root leaf bases in early summer.
• OTHER NAMES *Phyllitis scolopendrium* 'Marginatum'.
• HEIGHT 12in (30cm) or more.
• SPREAD 12in (30cm) or more.

Asplenium scolopendrium Marginatum Group

Z 4–8

ADIANTUM VENUSTUM

Habit Spreading, with creeping rhizomes.
Leaves Semi-evergreen, with black stipes and triangular fronds, to 32in (80cm) long, divided into fan-shaped pinnules. Pale green, pink-tinted on emergence.
• TIPS Grow in moist, humus-rich, acid soil. Propagate by carefully dividing in early spring or sow spores in summer.
• HEIGHT 6in (15cm).
• SPREAD indefinite.

Adiantum venustum
Himalayan maidenhair

Z 4–8

ASPLENIUM NIDUS

Habit Stiffly upright.
Leaves Evergreen, almost stemless, broad, lance-shaped, in a shuttlecock-like rosette. Glossy bright green.
• TIPS Grow indoors in cool climates, in coarse potting compost with added sphagnum moss. Sow spores in late summer.
• HEIGHT 2–4ft (60cm–1.2m).
• SPREAD 1–2ft (30–60cm)

Asplenium nidus
Bird's-nest fern

Min. 41°F (5°C) Z 11

NEPHROLEPIS EXALTATA

Habit Vigorous, erect.
Leaves Evergreen, linear, on wiry stalks. Bright green segments.
• TIPS Prefers damp and shade, but stands drought and waterlogging. Divide in summer or autumn. An excellent house plant.
• HEIGHT 3ft (90cm) or more.
• SPREAD 3ft (90cm) or more.

Nephrolepis exaltata
Boston fern, Sword fern

Min. 41°F (5°C) Z 11

ATHYRIUM NIPONICUM

Habit Clump-forming.
Leaves Deciduous, oval, divided into oblong segments. Gray-green, purple-tinged, with dark purple stalks and midribs.
• TIPS Needs a sheltered site, in neutral to acid soil. Sow spores in summer or divide in spring.
• OTHER NAMES *A. goeringianum*
• HEIGHT 12in (30cm)
• SPREAD 12in (30cm)

Athyrium niponicum
Painted fern

Z 3–8

PSILOTUM NUDUM

Habit Branched, erect, or pendulous if epiphytic.
Leaves Tiny, triangular, evergreen, with triangular, branching, pale green stems. Leaves bear yellow sporangia.
• TIPS Grow indoors in cool climates in warm, humid conditions. Sow ripe spores or divide in early spring.
• HEIGHT 24in (60cm).
• SPREAD 18in (45cm).

Psilotum nudum
Skeleton fork fern

Min. 55–59°F (13–15°C)

CARING FOR PERENNIALS

IF HERBACEOUS PERENNIALS are to give of their ornamental best, it is essential to match the plants' individual needs with the growing conditions that exist in the garden. Perennials originate in many areas of the world, from a range of climates, habitats, and soil types, so whether the site is sheltered or exposed, sunny or shaded, damp or dry, or on poor or fertile soil, there is always a number of plants that will thrive in a given set of conditions. A thorough site survey to assess soil type, exposure, and local microclimate may reveal that different areas of the garden provide a variety of growing conditions. A south-facing border, for example, is perfect for sun-loving plants, while a site beneath shrubs or trees, or a north-facing wall, suits shade-lovers. Damp, low-lying areas of the garden, provided that they are not sited in a frost pocket, may prove ideal for bog plants and natives of other moist habitats. Borders at the base of a wall are usually fairly dry, due to rain-shadow effects, and since they are also usually warm and sheltered, they can provide a perfect niche for plants that are not fully hardy or that require good drainage.

SELECTING PERENNIALS

SOIL PREPARATION AND PLANTING

Few gardens are blessed with the ideal fertile, moisture-retentive, and well-drained loam that suits the majority of herbaceous perennials. However, the drainage, aeration, fertility, and moisture-holding properties of most soil types can be improved by the incorporation of well-rotted organic matter. This is best done in the season before planting to allow the soil to settle. Very wet soils can be improved by the installation of drainage systems, and soil acidity or alkalinity can be modified to a degree by either liming acid soils or by adding well-rotted organic matter or acidifying chemicals to alkaline soils.

Pre-planting clearance of all weeds is essential, since they compete for light, moisture, and nutrients. Where the ground is infested with perennial weeds spray off in the season before planting with a systemic herbicide that also kills their roots. This is most effective when the weeds are growing strongly, usually in early summer. Although this may mean delaying planting, patience at this stage will be amply rewarded later. Repeated applications may be needed to remove persistent weeds like bindweed, quack grass, or thistles. A few perennial weeds can be forked out carefully. Annual weeds may be hoed or sprayed immediately before planting.

Selecting plants

Most perennials are now sold container-grown. Look for healthy, vigorous top-growth with no sign of pests, dieback, or abnormally colored leaves, which may indicate nutrient deficiencies. If buying early in the season, select plants with strong emerging shoots or few fat healthy buds in preference to those with many small, weak buds or shoots. Check the roots and look for a strong system of healthy roots that almost fills the pot. Avoid plants with a mass of tightly coiled roots or those with large roots pushing through the drainage holes. Examine the soil surface for perennial weeds or mats of mosses or liverworts. This may indicate that the plant has been in the container too long, and may have suffered nutrient deficiency or waterlogged conditions, in which case the roots may have rotted or died back.

DIVIDING LARGE PLANTS

1 *When buying easily divided perennials like this aster, choose large plants with several strong shoots. They prove their value since they will yield several plants for the price of one.*

2 *Gently tease the roots apart to make several small sections, each with its own roots. These can be planted immediately in groups or, if the divisions are small, potted up and grown on until well established.*

How to Plant a Container-Grown Perennial

1 In a prepared bed, dig a hole 1½ times wider and deeper than the plant's root ball. If necessary, break up the soil at the bottom of the hole so that it is friable and permits free drainage.

2 Water the potted plant well to ensure that the soil is evenly moist, and allow to drain thoroughly. Then slide the plant gently out of the pot, taking care not to damage the roots or disturb the root ball.

3 Gently scrape off the top 1¼in (3cm) of soil mix to remove weeds and weed seeds. Gently tease out the roots at the sides and base of the root ball, taking care not to break or damage them.

4 Set the plant in the hole, and adjust the depth by back-filling, so that the plant crown is at the correct depth. Back-fill gradually, firming gently as you go, then water thoroughly.

When to plant

Container-grown perennials may be planted at any time of the year provided that the soil is workable. In the drier months, however, they will need conscientious aftercare until they are well established, especially with regard to watering. The best seasons for planting are autumn and spring. Autumn planting allows plants to establish quickly before the onset of winter, since the soil is still warm enough to permit good root growth, and is likely to remain moist, without the need for additional watering, until they are well established. In cold areas, spring planting is better for perennials that are not fully hardy or for those that dislike wet winter conditions, such as cultivars of *Schizostylis coccinea* or *Cosmos atrosanguineus*. They then have a full growing season to become established before their first winter.

Bare-rooted plants should be replanted as soon as possible after receipt. Although occasionally offered by nurseries during the dormant season, the most common source of bare-root plants will be friends carrying out routine lifting and dividing of established clumps, usually during spring or autumn. A few perennials, such as hostas, may be transplanted during the growing season.

How to plant

Always plant into well-cultivated, weed-free soil and, if necessary, remove any weeds that have escaped the herbicide spray with a hand or border fork. Take care to position plants at the correct depth (see below). Most perennials should be planted with the crown at ground level, at the same depth as it was in the pot. Those that are prone to rotting at the base, or with variegated foliage that may revert, should be planted with the crown slightly above ground level. Some plants, such as those with a tuberous root system, are planted deeply, about 4in (10cm) below the soil surface.

To plant container-grown plants, first water the plant well to ensure that the

Planting Depths

Most perennials are best planted with their crown at the same level as it was in the pot. A number grow better if planted higher or deeper, depending on their individual needs.

HOSTA

Shallow
For plants needing moist soil, set the crown 1in (2.5cm) below soil level.

POLYGONATUM

Deep
Plant the crown of tuberous-rooted species 4in (10cm) below soil level.

ASTER

Ground level
Plant most perennials with the crown level with the soil surface.

SISYRINCHIUM

Raised
If plants are prone to rot at the base, set the crown just above ground level.

Transplanting Seedlings

Lift self-sown seedlings carefully when still small. Retain the soil around their roots so as not to break up the root ball. Transfer to the flowering site or nursery bed, firm in, and water thoroughly.

soil is evenly moist, and allow it to drain thoroughly. This is especially important for plants in a peat-based soil mix. Once peat dries out it re-absorbs moisture very slowly, even when surrounded by moist soil, and this often results in the loss of the plant through lack of water at the roots.

Dig a planting hole one-and-a-half times the width of the pot, and adjust the depth so that the crown of the plant is at the appropriate level. Remove the plant carefully from its pot, and loosen the potting mix at the base and sides of the root ball, by gently teasing out the roots with your fingers. Take care not to damage the roots. Set the plant at the appropriate depth and replace the back-fill gently but firmly. Loosen the soil surface lightly with a hand fork and water in thoroughly. For bare-root plants, the planting technique is essentially the same, but it is vital that the roots never dry out before re-planting. If necessary, store them in moist sand, peat, or compost until ready to plant.

Many perennials will produce large numbers of self-sown seedlings where conditions suit them. These may be transplanted directly to a new flowering site, or grown on in nursery beds. Before lifting, prepare the new planting site and dig a small hole to receive the young plants, allowing plenty of space for both the roots and top growth to develop. Lift gently with a hand or border fork, taking care to not to break up the root ball and to retain as much soil around it as possible. Replant immediately, firm in, and water thoroughly. Shade the plants in sunny weather and water regularly until well established.

Planting in containers

Growing perennials in containers can be a versatile and very attractive way of displaying a range of plants. It also offers the opportunity for growing plants that would not thrive in the open garden, either because the soil type is unsuitable, or because they are not sufficiently hardy. When planting containers with more than one type of perennial, it is important to select those with similar cultural requirements. Consider also the eventual size and shape of the selected plants to ensure that their top growth forms a balanced composition that is in proportion with the dimensions of the pot.

The range of containers is diverse, from terracotta or plastic pots to wooden tubs and ceramic urns. Whatever the style of container, it is essential that it has drainage holes to permit free flow of water and prevent waterlogging. It must also be sufficiently deep and wide to accommodate the plant roots. If the container is to be sited permanently outdoors, it must be made of frost-resistant materials, and even then may need additional insulation in winter, both to preserve the pot and to prevent soil from freezing around the root ball. Suitable materials include burlap, bubble wrap, old blankets, or horticultural fleece.

If planting a large container such as a stone urn, lead trough, or heavy terracotta pot, set it in position before planting, since it will be cumbersome to move when filled with potting mix. Stand the container on bricks or commercial "pot feet" to ensure unimpeded drainage from the bottom. Bear in mind that containers need frequent and regular watering during the summer months, so, if possible, site with easy access to a water source. Terracotta pots, although nearly always more attractive, dry out more quickly and need more frequent watering than plastic ones.

Most modern potting mixes, which are usually formulated to include a slow-release fertilizer, are suitable for container planting. Ericaceous and acid-loving plants need a lime-free (ericaceous) potting mix. For plants that need sharp drainage, incorporate additional grit (up to one-third by volume). Soil-based potting mixes have the advantage of being heavier than those with a peat base, lending additional stability to the pot. They also tend to hold nutrients better and are more easily moistened again, if accidentally allowed to dry out.

Cover the drainage holes with a piece of mesh netting or screening and cap with a layer of fibrous material, such as sphagnum moss, to prevent the soil mix being washed down to block the drainage holes. Fill the pot so that the surface of the soil mix is at least 1–1½in (2.5–4cm) below the pot rim, to permit thorough watering. Plant as for perennials in open ground and keep well-watered, especially during the establishment period. Top-dressing with a 1in (2.5cm) layer of gravel looks attractive, keeps the foliage free of soil splash, and helps conserve moisture.

Planting in Containers

1 *When planting in a container, group the plants on the surface of the soil mix when still in their pots to determine their spacing and arrangement. Then plant, firm in, and water thoroughly.*

2 *A few months later, the plants have grown and developed to form an attractive display, with a well-balanced graduation of height and form, and good contrasts of color and texture.*

Routine Care

Most perennials grow well with very little maintenance, but certain routine tasks, such as weeding or deadheading , will help to keep them looking attractive and in good health throughout the growing season.

The amount of water that plants require depends on the soil type, climate, and seasonal weather variations, as well as the individual plant's tolerance of dry conditions. The majority of perennials need regular watering while they are establishing themselves, but once they are established, provided that they are grown in appropriate conditions, they generally need only additional irrigation during prolonged periods of warm, dry weather. This is best applied in the evening, when water evaporates more slowly although you may encourage foliar diseases. Bear in mind that such irrigation must be copious, and sufficient to wet the soil well below the natural root zone. If only the soil surface is wetted, roots will grow upward to seek moisture, making them more vulnerable to damage by heat and drought. If established plants do wilt, they usually recover fully after prolonged rainfall or may go dormant until the following growing season.

In some areas, there may be legal restrictions on irrigation at certain times of the year, so in this case, other means of conserving soil water must be used. The most effective way of doing this is by incorporating plentiful well-rotted organic matter when preparing the bed, followed by regular mulching. On established beds, apply an annual mulch of organic matter, 2–3in (5–7.5cm) thick, onto the surface of moist soil in early spring, avoiding the area immediately around the plant crown. Suitable materials include spent mushroom compost, garden compost, well-rotted manure, or commercial mulches such as cocoa-shells or bark chips. All help to conserve soil moisture by reducing surface evaporation and by improving humus levels in the soil, since they will be incorporated into the soil when they eventually break down.

Mulching also helps to keep down weeds in the border, which is essential if plants are to grow and thrive. It prevents most weed seeds from germinating by depriving them of light, and any wind-blown seedlings are easily removed from the loose surface of the mulch with a hand fork. Any perennial weeds that occur must be dug out carefully with a hand or border fork. If established clumps become infested with perennial weeds, lift the whole plant, wash the soil off the roots, and tease out the weed species. Replant immediately, ensuring that no trace of weed roots remains in the planting site. It is usually impractical to spot-treat weeds with a spray of translocated herbicide without risk of damage to surrounding perennials. An

Mulching

Clear any weeds and apply a 1–2in (2.5–5cm) layer of mulch, such as garden compost or bark chips, to moist soil. Take care not to damage the young shoots of the plant (here a peony).

alternative is to use a "weed wiper" or "weeding glove" according to the manufacturer's instructions.

Organic mulches also provide some nutrients and are very important in maintaining the health and fertility of the soil. When planted into well-prepared and well-mulched soil, most perennials need little additional feeding, other than an annual top-dressing of bonemeal or a balanced slow-release fertilizer in spring. This is best applied after rain to the surface of moist soil. In dry conditions water thoroughly first, then work the fertilizer gently into the soil surface with a hand or border fork. Do not let the fertilizer come into contact with the leaves, since it may scorch them. Plants such as *Rheum* or *Hosta*, which are grown mainly for their foliage, benefit from the occasional application of a high-nitrogen liquid fertilizer during the growing season to help produce large, lush leaves.

Improving flowering

There are several ways of improving the number or size of flowers borne by perennials. Although most perennials produce many vigorous shoots in spring, some may be weak and spindly. If weak shoots are thinned at an early stage of development, the remaining shoots will be sturdier and usually produce larger flowers. When the shoots reach about one-quarter to one-third of their eventual height, pinch out or cut back the weak shoots at the base. This technique may be used with plants like delphiniums, phlox, goldenrod, and asters. Stopping is a similar technique that involves pinching out the growing tip of each stem, to produce sturdier growth and to prevent the plant from becoming tall and leggy. It also encourages the development of buds in the upper leaf axils, and is usually used on plants such as *Rudbeckia* and *Helenium*.

How to Thin Perennials

Thinning
Thin young shoots (phlox) when no more than a third of their final height. Remove one shoot in three by cutting or pinching out the weakest shoots at their base.

How to Stop Perennials

Stopping
Stop shoots (here an aster) by pinching out the top 1–2in (2.5–5cm) of the stem tip, when plants reach about one-third of their final height.

Deadheading to Prolong Flowering

Delphinium
After flowering, when new basal shoots are visible, cut back the flowered stems to ground level. Delphiniums must be fed and watered well to produce a second crop of flowers later in the season.

Phlox
Remove the terminal flower head as the flower begins to fade, cutting back to where sideshoots are produced from the leaf axils lower down the stem. This will encourage further sideshoots to flower.

Deadheading

Unless a plant produces decorative seedheads, or seed is needed to raise further plants, most perennials are best deadheaded as the flowers fade. This prevents the plant from expending energy in the production of seed, and it then puts on new vegetative growth instead, giving rise to strong plants that bloom well the following year. In many cases, deadheading also encourages a second crop of flowers on sideshoots, thus prolonging the flowering season. For some plants, such as *Centaurea* and delphiniums, the flowered stems are cut back to the base when the first flowers have faded. The new shoots that develop may then produce another, lesser crop of flowers later in the season.

Cutting back

A number of evergreen or semi-evergreen, sub-shrubby perennials, such as the marguerites (*Argyranthemum frutescens*), should be pruned annually in early spring. If left unpruned, they tend to produce bare, woody stems with a tuft of foliage at the top, creating a leggy and unattractive habit. Using pruners, cut back the main stems by about half of their length to remove any twiggy, semi-woody and messy growth. This will help maintain a dense mound of attractive foliage and encourage the production of strong new shoots that will then produce a succession of flowers throughout summer and autumn.

Autumn clearance

In autumn, once the perennials have finished flowering, cut down all top-growth to the base and remove all dead or faded leaves and stems. Clear any residual weed growth to leave the beds and borders neat and clean. In very cold areas, or if plants are not fully hardy, the top-growth may be left in place until early spring, since it offers the dormant crown some protection against winter cold. Some perennial plants, such as *Sedum spectabile*, some astilbes, and many grasses, have foliage or flower heads that remain attractive even when brown and dry in winter. These may be left in place during the winter months, but they are best removed in late autumn or just as new growth begins in spring.

A number of plants, such as *Cosmos atrosanguineus*, that may not be fully hardy in areas with cold wet winters, may be lifted in autumn and stored in frost-free conditions overwinter, to be replanted when the soil warms up in spring. This technique may also be used if autumn planting has been delayed by prolonged spells of wet weather, and is especially useful if transplanting perennials to a new garden, for example, when moving house. Lift the plants when dormant and pack into boxes or crates of damp compost or bark so that the roots do not dry out. Store in a cool, dry, frost-free place.

Spring operations

Just before new growth resumes in early spring, cut back any dead material that has been left *in situ* overwinter. Protect emerging new growth from slugs and snails; this is especially important for species with fleshy shoots like *Veratrum* or *Hosta*. Tall or fragile perennials need staking, and this is most easily done in early spring before the new growth is well-developed. Most forms of staking, although initially obtrusive, will be masked by foliage as the plants reach their final dimensions. Match the type of support used to the plant's habit of growth (see p.316).

CUTTING BACK IN AUTUMN

In autumn or early winter, at the end of the flowering period, cut down all top-growth to ground level (here Rudbeckia*) and remove all faded leaves and stems. Clear any weeds from the surrounding soil and leave the beds and borders neat and tidy.*

STORING PLANTS

Lift dormant plants in winter and place them in a dry, frost-free place in boxes half-filled with moist bark or compost. Cover the roots with more bark or compost to keep them from drying out.

STAKING TALL AND FRAGILE PERENNIALS

Single stake
For tall, single-stemmed plants such as this delphinium, insert a cane two-thirds of the plant's height as growth reaches 8in (20cm). Tie in the stem loosely with soft twine.

Link stakes
For tall, clump-forming plants, such as the Aster *shown here, push link stakes deep into the soil, and raise them gradually as growth proceeds.*

Ring stake
For low to medium-sized clump-formers, like peonies, use a grow-through ring stake. Set in position early in the season and, if necessary, raise the stake as the plant grows.

Ring of stakes
For weak-stemmed plants that are inclined to flop (here Centaurea*) encircle the clump with split stakes, and loop soft twine around and between the stakes and stems.*

Perennials in containers

Plants grown in containers need more care than those in open ground since they have limited supplies of food and water. During the growing season, keep the soil mix evenly moist, but never waterlogged. In periods of warm, dry weather, plants will need daily watering. Once they are well established and in full growth, apply a balanced liquid fertilizer every two to three weeks. Lift and divide the plants every year or two in spring or autumn, and replant into fresh soil mix. If the container is to be re-used, wash it well before replanting, or pot up into a larger container. Trim the roots of shrubby perennials by about a quarter before repotting. In cold areas, move slightly hardy and tender plants into the greenhouse in autumn. Protect them until the spring, and set out again only when all danger of frost has passed.

Maintaining Perennials in Containers

1 Rejuvenate container-grown perennials in spring or autumn. Lift out and separate the plants carefully and shake the soil mix from their roots.

2 Discard old soil mix, and refill container with fresh mix to within 4in (10cm) of the rim. Divide and arrange overgrown plants.

3 Plant the container, filling with more fresh soil mix around the plants, to within 1–1½in (2.5–4cm) of the pot rim. Firm with your fingers.

4 Finally, top-dress with a balanced slow-release fertilizer and mulch with gravel or bark chips. Water thoroughly, so that the soil mix is evenly moist and water runs through the drainage holes at the base. The plants shown here are bergenias, a Pachysandra, and a hosta (now dormant), all of which are ideal for a shady patio or terrace.

PROPAGATION

There are several ways of propagating herbaceous perennials. Growing from seed is ideal where large numbers of new plants are required, although it is usually only suitable for species, since most cultivars will not come true from seed. For most perennials, division is the easiest and most frequent means of increase. This and the other vegetative methods described here should be used for increasing almost all cultivars.

Seed

Raising plants from seed is a simple and inexpensive means of raising large numbers of plants. If collecting seed from the garden, bear in mind that most species will show natural variation in habit, vigor and flower color, so collect only from strong plants with good flower form and color. The seed of early flowering species usually ripens by midsummer, and is best sown as soon as it is ripe, since this is when it germinates best. The young plants can be overwintered in a nursery bed or cold frame, depending on hardiness. Sow seed of later-flowering species when it ripens in autumn; a few may germinate immediately, but most will sprout in the following spring. Alternatively, store ripe seed in a cool, dry place and sow in spring. The seed of some genera, notably *Paeonia* and *Helleborus*, may remain dormant for long periods unless suitable conditions are provided, or occur naturally, to break dormancy.

Other seeds need a period of exposure to cold or to light to break dormancy, while those of many in the pea family have a hard seed coat that needs soaking or scarifying to allow it to imbibe the water necessary for germination.

COLLECTING SEED

Collect ripened seedheads and shake seed out directly onto a piece of paper, or enclose the pods upside down in a paper bag so that seeds fall into it. Store in a cool, dry place until ready to sow.

Pre-germination treatments

Seeds that need exposure to cold to break dormancy may be sown in autumn or winter. It is usually most convenient to sow them in containers placed outdoors in a cold frame or open frame, where they will germinate in spring. Alternatively, mix seed with damp seed soil mix in a plastic bag, and place it in a domestic refrigerator at 34–41°F (1–5°C) for 4–12 weeks. Check regularly for signs of germination (usually the appearance of the white root tip), then sow immediately.

Peony and *Trillium* seeds usually need two periods of cold to break dormancy. After the first winter the roots appear and, following the second winter, the shoot growth emerges. Seed is sown in autumn in the normal way, but is left in the cold frame for two winters.

Scarify seeds with hard coats either by rubbing them gently between two sheets of sandpaper (for small seeds) or by nicking the seed coat with a sharp blade (for larger ones). Alternatively, hard seed coats may be softened by soaking for up to 24 hours in hot, not boiling, water. As the seed imbibes water, it swells slightly but visibly. It is then sown immediately in the normal way. Seeds of *Baptisia* and other legumes, *Arum*, and *Euphorbia* are treated in this way.

Sowing seed in containers is the most convenient technique; a plastic half-tray, or 5in (13cm) pot, will accommodate sufficient plants for even the largest garden. Most commercial seed soil mixes are suitable, but if seedlings are to be kept in containers for any length of time after germination, use a good-quality soil-based one. Fill the container with mix, level off, then firm with a presser so that the soil surface is about ½in (1cm) below the container rim. Sow seed thinly (about ¼in/0.5cm apart); sowing too thickly results in spindly seedlings that are prone to damping off.

In general, seed needs to be covered to its own depth with sieved soil mix; leave those that need light to germinate uncovered (e.g. gentians). Label clearly with the plant name and sowing date, and water well, either using a can with a fine rose, or by standing in a tray of water until the surface is moist. Cover with a sheet of glass and place in a cold frame. Shade from hot sun with newspaper or shade netting. Remove the cover and reduce shading once seeds have germinated. If seeds need chilling, top-dress containers with fine grit and plunge them in an open frame.

Raising Plants from Seed

1 Fill a 5in (13cm) pot with damp seed soil mix and firm gently with a presser, to about ½in (1cm) below the pot rim.

2 Using a clean, folded piece of paper, sprinkle seed thinly and evenly onto the soil surface (shown here are chrysanthemum seeds).

3 Cover with a shallow layer of finely sieved seed soil mix. Label and water from below until the surface is moist.

4 Cover with glass or clear plastic to retain moisture. Place in a cold frame until seeds develop 2 pairs of leaves.

5 Prick out seedlings into pots or trays. Handle them only by their seed leaves; the stems are easily damaged.

6 When seedlings have developed into young plants with a good root system, plant out or pot on as appropriate.

Dividing perennials

Propagating by division, as described here, is the most usual means of increasing perennials that have a spreading rootstock and produce many shoots from the crown. By removing any old or unproductive parts, division can also be used to rejuvenate plants that lose vigor with age, become overcrowded, or die out at the center of the clump.

Most plants should be divided during their dormant phase, between late autumn and early spring, but not in very cold, wet, or dry weather, since the divisions will not re-establish well in

How to Propagate Perennials by Division

1 *Lift the plant to be divided gently, taking care to insert the fork beyond the immediate root zone, to reduce the risk of damaging fine roots. Shake off the surplus soil. The plant shown here is a helianthus.*

2 *Plants with a tough, woody rootstock are separated into sections by chopping through the crown with a spade. For very tough plants, set the spade in position and stand on it to apply your full body weight.*

3 *If possible, divide the plant into sections by teasing the roots apart gently by hand. Retain only the healthiest and most vigorous sections, each with several new shoots or growth buds, and discard the remainder.*

4 *Cut back any old or dead top-growth, and replant the divisions at the same depth as the original parent plant. Firm in gently and water thoroughly. Continue to water regularly until re-established.*

these conditions. Division of fleshy-rooted perennials is best left until the end of their dormant season. In early spring, the new buds will have begun to sprout, thus giving a good indication of the most vigorous, and therefore most suitable, material for replanting.

First lift the plant to be divided, levering it up gently with a fork, being very careful not to damage the roots. Shake off any loose soil and remove dead leaves or stems to reveal the next season's growth buds. Discard any old, unproductive or damaged sections of the clump. For fleshy-rooted plants, it is advisable to wash off the soil from the roots and crown so that all buds are clearly visible; they are then less likely to be damaged when they are divided.

Many fibrous-rooted perennials are easily divided by teasing apart sections of the clump by hand (see left), and this is preferable wherever possible. Where the fibrous roots are tough and congested, insert two garden forks back to back near the center of the clump with the tines close together. Separate the roots into sections by levering the fork handles backward and forward.

Alternative Method

The technique of dividing fibrous-rooted, herbaceous perennials with garden forks, as shown here, is an old and traditional one. It can seem awkward at first, but is an invaluable technique once mastered. Set the forks back to back, so that they touch where the top of the tines meet the shaft. This acts as a leverage point as the fork handles are moved backward and forward to force the roots apart.

Dividing Hostas

1 *Divide large hostas with tough rootstocks in early spring, using a spade. Aim to produce sections with several buds. A section with six or more buds will produce a moderate-sized clump in its first year.*

2 *Smaller hostas that have looser, fleshy rootstocks may be separated by hand, or forced apart using forks back-to-back. Divide in early spring. Each section should have at least one eye, preferably more.*

Plants that form woody clumps or that have thick solid roots, like hostas, are cut into sections with a spade or knife. Trim each division cleanly with a sharp knife to remove any damaged or rotting roots. Make sure that each section has at least two growth buds. Dust all cut surfaces with an appropriate fungicide and replant divisions as soon as possible. Large divisions should be replanted directly into their final flowering site, and will usually re-establish quickly. Smaller divisions may be grown on in a nursery bed, or potted up until they begin to grow vigorously. In general, divisions are best planted at the same depth as the original plant, but any that are prone to rotting at the base are best set slightly above the soil surface (see Planting Depths, p.309). After planting, water the plant in thoroughly, taking care not to wash away any soil from around the roots.

If replanting is delayed for any reason, it is vital to keep the roots moist. Dip them briefly in water and store the divisions in a plastic bag in a cool, shady place until you are ready to replant.

Division of Rhizomatous Plants

1 Lift the plant to be divided (here an iris), inserting the fork well away from the rhizomes to avoid damaging them. Shake loose soil from the roots and separate the rhizomes into manageable pieces by hand.

2 Cut out any old or diseased rhizomes and discard them, then, using a sharp knife, slice off the newer, more vigorous rhizomes from the clump and trim off their ends neatly.

3 Dust the cut surfaces with fungicide. Trim long roots by about one-third of their length. For irises, cut the leaves to a miter, no more than about 6in (15cm) long, to reduce wind-rock.

4 Plant the rhizomes at least 5–6in (12–15cm) apart. For irises, the rhizomes should be only half buried, with leaves upright, and preferably with the rhizomes facing the sun.

If the delay is likely to be longer than a few days, it is a good idea to store plants in a box of moist bark or compost (see p. [illegible]).

The technique for plants with thick rhizomes, such as bergenias or rhizomatous irises, is slightly different (see left). Split the clump into pieces by hand, then cut the rhizomes into individual sections, each with one or more growing points. Plants with long, narrow, upright leaves, such as irises, are susceptible to being blown about by the wind during the time they are becoming re-established. To reduce the risk of this happening and knocking over the new plants at such a critical time, the leaves are trimmed to a miter, about 6in (15cm) long; they will be replaced by new leaves once the young roots have become established and growth resumes.

Dividing peonies

Herbaceous peonies must be divided with special care, since they resent root disturbance and dislike being transplanted. Divisions re-establish very slowly and may take several growing seasons before they are large enough to resume flowering. They are, nevertheless, well worth a patient wait, since once established they continue to bloom for many years in the same site. For best results, lift and divide the plants toward the beginning of their dormant season in early fall, when the new buds are beginning to swell and are clearly visible. Cut the crown into sections, each with several buds, with a clean, sharp knife, taking care not to damage the thick, fleshy roots. Dust the cut surfaces with fungicide and replant immediately. Prepare the new planting hole by digging deeply, incorporating bone meal and very well-rotted manure or compost to the bottom of the planting hole. Replant the divisions at the same depth as the original parent plant.

Dividing Peonies

1 *Lift the plant in early fall, when healthy growth buds are visible on the crown. Cut the crown into sections, each one with several buds.*

2 *Dust the cut surfaces of the divided sections with fungicide to discourage fungal infections and rot.*

3 *Plant out the divided sections at least 2ft (60cm)) apart. The buds should not be visible at the surface of the soil. Firm in gently and water thoroughly.*

Stem-tip cuttings

Herbaceous perennials that are difficult to divide successfully, such as *Argyranthemum* and *Erysimum*, can be increased by taking stem-tip cuttings. Cuttings can be taken at any time during the growing season, provided that suitable shoots are available.

Select the strongly growing tips of non-flowering shoots and reject any that are thin, weak, leggy, or damaged. They should be inserted as soon as possible, and must not be allowed to wilt. They are best taken in the early morning, when plants are at their most turgid, and placed into a sealed, opaque plastic bag until insertion.

Take cuttings 3–5in (7.5–12cm) long, with pruners or a clean, sharp knife, cutting just above a leaf joint. Trim the cuttings to just below a node and remove the leaves from the lowest third of the stem. Insert the cuttings, almost to the lowest leaves, into prepared pots of commercial propagating soil mix, firming in gently with the fingers. Ensure that the leaves do not touch each other and that air can circulate freely.

Water using a can with a fine rose, and treat with liquid fungicide. If possible, place the pot in a mist unit or propagator to maintain high humidity. Alternatively, cover the cuttings with a plastic bag or tent, supported by wire hoops or stakes, to keep the plastic well clear of the foliage. Any condensation that forms on the foliage may lead to fungal infection and the loss of the cuttings. Shade the cuttings in hot weather to prevent the leaves from scorching or wilting, but remove shading as soon as possible to admit maximum light. Cuttings will become drawn and leggy in poor light. Inspect them daily and remove any fallen or dead leaves to reduce the risk of fungal infections. Keep the soil mix moist but not wet.

The cuttings should root within about three weeks. Admit air gradually to wean them from their humid environment, then pot up singly and grow on before planting out into their flowering site.

Stem Tip Cuttings

1 Select short lengths of soft, non-flowering shoots, about 3–5in (7.5–12cm) long. Use the tips of strong healthy shoots, and cut them just above a node. The plant shown is a penstemon.

2 Trim the lower end of the cutting just below a node, with a straight cut, reducing the length to about 2–3in (5–7.5cm). Remove the leaves from the lowest third of the cutting.

3 Insert the cuttings around the edge of the pot. Space so that the leaves do not touch. Cover with a plastic bag supported by hoops or stakes to keep it clear of the leaves.

Basal stem cuttings

Propagating from basal stem cuttings is a technique used for plants with pithy or hollow stems, such as lupines (*Lupinus*) and delphiniums, and those such as chrysanthemums and cultivars of *Anthemis tinctoria* that produce soft new shoots from the base in spring. This type of cutting is usually taken in midspring, from the base of the plant at or just below soil level. To produce cutting material earlier in the season, plants may be lifted and planted in boxes of potting soil mix and forced into growth in a heated greenhouse. When cuttings have been removed, the plant may be returned to the open garden.

Select strong healthy shoots of which the first leaves have just unfolded, and remove them with a sharp knife, cutting as close to the base as possible, so that part of the firmer, semi-woody basal tissue is also included. Trim off the lowest leaves, treat the base of the cutting with hormone rooting preparation, and insert in a commercial cutting soil mix, either singly in individual pots, or several to a tray or pot. Firm, water well, then transfer the containers to a cold frame or propagator. Alternatively, enclose them in a clear plastic bag, kept clear of the cuttings with stakes or wire hoops. Shade the cuttings from direct sun to prevent scorching or wilting of the leaves.

Check the cuttings every few days, and remove any faded or fallen leaves to reduce the risk of fungal infections. Keep the soil mix evenly moist, but not wet, and wipe the glass or plastic covers clean to remove condensation.

Basal cuttings should root within a month. Once rooted, tip them gently out of the pot and separate them carefully, retaining as much soil around the new roots as possible. Pot them up into individual pots using a suitable soil-based potting mix. Grow on until large enough to set out in their final flowering site. Plants that are not fully hardy must be hardened off and planted out when all danger of frost has passed.

Basal Stem Cuttings

1 *Take cuttings (here a chrysanthemum) when the shoots reach about 1½–2in (3.5–5cm). Remove close to the base with a small portion of basal wood. Delphinium cuttings should be 3–4in (7.5–10cm) long.*

2 *Remove all the basal leaves then trim the base of the cutting, making a straight cut with a sharp knife. Treat the cut end with hormone rooting preparation.*

3 *Insert the cuttings into a prepared pot of damp propagating soil mix. Water well. Place in a propagator or use a plastic bag supported by hoops or stakes to keep the plastic clear of the leaves.*

Root cuttings

This method is used for perennials such as *Acanthus* and *Papaver orientale* that have thick fleshy roots. It is also useful for the non-variegated cultivars of border phlox that are susceptible to a nematode that affects the top-growth, but not the roots. Variegated cultivars produce only green foliage plants from root cuttings.

Root cuttings are best taken when the plant is dormant, usually in winter.

The technique for thin-rooted plants, like *Anemone hupehensis*, *Campanula*, *Phlox*, and *Primula denticulata*, differs slightly from that shown below. Make cuttings 3–5in (7–12cm) long, so that there is sufficient food storage for the developing cuttings. Lay them horizontally on the surface of damp soil mix in a tray, and cover to at least their own depth. Then treat as for standard root cuttings.

Propagating Perennials by Root Cuttings

1 *Lift the parent plant (here an acanthus) when dormant, and wash the soil from the roots. Select roots of pencil thickness and cut them off with a sharp knife close to the crown. Trim off any fibrous roots.*

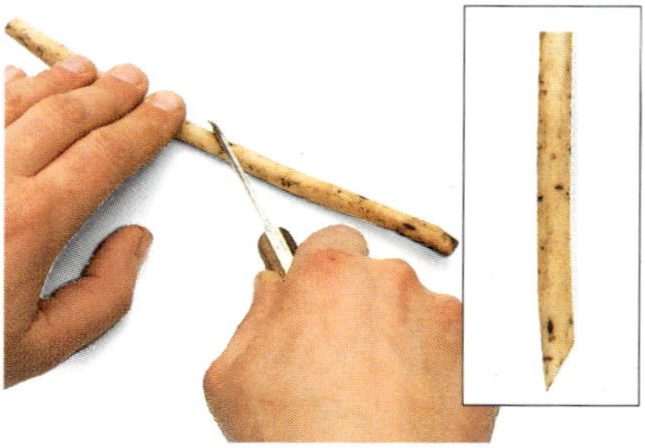

2 *Cut the roots into sections, 2–4in (5–10cm) long, with a straight cut at the top of the root, and an angled cut at the bottom. New shoots appear from the top of the cutting; be sure to insert the right way up.*

3 *Insert cuttings vertically into pots of damp cutting soil mix, with the top end of the cutting flush with the surface. Firm, water well, and top-dress with coarse grit. Label and place in a cold frame.*

4 *When the cuttings have developed young shoots, pot them up into individual pots filled with soil-based potting mix. Label each pot clearly, and grow the new plants until large enough to plant out.*

Grafting

A few perennials, such as *Gypsophila paniculata* 'Bristol Fairy', do not root readily from cuttings and are are increased by grafting onto seedling understock of the species. Lift plants of the cultivar to be propagated in autumn, pot up, and grow in a cool greenhouse. They will then produce new shoots in mid- to late winter, the optimal time for grafting.

Lift 1–2 year old stock plants of the species in mid- to late winter. The principle is to graft strong healthy shoots of the scion (the cultivar) onto strong roots of the rootstock (*Gypsophila paniculata* species). In ideal conditions, the graft union should form within six weeks. The grafted plants can then be potted up and grown on in frost-free conditions, to be planted out in early summer when danger of frost has passed.

Propagation by Grafting

1 Select and prepare the rootstock. Cut a straight piece of strong, healthy root, ½in (1cm) thick and 3½in (9cm) long.

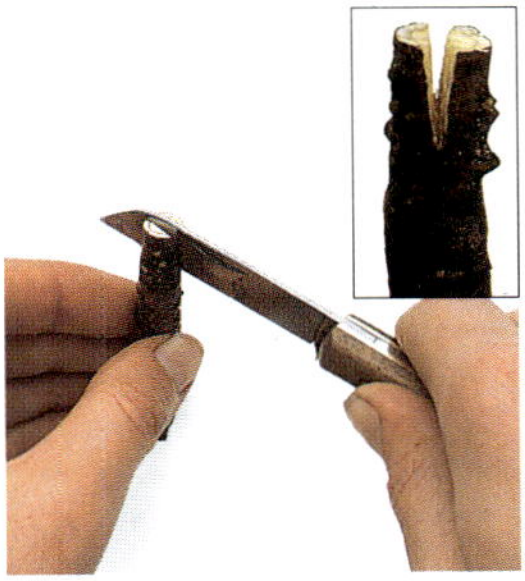

2 Remove fibrous roots, shorten lateral roots to ½in (1cm), and cut a ½in (1cm) incision into the straight-cut top of the stock.

3 Select a vigorous shoot from the scion, ⅛in (3–4mm) thick, 1½–3in (3–7cm) long. Trim the lower end to a wedge shape.

4 Insert the stock into a 3in (6cm) pot of damp cutting soil mix. Place the scion into the vertical incision in the stock.

5 Bind the graft union with plastic tape or raffia to hold the scion firmly in position. Label and water well.

6 Cover with a plastic bag supported by stakes. Place in light, warm conditions until new shoots appear above the union.

GLOSSARY OF TERMS

Italicized words have their own entry.

ACID (of soil). With a pH value of less than 7, or lacking in lime; see also *alkaline* and *neutral*.
ALKALINE (of soil). With a pH value of more than 7, or lime-rich; see also *acid* and *neutral*.
ALPINE HOUSE. An unheated, well-ventilated greenhouse used for cultivating alpine and bulbous plants.
ALTERNATE (of leaves). Occurring successively at different levels on opposite sides of a stem. (Cf *Opposite*).
ANEMONE CENTERED (of flowers). Flowers or flower heads in which the central petals or flowers (modified *stamens*) form a cushion-like mound and the outer rim or petals or ray florets are flat and spreading, as in some chrysanthemums.
ANTHER. The part of a *stamen* that produces pollen.
AWN. A sharp point or bristle, commonly found on grass seed and flower heads.
AXIL. The angle between a leaf and stem where an axillary bud develops.
BACKFILL. To fill in a planting hole around a plant's roots with a soil mix.
BRACT. A modified leaf at the base of a flower or flower cluster. It may resemble a normal leaf or be reduced and scale-like in appearance. It may also be large and brightly coloured.
BULBIL. A small bulb-like organ, often borne in a leaf axil, occasionally on a stem or in a flower head.
CALYX. The outer part of a flower, usually small and green but sometimes showy and brightly colored; it is formed from the sepals and encloses the petals in a bud.
COMPOUND LEAF. A leaf that is divided into two or more leaflets.
COROLLA. The part of a flower formed by the petals.
CROCKS. Broken pieces of clay pot, used to cover drainage holes of pots in order to provide free drainage and air circulation to the root system and to stop the growing medium from escaping, or blocking, the holes.
CROWN. The basal part at soil level of a *herbaceous* plant where roots and stem join and from where new shoots are produced.
CULTIVAR. A contraction of "cultivated variety" (abbreviated to "cv"); a group (or one among such a group) of cultivated plants clearly distinguished by one or more characteristics and which retains these characteristics when propagated.
CUTTING. A section of a plant which is removed and used for propagation. For the various methods see *Guide to Perennial Care*, pp.324–327.
DEADHEADING. The removal of spent flowers or *flower heads*.
DECIDUOUS. Losing its leaves annually at the end of the growing season; semi-deciduous plants lose only some leaves.
DIEBACK. The death of tips or shoots due to damage or disease.
DISBUDDING. The removal of surplus buds to encourage production of high-quality flowers or fruits. See also *stopping*.
DIVISION. A method of propagation by which a plant clump is divided into separate parts during dormancy. See *Guide to Perennial Care*, pp.320–323.
DORMANCY. The state of temporary cessation of growth and slowing down of other activities in whole plants, usually during winter.
ELLIPTIC (of leaves). Broadening at the center and narrowing toward each end.
EPIPHYTE. A plant that grows on another without being parasitic, obtaining nutrients and moisture from the air without rooting in soil.
EVERGREEN. Retaining its leaves all year round, although losing some older leaves regularly throughout the year. Semi-evergreen plants retain only some leaves or lose older leaves only when new growth is produced.
EYE. The center of a flower, of particular note if different in color from the petals.
FALLS. The drooping or horizontal petals of irises.
FLOWER. The part of the plant containing the reproductive organs usually surrounded by *sepals* and *petals*.
FLOWER HEAD. A mass of small flowers or florets that together appear to form a single flower e.g. daisy.
FLORET. A single flower in a head of many flowers.
FRIABLE. Soil of a crumbly texture, able to be worked easily.
GENUS (pl. genera). A category in plant classification, consisting of a group of related *species*.
GLAUCOUS. Blue-green, blue-gray, gray, or with a bluish, grayish, or whitish bloom.
GLOBOSE. Spherical.
GRAFTING. Method of propagation by which an artificial union is made between different parts of individual plants. See *Guide to Perennial Care*, p.327.
HABIT. The characteristic growth or general appearance of a plant.
HERB. A plant grown for its medicinal or flavoring properties or for its scented foliage.

HERBACEOUS. Non-woody plant of which the upper parts die back to the rootstock at the end of the growing season.
HUMUS. The organic residue of decayed vegetable matter in soil. Also often used to describe partly decayed matter such as leafmold or compost.
HYBRID. The offspring of genetically different parents, usually produced accidentally or artificially in cultivation, but occasionally arising in the wild.
INCURVED. Applied to *petals* and *florets* that curve inward to form a compact, rounded shape.
INFLORESCENCE. A group of flowers borne on a single axis (stem) e.g. *umbel*.
LATERAL. A side growth that emerges from a shoot or root.
LEAFLET. A subdivision of a compound leaf.
LINEAR (of leaves). Very narrow with parallel sides.
LIME. Compounds of calcium; the amount of lime in soil determines whether it is *acid*, *neutral*, or *alkaline*.
LOBE. A rounded projecting segment or part, forming part of a larger structure.
MICROCLIMATE. A small, local climate within a larger climate area, such as a greenhouse or a protected area of a garden.
MULCH. A layer of organic material applied to the soil over or around a plant to conserve moisture, protect the roots from frost, reduce the growth of weeds, and enrich the soil e.g. bark chips, rotted manure, garden compost, black plastic, gravel.
NEUTRAL (of soil). With a pH value of 7, the point at which soil is neither acid nor alkaline.
ORGANIC. 1. Compounds containing carbon derived from decomposed plant or animal organisms. 2. Used loosely of mulches, soil mixes etc. derived from plant materials.
PALMATE (of leaves). Having four or more leaflets growing from a single point, as in horse chestnut (*Aesculus hippocastanum*).
PERENNIAL. Living for at least three seasons; commonly used of *herbaceous* plants, and *woody* perennials, i.e. trees and shrubs.
PETAL. One portion of the often bright and colored part of the *corolla*.
PETIOLE. The stalk of a leaf.
PHYLLODE. An expanded leaf stalk, which functions as, and resembles, a leaf blade e.g. asparagus.
PINCH OUT. Remove the growing tip of a plant, with finger and thumb, to induce the production of sideshoots or the formation of flower buds.
PINNATE (of leaves). A compound leaf in which the leaflets grow in a row on each side of the midrib.
PROPAGATOR. A structure that provides a humid atmosphere for seedlings, cuttings, or other plants being propagated.
PROSTRATE. With stems growing along the ground.
RECURVED. Of petals or leaves, curved backward.
REVERT. To return to an original state, as when plain green leaves are produced on a variegated plant.
RHIZOME. Underground, creeping stem that acts as a storage organ and produces leafy shoots.
ROOT. The part of a plant, normally underground, that functions as an anchorage and through which nutrients are absorbed.
ROOT BALL. The roots and accompanying soil or soil mix visible when a plant is removed from a container or lifted from the open ground.
RUNNER. A horizontally spreading stem that runs above ground and roots at the nodes to form new plants. Often confused with *stolon*.
SEPAL. Part of a *calyx*. Though usually green and insignificant, it may sometimes be showy.
SPATHE. One, or sometimes two, large *bracts*, that surround a flower cluster or individual bud.
SPECIES. A category in plant classification, the rank below *genus*, containing closely related, very similar individual plants.
STAMEN. The male floral organ, bearing an *anther* that produces pollen.
STIGMA. The area of the female flower part that receives pollen.
STOLON. A horizontally spreading or arching stem, usually above ground, which roots at its tip to produce a new plant. Often confused with *runner*.
STRATIFICATION. The storage of seeds in warm or cold conditions to break dormancy and aid germination.
STOPPING. The removal of the growing tip of a plant (by finger and thumb) to induce the production of sideshoots or the formation of flower heads. Also known as "pinching out".
STYLE. The part of the flower on which the *stigma* is carried.
SUB-SHRUB. A plant that is *woody* at the base, but whose shoots die back in winter.
TUBER. Thickened, usually underground food-storage organ, derived from a stem or root.
UMBEL. A usually flat-topped or rounded flower cluster, in which the individual flower stalks rise from a central point. In a compound umbel each primary stalk ends in an umbel.
VEGETATIVE GROWTH. Non-flowering, usually leafy growth.
WHORL. Where three or more organs, e.g. leaves, arise from the same point.
WIND-ROCK. The destabilizing of a plant's roots by wind.
WOODY. With branches of hard, woody fibers, that persist, unlike soft-stemmed herbaceous plants. A semi-woody stem contains some softer tissue and may be only partially persistent.

INDEX

Each genus name is shown in **bold type**, followed by a brief description. Species, varieties, and subspecies are given in *italics*; cultivars are in Roman type with single quotes. Common names appear in parentheses.

A

C

E

F

ACKNOWLEDGMENTS

Key: t=top; b=bottom; r=right; l=left; c=centre; cra=centre right above

The publishers would like to thank the following for their kind permission to reproduce the photographs:

A-Z Botanical Collection Ltd/Neil Joy 300cr
Gillian Beckett 301tl
Deni Bown 303b, 305br
Pat Brindley 299tl
Derek Gould 21cr, 86bl, 199t, 251cra, 261cr
Mike Ireland 216bl
Marc King 138b
Andrew Lawson 57tr, 107br, 117tl, 124bl
Photos Horticultural Picture Library 26br, 82b,96cl, 197tr, 266br
Harry Smith Collection 34r, 83cl, 97cr, 202br, 208tr,213tr, 221cr, 273cra, /Polunin Collection 302br

Special photography: Eric Crichton, John Glover, Jerry Harpur, Andrew Lawson, Andrew de Lory, Howard Rice

Index: James J. Parker

Design assistance: Mark Tattam

In addition to the above, the publishers would also like to thank the staff of the Royal Horticultural Society Publications

Abbreviations

C	centrigrade	in	inch, inches
cm	centimeter	m	meter
cv.	cultivar	mm	millimeter
F	fahrenheit	oz	ounce
f.	forma	sp.	species
ft	foot, feet	subsp.	subspecies
g	gram	var.	variant